Practical
Apartment
Management

Professional Review

Diana L. Accardi, CPM®

Nancy A. Bishop, CPM®

Natalie D. Brecher, CPM®

Laurence C. Harmon, CPM®

Caroline Scoulas

Senior Editor, Education Publishing

Practical
Apartment
Management
Fifth Edition

Edward N. Kelley, CPM®

IREM **Institute of Real Estate Management**
CHICAGO

The photograph in Exhibit 10.2 is reproduced with permission from Rockford, Inc., AMO®, of Edina, Minnesota.

© 2004 by the Institute of Real Estate Management
of the NATIONAL ASSOCIATION OF REALTORS®.
First Edition published 1976. Fifth Edition 2004.

Library of Congress Cataloging-in-Publication Data

Kelley, Edward N.
    Practical Apartment Management / Edward N. Kelley.--5th ed.
    p. cm.
    Includes index.
    ISBN 1-57203-094-1 (soft cover)
    1. Apartment houses--Management. I. Title.

TX957.K44 2003
647'.92'068--dc22

                                                                        2003055882

Printed in the United States of America.

1 2 3 4 5 6 7 8 9 10 Printing / Year 13 12 11 10 09 08 07 06 05 04

To Marlene,
my very special partner

Preface

Almost four years ago to the day, I sat down to write the Preface for the fourth edition of *Practical Apartment Management*. As part of that message, I added the obligatory language warning about how things could or would change in the years to come. I had in mind some progress in our management practices, further leaps in technology, continued advances in rental property design and functionality, and a continuation of a healthy real estate investment climate. Many of these changes have arrived; more of them were in the form of jolts, and many were not at all what we expected or wanted.

In that time, the rental industry has evolved from tight vacancies and nice profits to the point of alarming rental availabilities and vanishing cash returns. Four years ago, others questioned my discussions about concessions and rent specials; they said such considerations are a thing of the past and will only date the book. This week, in a distance of two miles, I saw nine rental communities with banners offering two and three months' free rent or $199 move-in specials. Conditions can certainly change.

I can think of at least a dozen factors that are currently affecting the reduced demand for rental apartments. These influences include job losses, fewer newcomers to the country, fewer divorces, better homeownership alternatives, bargain mortgages, and the quest to get away from outmoded accommodations. Some of these will lessen with time and an improving economy while others will continue to burden the rental industry. Owners and managers are now faced with the reality of some difficult times and decisions. It might be the time for a hard, fresh look at rental policies, practices, and pricing—and especially the product itself.

My plan in writing this fifth edition of *Practical Apartment Management* has been to identify and walk through, step by step, the various disciplines and practices involved in successfully managing rental apartments. Some discussions take the form of a review; others will explore and debate different approaches to common situations. Then there will be many sections where I write with more authority and explain my experiences using different management and marketing techniques. I even point out things that simply no longer work that way. Intermixed are suggestions, predictions, and even some guesses as to where we are heading and how to best prepare for it.

Practical Apartment Management isn't just for full-time professionals charged with running large developments. In fact, the book serves as a guide to thousands of owners of small rental properties. After all, the problems and situations that arise in managing rental property are really much the same whether it is large or small. The difference is in the frequency of occurrence. A manager of a small property might not experience a single resident who totally "trashes" an apartment in a five-year period while those handling buildings with hundreds of units may see the problem several times each year. The steps to minimize these occurrences and to rectify the problems when they occur are really the same, almost without regard to the property's size. In many respects, the book's value to owners and managers of smaller properties might be even greater. For those individuals managing very large properties, the learning curve is quite steep, and it does not take long to become grounded in many of the ways things can go wrong.

One of the biggest obstacles in evaluating and implementing new ideas and procedures is simply finding the time to do it. Office and paperwork ground so many managers that time actually spent at the property is almost nil. The difference between the old and new ways of managing apartments is the computer. Throughout this book, the reader will be reminded of the many tasks that can be relegated to or handled by this ever-advancing device. It accomplishes in seconds what took hours to do just a few years ago. Budgeting, rent scheduling, "what-if" financial scenarios, alphabetizing, letter writing, maintenance scheduling, rent collections, communications, and reporting are a tiny listing of the tasks being performed by computers. This book points out many other management-related tasks that can be handled automatically and electronically, freeing more time for planning, action, and original thought.

My hope is that this new fifth edition of *Practical Apartment Management* will provide you with a fresh look at the business of managing rental property. You will probably relate to some of my experiences and argue with others. My goal is to nudge you from your routine and to encourage you to try some entirely new approaches. The rental customer is crying out for new and better accommodations and nicer treatment. *Practical Apartment Management* can be your guide to that end.

ACKNOWLEDGEMENTS

The most important person in the planning, writing, editing, and final production of *Practical Apartment Management* is Caroline Scoulas. She is the Senior Editor of IREM and quarterbacks so many of its books and publications.

When I received the call that it was time to begin writing the book's fifth edition, my first question was: Will Caroline Scoulas be available to help me? Over the years, I have worked with many book and magazine editors, but none the equal of Caroline. Her skills, interest, energy level, and dedication are an absolute pleasure to witness. She doesn't ask you to compromise your thoughts and ideas, but she does insist on an accurate and balanced text. The messages in this book are mine, but the words that best express them are often Caroline's. She is an extremely talented, warm, and wonderful person. Thank you, Caroline, for your help, patience, and friendship.

Next, I would like to recognize a number of property management experts who undertook the challenge of acting as reviewers for this new fifth edition. They were chosen because of their long experience in apartment management and their geographic diversity. They were asked to read through the text line by line, to raise questions and challenge principles and practices, and to offer suggestions to make the book as accurate and informative as possible. These reviewers did their job. They made me prove-up facts and figures and alerted me to different practices and industry techniques as well as changing local laws. I want to thank the following individuals for taking their time and adding their expertise in making *Practical Apartment Management* a valuable and important industry publication: Diana L. Accardi, CPM®, Vice President of Property Management for Omni Apartment Communities in Denver, Colorado; Nancy A. Bishop, CPM®, Broker Associate with Howard Bishop and Company, also in Denver; Natalie D. Brecher, CPM®, Principal of Brecher & Associates Incorporated in Redondo Beach, California, and Laurence C. Harmon, CPM®, CRE, of McGough Development LLC, in Roseville, Minnesota.

While writing this manuscript, I made countless calls and visited owners and managers of rental properties in many cities and towns. I wanted to garner their reaction to the changes that are occurring in the daily operation of their properties. What do renters want? Where have so many renters gone? What's making the business easier or tougher? How are new laws affecting rental operations? I asked for and received candid answers from these people who work in the trenches every day. Owners, managers, and leasing and maintenance personnel unselfishly took their time to show and explain how they were approaching and solving today's marketing and management challenges. In particular, I would like to recognize the following CERTIFIED PROPERTY MANAGER® (CPM®) Members of IREM for their help and advice: Barry Katz, Jules Gallanter, Ted Amdur, Lino Strazz, Paul Petrie, Bob Hohmann, and Jim Pio. I also asked friends and associates for their insights regarding accounting, legal, and other rental market issues—Joseph Batdorf, Morrie Much, and Frank Wagner were especially helpful. Many of these individuals took the time to read and critique text segments. I send a special thank you to each of them.

I am also grateful to John Rocheford of Rockford, Inc., AMO®, for granting us permission to use a photograph of one of the properties his firm manages and to Gretchen Huetteman, Chapter Administrator of the IREM Minnesota Chapter, for making the arrangements.

Edward N. Kelley, CPM® Emeritus

About the Author

Edward N. Kelley, CPM® Emeritus, has made property management a life-long endeavor. What started out as a part-time job blossomed into a remarkable series of achievements and successes. Mr. Kelley has pioneered and led the industry in a variety of areas: A great many of the marketing and management techniques that are common to the industry today got their start as one of his innovations.

In a career spanning 45 years, Mr. Kelley has had executive management responsibilities for billions of dollars worth of investment real estate. These include more than 150,000 apartments, many millions of square feet of office space, and commercial properties and hotels. These properties are spread over 137 cities, in 38 states. Mr. Kelley was a pioneer in the management of the country's very first condominium developments. He has undertaken numerous rehab and restoration projects including some with national historic registry status. His property management firm has gained a wide reputation in banking circles for its successes as a turnaround specialist. For more than twenty years, Mr. Kelley has also been the primary real estate consultant to a major university.

Mr. Kelley is a CERTIFIED PROPERTY MANAGER® (CPM®) and has been awarded the distinction of CPM Emeritus status. He has been active as a CPM Member of the Institute of Real Estate Management (IREM) for 40 years and has served on many of its committees and councils including Regional Vice President for three years. He is a former President of the Chicago Chapter of IREM. Mr. Kelley has twice received the Author of the Year Award from the *Journal of Property Management.* He was honored as the first recipient of the IREM Foundation's Louis I. and Y. T. Lum Award for his dedication to advancing professionalism in the industry and his many contributions in real estate education. For many years, Mr. Kelley was a popular Senior Instructor on the National Faculty at IREM; he also received the Lloyd D. Hanford Sr. Distinguished Faculty Award.

Mr. Kelley's writings and seminar presentations have enjoyed a wide audience. In addition to *Practical Apartment Management*, he has written other texts dealing with investment analysis and apartment marketing. He has written many computer software programs designed to analyze economic feasibility, forecast optimum rents, schedule maintenance tasks, and track rental prospects. His articles, which appear in industry trade publications, deal with subjects such as apartment marketing, upgrading and renovation, resident retention, rent setting, collections, and staff training and motivation. Mr. Kelley is a very accomplished speaker, and his programs as a headline speaker at the industry's major trade shows and conventions draw sellout audiences.

Contents

Chapter 1   **Getting Started** 1
The Business of Apartment Management   1
Types of Residents   7
Goals of Ownership   15
Ownership Disadvantages   19
Forms of Ownership   20
Types of Managers   24
Real Estate Investment Economics   27
The Management Agreement   32

Chapter 2   **Hiring and Managing the Property Staff** 37
Hiring   37
Employee Policies   41
Managing Your Staff   59

Chapter 3   **Property Policies** 65
The Office   67
Recreational Facilities   71
Supporting Amenities   72
Parking   75
Security and Protection Issues   76
Safety and Health Concerns   80

Chapter 4   **Leasing Policies** 83
Resident Selection   83
The Application Process   90

Chapter 5   **The Lease Agreement** 101
Terms of Occupancy   102
Special Provisions   108
Other Common Lease Clauses   110

Chapter 6   **Policies for Residents** 114
Communications   114
General Resident Policies   116
Problem-Solving   122
Improving Occupancy Durations   129

Chapter 7   **Rent Payments** 135
Rent Payment Policies   135
Rent Collection Policies   138

Chapter 8   **Maintaining the Property** 144
Getting Acquainted with Your Property   146
Documenting Property Assets   147
Conducting a Maintenance Inspection   152
The Apartment   162
Ongoing Maintenance of the Property   167
Deferred Maintenance   178
Supplies and Parts   179
Getting the Right Start   180

Chapter 9   **Preparing a Marketing Campaign** 182
Understanding Why People Rent   182
Market Identification   185
Marketing Tools   192
Finding Prospects: Other Sources   208

Chapter 10   **Advertising and Promotion** 213
Advertising Media   213
Traffic Builders   231
Public Relations   232

Chapter 11   **Converting Prospects to Residents** 234

The Telephone Inquiry   236
Preparing for the Visit   239
The Prospect's Arrival   243
Evaluating Results   251

Chapter 12   **Setting and Raising Rents** 254

Cash-on-Cash Return   254
Income Groups   255
Setting Rents for the First Time   258
Making Adjustments   269
Raising Rents in Established Properties   276
Determining Rent Increases   280

Chapter 13   **Upgrading and Renovation** 288

Planning Ahead   289
Four Levels of Rehab   296
Adding Amenities and Upgrades   300

Chapter 14   **Insuring the Property** 303

All Risk Coverage   305
Insuring Against Property Loss   305
Insuring Against Other Claims   308
Workers' Compensation   311
Handling Insured Losses   312
Risk Management   315

Chapter 15   **Budgeting and Planning** 317

Types of Budgets   318
Preparing a Budget   323
Budget Analysis   330
Business Plan   333
Management Plan   335

Chapter 16   **Computers, Accounting, and Record Keeping** . . 336

Computers   336
Accounting   337
Records   346
A Final Word   350

Glossary   351
Index   373

Albert Einstein's *Rules of Work:*
  Out of clutter, find simplicity.
  From discord, find harmony.
  In the middle of difficulty lies opportunity.

1

*The value of investment real estate is in direct proportion
to its ability to produce net operating income.*

Getting Started

Some 33 percent of the 105 million American households rent the place where they live. Assume a very conservative $550 monthly rent, and you have almost $229 billion changing hands each year. Slightly more than one-half of the nation's total rental housing stock is contained in a myriad of small properties. Management attention to these units requires only a few hours each month. The remainder, some 16 million rental units, is in larger apartment properties, and they provide the career opportunities for tens of thousands of professional managers. By some estimates, this segment of the rental market is expected to grow about ten percent per year through 2010.

The Business of Apartment Management

Real estate management offers a career opportunity with an ongoing growth potential. As an apartment manager, you have control over your destiny, and your proficiency can mean the difference between mediocre and dramatic results.

Real estate management is one of few occupations in which a single individual can make a difference. Even working for a large management firm, an enterprising manager can quickly emerge as a rising star. You are not locked up in some corporate tower with a sea of padded workstations. You are in the field, charged with the success or failure of some very valuable real estate. How you handle the challenge can be measured in many ways. With your initiatives, you can succeed where others have failed. Within months, you can begin restoring an apartment community's fiscal and physical viability, its direction and reputation. Many properties are valued in the millions of dollars, and owners will pay handsome rewards to individuals who can produce positive results.

Much of the rental housing stock in the United States is past its prime, and decision time is fast approaching. Some will fall under the wrecking ball to free the land for better uses. Others will undergo some creative upgrading that will improve their competitiveness. The apartment manager will play a very important role in this renaissance. A manager who understands the neighborhood's demographic forces and the property's competitive niche is in an ideal position to forecast future market needs and identify properties that are the best candidates for renewal.

As individual managers perfect their craft, their value in the job marketplace increases correspondingly. In time, creative managers will be in a position to apply the learned skills for their own account. By starting small and taking some risks, an apartment manager has one of the best opportunities of building some serious personal wealth.

Property Location.   Virtually every discussion dealing with the subject of real estate quickly underscores the importance of a property's location. This book is no exception. It is location that will dictate much of the success or failure of a given property, not the skills of or programs introduced by the owner or manager. You can apply the basics outlined in this book to an ordinary property in an excellent neighborhood and make it very successful. On the other hand, you can invest a great deal of money, imagination, and energy into a property in a declining or marginal location and realize only limited success.

For those unseasoned real estate investors and developers who disregard this warning, a natural trap awaits: Properties and land in poor locations are comparatively inexpensive and, thus, appear to be bargains. Realizing that it may be difficult to find buyers for their poorly situated real estate, sellers are inclined to take back financing or offer other purchase incentives. To many novices, a lower price and special purchase arrangements are irresistible. Nevertheless, poorly located property is seldom a bargain and usually produces mediocre profits at best.

As a real estate manager, you will frequently be offered opportunities to increase the value of investment real estate by applying your creative skills. You must understand that even the most highly skilled manager will find it nearly impossible to overcome the negative forces of a poor location. Every property can be improved, but the real turnaround success stories always start with ailing properties in choice or improving locations.

You might ask, at this point, just what defines a poor location? Generally, it is a neighborhood of buildings that can no longer attract caring residents. The buildings are undergoing an accelerated rate of decline. Often the neighborhood's infrastructure is being allowed to decay. As the resident profile declines, incidents of drugs, gangs, crime, and domestic disturbances increase. A level of fear and disgust finally drives away those who have other options. These vacancies are filled with replacements who have less pride and more personal baggage.

Types of Rental Properties.   Building height is a good starting point to distinguish different types of apartment properties. Where land is relatively cheap and the developer is under little or no pressure to increase the number of housing units per acre, shorter buildings can be constructed and spread out over a large area. Where land is expensive, developers must find ways of getting more units onto the land, so taller buildings are constructed. In this book, buildings of various heights are identified as follows:

- *Low-rise.* Buildings with one to four stories. Elevators are the norm in four-story buildings and are often included in two- and three-story designs.
- *Mid-rise.* Buildings with five to nine stories. Elevator service is assumed unless otherwise stated.
- *High-rise.* Buildings with ten or more stories.

The first years of the twenty-first century have brought a continuing series of changes and improvements to the look and layout of rental apartments. Villas, manor, and coach-houses are different names for housing that is designed to use multi-level layouts. Frequently, two or more units are interwoven on different floor levels. In other words, the design of a two-story unit may be staggered, placing its second floor space on top of a single-story unit. This design produces some interesting layouts and can permit the architect to squeeze more dwelling units onto the site—a cost-saving and revenue-increasing measure. Stacking identical apartments in uniform tiers is becoming less common. The old "city row house"—a two and one-half or three-story unit with a direct, outside entry and a very narrow floor plan—is also finding acceptance in both urban and suburban locations.

The method of construction often serves as an indicator of the building's complexity. "Stick-built" buildings are much simpler and less costly to build than reinforced concrete structures. A big difference is the mechanical systems, which are typically centralized in concrete structures and involve rather sophisticated equipment and controls. Elevators, sprinkler systems, trash compactors, pressurized corridors, and annunciator panels are just a sampling of the extra components you must oversee as the manager of these larger and sturdier structures.

In suburban and outlying areas, the traditional two-story garden apartment developments are losing their preeminence to taller and much denser building designs. The cost and scarcity of suitable sites are forcing many of these changes. The convenience of elevators is becoming more common in low-rise buildings. Garage or at least covered parking is quickly becoming a "must-have" feature. Crowding more units and facilities onto an already "tight" site is being partly camouflaged by intricate land layouts and mature landscape designs.

Whenever possible, newer construction and properties undergoing major renovation have transferred most utilities to the resident via individual metering. Electricity, heating fuel, and in many cases water are now billed to each resident.

Unit Size, Area, and Layout.   A prospect setting out to rent an apartment is interested in unit size (number of rooms), apartment layout (functionality of the space) and, to a lesser degree, the unit's area (square footage).

Apartment size is expressed by the number of bedrooms and bathrooms a unit contains (sample abbreviation: 2BR/2B) or by its total number of rooms.

Small bedroom-less apartments are called *efficiencies* or *studios*. (In the Southwest, a studio can refer to a small apartment with two levels.) Most often an efficiency apartment contains a small walk-in or Pullman kitchen (a kitchen built along a wall), a combined living-dining room that also doubles as a sleeping area, and a bathroom. A larger efficiency apartment layout— the *convertible*—is also popular, especially in expensive urban locations. The identifying feature of a convertible is an alcove off a large living room that serves as a sleeping area.

There is a prescribed way to make a *room count*. The kitchen, no matter how small, is considered one room. A living room is counted as a room, as is a separate formal dining room. A living and dining room combination is counted as one and one-half rooms, unless the combined space exceeds 300 square feet, in which case it is counted as two rooms. Dining or dinette space smaller than 100 square feet is regarded only as a half-room. Each bedroom with its own separate entry off a hall is counted as a room. A den or family room is also counted as one room. A bathroom that contains a toilet, washbasin, and tub or shower stall is a full bath; a bathroom with just a toilet and basin is classified as a half-bath. Neither is included in the room count, nor are outside patios or balconies, or closets, no matter how large.

Most apartment managers have adopted a short-cut method to determine an apartment's room count. This approach assumes that all apartments contain two and one-half rooms plus the number of bedrooms. An efficiency apartment, for example, would equal just two and one-half rooms since it has no bedroom, while a one-bedroom apartment would be equal to three and one-half rooms—two and one-half rooms for the apartment plus one for the bedroom. This system is much easier and surprisingly accurate.

The area of an apartment is stated in terms of its *rentable square feet.* This measurement is determined by multiplying a unit's length by its width. No deduction is made for partitions, plumbing chases, or other small niches. Neither should an apartment's square-foot area include balconies, patios, or unheated sun porches.

To a seasoned renter, an apartment's layout is really more important than its square footage. When comparing two apartments of identical area, one layout is often more functional than the other. Some layouts simply accommodate furnishings and belongings better than others and are more desirable because of their distribution of space. Newer apartment layouts share space very effectively. An island rather than a wall may separate the kitchen from the living room. Hallways take up much less space than they did in the past. In two-bedroom suites, bedrooms are placed at opposite ends of the apartment (two-bedroom split), whenever possible, to provide increased privacy for roommates, parents and children, or visiting guests.

Unit Mix. Almost every rental property contains a number of different-sized apartments. This distribution, whatever it is, is referred to as the unit mix. The unit mix can greatly affect the character, ultimate use, direction, and success of a particular property type. Any one of the property types described would take on a different character if it contained only one size of dwelling unit. For example, a building with only efficiency units would have a distinctly different resident profile than one with only two-bedroom units.

A building's location and intended market should influence the builder's decision when establishing the optimum unit mix. Differing economic conditions also affect the desirability of and demand for particular unit sizes. During periods when the economy is depressed, efficiency apartments and convertibles enjoy their greatest demand. Many people decide to scale down their living accommodations to small apartments in desirable buildings rather than move to one-bedroom apartments in older, less-expensive buildings or lose privacy by taking in a roommate to help share costs.

During down economies, even the mainstay one-bedroom apartment suffers vacancies as people opt for the less-expensive efficiency units or choose to share the rent for a two-bedroom apartment with a roommate or return to their parents' homes in a cost-cutting effort. Families who need two bedrooms will settle for apartments with one bath instead of the more desired two. Likewise, two- and three-bedroom townhouses will be in short supply as occupants wait for the economy to improve before they purchase a home.

At any point in time, economic conditions will affect the demand for the various types of units, so the definition of the optimum unit mix will always be changing. There is no ideal unit mix that always maintains the same level of demand. The goal is to provide a wide range of unit types, in varying percentages, to sustain a healthy occupancy and demand over a rental building's long life.

Managers seldom have the chance to establish the unit mix of a development. Still, they should be aware of the differences among unit types and their respective advantages and disadvantages.

Apartment Numbering.   A building should be identified by either an address or a special name, never by its construction project number or a single letter. Apartments should be identified by numbers that refer to their floor. Consider the difference between these two addresses: Apartment 802 at 415 Forest Park Circle and Apartment 14 in Building D.

Standard practice is to have the first part of an apartment number identify the floor and the last part refer to a specific apartment. Whenever possible you should employ the traditional numbering system. This would have you begin with the northernmost and/or easternmost apartment and proceed clockwise. For example, apartment 302 would refer to the second apartment (from the starting point) on the third floor; apartment 2102 would mean the same apartment on the twenty-first floor.

In some jurisdictions, the local fire department may dictate addresses and identifying signs for apartment properties. It is common for the U.S. Postal Service to also become involved in address approval processes.

Nonyield Space.   Every apartment building contains some nonyield space. This space costs money to build and is essential to the operation of the building, but it does not produce direct revenue. Obviously, the less nonyield space the better.

The ratio between a property's gross building area (length times the width of the structure[s] times the number of floors with living space) and the rentable area (the sum of the areas of all the apartments) is termed the building's *efficiency factor.* For example, a property with a gross building area of 100,000 square feet and a rentable area of 85,000 square feet has an 85-percent efficiency factor:

$$\frac{85,000 \text{ sq ft Rentable Area}}{100,000 \text{ sq ft Gross Building Area}} = 85\% \text{ Efficiency Factor}$$

Efficiency factors of apartment buildings vary for a number of reasons. Some architects are more skilled than others at minimizing nonyield space. On the other hand, a designer may intentionally provide more nonyield space than is necessary in a luxury building to establish a feeling of opulence through conspicuous waste (e.g., large lobbies or extra-wide corridors).

Generally, the most efficient housing type is one with its own separate entry such as a townhouse. Its efficiency factor is usually in the mid-90-

percent range, with losses due only to the exterior wall thickness and any outbuildings such as storage, laundry, or recreation facilities. High-rise and mid-rise buildings have comparatively lower efficiency factors than do walk-up apartments. This is due to their greater proportion of interior common spaces plus their space-consuming mechanical equipment areas.

Climate also has an impact on efficiency. Properties in northern regions usually have much lower efficiency factors than do those in southern regions because of vestibules and interior corridors that are added as a buffer against the elements. These properties also frequently require additional nonyield space to house larger heating, ventilation, and other mechanical apparatus. In northern regions, efficiency factors between 70 and 85 percent are common. Buildings in warm or moderate climates typically enjoy an efficiency factor in the range of 85 to 90 percent.

Rental Cycles. An airline pays close attention to the number of take-offs and landings for each of its planes. Rental car companies decide when to retire a car by its odometer reading and by taking into account the number of times the car has been leased. Rental apartments are not much different. If records were available for a large sampling of apartments from their first rental to their last, I am convinced they would show a definite correlation between the number of "occupant cycles" an apartment experiences and its useful life. The wear and tear comes more from the ins-and-outs than from the continuous days of occupancy. You will see this principle woven throughout this book as we discuss resident retention, turnover, maximizing returns, and the life of the property.

Types of Residents

The life of a residential property closely reflects the people who have occupied it. Because residents add a dimension to the character of a property, it is necessary to understand the resident's role, differentiate between the various types of residents, and apply management skills to guide a property's character through sensible resident selection.

Before discussing different types of residents, let's address the issue of word choice: How do you identify the people who live in the properties you manage? There has been a movement to replace the word "tenant" with another designation such as occupant, resident, or lessee. Some even refer to tenants as customers. This tendency is, in part, a response to the commonly held opinion that a tenant is a second-class citizen—a view held by many Americans in the early days of rental property. It is also an effort to deemphasize the financial relationship between owner and tenant (notice that I also choose to use the word "owner" rather than "landlord" because the latter carries some negative connotations).

Such a negative view is, of course, inaccurate. Many of the world's largest corporations are tenants in the premises they occupy. Nevertheless, it is important for the apartment manager to be aware of the sensitive nature of the word and to use it with discretion—especially in conversation. This is why I have chosen to use the words "resident," "occupant," and "renter" with a fair degree of frequency.

The fact remains that "tenant" is really the only word in the English language that specifically refers to a person who gains the privilege of occupying land or a building by paying rent. After all, every tenant is a resident, but not vice versa. There are hundreds of years of landlord and tenant laws, but no owner and occupant laws. As a result, it is absolutely necessary to employ the word "tenant" in legal contexts such as lease documents.

There are many types of residents: singles and families, students and the elderly, never-nesters and empty-nesters, and so forth. Since experience has demonstrated that each of these groups can be expected to behave in a certain predictable way and make certain demands, managers of residential rental properties must be able to recognize the resident groupings. The type of resident for which a building is designed will affect many aspects of management, including marketing, maintenance, and resident relations.

Some people may object to categorizing residents, claiming that every one is an individual human being and must be treated as such. True, residents are individuals. Still, insurance companies categorize people by height, weight, gender, medical history, occupation, etc., on the principle that groups demonstrate certain tendencies. Scientists make similar generalizations when studying behavior. It is important for the apartment manager to give some thought to the different types of apartment residents and to understand their different characteristics. Residents can be grouped in two broad categories:

> *Renters by choice.* These are renters making the decision that renting their housing is the way to go. As a group, they stay longer, cause fewer problems, and make better residents. They back up their decision with commitments of money, time, and energy.

> *Renters by circumstance.* To those in this grouping, renting is often a compromise, an alternative, a substitute or temporary convenience. They are not necessarily happy with renting; it is just what works best for them at a particular point in time.

The chart in Exhibit 1.1 illustrates the relative size of these two groupings.

Renters by Choice. Career professionals, settled people without children, couples whose children have grown and left home, and many retired people are renters by choice. For some, the situation is one in which the extra space available in purchased housing is not needed. Others want the freedom provided by renting (sometimes referred to as the "lock and leave

Exhibit 1.1
Decision to Rent

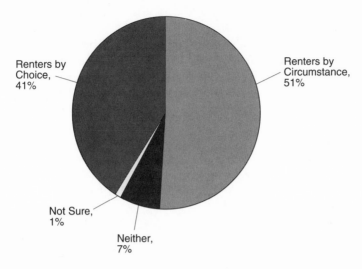

Renters by
Choice,
41%

Renters by
Circumstance,
51%

Not Sure,
1%

Neither,
7%

Source: Fannie Mae, 2000.

set"). Still others choose to rent because it is the most economical means of living in the area of their choice. (The preponderance of renter households are in the younger age groups, as can be seen in Exhibit 1.2.)

Their choice, however, is not necessarily absolute. If high-quality rental housing and its accompanying services are not available, renters by choice will be swayed to buy, and they are particularly attracted to cooperative and condominium units where exterior maintenance is provided. In increasing numbers, townhomes and other styles of attached housing are also being purchased by former renters. Almost all of these units provide private attached garages, which have become an essential need for so many. Owners and managers must be alert to the fact that renters by choice demand quality accommodations and will be constantly wooed by real estate brokers offering housing for sale.

Still, the resident types described below have one thing in common: They prefer to rent. Their priorities, lifestyles, and stage in life are such that the desire to become homeowners is negligible, perhaps entirely absent. Many long-term property owners are deciding that the time has come to sell and "cash out" their equity providing them with a retirement nest egg and saving their heirs the real estate-related problems of settling their estate. Some are convinced that, in the long run, there is greater economy in rent-

Exhibit 1.2
Renters as Percentage of Households (by Age)

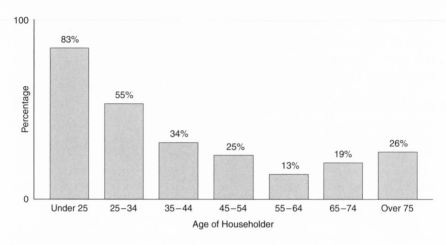

Source: U.S. Census, 2000.

ing. Others do not want to cut grass or handle maintenance chores any longer. In any case, these people are making a conscious decision in their choice to be a renter.

Empty-Nesters. Typically, these are married couples who have raised their children—perhaps in single-family homes—and have chosen the carefree ways of apartment living. They invest in furnishings to provide comfort and convenience. They pay the rent promptly, live in peace and harmony with neighbors, and pose few management problems. As the most selective of all renters in choosing their living quarters, they insist on quality in housing, services, and management. Before renting they shop around, since they are looking for accommodations that will remain satisfactory for the long run. They seek—and are willing to pay a premium for—quality, value, and service.

Empty-nesters potentially make up a large and increasing segment of the rental market. Unfortunately for the apartment manager, many empty-nesters are buying townhouses, coach houses, manor houses, and condominiums rather than renting. They have learned to enjoy the appreciation in value and the tax benefits of owning, and they regard ownership as the preferred alternative. Others are concerned that their neighbors in a rental community will not be of the same caliber as those in a more carefully controlled "home-owner community."

Career Professionals.   The number of established career professionals is also increasing. A relatively homogeneous group, their lifestyles are career-oriented. They have chosen to be renters rather than homeowners. The character of their homes is important to them and to their circle of close friends. They tend to choose apartments in neighborhoods that are convenient to work and entertainment activities. Because of their career orientation, these residents may move from time to time, so their occupancy does not offer the same stability that empty-nesters provide to management.

Senior Citizens.   Senior citizens—married and unmarried—who have regular retirement benefits are also renters by choice. They tend to make little noise, pay bills promptly, and keep their homes clean. Such people are also inclined to choose small apartments, especially when they are constrained by fixed incomes that have been diluted by declining yields and losses from investments. Budgetary limitations may keep senior citizens from living in preferred neighborhoods; still, they will be discriminating about finding a place where basic daily needs can be met. Managers learn that there are some specialized challenges associated with the aging of senior citizens which require extra concern and attention

Senior citizens are on their way to becoming the fastest-growing segment of the U.S. population, and many will choose to rent their housing.

Renters by Circumstance.   Offsetting renters by choice are those who rent because of their current circumstances. A student attending college away from home, for example, needs temporary housing. Families and individuals arriving in the United States for the first time are, more often than not, renters. Many young families want a place to live until they can save enough money to make a downpayment on a home, and singles who anticipate being married someday often do not want to be tied down to a house. In each of these cases, rental housing is occupied on an interim basis. Decisions about ultimate living arrangements are still to be made. Because of the temporary aspect of the choice to rent, there is a reluctance to commit time, money, and energy to create a home-like environment. When rental units are occupied without an ongoing commitment, management problems increase.

From management's point of view, the duration of occupancy and the absence of costly problems measure the desirability of different groups of renters by circumstance. After all, with good service, renters by circumstance may be transformed into permanent renters by choice. Every time the need to re-rent is avoided, net operating income (NOI) increases. (The economics of turnover and resident retention are discussed in Chapter 6.)

Families with Children.   The total number of families with children has declined somewhat but still remains a meaningful segment of the rental market. This becomes increasingly true when the cost of buying and maintaining a single-family home rises faster than most families' ability to meet these expenses. Renting often becomes the interim solution while a family postpones its goal of homeownership.

Families with children are less mobile than other residents, meaning that the need to deal with move-outs will be minimized. Also, the rate of skipouts (residents who leave without paying rent) tends to be lower with families. With a creative management program that channels the energies of youngsters in productive directions, an apartment manager can take advantage of the relative stability of this segment of the market.

Families with children may be renters by circumstance, but there are a lot of them. Also, the Fair Housing Amendments Act of 1988 prohibits discrimination based on *familial status* (the only exceptions are made for housing that satisfies specific requirements for older persons). Thus, it is not merely prudent to consider including families with children in your apartment community, it is required by law.

One- and Two-Person Households.   The people in these two categories represent the vast majority of all renters. According to the U.S. Census, in fact, single people living alone account for about 47 percent of all households. Two-person households are the second largest grouping with 27 percent. Both of these groups are maturing, with an average age well into the thirties. As these groups age, their lifestyles will mellow, their possessions will grow in number, and their abilities to discern quality accommodations will sharpen.

A substantial number of these people will not become homeowners; renting will be their way of life. While these people may start out moving from one property to another, they eventually find themselves looking for a place to call home for a number of years.

When interest rates and mortgage terms are particularly attractive and when the desire to have the latest in housing features and designs can only be satisfied by "for sale" housing, this segment of the housing market can quickly shift from renting to ownership.

Immigrants.   Often overlooked in a discussion of types of residents, immigrants make up a very sizeable segment of renters by circumstance. Many are uncertain about their long-range plans and often lack the resources to even begin thinking of ownership. Most need time to acclimate to a new country and society. Some will start out sharing accommodations with others; but in time, they will seek their own quarters, and the first step will be that of a renter. As in past decades, immigrant households often accept housing in deteriorating neighborhoods, and this grouping has done much to boost occupancies in buildings that are long past their prime. But this does not last for long. In time, they become established and identify better neighborhoods then set their sights on a home of their own. Conversations with home sellers will confirm that a sizable segment of homebuyers are foreign-born and relatively recent arrivals.

Divorced and Divorcing.   The U.S. Census Bureau reports that, on an average day, there are more than 3,000 divorces. One or both of the marriage partners in this grouping will often become a renter by circumstance, at least for a time. The resident profile of many rental communities shows a considerable percentage of separated or divorced individuals. Their situation is in transition: They are often struggling emotionally and financially, and rental housing often best satisfies their current needs.

Students.   The most temporary of all resident types is the student. Students come in large numbers to college towns, bringing with them few possessions and even less money. Their stay is short. This, and their lack of commitment to the place they are renting, presents management problems that only those who specialize in the student market will care to face. Occupancy terms are for nine months or less. Rent collections are often challenging. Wear and tear creates enormous maintenance problems. There is also the competition to cope with because the colleges themselves may offer lower-priced housing (dormitories, student and staff apartments, etc.). In periods of declining school enrollments, investment properties that rely on student renters are left with more and more vacancies.

Income Groups.   The discussion of resident types so far has made no reference to income. It is a sensitive subject that will be addressed in more detail in Chapter 12 when I discuss setting and raising rents. One fact is clear: Managing housing for low-income residents is different from and can be more demanding than managing apartments occupied by those more able to afford housing. It is beyond the scope of this book to deal with the socio-economic reasons for this observation, but for completeness, the matter must be mentioned.

It should also be stated that the management of a property that has been financed with government subsidies or has residents whose rents are subsidized requires a thorough knowledge of the regulations established by the U.S. Department of Housing and Urban Development (HUD) or other governmental housing agencies.

Categorizing the people who comprise the rental market, especially using a small number of classifications, is arbitrary and obviously very general. The exceptions to these descriptions are many and varied. In the final analysis, the quality and desirability of each resident can be gauged only by the individual's performance. (A method of rating residents' performance that I

Rating Residents

One of the most frequently asked questions in the management business is "What makes a good resident?" From my experience, I have come to the conclusion that residents can exhibit up to five separate, but equally important, attributes. While some residents may demonstrate only one—or none—of these attributes, the majority will exhibit at least two or three (i.e., somewhere in the middle). The success and future of a rental community greatly depends on how its residents measure up. The five resident attributes are:

1. **Willingness to invest in their homes.** Some residents move their possessions in and start living. Others see it as their home and spend time and money adding custom touches such as special window coverings and furnishings to fit the unit's niches. These residents invest to add warmth and to personalize their homes.

2. **Setting up permanent housekeeping.** This means a "we are here to stay" attitude—fully unpacking, hanging pictures, adopting a decorating theme, and adding accessories. They register their children in school, change their car license and voter registration, notify friends and family of their new address, and join the community.

3. **Social compatibility.** Multifamily housing puts residents in close proximity to one another. Do they exhibit common courtesy and civility? Do they get along with members of their families and their neighbors? Is there evidence of sharing? Do they avoid encroaching on others?

4. **Financial stability.** Does the resident pay the rent (and other financial obligations) on time? It is safe to say that a majority of problems with residents are centered around money. Financial pressure can transfer itself to most aspects of normal living. Are the resident's finances stretched too thin?

5. **Understanding of the need for rules.** Some residents believe the rules are meant for the "other guy." Excessive noise, rowdy friends, littering, and other selfish behaviors are characteristics of troublesome residents. Others understand the need for rules and do their best to live within these constraints.

Accurately gauging each resident can be difficult, and the process is somewhat arbitrary, but it is important that managers try to do this if they are to understand the tenor of the apartment communities they manage.

To demonstrate this principle, suppose you are the manager of a small, ten-unit property. You carefully consider each of the ten residents and which of the five attributes they exhibit. Assuming the ideal resident would have five stars, you would take one star away for each attribute a particular resident does *not* exhibit. There is no need to be harsh in your rating, but you should try to be fair. (Knowing what you know now, you might ask yourself: Would I choose this resident again? Are there problems that are severe enough to not renew someone's lease?) The results of your evaluation might look something like the following:

Rating Residents *(continued)*

Apt	Commentary	Rating
101	Top resident; exhibits all five attributes	★★★★★
102	Struggles to meet the rent; otherwise a responsible resident	★★★★
103	Continually complains; slow in paying rent	★★★
104	Apartment is damaged, slow in paying rent; potential trouble	★★
105	Has had repeated fights with neighbors; eviction proceedings started	★
106	Has little furniture; neighbors complain about noise	★★★
107	Problems with children, rent, and unit condition	★
108	Sheets hung at windows; noisy	★★★
109	Has little furniture; dog barks a lot	★★★
110	Argues with neighbor but has not disturbed other residents	★★★★

Together, these ten residents were given a total of thirty stars or an average for the property of three stars per resident. This indicates a middle-of-the-road resident profile. It calls out for greater resident selectivity and indicates a need for undertaking an improvement program. This property is at a balance point, and one or two more two-star residents could easily put this property "on the skids." The problem residents and those that are less stable can drive out the four- and five-star residents. On the other hand, careful selection and an improved property could help to attract additional four- or five-star residents.

The example contains only ten units, and the average is easily skewed by a change in the ratings of one or two residents. Changing the ratings for a much larger property occurs more slowly.

There are many properties that can barely muster an average of two stars per resident. When a mid-to-large size property has an average score of just one or two stars, the situation is very difficult and sometimes irreversible. This generally indicates that the property is in a state of decline and may be coming to the end of its economic life. On the opposite end of the spectrum, properties that enjoy a four-star average resident profile need a constant infusion of capital and special resident services to keep the property at that level. Properties in the mid-range could start a downward slide without better resident selectivity and serious upgrading.

have used and found workable is described in the accompanying sidebar. Throughout this book, references to the quality or caliber of residents will reflect this rating system.)

Goals of Ownership

When you undertake the management of a real estate investment for either yourself or others, the first order of business is to understand exactly what you expect to accomplish. If you are being hired by the owner of an apartment community, what does he or she want? "To make as much money as possible" is not a very precise answer, and it is one that will not help you very much in preparing a management plan. Some owners need regular monthly income while others would rather reinvest surplus money into the property in hopes of dramatically increasing the ultimate resale value some time in the future. An owner may have several goals for an investment property. Over time, these may change. They may even conflict with each other. It is the manager's duty to ascertain, clarify, and continually verify owners' goals. Let's explore some of the more important goals of ownership and their differences.

Periodic Income.   This means a steady return in the form of cash. An owner risks the cash invested (equity) when purchasing real estate. In return, the ownership entity expects to receive monthly, quarterly, or annual cash dividends that represent the profits or surplus revenue derived from the property's operation. Investors certainly have other choices besides income-producing real estate. Alternatives include certificates of deposit (CDs), treasury notes and bills, corporate and government bonds, stocks, annuities, investment trusts, and money market accounts that can yield regular income. Many of these are insured, guaranteed, or backed by years and years of payment patterns. However, many time-proven investments have failed for a number of reasons (accounting fraud, corporate malfeasance, bankruptcies, business failures, etc.). Other investments are subject to fluctuations, and sometimes these are wild and unpredictable. Investment real estate must be included with the unpredictable, and it is also highly sensitive to market "winds" and the impact of management skills. Those seeking regular and predictable returns often opt for buildings with long-term commercial or industrial leases held by creditworthy tenants rather than risk the frequent turnover experienced with rental apartments or small offices.

The *rate of return* on investments is generally dictated by the probability of predictable and sustained periodic earnings. In other words, an investor will usually seek a much higher return if there is a degree of uncertainty about either the rate of earnings or the recapture of the original equity invested.

Today, investors are searching for cash generators. They are looking for apartments and other types of rental real estate that will produce a steady flow of cash as a return or reward for invested capital. Often, asking prices are too high for what may be described as barely marginal real estate. Whenever there are too many bidders, the price of the property goes up, which of course, lowers the rate of return. The alternative is to look for properties that have been poorly managed or ones that have been so loaded down with debt in the past that they have a dismal record of returning any cash. Many properties fall into this category. Be aware that finding the right property in terms of location and income-generating potential is the hardest part of the investment process.

In the past, the stock market has raised huge sums of investment capital, and a few firms have emerged as real estate giants, some with portfolios containing hundreds of thousands of apartment units spread throughout the

United States. Their ability to maintain management control over such huge and widely diverse portfolios has not been proven conclusively.

Appreciation in Value. The term "playing long ball" is sometimes used to describe investors in search of real estate investments that produce little or no cash return but have the potential to grow significantly in value sometime in the future. These investors often have successful careers in other fields and look to real estate investment as a way of "parking" surplus cash and providing for a payoff down the road. People who speculate with vacant land are likewise looking for investment appreciation as the reward. Others wait for an economic upturn after purchasing buildings in up-and-coming locations or properties that need an infusion of new money and imagination. Some investors pay too much to capture a trophy building in a prime neighborhood and are forced to wait for rents and values to catch up.

There is considerable difference between the management techniques employed to satisfy the goals of an owner who is more interested in the property's ultimate appreciation in value and those employed to satisfy the owner who is only concerned with the monthly cash return. Usually, the management techniques employed for an owner who is looking solely for periodic return require a more short-term outlook than would those employed for an investor who is speculating and building for the future. Also, the investor seeking appreciation in value is more likely to invest in capital improvements to the property.

Control of Investment. Ownership of rental real estate offers investors one of the highest degrees of physical and financial control. When you purchase stocks or bonds, you are clearly at the mercy of many influences over which you have absolutely no control. When a particular stock plummets or panic selling begins in the market, investors may not see the warning until it is much too late to avoid losses. Bonds, gold, and collectibles often follow patterns that are difficult to predict and impossible to control. With real estate, however, the investor possesses some control. If there is a surplus of unfurnished apartments in the market, the answer may be to offer some units as furnished or corporate rentals. If two-bedroom apartments with one bathroom are slow to rent, perhaps the second bedroom can be modified into a computer center or an extension of the living room. The owner or agent can attract more customers by adding some landscaping punch to the entranceway. An apartment operator can always exercise control over occupancy levels—and sometimes influence profits—by adjusting rental rates.

Some aspects of real estate are beyond the investor's control. Real estate markets, mortgage rates, and property availability are a few examples. Tax laws, environmental and safety issues, and neighborhood influences all change; they too are usually beyond the immediate control of the real estate investor. Nevertheless, real estate offers a higher level of control than most other forms of investment. You, as a manager, will be called upon to participate in that control.

Pride of Ownership.   For many people, being able to demonstrate success and a high level of achievement is something to be coveted. Over the centuries, real estate has been used by many successful people to display their wealth and power within a community. While considering this concept, several names probably come to mind—people who have named towers, developments, or even entire communities after themselves. On a less grand scale, there are many real estate owners who are more motivated by the pride they have in their properties than by the dollars they can earn. As a manager, you will probably come in contact with the type of owner who regularly sacrifices maximum profits while making a property more and more of a showcase. To such an owner, decisions regarding an effect on the property's appearance always seem to outweigh the immediate effect on the bottom line. All the same, it can be said that pride of ownership is another form of value appreciation; meticulously maintained properties almost always command premium prices at resale.

For Use by Owner.   This ownership goal is not nearly as prevalent in rental apartments as it is with office, commercial, or industrial real estate, but it does occur. There are owners who prefer living in multifamily buildings and do not want to trust their lifestyles to the typical landlord. Usually, properties that are used in part by their owners have better locations. Also, a much more strict set of criteria is used to screen prospects who wish to rent in these properties. One of the most difficult assignments a manager can undertake is handling the affairs of a rental apartment property in which the owner or owners reside. This arrangement usually involves two sets of rules—one set for the owners and a distinctly different set for the rent-paying residents.

Financing Leverage.   One of the attributes of real estate ownership is that an investor can leverage a considerably larger investment through borrowing. In its heyday, mortgage financing of 90 percent, and even 100 percent, was not uncommon. An investor who made a relatively small cash downpayment could control real estate worth much more. Any cash return was substantial when compared to the actual cash at risk. Books and television shows were created to show the world how to become rich using *other people's money*. Leverage or mortgage borrowing works best when the cost of the money (the interest rate) is close to the earning rate of the property.

The problems begin to escalate quickly, however, when a property can earn only 5 percent, and borrowing the money costs 7 percent or more. This is called negative leverage. Another sure indicator of trouble is when the mortgage payments are so high that they begin to siphon money away from needed operating funds. During inflationary times, many owners may burden their properties with additional debt in order to gain the advantage of acquiring cash immediately while allowing them to pay back the debt with cheaper, inflation-diluted dollars. Managing investment real estate that has been the subject of such financing schemes and extremes is a most difficult undertaking. After the debt has been "serviced," there is often little money left to operate the investment properly.

Income Tax Shelter.　For a period of some 40 years after World War II, real estate enjoyed a unique tax advantage over almost all other investment ventures. Owners were allowed to recover the cost of their investment—often at an accelerated rate—and offset any resulting losses against their other income, including salaries and the like. Tax laws allowed investors to be creative and aggressive in their interpretation of these regulations. High tax bracket investors often paid premium prices to acquire properties that could serve as tax shelters. The tax-saving aspects of real estate ownership neutralized many basic considerations of a purchase, such as location and the property's ability to generate periodic returns. Many managers were hard pressed to meet the challenge when investors insisted that tax-driven investments continue to "stay open for business" despite their inability to meet normal operating expenses, just to avoid the negative consequences of *recapture* if the property should fail and fall into receivership.

Tax shelter reform legislation now limits the advantages and excesses of *paper losses,* returning real estate investors to the time-proven basics of prudent investing.

Hedge on Inflation.　Whenever there is a hint of inflation and its erosion of the buying power of the dollar, investors begin a shift to collectibles; and one of the most popular and most tangible is investment real estate. Rents historically parallel inflation, thereby protecting the earning power of real estate. Single-family homes often lead price increases in an inflationary period and reach a point at which they become unaffordable. When homes become less affordable, the alternative generally is renting. This strengthens the income potential of rental apartments.

Ownership Disadvantages

There are also disadvantages to purchasing real estate as an investment. A wrong decision in the original purchase or in the method of operation may be enough to wipe out the investment. Changing market conditions, as well as local laws and ordinances, can adversely affect the situation. Rent control, specialized health and safety requirements, and significant changes in property tax rates, for example, can be damaging blows to real estate investment. More than that, real estate ownership means loss of the liquidity of investment capital. For example, while stocks, bonds, and savings accounts can be cashed quickly when funds are needed elsewhere, real estate often requires a minimum of 60 days and usually much longer to liquidate — and then perhaps at a loss because of the quick sale.

Ownership of income-producing real estate involves business management problems that do not arise in most other forms of investment. In addition to the professional management needed to operate the property, there must be supervision of the management itself. More than that, investors in real estate face the fact that bricks and mortar do not last forever. Ultimately, all that will be left is the land itself.

Despite these formidable shortcomings and the fact that many owners are not making money on real estate investments, private investments in multifamily housing properties still offer opportunities for profit. In fact, it can be said that real estate of any kind provides an attraction shared by no other form of investment. This is because land, with or without improvements, is something tangible and inexhaustible that historically has appreciated in value.

Forms of Ownership

The form or structure of the entity that holds title to the property is independent of the type of property, its location, or the resident who selects it for occupancy. Here are some of the more common forms of apartment ownership together with a short description of their unique features or approaches to ownership.

Sole Owner.   Of the 2.7 million rental properties in the United States, according to U.S. Census figures, individuals and husband/wife owners account for more than 80 percent of the total. The great majority of apartment properties contain fewer than five units. Many may have been acquired using earnings from other business or employment income, while some were inherited. Others were created by dividing existing spaces. Most are being held as a form of investment for the production of income and value appreciation.

Partnerships.   When two or more entities invest in a property, you have the makings of a partnership. All partners in an ordinary partnership are general partners. By having more people involved, the risks to each individual are reduced, and larger purchases can be made that may be more profitable because of the economies that come with size. In the case of partnerships, there is always the problem of how to control and deal with disenchanted partners. Written partnership agreements help but are rarely adequate when disagreements arise.

Some partnerships are formed involuntarily through inheritance. These arrangements can be most difficult for the real estate manager because the goals and objectives of the various partners and their attitudes toward risk often are at odds. Hence, the manager is thrust into the position of mediator. This generally is not as big a problem with voluntary partnerships whose participants have similar goals and objectives, although even here disagreements do occur.

For years, attorneys have structured limited partnerships (LPs) as a popular form of real estate ownership. Unlike the *general partnership,* with partners whose liability is not limited, the *limited partnership* involves two classes of ownership: one or more general partners and the limited partners. Essentially, the general partner is the quarterback who organizes and calls the plays (i.e., controls the property and makes up any operating losses that may occur). Meanwhile, limited partners invest capital in an agreed-upon amount, and this amount becomes the limit of their liability. The limit, however, applies only so long as the general partner is solvent and performs as expected. If the general partner fails to do this, the limited partners, who otherwise are passive investors, may have to assume responsibility to protect their investment; however, they are under no legal obligation to do so. Managers of properties owned by limited partnerships take their direction from the general partners, not the limited partners.

The ownership form of choice for multiple owners is the *limited liability company (LLC).* It has many of the same attributes as the limited partnership but generally allows more flexibility in its organization and partnership structure. It is taxed the same as other partnerships. It allows for multiple classes of ownership that all enjoy limited liability. The partners are called *members,* and the partner in charge is usually referred to as the *manager member.* The rules governing limited liability companies vary from state to state, some of which impose rather onerous fiduciary responsibilities.

Structuring real estate partnerships is a carefully honed specialty that requires years of legal and tax experience.

Joint Venture.   This is not a legal form of ownership, per se, but a term used to describe an arrangement in which the skills and assets of two or more individuals or entities are brought together for one specific project. Typically, one side furnishes the investment capital while the other furnishes services or know-how. Builders and developers frequently supply their construction knowledge and capabilities while their joint-venture colleagues provide the cash. Many large lending institutions and other major corporations have funded such operations as investments. No rules dictate how profits are split, as each case is negotiated separately. The success or failure of a joint venture rests solely with the attitude and skills of the participants.

Corporate Ownership.   There are several different types of corporations: A corporation can be privately held or publicly traded, for-profit or not-for-profit; it can have C corporation or S corporation tax status. All corporations are legal entities that are chartered by one of the states.

There was a period when mainstream corporations decided to enter the business of owning multifamily rental housing. These attempts at diversification were often not successful—despite the general tendency for real estate to appreciate in value with the passage of time. Real estate entrepreneurs and developers succeed more often than not because of a certain degree of daring. They move quickly in ways that are dynamic, even flamboyant. These are not operational characteristics of corporations, especially large ones whose structures prevent their making intuitive decisions. Some major corporations have suffered substantial losses and have withdrawn from their investments in rental apartments.

A few large corporations have entered the multifamily housing business, not as an investment, but as a way to provide convenient, safe, and clean residential accommodations for their employees. In some cases, special holding companies may be formed to avoid the appearance of creating a "company town."

Insurance Companies and Lending Institutions.   Many of these types of companies in the United States have ownership stakes in residential rental housing. Insurance companies, financial institutions, and the government itself have many billions of dollars invested in rental apartments. Some ownerships are involuntary, the consequence of having to foreclose on delinquent accounts. Ownership that develops in this manner is usually the interim or caretaker type. The goal is to wait out the bad times and resell the investment at a price that minimizes any loss. The difficulties of managing a property associated with financial failure are quite unique and often very frustrating.

Increasingly, insurance companies and financial institutions are acquiring real estate as investments. Typically, they limit their investments to top-quality modern properties in strong and growing markets. They add rental real estate to their portfolios to produce income and gain value from appreciation. Local real estate managers with top reputations are frequently selected to handle these properties. These institutions tend to be quite demanding about how their properties are managed; even so, this is a coveted segment of the real estate management business.

Real Estate Investment Trusts.   Real estate investment trusts, referred to as REITs (pronounced "reets"), are well into their second go-around as a real estate ownership entity. By pooling funds to create substantial investment capability, REITs give small investors the profit opportunities and advantages that come from large-scale real estate ownership. The REIT investor is passive, however, and has almost no voice in the management of the real estate. Also, by law, the REIT must distribute 90 percent of its income to the investors.

REITs get approval from the Securities and Exchange Commission (SEC) to make a public offering of *shares of beneficial interest*. The funds generated are used to purchase real estate (i.e., equity REITs) or provide mortgage funding for real estate properties (i.e., mortgage REITs); still others have combined goals (i.e., hybrid REITs). Investment in a REIT is subject to many of the same fluctuations as the stock market and is not tied exclusively to the values of the properties themselves. Thus, an important attribute of real estate ownership is missing.

Back in the early 1970s, REITs got off to a bad start, plunging many millions of dollars into real estate without proper research and knowledge. When rental real estate went through a major decline in the mid-1970s, considerable losses were incurred. Not much was heard about REITs until they made a big comeback in the early to mid-1990s. Since that time, REITs have rebuilt their image in the investment community, and today their portfolios reflect a healthier and more conservative investment attitude.

At this writing, there are more than 30 major publicly traded REITs that specialize in rental apartment properties. The value of these properties is into the many billions of dollars. Some REITs aggressively seek new investment capital to fund future purchases. With attractive mortgage rates and higher rent levels, REITs often pay substantial prices to acquire properties while maintaining their ability to deliver attractive quarterly returns to investors. Some REITs offer their shares in trade for rental properties. This helps the property owner delay and spread out the payment of capital gains taxes. REITs have become an extremely large and important owner of rental apartments. Just how their future growth will progress depends on both their reception in the stock market and the operation of their real estate.

Managing REIT properties is not typically contracted to local real estate management firms. Normally, a management division handles the property operations in house.

Common Interest Real Estate. Condominiums, cooperatives, townhouses, and zero-lot-line developments are forms of common interest real estate. They operate for the mutual benefit of the owners and not for profit. In recent years, accountants have taken to referring to this real estate type by the acronym CIRA (pronounced "sear a") for *common interest realty associations*. Buyers of common interest real estate hope their investments will appreciate, but they are primarily users, not investors.

Common interest real estate presents a most difficult challenge to professional management. This is because the two essential ingredients for successful management are lacking.

The first ingredient is *knowledge of the property*. To be successful, the real estate manager must know more about the property than anyone else — especially the residents. This is very difficult to do when the owners live in the building and the manager does not. The manager may be forced to assume a defensive posture when unit owners constantly search out problems and flaws in both the property and its management and complain about their findings.

The second ingredient is *authority*. The management of a business enterprise is most successful when there is only one boss. However, most common interest real estate developments are operated by an association with an elected board of directors and a collection of committees—in spite of the fact that they have hired professional management. Instead of restricting themselves to major fiscal matters and long-range policy, the board and its committees often feel compelled to get involved in day-to-day operating problems. This is less true in upscale condominiums whose units typically are owned by successful businesspeople more accustomed to delegating authority. The problem lessens with time as these associations stabilize and the succeeding boards come to realize that professional managers possess the skills to operate their property. Unfortunately, it usually takes several changes in management before the board begins to mellow. About that time, major physical problems affecting the structure begin to develop, again raising the interest and involvement of the resident-owners.

Managing common interest real estate is one of the more difficult management disciplines. It requires a highly organized person with extreme patience and a knack for follow-through.

Foreign Ownership.   Balance-of-payment deficits sent hundreds of billions of U.S. dollars overseas. Many foreign investors chose to return those dollars by investing in American real estate. Very high prices were paid for some top quality properties. Most of the activity centered on hotel, commercial, and industrial properties, with only limited money being invested in rental apartments. Apartments were often avoided because of the intense daily management required to operate them and some fears about possible rent control. Later, many foreign investors were disappointed with minimal returns and slow increases in value. This, together with financial problems in their home countries, has slowed a good deal of foreign investment.

Types of Managers

A real estate manager is primarily an *agent*—an extension of the owner he or she represents. The owner's interest always should be uppermost in the professional manager's mind. When faced with decision-making, the manager ought to ask: "What would I do if I owned this property?" The manager who has acquired experience and specialized skills is in a much better position to produce a qualified answer than is the owner. The manager assumes the role of a professional substitute for the owner.

The basic goal of the real estate manager is *to produce the highest possible net operating income (NOI)*. This is defined as collections less operating expenses. Some owners would like the manager's role expanded to include production of the largest possible *cash flow,* which is NOI less debt service (mortgage payment). The amount and payment of debt service has little to do with successful management. The real estate manager who has produced maximum rent collections and has kept operating expenses to an effective minimum has done the job, regardless of the debt service the owner must pay.

So with the goals and responsibilities of management in mind, let us look at what is involved in managing a property. First, a professional real estate manager must be equipped with a storehouse of information about the property and its location, the market area, operating expenses, maintenance techniques, reporting procedures, and a host of other items. The principal ingredients that make a capable manager are common sense, resourcefulness, organizational skills, and a willingness to work hard. The sole purpose of this book is to offer managers time-tested knowledge that has been gained by others through years of experience.

Managing profit-producing housing is more demanding and more fulfilling than is caretaker or not-for-profit management. In fact, managing caretaker or not-for-profit properties can be very frustrating because of the absence of a material goal. The most exciting part of the management business is the handling of investment properties for profit.

The differences between the types of managers really reflect varying degrees of knowledge possessed at the different levels. Granted, the amount of authority also changes, but this is just a further reflection of a particular manager's skill and experience.

Managers are employed in one of two ways, either as direct employees of owners, who can be individuals, partnerships, corporations, or even the government, or as employees of real estate companies that are in the business of real estate management. The first category covers the greatest number of managers.

The managers described below may belong to either group. The success or failure of privately financed investment real estate falls on their shoulders. Those who learn their lessons well will be rewarded both financially and in the satisfaction of performing a vitally needed service.

Executive Property Manager. An executive property manager is a supervisor who oversees and directs other property managers who are in the field handling the operational affairs of various properties. The executive's primary concern is with running a business that manages properties rather than with the direct management of those properties. Knowledge for this position is usually acquired from long and broad experience in the actual management of investment real estate. This knowledge is used to establish long-range policies and fiscal plans and to guide the company's property managers in resolving difficult situations.

The executive property manager is frequently an officer of the company and, in fact, might be its owner. This position is typically compensated by a regular salary although additional incentive bonuses are common.

Asset Manager.   Asset managers provide finely tuned skills in the planning, analysis, and financial tracking of investment real estate. These managers are often charged with the long-range planning and preparation of business plans for rather substantial investment portfolios. It is common to combine the use of an asset manager with a full complement of management personnel. For example, a 200-unit apartment community might have a site manager who works for a supervising property manager who, in turn, reports to an executive property manager. If the property is owned by an institution, there might be an asset manager who is coordinating that 200-unit property with the other properties in his or her portfolio. Responsibilities of the asset manager may include capital improvements, cash management, market analysis, rent structuring, and budget tracking, plus short- and long-range goal attainment; and sometimes they are consulted regarding acquisitions, financing and refinancing, and dispositions. Asset managers employed by corporations and institutional investors are typically compensated by a salary.

Sometimes a property owner will hire an asset manager to directly supervise (or at least monitor) the activities of those who are actually involved with the day-to-day affairs of a property. Asset managers often deal with rental properties that are located in widespread geographic areas with many divergent customs, laws, and market influences. The staffs of individual properties frequently become frustrated when supervising asset managers try to streamline their procedures into textbook guidelines, ignoring local market nuances.

Rental housing is a consumer product that is emotional as well as volatile. Careful tracking of rents and expenses, along with comparative studies of neighboring properties, will frequently help an analyst to develop a financial plan; but there is no substitute for a thorough understanding of the property and its marketplace. This knowledge comes with years of hands-on experience. Hence, the asset manager whose analytical skills are combined with day-to-day property involvement has the best chance of delivering significantly better bottom-line results.

Property Manager.   The property manager is the chief operating officer or administrator of a single property or a group of properties. A property manager is responsible for fiscal planning, setting rents, establishing marketing and maintenance procedures, supervising site managers, and reporting to and maintaining liaison with owners and superiors.

Property managers may be employees of a real estate management company and compensated by a salary and, possibly, incentive bonuses.

However, this title also applies to individuals who contract directly with property owners and are compensated by a management fee under a written management agreement.

Site Manager.   The front-line operator of the property is the site manager. The responsibilities of this position include day-to-day dealings with residents, renting units, making collections, and follow-through supervision of maintenance. The site manager is truly the person on the firing line. This manager has the greatest impact on the daily operation of a property.

Site managers who are employed by real estate management companies are primarily compensated by a base salary. Total compensation may include an apartment at the managed property plus commissions and/or bonuses.

Some people refer to the site manager as the on-site or resident manager, which implies that the person lives on the site. This is not always true. The place of residence has nothing to do with the responsibilities of this position. In this book, the term "site manager" will be used to refer to this level of management.

"Ma and Pa" Management.   So-called ma and pa management, originally popular in furnished apartment buildings, is on its way to extinction in the apartment business. Historically, one spouse would perform the renting and bookkeeping duties while the other would handle maintenance tasks and perhaps some collections problems or minor disturbances. Compensation took the form of individual salaries and free housing.

While less expensive in the short run than professional management, this arrangement is frequently inadequate and ineffective in today's demanding times—especially for major investments.

Real Estate Investment Economics

The management of investment real estate revolves around collecting rents, maintaining the property, and paying for needed products and services. Because the property's income and expenses have many different components, and these are related to each other in specific ways, it is appropriate here to discuss the terminology involved. We will begin by charting the flow of income and expenditure items common in most investment real estate today (see sidebar). All of the items are interrelated, and each has an effect on the final item—cash flow. Also, while street rent is not a part of the income and expenditure flow chart, it is typically presented above the scheduled receipts for purposes of comparison. What follows is a brief explanation of how each item affects the cash flow and, ultimately, the return to the investor, beginning with street rent.

Income and Expenditure Flow Chart

Scheduled Receipts (Gross Potential Income)

Less	Vacancy and Collection Losses
Plus	Unscheduled, Sundry, or Ancillary Income
Equals	*Actual Receipts, Collections, or Effective Gross Income*
Less	Operating Expenses
Equals	*Net Operating Income (NOI)*
Less	Debt Service or Mortgage Payments
Equals	*Cash Flow*

Street Rent.   This is the rent that will be quoted to new prospects and that which renewing residents will pay. It is also referred to as market or optimum rent. For example, consider the situation in which all of the apartments in a 24-unit building are occupied and have varying lease expirations. The *street rent* is the rental rate you plan to achieve when these leases expire or a unit suddenly becomes available due to a resident move-out. Establishing the next rent level for each unit is very important because it helps to prevent leasing personnel from re-renting vacant units today at yesterday's rate. The total street rent includes rent values for every unit in the development, including models, employee housing, office space, and any unrentable units. Street rent is the rent you would be trying to get if everyone moved out of your building today. It is always helpful to contrast the rent you are getting with your target rent. (Rent setting is discussed in Chapter 12.)

Scheduled Receipts or Gross Potential Income.   These two terms are synonymous and identify the current total *rent roll*. Included in this total is the monthly rent of each unit under lease (actual or contract rent) plus the current street rent value of each vacant and non-revenue-producing unit. (Annual gross potential income is the total monthly rent multiplied by twelve.)

Vacancy and Collection Losses.   This item reflects the amount of money that is lost, or is expected to be lost, as a result of vacancies and collection losses. Vacancy and collection losses are a fact of life in the rental housing business. As strange as it may seem, 100 percent occupancy usually means that a property is not achieving its maximum rent potential. While full occupancy month after month may be the result of the property's exceptional location, facilities, and services, it is just as likely to be a signal that rents are too low.

There are two distinct types of vacancies—*physical vacancy* and *eco-*

nomic vacancy. When vacancies are reported, they are usually physical vacancies (unoccupied units available for lease). Economic vacancy indicates
the percentage of units that are not producing income. The following
rule of thumb can be employed with properties of 100 or more units that
are experiencing moderate vacancies (between 4 and 8 percent): The economic vacancy rate will usually amount to twice the physical vacancy rate.
Therefore, a property with a 5 percent physical vacancy will usually suffer
a 10 percent economic loss.

Economic vacancy almost always exists, even if there is no physical vacancy. This occurs for a number of reasons. If an apartment is rented in
March for occupancy in May, it is not listed as a vacant apartment available
for rent, yet it generates no income for the month of April. If a resident is
behind in rent payments, there is no income, but the unit is nonetheless
classified as occupied. Those apartments given to employees or used as
models or for office or storage space, in addition to unrentable or cannibalized apartments, are not available for rent yet produce no income. Finally,
vacancy problems frequently center on the most expensive units. This creates a disproportionate dollar loss when compared to the actual number of
vacant apartments.

In determining vacancy and collection losses, the apartment manager
should be interested not only in the number of units that are vacant and
available (physical vacancy), but also in the number and value of units that
reasonably can be expected to be non-revenue-producing. I have found that
in larger properties, it is practically impossible to operate regularly with less
than 5 percent economic vacancy. Even in a fairly tight market, an economic
vacancy of 7 to 9 percent is more realistic. In privately operated student
housing, an economic vacancy of 20 percent is more the standard, and this
assumes zero physical vacancy at the start of the fall term.

There is a tendency to group physical vacancies and analyze them as a
total. This can result in misreading a marketing problem related to the desirability of individual unit types. Vacancies should always be detailed by
unit type, indicating the total number of each type in the property, the number of each type of unit that are vacant, and the vacancy expressed as a percentage of that total (Exhibit 1.3). It is even more important to do a monthly
listing of vacant units and to keep a running total of rent lost from the day
each unit was last rented. Some computer programs track the number of
days each unit has been vacant, but that fact is not nearly as telling as the
amount of money lost. Some units will suffer enormous losses in between
rentals. It is crucial to learn why.

Unscheduled, Sundry, or Ancillary Income.   Any one of these three
terms may be used to identify income that is derived from a source other
than rent. Ancillary income includes money or commissions received from
sources such as laundry concessions, occasional rentals of party rooms or

Exhibit 1.3
Vacancies by Unit Type

No. of Units	Unit Type	Vacancies	Percent
15	Efficiency	1	7%
33	One Bedroom	3	9%
18	One Bedroom, Den	0	0%
27	Two Bedroom, 2 Bath	7	26%
7	Two Bedroom, 2 Bath, Townhouse	0	0%
100		11	11%

recreational facilities, key deposits, charges levied for NSF (non-sufficient funds) checks, forfeited security deposits, settlements, and resident damage reimbursements.

Actual Receipts, Collections, or Effective Gross Income.   These three terms are used interchangeably to refer to the net amount of income collected after subtracting for vacancy and collection losses and adding the unscheduled or ancillary income.

Net Operating Income (NOI).   Occasionally, some real estate practitioners will attempt to coin a new phrase to replace the term net operating income (NOI), but this term has survived and is used and accepted almost universally. It represents the amount of money that remains *after operating expenses are subtracted from actual receipts* (see sidebar).

Net operating income is the primary measure of a property's performance. The apartment manager understands that it is his or her responsibility to produce the highest possible NOI over the economic life of the property. In other words, the manager works to maximize collections and minimize operating expenses. This, of course, must be done in such a way that it does not jeopardize the long-range economic potential of the particular property.

Real estate appraisers and investors value income-producing real estate in direct proportion to the property's ability to produce NOI. The primary method of arriving at a value for rental real estate is the *income capitalization* approach. Using this approach, investors, appraisers, managers, lenders, and others arrive at a property's value by selecting a desired yield or *capitalization rate* and dividing that rate into the property's NOI. The formula is:

Operating Expense Categories

Utilities
Services and Supplies
Payroll and Related Costs
Management, Administration, and Promotion
Real Estate Taxes and Insurance
Maintenance and Repairs

$$\frac{\text{Net Operating Income (I)}}{\text{Capitalization Rate (R)}} = \text{Value (V)}$$

In most real estate training sessions, this formula will be introduced as the *IRV formula* to help students remember the math components.

In a given marketplace, capitalization or "cap" rates fluctuate much the same as interest rates. If there is a lot of money available to be invested, there will be downward pressure on the available yields. In other words, when investors find the profit potential better in income-producing real estate than in other alternatives, money will flow to it and cap rates will decline. With the fall of cap rates, there is a corresponding rise in the prices being paid for investment properties. Upscale properties in stable neighborhoods are obviously less risky than deteriorating properties so it follows that investors will accept a lesser return, sometimes significantly less.

As an example, let's assume that a property has NOI of $360,000 and the prevailing capitalization rate is 8 percent. Applying the formula, we arrive at the following estimate of value:

$$\frac{\$360,000}{.08} = \$4,500,000$$

Continuing the example, suppose the manager is successful in combining rent increases with a series of skillful cutbacks in operating expenses. These changes increase the NOI to $400,000 per year. Using the same cap rate of 8 percent, the property now becomes more valuable:

$$\frac{\$400,000}{.08} = \$5,000,000$$

As you might imagine, investors search for skilled managers who have the ability to "create value" by instituting changes that will bring about steady and sustained increases in NOI and, hence, increase the value of their properties.

Debt Service or Mortgage Payments.   The terms debt service and mortgage payments are used synonymously to describe payments of principal and interest on outstanding loans. Most real estate people isolate mortgage payments because they are considered an owner obligation and are not used to arrive at the property's NOI.

Cash Flow.   After the mortgage principal and interest payments are deducted from the NOI, the amount of money remaining is termed cash flow. Most owners and investors have an ongoing interest in this amount because it represents pre-tax spendable income. While cash flow is tracked and can be distributed monthly, it is usually expressed as an annualized amount. The *annual cash return* divided by the cash equity invested indicates the property's *cash-on-cash return* or *yield*.

$$\frac{\text{Annual Cash Return}}{\text{Cash Equity}} = \text{Cash-on-Cash Return}$$

As an example, if an owner's equity amounted to $1 million and the amount of cash generated in a year was $65,000, the owners return would be 6.5 percent.

$$\frac{\$65,000}{\$1,000,000} = .065\ (6.5\%)$$

To an owner, the cash-on-cash return is often the primary concern and therefore the method of choice in measuring investment performance.

Be aware, however, that the investment real estate industry has also devised a whole collection of other methods and formulas to arrive at values and returns. Some of these will deal with after-tax consequences and the property appreciation. You are encouraged to continue studying the economics of real estate investment. A full understanding of the financial potential of multifamily rental housing is critical in rounding out your real estate education.

The Management Agreement

When any one of the real estate manager types is employed directly by the property owner, the duties and responsibilities are commonly spelled out in a job description. When the manager is an employee of the management company that is acting as the managing agent for the owner, the duties and responsibilities are defined in what is referred to as a *management agreement*. At its most basic level, this document accomplishes several functions:

- It serves as an employment contract between the owner and the managing agent.
- It establishes an agency relationship, giving the managing agent the right to act on the owner's behalf and to assume obligations in the name of the owner.

- It spells out the rights, responsibilities, and limitations of the managing agent.
- It stipulates the managing agent's compensation.
- Finally, it provides for the agreement's termination.

To undertake the management of real estate without a management agreement is hazardous. The main reason for having an agreement is that it sets out everything in writing, thereby reducing the chances of misunderstandings. The agreement is as much for the managing agent's protection as it is for the owner's. While a preprinted management agreement form can be used, it is often necessary to tailor the provisions to the arrangement for the particular property. It is advisable to have the finalized document reviewed by both parties' attorneys before it is signed to ensure, among other things, that it complies with applicable laws.

Powers.   A managing agent is far more than the owner's representative. The *agent,* in effect, acts for the owner and has the same powers as the owner would have.

As the owner's agent, the manager has the authority to set rents; to execute, extend, and cancel leases; and to make settlements with residents. The authority to collect money and spend it on behalf of the property is also granted. The manager has a *fiduciary* responsibility to the owner to act honestly and in good faith, which requires a precise accounting of collections and expenditures.

The management agreement also gives the agent the authority to execute contracts for building services, keep the property in good condition, and make repairs. What is spent on maintenance and repairs may be limited by a dollar amount, beyond which the owner's further approval is needed. The exception to this would be emergencies when life or property is threatened and immediate action is required.

The manager also has the authority to hire, fire, and supervise personnel. Employees who work at the property are generally employees of the property owner, not direct employees of the managing agent. However, even when this is the case, the agent may be considered an alternate employer because of the authority to hire, fire, and supervise. For instance, a manager may be held responsible for observing all requirements of the federal and state Wage and Hour Laws. This obligation cannot be avoided, even though the personnel are employees of the owner. Along with the manager's authority to hire, fire, and supervise, there is a corresponding responsibility to see that all employment conditions required by the law are fulfilled. The owner can hold the manager responsible for fulfilling all of these obligations.

The extent and limitations of the agent's authority to act on the owner's behalf should be set forth clearly in the management agreement. This authority is needed for three specific reasons:

1. *To establish the manager's authority to execute a lease.* A tenant may challenge your authority to do so. By referring to the management agreement you can validate this authority.

2. *To meet Internal Revenue Service requirements for filing employee tax payments.*

3. *To distribute net proceeds to the owner or owners.* This can be complicated. You must get specific direction from all of the owners for any percentage distribution of net proceeds. It is not uncommon for a managing agent to receive a contract from two owners, only to discover later that there are other owners who demand their share of the proceeds. The only protection you have is to identify all of the owners and make sure they all sign any distribution instructions.

Independent Contractor.   You may be asked to sign an agreement that is not the typical form management agreement but a contract that identifies you as an independent contractor. This is a rather common request when contracting with lending institutions with foreclosed properties or major investment institutions that own apartment properties. The reason for this is that these institutions often do not want someone to be acting in an agency capacity; they prefer a hired vendor. There is a world of difference between the status and liability of an independent contractor and that of an agent. Such a document should be carefully reviewed with an attorney to determine whether or not this change in capacity is acceptable. Many independent contractor contracts are thinly veiled agency agreements that will be interpreted as such by the courts. Be sure to seek a professional legal opinion before proceeding.

Obligations.   The manager's overall obligation is to act in a professional manner with the owner's interest as the first objective. Most management agreements place obligations on the agent to:

- Ensure that the property achieves maximum occupancy.
- Collect rents.
- Pay bills incurred for the property.
- Submit a report to the owner of collections and disbursements.
- Make sure that the necessary property and liability insurance is maintained.
- Pay real estate taxes from building funds.
- File employee payroll tax returns.
- Maintain the property with building funds.
- Notify the owner of the property's shortcomings and defects as well as citations.
- Maintain records such as leases, tax payments, mortgage payments, original paid invoices, and insurance policies, all of which are the

owner's property. However, correspondence files and books of account that the agent generates in the course of managing the property remain the property of the agent, not the owner. This does not imply that the owner cannot access these records. Many states' departments of licensing require a real estate broker or real estate manager to maintain such files.

Associated Risks.   A managing agent is exposed to certain risks. The *hold-harmless* provisions of the management agreement are designed to minimize these risks by placing many responsibilities on the owner and providing for the payment of legal defense in certain matters, unless the agent has been negligent. These matters generally include:

- Actions stemming from the owner's refusal to advance needed funds.
- Building code violations.
- Civil rights lawsuits.
- Wage and Hour Law claims.
- Occupational Safety and Health Act (OSHA) claims.
- Lawsuits in general.
- Harmful or improper acts of employees.

It is also possible for an agent to create liabilities for the owner when acting on the owner's behalf. For example, if the managing agent commits an unlawful act (e.g., a fair housing violation in particular), both the agent and the owner are liable.

Compensation.   The most common method of compensation for real estate management is a flat percentage of total collections from a property's operation (less security deposits). It is also routine to have an established "floor," so that the managing agent is guaranteed a minimum fee. This method is traditional and it gives the agent an incentive to collect the maximum rents.

In addition to covering the managing agent's fee, the agreement should also spell out who pays for on-site administrative help. Usually, this is the responsibility of the owner, not the managing agent.

Finally, the agreement should contain any specifics on commissions for renting apartments and bonuses for lease renewals.

Termination or Cancellation.   The management agreement can be terminated in one of four ways:

1. When the term of the agreement expires.
2. By notice from either the owner *or* the managing agent according to contract provisions.
3. By mutual agreement. If cancellation is negotiated, one party may ask for payment from the other in return for early termination.

4. When the purpose is ended. A common reason for terminating agreements is the sale of the building. Owners retain agents to manage their property; but if a property is sold, the purpose is gone, and the contract normally is ended. The managing agent may seek protection against early termination by having the agreement state that sale of the property does not affect the contract, or if the building is sold, that the agent will receive a specified sum as liquidated damages.

The management agreement is an important document, one that should be kept in a safe place. However, it does not guarantee continuous employment. Only effective performance will do that.

2

When hiring, look for . . .
a pleasant appearance and manner,
willingness to learn and work, and
a high level of common sense.

Hiring and Managing the Property Staff

It is the property staff who must make things work. Personnel policies alone will not make employees work harder or more skillfully; however, they will help minimize disputes and confusion while ensuring uniform treatment of employees and establishing a professional level of employment practices. The following discussion focuses on the key areas these policies should address.

Hiring

Before making any hiring decisions, it is essential to check the qualifications of all applicants. Be aware that federal law prohibits discrimination in employment. Complaints by applicants or employees claiming discrimination can be filed through a state commission, an office of the Equal Employment Opportunity Commission (EEOC), or federal court (state laws on filing vary). It is important to treat all potential employees the same so that none of your actions can be interpreted as discriminatory. The inclusion of the "EOE" (Equal Opportunity Employer) abbreviation in your advertising and application materials is recommended. Know the laws as they apply to your situation.

Screening Applicants.   Obviously, it pays to find the right employees, and there are means to locate the best people. The following items are some tools to consider.

- *Application form.* Be aware of what you are legally permitted to ask and what you cannot ask; check federal, state, and local laws governing hiring. In most cases, the standard application form you purchase from local stationery or office supply stores will meet current requirements. (If you make changes to a standard form, your attorney should approve the revised form before it is used.)

- *References.* Talk to the applicant's previous employers (as many as possible) or to a reference who is not a relative. Ask the previous employers to list the applicant's strong and weak points. This is especially relevant if the applicant has worked in real estate management before. Pay particular attention to the answers you get. I should point out, however, that this will be a difficult task. Previous employers may refuse to provide information about anything other than the person's period of employment and salary.

- *Credit bureau.* A credit bureau check can provide information regarding judgments, bankruptcy, and general credit history. However, this information should not be used in making the hiring decision unless it is relevant to the job (e.g., if the employee will have access to money or merchandise). If credit information is used for hiring, there are specific disclosure requirements that must be followed as outlined in the Fair Credit Reporting Act (FCRA). It is illegal in most states to refuse employment because of an employee's past credit history; therefore, a credit check is of limited value and may only serve to forewarn you that there could be trouble ahead. (Applicants must be advised that a credit check will be made, and you should obtain their *written* permission beforehand.)

- *Criminal background check.* This may be done when required by business necessity (e.g., to meet bonding requirements) or by state law. Prior convictions should not be an absolute bar to employment. Consideration must be given to the nature of the position being filled, the seriousness of the prior offense, and how recently the offense was committed.

    It is increasingly common for criminal background checks to be done on a wider basis. Employers are responsible for employees' behavior in the workplace—they can be held liable if an employee is harmed by a co-worker. In apartment management, having access to occupied apartments creates potential for residents' to be harmed financially (theft) or physically injured (assault) by a staff member. As with a credit check, the job applicant should be asked for *written* authorization to conduct a criminal background check.

- *Bonding*. Any employee who deals with money or is responsible for major expenses should be bonded.

- *Tests.* Some companies require applicants to take a battery of psychological and personality tests. These have their limitations but may be useful in giving you more insight regarding the applicant—in particular, how an individual would "fit" with the property team. Tests can also be obtained (or written in house) to determine applicants' skills in math, writing, maintenance, and other areas.

  Drug testing has become a very common requirement in the hiring process. (It may also be desirable or appropriate to conduct drug tests periodically after employees are on the job.) Many establishments that post hiring notices at their entrances include the warning that all applicants will be tested for drugs. An executive property manager with a major firm told me that his company requires drug testing of all prospective employees. What surprised him was the high percentage of individuals who went ahead with the application process, even after being warned of the policy, and indeed tested positive.

- *Polygraph tests*. Federal law now prohibits the use of employee lie detector tests in most business situations. This practice, when used previously, almost always had a negative effect on employee morale. However, in situations in which the employer has suffered an economic loss, polygraph tests are permissible after notice is provided and a number of other restrictions have been met.

  Taking a little extra time in carefully performing reference and background checks prior to making hiring decisions will certainly help, but it will not eliminate future problems. In thinking through my experiences with employee dishonesty, I am reminded that most cases resulted from either the lack of a policy or the lack of enforcement of what should have been an everyday security measure. In other words, management simply left the door wide open to tempt and permit a loss. The second shortcoming is a general disbelief that a trusted employee would ever be involved in a dishonest act.

Matching the Individual to the Job.   Employees must fit the apartment community. The reverse is also true. Before you make a decision regarding employees, you should sit down and write a description of the types of people who currently reside there.

Your choice for a manager should be shaped by your resident profile. The manager should be comfortable with the rent levels being charged. For example, if the rents are in the range of $1,200 a month, your manager should be comfortable with that figure. The subject of value will constantly surface; it is essential that the manager is not intimidated by a high rent or, on the other hand, does not belittle the residents because the rent level seems low.

The same advice should be followed when choosing leasing agents. If a leasing agent is at all troubled by the rent level, it will be virtually impossible for that agent to help a prospect over the decision hurdle or, for that matter, to understand the motivations of people in higher income brackets.

The leasing agent's demeanor should be compatible with your resident profile. People often need help and counsel in making major decisions about housing, but they are likely to be slow to take advice from someone who is not in or near their age-range or who is not near their achievement level. An inexperienced leasing agent cannot be expected to provide the right touch or invoke the necessary urgency with an established, sophisticated renter. You should not confuse a very helpful, energetic, and highly personable clerk with a professional leasing agent who can make the difference between a signature on a lease and prospects who leave "to think about it." When times are tough, the compatibility of the leasing agent with the desired customer is critical. This is especially true at the high end of the market.

Demeanor is all the ways a person presents himself or herself, including personal appearance. There are probably those who will say that making a judgment based on *appearance* is illegal, but appearance is crucial to your employee selection process. There are a number of individuals who are determined to make a statement or set themselves apart with some unique dress or hairstyle or conduct. They are entitled to present themselves as they see fit, but not as your representative. People who have decided to separate themselves from the mainstream present a distraction in the people-contact business. Business will surely suffer if your present and future customers are expected to interface with such employees.

Having and enforcing a dress code—and informing job applicants of this requirement when they are being interviewed—can help avert problems.

Finding Qualified People.   When economic times are good, one of the toughest tasks is to find people who are ready, willing, and able to work. So many of the people who apply for apartment management positions have been around the industry for years, continually moving from job to job. Some have their own set of rules—e.g., they won't work weekends. Some have attitudes that will not help resident relations. One of the best ways to expand your employment pool is to look outside the apartment industry. Department stores are an excellent place to look. These workers generally dress well, are well-spoken, used to varying workdays and hours, trained in customer satisfaction, and often underpaid by real estate management standards. Hotel and motel workers have many of the same attributes. Other good sources include similar "high touch" employment situations such as restaurants.

Finding qualified apartment maintenance people is one of the more difficult tasks. These positions are also ones with rapid turnover. My company has had some success with help wanted ads seeking retired plant maintenance workers. Although they may be older, and will probably decline a 40-hour work schedule, many are skilled mechanics. Some are bored with retirement; others want to augment their income, and some just want to get out of the house for a few hours. If you are flexible, this can be an excellent means of finding people with skill, time, tools, and a refreshing attitude. Many also pass on their skills and techniques to the younger staff members.

Job Descriptions.   A job description is rarely a complete list of job responsibilities. Although most personnel manuals recommend that you have job descriptions, it is important to be aware of the problems they may create—difficulties can arise from the restrictive nature of any finite job description. Management personnel are called upon to perform a variety of duties, some of which cannot be anticipated or formalized into a job description. An employee may balk at a request to perform a certain activity because "it wasn't in the job description."

When you put a job description in writing, be sure to use broad terms. In addition to identifying the duties and responsibilities of the position and the knowledge and skills required to perform the work, a written job description should include reference to "other duties as may be assigned." This will avert claims of tasks not being specified in a job description.

Employee Policies

Policies are necessary tools for managing any staff. As is the case with other policies in apartment management, employee policies are usually developed by or in cooperation with the property owner. It is a good idea to provide employees with a handbook that outlines your expectations as an employer along with guidelines for behavior on the job and explanations of the benefits provided.

Scheduling.   When scheduling staff, you should remember that those who work in the apartment management business must be able to effectively serve both prospects and existing residents. It is amazing that some residential management professionals will complain of poor rental results and search for ways to increase prospect traffic, but they will not work on one of the most important days of the week, Sunday. Granted, there are situations in which Sunday is not an active rental day, but these are rare occurrences indeed. More often than not, a manager will say that Sunday is not an important rental day in his or her area when, in fact, rentals could be brisk on Sunday if the rental office was just open. The real estate management industry would do well to follow the lead of "home sales brokers." I am sure you have noticed that Sundays are their day of choice when hosting open houses. Also, most retail outlets are regularly open Sundays as are customer service and support functions, and Internet sites are accessible around the clock. Sundays are important. Your Sunday staff must be top notch. A property simply cannot afford to have the rental office staffed with part-time leasing agents during the times when most prospects do their serious looking. Some managers choose not to work on Sunday, even though the office is open. Sunday may not be producing any better results than other days, but it might be because the second-string staff is on duty then.

Besides leasing, there are many other duties that can be better accomplished on Sunday. For example, most managers complain that they do not have blocks of uninterrupted time in which they can accomplish much-needed planning or paperwork. Between 9:00 and 10:30 A.M. on Sunday morning, the manager is almost guaranteed some "quiet time." Sunday is also an excellent time to get out and meet the residents and handle lease renewals or solve problems. This does not mean a six-day week. The workweek of many managers runs from Sunday through Thursday.

Just as the presence of the manager is needed on Sunday, the property should have the benefit of its maintenance chief all day on Saturday. Many residents are reluctant to have people in their apartments when they themselves are not present. If they are experiencing a complicated or intermittent problem that is best explained in person, Saturday is often a perfect time for a maintenance visit. Saturday service in an apartment community is a must if you plan to retain the maximum number of existing residents. The convenience of your maintenance staff should not be a factor in deciding the level of service you are offering to your customers. The Saturday schedule should not be a partial day for maintenance even though the rental office may not be open the full day. Typical hours for maintenance staff might be 8:30 A.M. to 4:30 P.M. Tuesday through Saturday.

Scheduling and Staffing Alternatives.   A great deal is being learned about apartment property staffing, and it is much different than what has been done in the past. Typically, an apartment owner or manager would decide on the number of staff positions needed to carry on daily operations. With the exception of some part-time leasing agents, most positions were full-time; and most of these people worked a conventional time slot, say, 8:30 A.M. to 4:30 P.M. Lately, there has been a shift to afternoon and even early evening hours. Maintenance and custodial personnel are often asked to work from 11:00 A.M. to 7:00 P.M. The advantages are several. Many repair calls do not come in first thing in the morning; they trickle in throughout the day. Calls coming in the afternoon often can be handled later that same day or scheduled for early evening, after the resident returns home from work.

Custodial work can also be performed later in the day, and you gain some important advantages. With conventional staffing, many residents often do not see or come in contact with the custodial staff. When you shift the schedule to the afternoon and early evening, people see the work being done. Staff members are around and about. This will have a very positive effect on security as well, since most thefts, vandalism, and social problems occur from mid-afternoon to early evening. With staff tending to daily custodial tasks throughout the property during these hours, the number of such incidents usually decreases.

Many tradespeople will take on side jobs to augment their incomes. In time, you can make arrangements with people willing to work on a part-time or as-needed basis. Many apartment communities have such arrangements with heating and air-conditioning technicians, plumbers, electricians, carpenters, carpet installers, and other service vendors.

Living On Site versus Off Site.   Living on site was almost standard for apartment managers in the early years of the rental apartment business. The managers, often a "Ma and Pa" team, handled rental and maintenance duties. This was basically a seven-day-a-week commitment. As apartment properties grew larger, their staffs grew as well. Living on site remained commonplace, but there were many exceptions. This section will examine the pros and cons of living on site.

With a manager living on site, someone is always available to handle the inevitable after-hours' problems. The manager can observe how different facilities are used or abused during peak activity times. Monitoring of parking patterns and night lighting is often ignored when the manager leaves for home at the end of the workday.

There are also distinct disadvantages to having someone live on site, burnout being perhaps the greatest. Working and living in the same place, especially in a business that involves a constant flow of problems, takes a heavy toll. Some managers become hermits and practically hide from residents in an attempt to preserve some semblance of a private life. Some become hostile in an effort to keep intrusions to a minimum, while others strike up acquaintances with existing residents that can affect their objectivity. All of these reactions will have a negative impact on the property. Many managers want to own their own homes. Others may have families too large for the apartments available. Rules requiring a manager or a maintenance chief to reside on site should be flexible. Sizable apartment communities can benefit from one or more staff members living on site, but they need not be the manager or maintenance chief. Latitude should be exercised when assigning on-site duties. (Note: State law may establish specific requirements in this regard. In California, for example, properties with 17 or more units must have a manager living on site.)

It is a problem when staff members think themselves better than the residents and prefer not to live with them; this is almost instantly detected by the residents. There will be associated costs when residents sense that the staff has a low opinion of them. Turnover is almost certain to increase—it is difficult for people to feel good about their homes when the property's management displays even a hint of a belittling attitude.

When staff members live on site, the location of their housing is the next decision to be made. Most managers live very close to the rental office or in a building that has a special view or some extra feature or appointment. This happens for two basic reasons. First of all, the manager's apartment may have been part of the initial construction package. Secondly, these early buildings often received very special treatment as they were being used to demonstrate the quality standards that were to follow.

With the passage of time, the grounds and buildings will begin to show wear, but the process is noticeably slower in the areas immediately adjacent to the on-site employee's unit(s). The reason for this .is simple: Because these areas and the various building components are in daily view of resident staff members, any needed corrections are promptly ordered. Many owners or supervisors who visit the property look only at the buildings surrounding the clubhouse and rental center and will quickly authorize repairs or replacements in these highly visible areas to avoid losing prospects as a result of a bad first impression of the apartment community.

Another sure indicator of trouble occurs when staff members choose to live in the very best units. To understand this, assume that an apartment community has 50 one-bedroom and 40 two-bedroom apartments plus 10 townhouses. The townhouses are in the least supply and probably in the greatest demand, plus they rent at top dollar. These units should be reserved for rent-paying residents. Staff should be assigned the most difficult units to lease, certainly not the most marketable ones.

Almost every apartment community of any size has one or more buildings that are more run down or suffer with a more troublesome set of residents than in the balance of the property. If the manager, maintenance chief, or other member(s) of the senior staff are housed in these buildings, an almost guaranteed improvement will take place within weeks. The presence of staff living in the building will bring the much-needed attention to problem areas, and the behavior of the residents will improve markedly—and immediately. It just happens . . . *try it*.

Exchange for Service.   The exchange of services for free or reduced rent is a practice that should be avoided. For example, a member of the police force might provide part-time security service to the apartment community in return for a rent reduction. Sometimes individuals offering maintenance or custodial services are compensated with different degrees of reduced rent.

This practice always increases in popularity when vacancies are abundant. It might start out looking like a bargain, but the property rarely ends up getting full value on a sustaining basis. I believe that trading labor or services for rent is unprofessional. The practice produces only marginal results and more than likely violates some important laws.

While a particular situation may warrant consideration of an exchange for service, as a general rule the manager should hire and pay for needed services. Following this path, the property will receive a better quality of overall service with better economy.

Socializing with Residents. All employees should be discouraged from socializing with residents. This policy is particularly hard on staff members who live on site, but it is necessary. Socializing with residents, becoming personally involved with them, or having occasional refreshments are all seemingly innocent practices that are bound to affect an employee's judgment. These types of fraternization are different from and go beyond maintaining friendly, but professional, relationships with residents. (Note: This perspective may be more difficult to maintain where contemporary management practices have the manager act more like a concierge.)

Posting Notices, Keeping Records. At this juncture, it is important to take note of some employee-related legal requirements. Managers must be aware of local, state, and federal regulations regarding the posting of certain notices and licenses. Here are some examples of commonly required postings.

- Local business license
- Real estate salesperson and broker's license
- Unemployment insurance notice
- Worker's compensation notice
- Occupational Safety and Health Act (OSHA) notice
- Equal Employment Opportunity (EEO) notice
- Fair Housing notice
- Employee Polygraph Protection Act (EPPA) poster
- Fair Labor Standards Act (FLSA) poster
- Age Discrimination in Employment Act (ADEA) poster
- Family and Medical Leave Act (FMLA)

These notices primarily address issues concerning prospective and existing employees. Such posters must be placed in an area accessible by your staff. Those notices that pertain to residents and rental prospects must be similarly accessible to their "audience." It is important to stay current: Laws change and there may be state regulations to keep in mind (e.g., your state Department of Labor probably has information-posting requirements).

There are also numerous laws that prescribe requirements regarding employee records, and these laws frequently change and expand. Some of these requirements are an outgrowth of the Occupational Safety and Health Act (OSHA) of 1970. OSHA includes definite record-keeping requirements for employers—including managing agents—and fines are imposed for violations. Since laws are changing constantly, the local office of the U.S. Department of Labor should be contacted for details. It is sound business practice to always maintain adequate employee records. Here are examples of items that should appear in the file of every employee, including part-time workers.

- Employee application form and documentation of reference and background checks
- Job description
- Current W-4 form for withholding tax
- Benefit application
- Time records
- Pay records, including regular pay, overtime, bonuses, commissions, and raises
- Vacation and sick-day records
- Social Security and Medicare payments
- Union benefits
- Accident reports
- Performance review and evaluation reports
- Promotions, transfers, layoffs, and discharges
- Commendations and complaints
- Records of disciplinary action
- Immigration and Naturalization Service (INS) Form I-9 (proof of citizenship)

The Americans with Disabilities Act (ADA) requires records with medical content to be kept separate from other employee records. This includes any prehiring physical examinations, workers' compensation benefits for job-related illness or injury, and other similar information.

Employment records should be maintained for at least five years after the employee leaves. Many management firms keep employee records indefinitely. In situations where the people working at an apartment community under your management are technically employees of the property and not of your company, prepare a duplicate set of records for your own files. By doing this, your files will be complete if you should lose the management account and be required to turn over the employment records.

Licensing.   Many states have real estate license law provisions which say, in effect, that persons who "lease or offer to lease" real estate must be licensed. In most states, this requirement does not extend to direct employees of the property owner, but it almost always includes employees of a managing agent. In the future, licensing requirements will become increasingly stringent and may include the licensing of real estate managers. Licensing requirements vary from state to state, and it is important to know whether the licensing specifications in your state include continuing education requirements. You need to be aware of the laws in your area and be alert for any changes in those laws. It is also wise to seek advice of legal counsel to ensure ongoing compliance with licensing requirements.

Compensation.   It is not unusual for real estate management employees to receive several forms of compensation, including salary or wages, free or reduced rent, free utilities, and other noncash items. Some owners hold the opinion that salary or wages can be lower if other noncash benefits are offered. Thus, as some owners put it, "You can hire a site manager for $1,500 a month, provide an apartment valued at $700 per month, toss in $100 worth of free telephone service and utilities a month, and claim to be paying the employee $2,300 a month." Let's see if this is true.

Free Rent.   The idea of giving an apartment rent-free to an employee came about in the days when empty apartments were more plentiful than money. When the practice started, it was common for employees not to report the value of their apartments as income; but that is not how the law reads now. The Internal Revenue Service (IRS) includes an apartment's value as taxable income, unless the employee is required to live on the site *for the owner's convenience.* When an apartment is provided for the owner's convenience, it is not counted as part or full compensation for services rendered. (In addition, some states also have rules regarding taxability of free rent.)

In most cases, providing a free apartment is simply a matter of giving the employee something extra to make up for an otherwise low salary or wage. Under those circumstances, the employee will have to pay taxes on the value of the apartment. So, "free" rent is not exactly free.

Now let's examine it from the employee's standpoint. Someone earning $2,000 a month normally would budget about $550 a month for an apartment. If you provide the employee with a unit renting for $800, the employee can only allocate the $550 value that he or she would normally spend on rent; the other $250 of value is nice, but the employee probably needs the cash to pay other living expenses. The disadvantage to giving an employee an expensive apartment is that some of the value cannot be appreciated. As noted in the discussion of economic vacancy in Chapter 1, removing a prime apartment from inventory negatively affects the property's income stream—i.e., effective gross income.

Employee Discounts.   One way to avoid the problems created by offering free rent is to rent the apartment to the employee at its regular value less a discount. This is a method used by retailers, and it results in the employees being aware of value. Also, a modest employee discount on rent may not be taxable compensation.

The IRS allows some flexibility when it comes to taxing the benefits of an employee discount. However, you should check with a tax law authority before establishing such a discount policy. The general rule in the apartment industry is that an acceptable discount would be roughly equal to the money spent on a per-unit basis for promotion plus an allowance for profit. Fifteen percent is a fairly common figure for this reduction. An apartment leasing to the general public for $700 per month might be discounted by $105 when rented to an employee without incurring income tax liability on the benefit.

Discounts should be offered to all employees equally; they cannot be used as a method of rewarding one set of employees and not others.

Free Utilities.   In some cases, the employees' utility bills are paid for by the property. It has been my experience that employees who receive this benefit seldom appreciate or credit this benefit as part of their income. Ask them what they earn, and they will quote their salaries or wages, ignoring the cost of extra benefits such as free utilities (or even a free apartment). Because they do not write the check, they often remain clueless as to the value received.

Other Noncash Benefits.   The same holds true of other noncash benefits such as telephone or cable TV service. Free gasoline for employee cars is another benefit that quickly becomes unappreciated or misused. A better strategy is to offer a mileage allowance.

Salary.   A manager is better off paying an employee a straight salary or wage and forgetting about free apartments and free utilities. The amount of the salary or wage should be set at a level that will attract the people you want. This level will vary from one area to another. When real estate management businesses underpay employees, they pay for it dearly in inefficient operations. An informed owner wants a manager who is competent and businesslike. There are no bargains in low wages.

Salary versus Commission.   The question of salary or a commission will come up when you set out to hire a leasing agent. My advice is to choose salary, but you should also be mindful of what is being done in your marketplace.

Commission would appear to have much in its favor. The apartment community only pays for results, and job positions that compensate with commissions rather than salary have a way of weeding out those who lack confidence in their sales ability. It is expected that a person will work harder when on commission and therefore make more money.

So where is the problem? There are several. First of all, the most confident and persuasive real estate people are selling houses, rather than leasing apartments, because the financial rewards are significantly greater. There are certainly some exceptions, as when individuals with good selling skills decide to "get their feet wet" in real estate by starting as leasing agents. In time, however, many of these people will "transition" into real estate sales. Unfortunately, many people who apply for a commission-only leasing agent position see it more as an interesting sideline rather than as a long-term career opportunity. To attract top-quality leasing agents, the commission per lease must be substantial. This way, they can average-out their earnings to cover the orientation and start-up period as well as the inevitable slow weeks. If the agent succeeds in obtaining large numbers of signed leases— either because of ability or market trends or both—the income achieved might possibly exceed what the manager is being paid. Obviously, this creates a whole new set of problems. Hard feelings and resentments can develop, making it difficult for managers and leasing agents to work together.

Commission-only leasing agents get paid exclusively for prospects who become residents. It does not take long to learn which prospects the manager will accept on the basis of income and past history. As a result, agents may steer an applicant's answers to fit the manager's expectations. Also, a commission-only leasing agent may refuse to handle resident calls, substitute as a receptionist, or even take a rent check from an existing resident during busy times in the office. Offering fixed salaries to your leasing agents not only provides them the security of a regular paycheck, but also allows you the freedom to assign additional duties.

When the pace of leasing is fast moving, there are usually few problems; but when prospect traffic falls off, leasing agents often go searching for greener pastures. When times are tough and you need the best staff, the commissioned agent's pay will be at its lowest; and you may be back hunting for new help. There are many individuals who will develop into top-notch leasing agents who need and want the dependability of a regular salary. You can sweeten an agent's paycheck with a small bonus after an exceptional week, but the fixed salary should represent most of the compensation package.

Salary and Wage Adjustments. Ideally, you should make it a policy to review salaries and wages for each employee at least once a year. At that time, you can determine whether an employee should be given a merit or cost-of-living increase. Individual performance and local job market conditions will help you decide the amount.

In keeping with what was said earlier about paying a competitive wage or salary, your policy should be to reward good performance and to pay employees well and in accordance with their responsibilities.

Overtime in general should be discouraged. When it becomes a routine occurrence, employees will come to expect overtime pay as part of their regular income and will be disappointed when they do not receive it. Try to streamline your operation with efficient planning and scheduling so all routine work is performed during a normal 40-hour workweek. There may be certain periods due to weather, untimely breakdowns, or seasonal traffic when short-term needs justify overtime. If the need for overtime becomes too frequent, you should add another staff position.

Incentives and Bonuses.   Regular incentives and bonuses are self-defeating. Employees learn to count on them and expect them. They become regarded as part of employees' regular income and lose all value as incentives for extra effort. For this reason, payment of any kind of regular bonus, including a holiday bonus, is discouraged.

Instead, consider specific incentive bonuses geared to short-range goals, such as leasing a certain number of apartments, obtaining renewals, or improving rent collections in a specific time period. Such incentives build excitement, improve employee morale, and vary the pace of activities. Employees usually welcome the challenge and respond with extra performance. Bonuses need not be paid in dollars; they can be just as effective in the form of merchandise, commendations, or travel. One of the most popular rewards is a "no questions asked" half or full day off work (with pay). This can be used at the employee's discretion. Some call it a "get out of jail card."

Wage and Hour Law.   It is absolutely essential to be familiar with the Fair Labor Standards Act (FLSA). This is frequently referred to as the Federal Wage and Hour Law. The requirements of this law are significant. Likewise, the penalties for failure to comply are severe. You can contact the Wage and Hour Division of the Employment Standards Administration of the U.S. Department of Labor to obtain information on the law and its requirements. *States may also have wage and hour laws, and the more stringent of the two will prevail.*

The comments in this section amount to a broad interpretation of the Federal Wage and Hour provisions. Specific wage and salary amounts have been avoided, as they are subject to change. Interpretation of specific situations by regional Wage and Hour offices will differ, making a complete discussion of the subject even more difficult.

The Federal Wage and Hour Law generally prevents paying a real estate management employee a fixed salary so that the employee can work unlimited hours each week without additional compensation. Almost all apartment buildings are covered by this law, which states that employees must be paid the minimum hourly wage and that you must compensate employees at the rate of time-and-one-half for all time worked in excess of 40 hours each week, with certain exceptions. Even if you pay employees monthly,

---

Exemptions from Overtime

The Federal Wage and Hour Law provides that certain employees meeting specific criteria can be exempt from the overtime provision. In real estate management, these exemptions come under one of two classifications—executive or administrative. The government has published a special booklet dealing with these exemptions (Regulations, Part 541). Copies are available from the Wage and Hour Division of the U.S. Department of Labor.

In a very broad interpretation of exemption requirements, a person must at least meet the following tests to qualify for exemption from the overtime provision.

1. The primary duties of the employee must be management related.

2. The employee must supervise two or more employees.

3. The employee must not spend more than 20 percent of the workweek performing manual or non-management-related activities.

4. The employee must receive a guaranteed weekly wage of at least a specified amount. This figure has two levels and is subject to change. The wage must be guaranteed at this level and must not be subject to deductions for sick time or short hours. The test of the minimum wage level may not include any apartment value.

I recommend a thorough reading of the government's pamphlet on this subject before determining which, if any, of your employees can be classified as exempt.

---

the federal agency simply will take the monthly salary, multiply it by twelve months, and then divide by 2,080 hours (40 hours a week × 52 weeks a year) to arrive at an hourly rate. (There are exemptions from the overtime requirement for certain executive and administrative personnel. These are outlined in the accompanying sidebar.)

You need to consider some implications of the Wage and Hour Law. Your objective is to minimize overtime pay, if possible. You can do this by giving compensatory time off within the particular workweek. This means that an employee who works 40 hours before the end of the week can be given time off for the rest of the week. You cannot give compensatory time off during the following week; the law says each week must stand on its own.

In most industries, the workweek begins on Monday and ends on Sunday. If you follow this system and you need employees to work on weekends—the time when most emergencies occur—you will probably end up paying overtime. You are better advised to declare your workweek to begin on Friday and end on Thursday. Then, if employees must work on the weekend, you have the less-hectic remainder of the week to grant time off to compensate for those extra hours. Such a policy can save you many over-time hours. If you do this, it is more efficient to pay employees weekly or every two weeks, because then your records will conform more easily to a standard workweek.

You should take the time to study how the federal government cal-culates minimum wages and overtime. The Wage and Hour people may consider both the salary and the value of an apartment when calculating the hourly rate and testing for the minimum wage. The apartment value only counts if the apartment is provided for the employee's—not the em-ployer's—convenience. If that is the case, the IRS will expect taxes to be withheld on its value.

Here's how you can test to see that you are meeting the minimum wage requirement. Assume you provide an apartment for an employee and that this apartment normally rents for $800 per month. Assume further that a reasonable profit and promotion allocation attributable to the unit is $120 per month. You then subtract this amount from the monthly rent ($800 − $120 = $680) to arrive at the apartment's discounted value, which is added to the monthly salary for the purpose of satisfying minimum wage require-ments. Continuing the example, a person receiving a monthly salary of $1,800 and an apartment with an adjusted value of $680 is effectively being compensated $2,480 per month or $29,760 per year. Dividing by 2,080, you arrive at an hourly rate of $14.31.

$$(\$1,800 + \$680) \times 12 = \$29,760$$

$$\frac{\$29,760}{2,080} = \$14.31$$

The foregoing formula shows the annual total of both salary and apartment value ($29,760) being divided by the 2,080 hours in the standard work-year, thereby producing the hourly wage for Wage and Hour calculations. This amount will be used to determine whether the minimum wage requirement is being met and for calculating premium pay for overtime hours. If the cal-culation had produced an hourly rate that was below the prevailing mini-mum wage, you would be required to increase the person's compensation to at least meet that amount. If your property is in a state that has a differ-ent minimum wage than the federal rate, the higher of the two rates will pre-vail. For tax purposes, the employee in the example will report the total of both the salary received and the discounted value of the apartment.

When computing overtime compensation, the government requires you to use the total hourly rate that includes the adjusted apartment value. This hourly rate is to be multiplied by 1.5 to arrive at the hourly wage to be paid for the time worked in excess of 40 hours during a particular work-week. (Finishing our example, this employee would be entitled to $21.47 [$14.31 × 1.5] for each hour worked beyond 40 hours.)

The preceding example is an extremely simplified illustration of one particular situation. It is imperative that you seek legal advice to learn how the Federal Wage and Hour Law—and possibly state laws—applies to your unique circumstances.

You must be very careful in keeping track of both wage levels and hours worked. If the government suspects you are violating the law, it can audit *all* of your employees' pay records for the past two years (in some cases, for the past three years) and hold you liable for any underpayment of the minimum wage plus any premium or overtime pay that was not paid during those years. If it can be proved that you acted willfully in underpaying your employees, the government can go back three years and force you to pay double the wages due.

The best practice is to have each employee fill out a weekly timecard detailing the hours worked each day. Employees should sign their cards at week's end. You should retain these cards as a permanent record and pay overtime when necessary.

The Wage and Hour Law should not be taken lightly. The law is written to protect employees, and their word often will be upheld against their employers'. You need to know and understand the law thoroughly and document your actions carefully.

Reporting to Work and Breaks.   You have a right to expect employees to be at work on time. Your policy should state that if an employee is sick or delayed, the supervisor must be notified no later than 30 minutes after the appointed starting time. Similarly, if an employee must leave work before the designated break, lunch period, or quitting time, the supervisor must be notified. Your policies should clearly state the number of violations of these rules that will constitute cause for dismissal.

An employee found not working commonly replies, "I am on my break." If you wish to eliminate this excuse, establish uniform time periods in the morning and afternoon for breaks. Typically, these might be from 9:45 to 10:00 A.M. and 2:30 to 2:45 P.M. You may also establish a set lunch period. At all other times of the workday, you should expect to find employees working.

Holidays.   Let your leasing personnel know right away that they will be expected to work on Sundays and summer holidays. Rotating schedules help shift weekend work assignments to most staff members. Thanksgiving, Christmas, and New Year's Day are poor rental days so you might just as well remain closed. A minimum maintenance staff will be needed for most holidays.

Vacations.   It is a good idea to establish a period in which any earned vacation time must be taken. An employee usually earns one day of vacation for each full month of employment, up to a total of ten days per year (employees with greater tenure should be allowed to accumulate additional vacation time). Employees should be required to take these vacation days within a certain period. For example, many management companies allow vacation time to be accumulated through April 30; employees then have to take their vacations before March 31 of the following year. This policy prevents employees from combining two weeks of vacation at the end of one year with two weeks at the beginning of the next to make a four-week vacation. The following are some other vacation policies to consider:

- Employees must schedule their vacations around those of other employees so that you are not left shorthanded at any time. If a conflict develops, seniority rules.

- Any vacation time not taken within the specified period is lost forever. It is not carried over into the next year or compensated by money.

- If an employee resigns without sufficient notice or after less than one year of employment, all accrued vacation time is lost.

- An employee who is terminated receives any accrued vacation pay as severance.

- If an employee dies, the heirs receive any accrued vacation pay.

State law may restrict practices related to carryover of vacation time and payment for accrued vacation time when an employee voluntarily leaves employment.

Death of a Relative.   You should consider granting up to three days off with pay (perhaps even up to five days in cases with special circumstances) if an employee's immediate relative dies. "Immediate relative" includes one's spouse, mother, father, mother-in-law, father-in-law, son, daughter, sister, or brother. If the employee needs more time, allow an authorized leave of absence. Absence due to the death of any other relative or friend should be without pay.

Sick Days and Personal Days.   It is virtually impossible to set a foolproof sick-day and personal-day policy. In many cases, with both spouses working, more employees might opt for personal time off to care for a sick child rather than take the traditional sick day. Some companies allow employees five such days during a calendar year. For each day they take, they are paid. For each day not taken, they receive one additional day of vacation, up to five days. Any time taken beyond five days is then without pay. Whatever policy you establish, be sure to carefully record time taken to avoid future disputes.

Employee Health Insurance. Employees of large management firms typically receive varying levels of medical coverage as a benefit of their employment. As in most other employment situations, the cost of hospitalization and other medical coverages is often shared by employer and employee. Smaller firms and individual properties, on the other hand, find it increasingly difficult to secure adequate and affordable medical and hospitalization coverage. Many do not meet the insurance companies' minimum group size. In these situations, additional compensation is often provided so that the employees can secure coverage on their own. Without some allowance for health insurance premiums, smaller companies and individual properties find themselves at a serious hiring disadvantage.

In some cases, employers are obligated to provide a Health Maintenance Organization (HMO) option. This requirement only applies to those employers who already provide health insurance benefits. Under the Health Maintenance Organization Act, an employer may be required to offer an HMO plan if the employees involved exceed a specified number and a written request has been received from a qualified HMO. An employer who fails to comply can be subject to substantial fines. The changing law in this area serves as a reminder that the entire insurance picture is in a state of flux. It is very important to stay up-to-date and seek professional advice.

Education and Tuition. Employers usually benefit from encouraging their employees to pursue education that will improve their on-the-job skills. This education can include formal day or evening classes, seminars, dinner programs, and short-term training programs. Administrative, leasing, and maintenance personnel, as well as managers, should be included in the education policy.

The policy must be thought out carefully and enforced, or you may find yourself paying for education that has no relation to the job. Some employers find this acceptable; they believe that any course an employee takes will pay off in better job performance.

The typical education policy requires an employee to obtain approval from a supervisor before enrolling in the course. The employee then pays for tuition, books, and other expenses in advance. When the employee presents evidence of having successfully completed the course (often with a grade of "C" or better), the employer calculates the reimbursement due using a predetermined percentage of the tuition cost (e.g., 75 percent). Books and other out-of-pocket expenses are sometimes reimbursed as well. Usually, a company will limit the number of courses or the total amount of reimbursement in a given year. This policy encourages the employee to make a personal financial commitment and take the course more seriously.

Professional Memberships. You may decide to encourage your employees to join a professional association, perhaps one with which you yourself are affiliated. In this case you can establish a policy to pay for part or all of the employees' membership fees and subsequent dues. Professional organizations provide a forum for exchanging ideas and an opportunity for members of your staff to learn about the industry through the experience of other real estate managers. Providing this benefit may be quite costly, but it frequently pays off in the form of a skilled and enthusiastic staff.

Uniforms. Policies on uniforms vary. Staff uniforms can range from a baseball cap and imprinted T-shirt to a full wardrobe for each job position, even accounting for varying weather conditions. The trend seems to be headed more toward the full uniform. Leasing personnel are often dressed in blazers. Maintenance people wear freshly laundered full uniforms. With so many service organizations outfitted in uniforms today, it is having an effect on the apartment industry. Consider FedEx, UPS, the airlines, and even oil change services. Fully uniformed maintenance and custodial workers present a much more professional appearance. Uniforms identify these workers as staff members, which comforts residents and wards off intruders. Uniforms also save wear and tear of the workers' own clothing. Providing and maintaining uniforms is an expensive proposition for employers, but it pays dividends in many ways.

Some firms have adopted the policy of "casual Friday," some extend it to everyday. This idea may be fine for a law firm or engineering company, but it is not right for service providers. Can you imagine the UPS driver arriving at your door on Friday in jeans and a sweatshirt?

Employee Identification. With the general feeling of concern that exists today, apartment properties are advised to provide clear identification for all of their employees. Those who will have contact with customers and will be entering apartments should wear picture identification badges. Others who handle chores on the grounds should ideally display badges with the property's name.

Tools. Maintenance personnel should be required to provide their own basic hand tools. If they are experienced, they will have the tools of their trade. Ask to see their tools before you make a hiring decision. Generally, craftsmen keep their tools in good condition and are proud to show them off. When you provide tools, make the workers responsible for their care and safe storage. The property will be expected to provide both power tools and all specialized and expensive tools. You must also provide appropriate safety equipment (e.g., goggles, masks, helmets) if the nature of an employee's work requires such items. Specifics are spelled out in the Occupational Safety and Health Act.

Radios. The work environment may be perceived as less-than-professional if workers are permitted to bring radios and play their favorite music or listen to sports or talk shows while they work. The rules you establish regarding radios should apply to both employees and vendors. The sound of a loud radio can be annoying to residents and visitors. You will not see employees or other outside workers in top hotels playing radios, even types equipped with headsets. Radios can be irritating and, worse, the distraction can lead to accidents.

Weapons.   It is important that you prohibit employees from carrying any form of weapon. This certainly includes guns, knives (other than small pocket knives), and clubs. Nor should weapons be stored in a locker or desk. These items can be misused, leading to tragedy and possibly a lawsuit against you and the property.

Personal Hygiene.   While this can be a sensitive subject to broach, it must be recognized that real estate management employees are service providers who are in direct contact with their customers. Employees with poor personal hygiene habits cannot be tolerated. If this problem presents itself, you as the manager must take immediate steps to see that it is addressed. There is no shortcut to solving this problem other than a face-to-face explanation and a demand for better hygiene.

Controlling Employee Purchases.   Apartment managers often establish accounts with local vendors such as hardware, electrical, and plumbing supply stores. This can create problems because employees may take advantage of these accounts to buy items for themselves. Some managers attempt to deal with this situation by setting a dollar limit on each order, but it is a simple matter for an employee to get around such a restriction by coming in at different times with smaller orders.

The recommended way to control purchases is to require vendors to refuse any orders that are not itemized on a written *purchase order* signed by the manager. This makes it more difficult for any unauthorized person to buy something for personal use. The same rule applies to purchases of capital equipment.

Gifts, Kickbacks, and Commissions.   I believe managers should have an absolute policy regarding gifts, commissions, and kickbacks in order to head off trouble and ensure that whatever they purchase from vendors is based on price and quality, not favoritism.

Vendors historically have offered management employees bonuses for orders, believing that the employees' traditionally low pay scale may tempt them to accept. Many companies that sell light bulbs, cleaning supplies, and chemicals, for example, continue to follow such practices. Some furniture leasing companies pay a bonus to the manager or leasing agent for every resident who becomes their customer and then may pressure the manager to let the furniture remain after a resident moves, hoping that the apartment will be re-leased with the company's furnishings in place. This practice saves the furniture company money because it does not have to pick up the furniture. Nevertheless, waiting for someone who will accept the furnishings may cost the property owner money in lost rent. You should also consider the fact that residents who have their own furnishings are often more stable than those who do not.

Commissions, gifts, and bonuses—indeed, any form of kickback from a vendor—are unacceptable for several reasons. First, they may encourage employees to order more than is needed in order to qualify for a gift. Second, employees may disregard quality, costing the property more money in the long run. Third, if there are any price reductions or bonuses, these rightfully should be credited to the building account in the form of a discount rather than going into employees' pockets.

To make sure that all relations with suppliers are on a strictly business basis, employees should be forbidden to accept any kind of money payments from them. They should also be instructed to refuse any free tickets to entertainment or sporting events and to turn down any free dinners or other invitations to socialize. However, you may wish to permit the acceptance of "token" gifts during the holiday season, possibly setting a maximum value limit on these.

Gifts or tips from residents should also be refused. They could lead to special treatment and unequal service, a source of many resident complaints. If holiday tipping and gift-giving to employees is already practiced, I recommend establishing a means of pooling these funds so the total can be divided among all the employees and individual residents are not identified.

Pilfering and Petty Theft.   Because of the supplies, equipment, cash payments, petty cash, and vending machine collections kept on the premises, a real estate management office is vulnerable to pilfering and petty theft. Employees should know that you realize this temptation exists and that you will use every means available to reduce losses. Furthermore, let them know that if they are caught pilfering, you will terminate their employment. If the theft involves a substantial amount, you should prosecute. Following are some steps you can take to reduce the possibilities of petty theft:

- *Keep supplies to a minimum.* If you order large quantities of popular supply items at one time, you can expect pilferage. Instead, give the vendor a blanket purchase order to obtain the quantity discount and then arrange shipments of small quantities as needed.
- *Store supplies in locked cabinets.* Give keys to only one or two people.
- *Buy bulk quantities.* It is easy to steal a gallon of paint or a quart of household cleaner. However, if you buy in larger containers, such as 30-gallon drums, theft becomes more difficult.

- *Bank money daily.* Do not hold checks or cash (other than petty cash) for more than eight hours. Keep petty cash in a locked desk.

- *Log all vending machine collections.* Normally, there will be little variation in monthly collections from vending equipment from one year to the next. If there is a sharp drop in this income, you can suspect theft.

- *Never authorize site personnel to sign checks.* They should only make deposits. Any exception to this recommendation creates the potential for accounting problems and money irregularities.

Managing Your Staff

The subject of staff management is an expansive one. Your level of management ability will depend on your aptitude in a wide variety of skills. For starters, a manager must be able to organize, communicate, solve problems, and relate to others. There is a proliferation of courses and books addressing this topic, and many of them can be helpful. For that reason, I will explore personnel management issues without devoting much time to general management techniques.

Employee Turnover.   Turnover of employees is expensive. With each change, the training process starts over again, and usually a little something is lost with each new training session.

Your residents notice such turnover. Finding new staff members with each trip to the office can be frustrating for residents who are then forced to update the chronology of their occupancy problems and to adjust to the new workers' personalities and temperaments.

The advice for achieving greater longevity is the same advice I will offer for selecting new residents: Slow down. Don't jump at the first hiring opportunity. Complete thorough background and reference checks. If a person has held a number of positions in the past year or so, you should be alert. The same is true if there are unexplained gaps in employment. Hiring and working with people involves personal chemistry. So, while it is possible that you will succeed where others have failed, the odds are not in your favor. You will solve an immediate problem if you can quickly replace someone who leaves your operation. Nevertheless, it is crucial to be aware that you waste time and money when you train someone who ultimately will not stay.

You need to assure yourself through investigation that the individual is capable of doing the job. It is a good idea to start out with an introductory period during which both parties can evaluate the hiring decision and whether it has resulted in a good match. A large company can offer advancement and a multifaceted benefit package. A single apartment community cannot compete on the same terms, but it can certainly respond with a good compensation program, greater individual recognition, and freedom from the politics of working for a large organization. Both employee and employer must be satisfied with the arrangement.

Hiring is often driven by a need for a particular strength. The four basic disciplines in the management of investment residential real estate are:

- Product preparation,
- Marketing and leasing,
- Organization, and
- Customer service.

Each of these areas demands unique strengths. Therefore, as the need for help within a given discipline changes, so does the need for a person with different skills and interests. Finding someone with a flair for all or most of the four disciplines usually does not work because few such people exist and those who do are often running their own operations.

The need for a particular skill often comes and goes in a fairly short time span. For example, consider an apartment community that has been allowed to deteriorate. What is needed in this situation is a manager who possesses considerable experience in identifying the work to be done and has the skill to direct people to orchestrate a general fix-up program. When the property is returned to acceptable standards, the skill needs begin to shift. Now, the property needs the talents of a person with carefully honed marketing and leasing skills. Later, as occupancy levels climb, the challenge becomes one of instituting operating systems and achieving financial stability so that the business can perpetuate itself. Lastly, a person is needed who relishes the principles of customer care and commitment to service. Reflecting on your own experiences, you will probably recall individuals who exhibited competence in one or two of the four skill areas and a defined weakness in the others.

Many of the larger firms recognize these different skill disciplines in their employees and shift specialists in and out of properties to answer particular needs. By doing this, they provide the talent to address the problem and avoid frustrating employees by insisting that they engage in tasks they are ill equipped for or uninterested in handling.

Shifting managers to different properties from time to time can be helpful and refreshing to both the residents and the manager. Apartment managers can find themselves in a rut that depletes their energy and enthusiasm. Some managers have actually cataloged their residents as troublesome or complainers. Transferring to another apartment community might just reset their energy meter. There will be all new things to learn at a different property, new shortcomings to be corrected, and new residents to get to know. While too much change is not good, some change may be just what is needed.

The Importance of Building Morale.   Morale is a hidden force that can push your efforts forward or stop any chance of success. Instilling positive morale requires the kind of leadership and motivational skills that are the envy of managers in all aspects of the business community. It is also the subject of countless training courses and books. The damaging effects of low morale and the ways the motivation level of your staff can be eroded need to be addressed. In a service-driven business, low morale is surely the beginning of the end.

Nonpayment or slow payment of bills does more damage to staff morale than anything else. When a maintenance worker is turned away at the hardware store because previous bills remain unpaid, the psychological damage is substantial. People need to feel good about their jobs, and they need to feel secure. If a small hardware bill is not paid, the newspaper has refused any more ad insertions, or units have been left unpainted because of a lack of money, there is no way the staff can feel secure or enthusiastic. Sometimes the owner of a group of properties will put on sales training or motivational sessions in an expensive hotel in an effort to brighten the spirits of the staff. Employees may want to attend, but they cannot sidestep the fact that it would be more helpful to use the money to pay bills. If there are problems with money, they must be dealt with at the highest level. Once the staff knows financial problems exist, much of the positive spirit in the office is lost.

Hiring or promoting staff members who are unqualified for their positions also damages morale. Relatives are sometimes given jobs ahead of staff members with much more experience. Nepotism is a dangerous practice. You should also be alert to the possibility of staff members having intimate relationships; office romances often cause breakdowns in morale and operations.

Displaying a lack of sensitivity is another way to harm employees' spirit. Firms whose policies ultimately cheat residents on their security deposits are in fact hurting their staff as well as their residents. People do not like unfair policies or methods. Employees may appear to support unfair policies (because they want to keep their jobs), when in fact they may disagree vehemently. This sets up a lack of respect that will weave its way through virtually every employee action.

Employee Burnout. Managers and maintenance people are often subject to burnout. Apartment management is a business of basics that must be repeated every day. Maintenance personnel are responsible for cleaning up the messes left by departing residents and are pressured to quickly put the apartments back into shape for the next round of rentals. The more the property is used, the greater the need for cleaning. Employees begin noticing that the good residents seem to leave and difficult residents seem to stay. Owners and managers must acknowledge the fact that all properties are subject to a continual process of decay. The older a property gets, the greater the operational costs. This usually coincides with a decline in the property's peak rent levels. Deteriorating conditions bring less-responsible residents, who often cause more damage and are even more transient. This cycling will continue at an ever-increasing pace unless there is a sustained and conscious effort to keep the property looking sharp.

Without a program of constant renewal, the employees will begin to bog down and the burnout syndrome gets its start. At that point, employees no longer put a lot of thought behind their actions. Suddenly, the excitement of maintaining and improving the property is gone. The challenge of learning what prospects want in their housing is lost. The rewards of resident comments and praise stop—and the winning attitude vanishes.

The way to defeat burnout is to constantly experiment with new property improvements. When a vacancy occurs, don't just apply a coat of white paint—try something special. You might change the carpet types or colors or add some new woodwork or built-ins. If you always plant geraniums in the front yard, try creating new flowerbeds with totally different arrangements. Redecorate the rental center or recreational facility, or start over completely and create the most provocative models you and your staff can. (In Chapter 12, we will explore other ways to update and improve apartment properties.)

As the manager, don't get caught waiting for others to come up with new ideas and innovations. In my 45 years in property management, I have never once been faulted for implementing new ideas and property improvements. Making progressive changes in your apartment community will pay dividends far beyond the prevention of employee burnout.

Managers of relatively small apartment properties often feel trapped, with little challenge and low pay. The job is simply a job, and the economics of a small property often do not justify an increase in compensation in spite of the manager's tenure, loyalty, and ability. The solution might be to add a second small property to the manager's portfolio. This solves many problems: It provides new and different challenges; it lessens the "trapped" feeling; it exposes the manager to a different resident profile, and it allows for increased compensation.

Employee Termination.   Most apartment managers are employees themselves, and they understand the family crisis that can result from losing a job. Terminating a fellow employee is a distasteful and often emotional situation. All too often the severance process is postponed in hopes that things will improve or that the employee might get the message and quit.

Sometimes a problem employee claims to be indispensable. Perhaps this individual knows something about your building equipment that no other staff person appears to understand. However, there are few things in an apartment building that cannot be quickly figured out by professionals. Certainly, nothing is so mysterious that you should put up with a difficult employee. In fact, terminating the so-called indispensable person almost al-

ways results in the discovery of a grand omission on the part of the departing employee. Correcting these problems obviously benefits the property.

Countless situations exist in which a valuable employee threatens to
quit. A good many of these threats are ongoing and often said in a joking
fashion. Nevertheless, the message is clear. When this happens, the time has
come to stop the comments or terminate the employee. You absolutely do
not need an employee who walks around telling others it is time to quit if
changes are not made. Allowing this to continue means you will lose control and respect. When it comes to an employee threatening to quit, my advice would be to grant one written warning (and no more than one) before
termination. Note that all your termination policies should be checked with
an attorney before they are implemented.

Before you terminate an employee, it is crucial to document the incidents that led to your decision to discharge—that way you will have the
proper records if a disgruntled former employee accuses you of wrongful
termination or discrimination. When you must terminate someone, handle
the situation with dispatch. If circumstances dictate severance pay, then issue a check and dismiss the employee. The final check should not be turned
over, however, until the employee gives back all keys, vehicles, tools, and
any other property belonging to the apartment community. If you are providing the employee with living quarters, naturally you must take possession of the space before handing over the final check. (Release of final
checks may be governed by state law. It is also important to know your state
laws because there may be notice requirements when living quarters are
involved.)

In general, do not give a two-week notice. If a person is being terminated, your best, safest, and most humane course of action is to make the
termination effective immediately. The terminated employee will only do
harm to your relationship with other employees, vendors, or residents during those two weeks. Also, it is absolutely foolish to have a person who is
leaving involuntarily train a replacement.

As a final note, you do not need to crush a person's self-esteem with a
recitation of every weakness and fault, nor do you need to quantify the
damage that has been caused to the property. It is sufficient to say that things
have not worked out. (This person now has the problem of having no job
and an interrupted income. There is no need to inflict more pain or embarrassment with a sermon.)

Labor Unions. In certain areas, particularly in major cities, labor unions
have tried to organize apartment management personnel, especially maintenance workers. Unions seek out the larger properties because the numbers of employees make it worth the effort.

The best approach is to help employees avoid the attraction of union
organizing in the first place. Some important ways of doing this are by hav-

ing fair and reasonable personnel policies that are applied uniformly, regular salary and wage reviews, good supervision, and communication with your employees. Give employees more advantages than they would have as members of a union, and you will eliminate any need for them to organize.

If a union does approach you with notice of its intention to organize, contact a labor attorney immediately before you take any action, including discussing the situation in any manner with personnel. This is not the time to get tough or make threats. The federal government has strict rules governing union organizing, and a labor attorney can best interpret these.

Note: Being an employer creates certain legal responsibilities. Policies regarding employees and their employment should be reviewed by legal counsel before implementation to avert problems of interpretation, minimize potential for liability, and ensure compliance with applicable laws.

3

*The easiest building to manage is an empty one;
all others will need some policies.*

Property Policies

Every business, large or small, is confronted constantly with situations and problems that demand decisions. One way of handling this decision-making responsibility is with policies, which are prepared answers to anticipated problems. Some policies can eliminate problems before they arise. Others will make it easier to deal with recurring problems swiftly and competently.

The development of proper policies is critical to the smooth functioning and successful management of multifamily housing. Every real estate management organization needs to have policies. Even a one-person operation needs them because it will face the same problems that the large management company faces. For the large company with hundreds or thousands of units to manage, problems are much the same in kind; they simply are more numerous. Without policies, management would have to make every decision on a case-by-case basis. Not having policies would not only lead to chaos but also be time-consuming and produce inconsistent results.

Policies help to eliminate all this. They clear the air. Policies let all persons involved know where they stand, what is expected of them, and what will be done when something goes wrong.

The right policies permit the scheduling of management activities on a routine basis and thus enable the manager to concentrate on the really demanding aspects of the business. Certainly policies have to be developed in accordance with the owner's goals and objectives, but the best policies are shaped by the expertise of a professional real estate manager. With policies, it is not necessary to spend time constantly reinventing the wheel, so work becomes more efficient. Once a pattern has been set, it can be followed until something occurs to indicate the policy is no longer useful.

Policies should be reviewed and changed when necessary. They are guidelines, not straitjackets. It is not possible to anticipate every contingency. From time to time, you will encounter problems that cannot be dealt with unless policies are bent a little or changed entirely. For the most part, however, policies will save you the trouble of making time-consuming decisions on an individual basis.

Policies are also important because they compel you to study your business and understand it thoroughly. Good policies cannot be made until you know everything about your business. When taking over a property for the first time, you must do a lot of creative thinking—just as a chess player does—to plan moves and consider alternatives.

Policies are important, not only for you, the manager, but also for all the other employees at the property and for prospects, residents of the building, and the property owner as well. Each has a right to know what to expect. The time to examine those expectations is before a crisis erupts, while there is time to reach a cool, dispassionate decision rather than being forced to act in haste.

To be useful, policies should be in writing and made available to everyone concerned. When policies are changed, the changes should be communicated to all appropriate parties. Dating your printed policies and including revision dates on all changed pages can prevent confusion.

Policies should be reasonable and enforceable. The manager's position will be weakened if policies are established that cannot be enforced, and he or she will appear dictatorial if the policies are unreasonable.

You do not have to rely entirely on your own ability to anticipate problems. In the very beginning, real estate managers had to innovate because there was no history of professional expertise. You are more fortunate—you can learn from the experiences of others.

The following discussion will focus on some policies that ensure high levels of efficiency. In a very real sense, much of this book is a delineation of policies that address the various aspects of apartment management. Special areas that call for policies will be pointed out, and alternative policies will be suggested. In some cases, specific policies will be recommended. However, it is up to the manager to determine the policies best suited to a particular situation.

To ensure an efficient management operation, general policies are needed in several major areas. Specifically, policies should cover the rental and management office, recreational facilities, amenities of the property, and parking. Your property policies and procedures for implementing them should be compiled into an *Operations Manual* that also includes policies regarding staffing, leasing, residents, maintenance, and all the other aspects of managing your apartment community.

The Office

Let's begin with policies that relate to the rental and management office. We will also note some of the decisions and practices that will facilitate implementation of your office policies and provide for smoother operations.

Office Location.   There may be several possible locations for the rental and management office. Since the purpose of the office is to serve both prospects and residents, it should be located where it will be easy to find, especially for prospects. From this standpoint, the closer the office is to the road or visitor parking lot, the better.

One of the best places to locate the office is close to or in the property's recreational facility. There are several advantages to this arrangement.

- It ensures that prospects will see the recreational facilities. In the later stages of a rental program, agents showing the property may skip this part of the tour.

- You can supervise the recreational facility without adding the extra staff you would need if the office and facility were separate.

- Finally, when the office is located in the recreational facility, you can easily check on its maintenance status and make sure the facility is kept clean at all times.

Unfortunately, in some properties, the recreational facility is closed or even locked during daylight hours. Having the office in the recreational facility ensures that the facility will be open when the office is open.

At apartment communities that have no recreational facilities, the office should be in an easy-to-find location—probably close to the main entrance. Ideally, the office will have a separate outside entrance so prospects do not have to enter the building lobby.

Some managers like the idea of making the rental office part of the model apartment or setting up the office in an apartment next to the model. When alternatives are available, these are poor choices. They breach security by bringing outside visitor traffic into the building and by having a commercial purpose intrude into a residential area. This is especially true in mid-rise and high-rise buildings that have a single main entrance.

Combining the office with the model apartment usually destroys the merchandising appeal of the model. If only one unit is available, it would be better to have only an office and no model.

One Office versus Two.   The function of the rental office, or, as it should be known, the rental information center, is to serve prospects; the function of the management office is to serve residents. For this reason, you may consider having two separate offices. However, it is generally better to combine the two functions in a single office because such an arrangement uses personnel more effectively. If there is only one person in an office during slack periods, there would be no staff present if that individual had to leave for a few minutes. When the two functions are combined, rental and management people can fill in for each other when necessary. This arrangement also allows the staff to gain a better understanding of the property's total operation. Possible exceptions are extremely large apartment communities.

Some managers prefer to separate the two functions in all cases to avoid the risk of having a complaining resident come into the office and discourage a prospect who overhears the complaint. Most managers do not encounter this problem frequently, especially when their properties are operated properly. If a resident complains, it is generally at the time of rent payment (usually early in the morning or late in the day) or just before a major holiday (like Thanksgiving or Christmas) when it is important to have things looking right for visiting friends and relatives. These are light leasing periods when prospects are not apt to be present.

If the thought of having residents and prospects running into each other is still a concern, a private area in the same office can be set aside for residents. The fact remains that a combined office is more efficient than two separate ones.

Office Appearance.   Despite the old saying, "You can't judge a book by its cover," people can and do judge by appearance. A disorderly management office, with service requests stacked in the file tray, half-empty coffee cups lying around, wastebaskets overflowing, and old plumbing parts on the floor, may make a rental prospect wonder just how well the rest of the property is maintained.

Maintaining an attractive appearance is essential. Desks should be clean and uncluttered. Coffee pots and cups should be kept out of sight, except when coffee is being served. If there are magazines for prospects to read while they are waiting, the copies should be current and appear fresh. Windows should be sparkling, and the floor should be cleaned or vacuumed daily. Good housekeeping in the rental office will pay off in increased prospect confidence.

Smoking is rarely allowed in business offices today. However, some apartment offices are one-person operations, and that person may sometimes smoke while alone in the office. After all, who will see and tell? Actually, just about everyone who does not smoke. A no smoking policy should mean just that.

Office Hours.   Again, because the office exists to serve prospects and residents, the hours of operation should conform to their schedules. Consider
prospects first. My experience shows that Sunday is the day when you can
expect the greatest activity. Some holidays are as important as Sundays. The
exceptions are Thanksgiving Day, Christmas, and New Year's Day when
most people stay home; but Easter, Memorial Day, the Fourth of July, and
Labor Day all bring out apartment hunters. Late Monday afternoons and
early weekday evenings are other prime times for rental prospects. In some
markets, Saturday is often a rather slow rental day because many people reserve it for grocery shopping, chores, and sports and social activities.

Knowing this, it is a good idea to keep the rental office open on Sundays and holidays in addition to weekdays. That means seven days a week.
Studies of prospect traffic often reveal that few people show up before
10:00 A.M. So generally, with rental hours from 10:00 A.M. to 6:00 P.M., you
will catch most of the prospect traffic. When establishing your hours, try
to settle on a set of times that is consistent from one day to the next. You
do not want your Office Hours sign to be confusing. Again, follow the lead
of major merchants. You will find they usually use just two sets of hours,
one for Monday through Saturday and then a slightly different set for Sunday. It is generally unwise to show apartments after dark. You may want to
extend your hours to coincide with the start of daylight saving time. Your
office hours should be posted at the office entrance and included in your
advertising.

It is not uncommon to find rental office hours that differ from business
hours. For example, even with rental hours of 10:00 A.M. to 6:00 P.M., the
workday might begin as early as 7:30 A.M. This allows the residents to visit
the office on their way to work and the staff to plan their workday and get
an early start on the day's problems.

Banks and landlords were probably two of the last holdouts against adjusting business hours to meet customer needs. Banking institutions today
are certainly open and ready to serve their clients at all sorts of odd hours.
Apartment managers should follow suit. You need to be open when the customer is most likely to have free time. That will include early mornings,
some evenings, and all weekends. Service is the apartment manager's goal.
If you need to change hours to better serve prospects and residents, do so!

Automated Telephones.   Funeral homes, car dealers, and apartment
properties are just three examples of businesses that should not even begin
to consider using automated telephones. Calling into a business that uses
one of these systems is one of the consuming public's most frustrating experiences. I know of many apartment communities that have removed these
phone systems after realizing the damage they do to customer relations.
Housing is a very personal matter, whether someone is considering a
change or has a problem needing attention in his or her current quarters.

When a machine answers and stops you because you do not know your party's extension or you are forced to listen to a long list of options, the frustration builds. If you cannot speak with a live person when you are trying to get leasing information, can you imagine what it will be like when you live there and have a problem? There was a big rush to install automated telephone systems, but with the aggravation they cause and the lack of promised savings, you can expect a turnabout. The best policy is to have a live person answer the telephone and, when the office is closed, have an answering service take messages and forward emergency calls.

Web Site.   Properties with 100 units and especially those with 200 units or more are well advised to establish a web site. It provides residents and potential customers with the ability to communicate with you at any time. What started out as an obscure system of networking has evolved into a high-speed, highly efficient information source and communication vehicle. Today, most businesses offer their customers and the public the ability to communicate via their web site. Most web sites include direct links to a variety of business features and applications.

The rental apartment industry now takes advantage of this tool in ever-expanding ways:

- *Leasing tool.* Photographs of the property's features, floor plans of apartment layouts, virtual tours, neighborhood highlights, maps and directions, and unit availability and pricing are a few such tools.

- *Emergency help.* Twenty-four hours a day, the web site can guide residents through steps to solve all manner of emergencies such as lockouts and appliance, plumbing, and electrical breakdowns. It should also list emergency phone numbers as well as departments, agencies, and groups to help in a wide variety of situations. It is a good idea to set up this page in a suitable format so residents can print out the information and keep it on file.

- *Frequently asked questions (FAQs).* Answers to many of the questions that residents have can be accessed at their leisure. This is a convenience to the resident and can be a considerable time saver to the office staff as well.

- *Repair requests.* The resident can report repair problems quickly and easily, and these requests can be integrated into the property's scheduling system.

- *E-mail.* Direct communications and replies are available.

- *Announcements and event notices.* A web site provides almost limitless opportunities to stay in touch with residents and to keep them informed of what is happening at the property and in the community at large.

- *Account information.* Using a protected password, residents can look up their account information and in some of the more sophisticated systems, they can even monitor their utility usage and charges.

This short listing is just a hint of what is now available for apartment web sites. You can expect the interactive communications and use of apartment web sites to grow exponentially as ideas and technology advance.

Use of a web site and e-mail implies immediacy. Office staff should be encouraged to check and respond to e-mail messages several times a day. Maintenance service requests submitted through the web site will be delivered to the office through the e-mail system. This will not only expedite scheduling of repairs, but allows for direct acknowledgment to the resident. Additional details can be asked for, if needed, and the entire string of messages stays together through completion of the repair.

Creating a web site requires understanding of how these sites work and what can and cannot be done with them. User-friendliness is imperative; otherwise, residents (and prospects) will not make use of your site. A web site should be created by professionals. If information will be added or changed frequently, and you do not have staff who are able to do this, site maintenance should be contracted out to ensure the contents of your web site are kept current.

A final note about web sites involves what is called *positioning.* Your own experience while using the Internet has likely shown that searches for web sites often are not successful. After expending the time and money to create and maintain a web site, it is essential to make sure that the major search engines (Google, Yahoo) are aware of your site and position it high in their listings. This is not free. It will involve setup and maintenance fees, which can be substantial. There are companies that can make and follow though with such arrangements.

Recreational Facilities

From a single room with a ping-pong table to a lavish clubhouse, all the property's recreational facilities need policies to govern hours of use, guests, and fees. Otherwise, these facilities will be uncontrolled, a situation that will irritate residents and reflect poorly on management.

In setting hours, consider residents' preferences as well as the effect on those who live near the facility. For example, it would not be wise to permit the clubhouse to be open until midnight if it is immediately adjacent to dwelling units. Recently, a number of rental properties have permitted use of the clubhouse facilities until well after midnight. The practice was adopted as a marketing tool to allow residents with unusual schedules to take advantage of the facility. The idea is great, but it has not been without problems. Some facilities have become hangouts. Gang activity, rowdy parties, drugs, and alcohol quickly destroy the attractiveness of such a facility. The use of keycards will help prevent some unauthorized access, but it will not help if the keycard is in the hands of an unsupervised youth.

Guests can be a problem. There is a thin line between being so restrictive that residents will be discouraged from having guests (and may move out for that reason) and being so relaxed that the entire neighborhood can use the facility. A policy that many managers have found workable is to limit guests to two at a time in the company of a resident.

Guest fees should be avoided if possible. Residents dislike them, and they make your place seem unfriendly. Guest fees are a negligible revenue source at best, and they create extra bookkeeping work.

The facility should not be staffed with any more personnel than absolutely necessary. Otherwise, you will establish a precedent that you may have to maintain. For example, unless you are legally required to have a swimming pool lifeguard, do not hire one unless it is a service you wish to extend indefinitely.

If your apartment community has a nice facility, make sure the established policies allow it to be used. Sometimes management is reluctant to let the residents use the recreational facility for fear it will become less "showable" to prospective renters. If people who live at the property cannot use this feature on a regular basis, it really has little value in the rental process or in retaining residents.

Basketball courts, pool tables, and the like are popular amenities at some apartment communities. However, if they are not controlled or managed carefully, these competitive activities can get out of hand. If you decide to have these types of equipment, you should be prepared to manage their use through policies and actions.

Finally, you should establish a policy governing use of the recreational facilities by special-interest groups such as political organizations or commercial enterprises. Generally such use should be discouraged.

Supporting Amenities

Most properties have supporting amenities designed to meet resident needs and make life more comfortable. You should carefully consider what policies are needed for these facilities.

Laundry Room.   This is a basic facility that is important in satisfying residents' daily needs and will certainly be of interest to prospects as well. In communities whose apartments are not equipped with a washer and dryer, you can expect the common laundry to see heavy use.

This facility should be equipped with the right number of washers and dryers. Defining equipment requirements has a great deal to do with your typical resident. The following will help as a guide.

Young families—One washer and dryer per 10–12 apartments
Career professionals—One washer and dryer per 12–16 apartments
Upper rent level—One washer and dryer per 16–20 apartments
Senior Citizens—One washer and dryer per 20–30 apartments

Dryers should be the single-load, stack-on variety rather than the large double-load models. The latter type is hard on clothes and does not offer the flexibility or revenue potential of the smaller dryers. Management should provide sorting tables, clothes hanging rods, and laundry tubs in adequate numbers for the size of the facility. The laundry room should be properly ventilated, brightly decorated, well lit, and cleaned daily. To encourage neatness, add one or more wide-mouth trash receptacles. For the convenience of your residents, a bulletin board is a good idea; but you should keep an eye on the items posted and remove the undesirable ones. The laundry room should remain open the maximum number of hours each day, depending on its location. For security reasons and to minimize the disturbance to nearby residents, 11:00 P.M. is a typical closing time. If conditions permit, consider keeping it open 24 hours a day for residents who work odd hours. It may be necessary to keep the laundry room locked at all times. If so, residents should be issued laundry room keys or keycards. Residents' apartment keys can also be designed to operate the laundry room lock.

Soap and detergent dispensers are often cheaply made and are subject to failure and pilferage. Residents who come to depend on them will become irritated when the machines are empty or not working. As a policy, you may choose not to install them. In the absence of dispensers, residents will bring their own supplies. You should also avoid having the management office make change; otherwise you might find yourself repeatedly interrupted. In my experience, most residents prefer using only one denomination of coin to operate the machines, even if it means paying a little more.

A lot is happening in terms of technological advances in central laundry rooms. The use of the debit card has become a standard, eliminating most problems of change-making and theft. Machine use is monitored by computer, and reports will indicate which machines are used the most, pinpoint the busiest times of the day and week, and provide an accurate accounting of the money earned.

Should the property own the laundry machines? From a financial standpoint, it is probably better to do so. However, the burden and expense of maintenance, plus the risk of damage or theft, are major drawbacks. If a manager deals with a concessionaire, he or she should reserve the right to approve prices charged to operate the machines. Otherwise, residents may become irritated and blame the manager if the concessionaire raises prices unreasonably.

Vending Machines.   Many residents appreciate soft drink and snack dispensers. These machines are best housed in a separate facility (preferably in or near the recreation room or clubhouse), in their own separate room, or in the laundry room.

The disadvantage of these vending machines is that they are subject to vandalism and theft. Because of this threat, some vendors choose to encase their machines in a cage-like enclosure or install heavy bars and locks to protect their equipment. This absolutely sends the wrong message to prospects and residents alike. If the machines require this level of protection, the property may be better off without the concession. These machines also create an ongoing maintenance problem and become faded and unsightly when exposed to the weather.

Public Telephone.   Pay telephones, especially coin-operated ones, are certainly on their way to extinction. These days it seems that almost everyone has a cell phone handy. However, there are still situations where a public telephone fills a need—for new residents to arrange telephone service, employees to make personal calls, delivery people, subcontractors. A public telephone should be located in an out-of-the-way spot. If it is inside, the telephone may become a gathering place and will probably collect litter.

If you feel strongly about having a public telephone indoors, a service area near the laundry room might be a good choice. The constant activity and the resulting lack of privacy will work to discourage people from spending too much time using the phone. Public telephones have been used and abused by gangs and drug dealers, but this is less likely when they are placed in highly visible locations.

Public telephones are subject to vandalism and seldom generate enough revenue to pay for themselves. Cost is also a consideration. Telephone companies offer different kinds of public telephone service. Public phones do not necessarily involve a monthly fee, but there are requirements that must be met (e.g., likelihood of use, a minimum number of daily calls). If these requirements cannot be met, the alternative is likely to involve installation fees as well as monthly charges. Obviously, phone companies are your source of information regarding service and fee structures. Private telephones are another possibility. These concessions often produce a nice income for the operators, but higher than normal charges become an aggravation to the user.

Storage.   A secure, well-kept, organized, and brightly lit resident storage facility is a building asset. Some apartment communities have a storage area that is nothing more than a large room where residents can store items at random, without benefit of lockers or any other separation. This arrangement has a major drawback: Even though the lease may have a disclaimer denying landlord responsibility for items stored in the facility, there still may be liability for theft or damage.

Many of the newer rental properties offer separate and secure storage facilities adjacent to each apartment unit. Others provide locked storage rooms with individual lockers or cages for use by their residents. Lockers should be identified by number to avoid confusion and to help the resident and management locate a particular one. To prevent residents from using unauthorized lockers or more than one locker, all vacant lockers should be kept securely locked until assigned. Many municipalities have become concerned about fire hazards which are often associated with storage rooms so these facilities are typically included during building fire inspections.

As an added convenience and as an extra income source, many rental properties offer supplemental *self-service storage* facilities of varying sizes to their residents and charge them additional rent. This feature is especially useful to residents who are downsizing and have extra possessions and to businesspeople who need quick access to such items as samples and sales literature. These facilities can be included in the building proper or in separate outbuildings. On a basis of rent received versus cost, these storage units make a great deal of economic sense.

Parking

Parking is one of the perennial problems of management. Unsupervised parking of automobiles, motorcycles, boat trailers, and bicycles is a major detraction from the neat appearance of a property. Carefully crafted policies can do much to alleviate the headaches associated with parking.

There is a very specific set of rules governing the provision of handicapped parking. Your property must comply by providing a certain number of spaces that are of a certain width plus an island divider. They are to be striped in blue and show the approved wheelchair glyph, with signs mounted at a given height identifying these spaces and detailing the amount of the fine for violators. Many managers locate these spaces at the main entrance of the building to assist the person using the space. This tends to open up a vista that better identifies the entrance, since these spaces are frequently empty.

I recommend that you do not establish reserved parking. This rule should always apply except where parking spaces are enclosed or specially delineated, as in high-rise garages, covered carports, or individual garages. The reason for this is that reserved parking is extremely difficult to enforce. Residents who have reserved parking spaces naturally expect them to be available at all times. If they find another car in their space, they may become upset and create a scene; this usually occurs late at night. Reserved parking that cannot be effectively enforced is bound to irritate residents. If you do reserve spaces, it is crucial that they not be identified by an apartment number for reasons of security.

If your apartment community has surplus parking, or if residents crowd the parking nearest the building entries, consider striping the remote sections of the parking lot to provide eleven-foot-wide spaces. Residents with nice cars will often trade proximity for the protection that a wider parking space offers.

Prospects may be discouraged if there are numerous motorcycles, campers, and boats parked in the lot. You can counter this by establishing separate parking areas for these vehicles. For motorcycles, construct a rack of 2.5-inch galvanized pipe and embed the ends of the pipe in concrete; motorcyclists will be receptive to this because they can chain their cycles to these racks. Set aside a remote area of the parking lot for boats and trailers. A row of boats lined up together not only solves a parking problem, but also gives your property a neat and organized appearance. Do the same for campers and recreational vehicles.

Junk autos should not be tolerated in your parking lot. You should check local ordinances before you do anything about this. In general, however, if there is a car in your lot that is not currently licensed and drivable, the owner should be asked to remove it. Autos being repaired in the parking lot may attract prospects who long to be auto mechanics, but this will also turn off other prospects. Your rules and regulations should prohibit auto repairs and maintenance. An exception is car washing. A policy that designates an area of the property for car washing allows management to control this activity.

Security and Protection Issues

The public is concerned about security for good reason: In a single year's time, one out of every twenty people is a victim of burglary, vandalism, mugging, robbery, or car theft. It is tempting for apartment managers to promise a higher level of security than is offered elsewhere. However, such a promise—either in the form of a direct claim or an implied commitment—should not be made without fully understanding the consequences. Prospective residents will not take the promise lightly; nor will the public, a judge, or a jury.

To begin with, promoting security may make prospects fearful or exacerbate fears that already exist. Promoting security may even cause prospects to think that the apartment community's security protection is not what it should be. Unfortunately, no residential property is truly secure.

Feeling secure has a lot do with a person's frame of mind. Hotels generally do a superb job of providing security, but they never promote it. Yet try something funny in a hotel lobby and watch how quickly the house detectives materialize. Hotels know that the suggestion of security is disturbing to guests, so they provide security quietly. Apartment managers would be smart to do likewise.

When you promote security, you not only raise people's fears, but you may very well incur a liability that would not normally arise. If a resident is

robbed, injured, or killed, you could be blamed because you did not provide the security that was promised. No matter how good the security system is, an injured party can always claim management could have done
more (e.g., doubled or tripled the guard patrols, increased surveillance,
trained personnel better). Many court cases in which this very principle was
the deciding factor have already been settled. Don't install systems that have
the appearance of "guaranteeing" security, and never mention security in
your advertising or promotional literature.

You are fortunate if you have avoided promoting security to date. If you
have been promoting some property safeguards, you will have to begin
working your way out of it. There is a definite risk in suddenly reducing
your security involvement. If you do, residents may claim you are reneging
on your security promise, especially if an incident should occur.

Security policies and requirements will vary from one location to the
next. One decision that seems to have set a precedent requires owners to
meet the standard of protection commonly provided in the community. This
would mean that if most of the buildings in the community have round-the-
clock security officers, your property should have the same; it is suggesting
that there is no need to provide more than what others are offering. Managers need to stay alert for local and higher court decisions and new legislation on this subject.

Maintaining a safe environment at the property is an extremely important aspect of apartment management. Among the topics that need to be
considered are locks and keys, security devices, patrols and surveillance,
and resident versus management responsibilities. The following discussions
highlight the types of decisions and challenges involved.

Locks and Keys.   What started out as a fairly straightforward subject has
become complicated and risk-filled. Modern rental communities were typically outfitted with apartment door locks that could be opened with both an
individual and a *master key*. Certain staff members would be issued a master key to facilitate access to all locked doors on the property. This is far
more efficient than constant trips back and forth to the office to secure and
return specific keys. What happens, however, if the master key is lost, stolen,
or ends up in the wrong hands? The correct response is to have the entire
property re-keyed. This is an extremely expensive and time-consuming undertaking. So, generally, when a master key turns up missing, little or nothing is done about it. Few want to admit to the problem and be held liable
for the increase in risk and expense. Often nothing comes of the missing
key, but not always. There have been some terrible incidents where these
keys have gotten into the wrong hands.

There is another risk with lock systems that utilize a master key, which
locksmiths have known about for years but which is now available to anyone with an Internet connection. With some simple instructions, a small file,

---

Accessing Vacant Apartments

There is a technique that I have found works well for gaining access to vacant apartments. Let's say that you find yourself with five vacant units. Have your maintenance staff install five lock cylinders that are all keyed alike. Make a batch of extra keys and issue them to the leasing and maintenance personnel. You might also give keys to certain trusted vendors such as painters, carpet cleaners, and window-covering people. This makes things very convenient, saves the chore of picking up and returning keys, and improves security. Few people find it worthwhile to break into a vacant apartment. The "mini-masters," as they are called, secure the apartments from curiosity-seekers and others but allow easy access by those who have work to do. Once the apartment is leased, a newly re-keyed cylinder is installed and a fresh set of keys is presented to the new resident. The "mini-master" cylinder is then reused on the next vacant apartment.

---

a handful of about 5 or 6 key blanks, and fewer than 50 probes, almost anyone can produce a master key to a building in about 15 minutes. Seeing this demonstrated can be very scary.

In order to minimize liability, the overwhelming trend in rental apartments is to abolish the use of master keys. Most of the industry giants have already done so. Instead, duplicate keys are coded and installed in a locked cabinet. Several manufacturers produce a variety of security systems designed to protect stored keys and accommodate the need to check them in and out. Unfortunately, in the day-to-day operation of an apartment property, these "fail safe" systems prove very cumbersome. More often then not, you will find the "key safe" open and the key code book sitting right there for quick and easy access.

It is becoming quite obvious that keys, especially those in multifamily dwellings, will not provide the level of security needed or expected. Hotels and motels faced much the same problem and turned to the electronic lock and keycard. You can expect the apartment industry to follow their lead, but utilizing a more durable form of magnetic or electronic key. These locks are much sturdier, and they are five times more expensive, but they can be reprogramed in seconds.

In the meantime, properties with conventional locks and keys must adopt an aggressive policy for the dissemination and storage of apartment keys.

Entry Restriction.   A chain device mounted on an entry door to restrict its opening to a few inches can be a source of real problems. Most of these devices incorporate weak chain links and screws that are too few and too short. Some of these devices are installed improperly by residents looking for an extra level of security. The links in the chain quickly break when the door is bashed or kicked-in. Hotels and motels learned this lesson years ago and have replaced the chain device with a heavy-duty slide-bar device that is much stronger and its mounting brackets are held with six hefty screws with long shanks.

What some people see as a feature of this slide-bar device is that the bar can be swung outward on its hinge to hold the door ajar. Housekeeping staff in hotels love this feature, but it is a problem waiting to happen if occupants or residents breach their security this way.

Other Devices and Equipment.   Quality, heavy-duty dead-bolt locks are a necessity today and often required by law. This protection can be incorporated into the primary locking system or it can augment the keyed passage lock already installed in the entry door. A wide-angle viewer is a requirement that should be installed in every entry door. Intrusion alarms provide the resident with another level of protection.

Apartment-to-lobby intercommunication and TV systems that allow the residents to screen visitors are important features in properties with a central entry point. All such security-related equipment must be kept in perfect working order.

Removable grills on ground-level windows and special locking devices for sliding glass doors have become common equipment in garden style rental apartments.

Property Patrols.   Whatever you provide to improve levels of security, make sure that it is done correctly and that you continue it once you begin. If you contract for security patrols, they should follow an intermittent schedule that cannot be readily tracked. Gatekeepers or community service personnel should not be dressed like guards and should certainly not carry weapons. A four- or six-cell Mag flashlight will serve as a level of self-protection during minor encounters. Canine patrols are absolutely unacceptable.

I am not in favor of giving an apartment rent-free to a law enforcement officer in exchange for part-time security during his or her off-duty hours. The apartment community rarely gets its money's worth, and having a squad car sitting in your parking lot during those off hours does not result in a feeling of well-being in the residents' minds—and it certainly does not improve a property's image.

Video Surveillance.   Surveillance cameras have become the norm in many commercial operations. Trained specialists can monitor multiple and rotating screens and quickly spot trouble or questionable happenings. However, without a "real time" person on duty, the benefit fades to a collection of scenes captured on videotape. There is most probably a degree of deterrence when cameras are placed about a property, but there might also be an implied promise that these images are being constantly monitored and that any needed help will arrive soon. One thing is for sure: Do not install phony cameras on the property.

Management Responsibility.   You should take immediate steps if you are aware of any criminal activity on your property that implies a breach of security. For example, if an intruder enters a unit through a faulty patio door, make sure that all the patio doors in your property are inspected and, if necessary, modified. If a resident is mugged in a dark area of the parking lot, increase the level of illumination there immediately. Even comparatively small incidents should earn your prompt attention. If a resident reports the theft of a car stereo or expensive wheel covers, take some decisive action. All steps you take to mitigate problems should be formally documented, as appropriate, and retained in management files so they will be available in the event of any related litigation.

When these types of problems occur on our properties, we often shift some of our groundskeeping and maintenance tasks to the early evening hours (which is when most problem activity takes place). Just the presence of uniformed staff members going about their business is enough to end most problem activity. If you choose to do nothing and subsequent crimes occur, you and the property owner are at a much greater risk of liability because you were aware of a problem and failed to act.

Resident Responsibility.   Most crimes in apartments occur because of resident carelessness—residents doing such things as holding the lobby door open for strangers, failing to screen callers before pushing the switch unlocking the door, or propping or leaving doors open for convenience. Residents should be reminded about the dangers of such practices. This is where newsletters and web sites are useful communication tools.

Police Involvement.   If you are experiencing security-related problems, call upon the police to help you search for a solution. They know the identities of perpetrators who commit certain crimes. The police will frequently provide assistance in the form of increased patrols. Keep residents informed by distributing police department literature. It is best that you do not reproduce security advice under the building's name as this may imply liability.

Safety and Health Concerns

An apartment manager's safety-related responsibilities are substantial. They involve maintaining a safe environment for residents, employees, and visitors. The manager must make sure basic equipment is provided and maintained—e.g., fire extinguishers, smoke alarms, carbon monoxide (CO) detectors, ground fault interrupters (GFI), emergency lighting packs, fire doors, and in some cases, sprinklers. It is also important for the manager to conduct regular safety inspections and develop evacuation plans. To reinforce your safety program, it is a good idea to publish safety suggestions and evacuation procedures in resident and employee manuals and update them as needed.

First Aid.   It is imperative that you have a complete first aid cabinet available and accessible. It follows that several staff members should receive training in basic emergency care and that a first aid handbook should be immediately available. A listing of telephone numbers of emergency transportation and care facilities should be prominently displayed in a central location.

Safety Equipment and Related Requirements.   You must insist upon appropriate safety gear such as hard-soled and toed shoes and safety eyewear when appropriate for the task. Other items include ear protection, rubber and latex gloves, masks and respirators, goggles and face shields, hard hats, approved ladders and scaffolding, and other safety equipment to protect employees as they go about certain tasks. The Occupational Safety and Health Administration (OSHA) publishes rules and guidelines about employee safety equipment, and it is up to management to stay in compliance.

OSHA also makes periodic inspections of rental properties, and they can be brutal. Splices in extension cords, painted ladders, and untrained workers are just a hint of the types of violations they are seeking. The fines can amount to many thousands of dollars, and the chances of having them waived on appeal are slim. OSHA requires that you post notices and maintain a log of all accidents and deaths. Failure to comply will prompt serious penalties.

The U.S. Environmental Protection Agency (EPA) is also interested in a number of areas. A few examples which might be found in rental apartments include:

Asbestos	Carbon monoxide
Lead	Hazardous wastes
Radon	Solvents, paints, glue
Pesticides	Oil spills and leaks
Air emissions	Underground storage tanks
Water pollution	Trash recycling
Ground Contamination	Water conservation

You need to be aware that there is specific federal legislation requiring disclosure of the presence of lead-based paint to residents and prospective residents.

Laws, Rules, and Regulations.   A friend of mine who runs one of the largest management operations in the United States told me that one of his busiest employees is a person he calls his "compliance director." This job entails tracking all of the rule changes that apply to the operation of rental apartments and making sure they are being complied with out in the field. The penalties and associated liability for noncompliance can be enormous. Often, these regulations are vague or over-reactions on the part of politicians who feel compelled to "do something." Nearly all of them require costly changes and added reporting duties.

Few apartment managers will have the help of a compliance director, so it becomes their responsibility to remain vigilant for changes and to see that new policies are implemented. In the past decade, there were literally hundreds of such changes on the national scene—not counting those promulgated at local levels. Here is just a tiny sample of some of the better known topics that underwent rule changes or were introduced in this time span.

Bio-hazard containment and handling	Entry gate safety
Lockout/tagout	Fire stair width
Safe place of refuge	Combustible insulation
Bloodborne pathogens	Mold
Ammonia use limitations	Smoke-free environment
Fluorescent tube disposal	Playground safety
Accessibility	Satellite dishes

Apartment managers need to be aware of existing laws and regulations and how they change. State and local rules and codes often have stricter compliance requirements than do federal regulations covering the same things. This is an area where professional advice (attorney, environmental consultant) should be sought to ensure that your policies and practices comply with the law.

4

Question on an apartment application form:
What is the make and model of your vacuum cleaner?
The better housekeepers always have an answer.

Leasing Policies

Before opening the door for business, we must identify a set of policies that will guide the leasing process. These need to be liberal enough so as not to unduly constrain the pace of rentals. They must also protect the continual well-being of the property, its image, and the rights and enjoyment of the majority of your residents. In this chapter, we will walk through the important policy-making decisions that will lead to a profitable and stable rental apartment community.

Resident Selection

By renting to the best-qualified applicants at the beginning, many management problems can be avoided. A thorough job of screening applicants results in a much higher percentage of residents who pay their rent on time, observe rules and regulations, and remain in your building year after year.

It should be emphasized that the law leaves few areas untouched when it comes to resident selection. Fair housing laws at all levels—federal, state, and local—exist to prevent discrimination. These laws are very clear and so are the penalties for establishing or following policies that effectively discriminate against people for such reasons as race, nationality, sex, religion, age, family status, or any physical or mental disability they might have.

Local laws vary; some exist to prevent discrimination against classifications of people other than those just listed (same sex couples may be protected, for example). Because these laws are constantly being expanded, it is extremely important to know what applies currently. You should also bear in mind that HUD tests to ensure that fair housing laws are enforced. (Testers pose as prospective renters.) Trying to get around these laws will surely shorten your career in the rental business and subject the property owner to potentially disastrous penalties.

There are some resident selection policies which can lead to an indirect and unintended violation of fair housing law. For example, based upon some of the negative attributes associated with student renters, a particular property adopts a policy banning all student renters. Next, a student applies and you reject him or her. If that student happens to be an African-American or belongs to a particular religious sect, your rejection might be seen, not as a student issue, but as a fair housing violation.

Resident selection policies can contain some interesting and surprising twists and turns. Careful monitoring of what is happening with interpretations of federal as well as state and local fair housing laws becomes increasingly essential.

In the next sections, we will explore a number of other determinants that should be included when considering the desired resident profile.

Fast In, Fast Out.   Many apartment communities pride themselves on their ability to approve a rental application in a single day or even within hours of its being submitted. Asked, "What's the rush?" you and the owner might answer, "the bottom line." An empty apartment is a liability, and in front of you stands an opportunity to fill a vacancy and increase the property's income stream. Technology exists that will provide an almost instantaneous credit history on most people. So, why not take advantage of it and hurry your approval? The answer is, because those in the apartment management business know, from hard, bitter experience, that the speed at which a renter moves in is almost always the same as when he or she moves out. Housing selection is one of the most important decisions a person makes. If a person delays the search for replacement housing to the very last minute, you are being sent a very important signal.

You can prove this to yourself with your own records. Look at the applications of the residents you have now and have had in the past three or four years. Using a spreadsheet, break them down into three classes:

- Those who moved in within 14 days of first submitting their applications,
- Those who allowed between 15 and 45 days prior to their move-in, and
- Those with move-in lead times of 45 days or more.

Now count their respective days of occupancy. You will most likely find a distinct pattern—i.e., that those who moved in with very little lead-time had very short stays. In a study we monitored, more than 83 percent of the parties whose move-in was in the 14 days or less category were gone on or before their first-year anniversary. If you are practicing the technique of quickly processing rental applicants, you can also expect the work and expense of re-preparing an inordinate number of apartments.

An easy way to minimize this problem is simply to slow down. If you ask for five to seven days to process the approval, you will find little resistance from applicants who have allowed a reasonable lead-time. In fact, many will appreciate your thoroughness and will not be overly concerned about the delay because of their confidence in their housing and credit history. Of course, the applicant with only days remaining on a lease can ill afford to chance an extended approval period and will typically opt to look elsewhere for fast-track approval. Adopting a slower approach to applicant acceptance will take some convincing because it does slow the pace of rentals. The payoff, however, is longer occupancies, more-qualified residents, and a bigger bottom line.

Automobile Insurance. One of the quickest ways to separate people who are living on the edge from those who are abiding by the law is to ascertain whether they have current automobile insurance coverage. One can almost assume that most of the unsightly, derelict cars parked at an apartment community are uninsured. The same people who observe the rules of civilized conduct will continue to do so when it comes to maintaining insurance coverage. This inquiry should probably be limited to general liability coverage, but that alone is an excellent indicator. If these autos are going to be driven on the grounds of the apartment property, a risk is present. It is not unreasonable to require *proof of insurance.* (You cannot assume because your state has a mandatory automobile insurance requirement that everyone complies with the law.)

Shaping Resident Mix. A variety of factors will determine who will reside at a particular apartment community. Among the things to be considered are whether you will lease furnished or unfurnished units, or both, and what policies you will set regarding pets and potentially troublesome possessions.

Unfurnished versus Furnished Units. Whenever there are prolonged downturns in the economy and unusual numbers of vacancies appear, managers begin considering the advisability of furnishing their apartments. They do this in an effort to maximize the potential market, hoping to attract couples and families who do not have furniture. Some of these people might be new to the area, or their circumstances are expected to be temporary.

Furnishing apartments brings an additional dimension to a property's product inventory. Nevertheless, furnished apartments can be a management burden and a drag on net operating income. Those who rent furnished apartments may have little commitment to their residences. Even when paying larger security deposits, people are not likely to care for somebody else's furniture as if it were their own. Consequently, furnished apartments need constant refurbishing. At the end of three years, an apartment community that had every unit furnished when it was new might only have enough furniture to properly fill half of the units because of breakage, abuse, wear, and theft. Moreover, furnishing apartments requires a substantial capital outlay, a cost that is seldom recovered through higher rent.

Under special market conditions, renting furnished apartments makes some sense. Student housing and seasonal occupancies in vacation areas are two such situations. Otherwise, people who want furnished apartments can easily satisfy their needs by renting furniture. These furnishings can be selected to suit individual tastes, and the burden of paying for and taking care of the furnishings is on the resident. If you are managing a building that already has furnished apartments, you may want to consider selling or donating the furniture.

Corporate Units.   Closely allied to furnished apartments are those units outfitted to serve the employees and visitors of corporate clients. There are countless situations in which businesses move their employees for a temporary assignment or a training session and decide against housing those employees in a hotel or motel. This may be a method of economizing or simply making life homier than staying in a hotel would be. Proximity to the business is an important criterion in selecting such housing, as are unit size and layout.

These apartments are almost always furnished by the apartment community, and the furnishings often include cooking utensils and linens. Providing housekeeping service a few days each week is also common. Rent for a fully equipped apartment with service often approaches twice what the same apartment would cost if it were unfurnished. Even at this higher rent, the renter's employer saves a great deal over the daily or weekly rate at a hotel or motel.

Those who use these units are generally four- and five-star residents. Most long-term stays involve the company's top talent, and these people rarely cause problems that would prompt complaints from other residents.

A final note: Hotel chains are well aware of this market niche and are better positioned and accustomed to handling the demands of this business. If apartment managers wish to attract and retain this type of business, they had best offer better service or more economical accommodations.

Pets.   Pets have long been a source of contention between apartment managers and residents. According to the U.S. Census, Americans care for some

---

Pet Policies and Fair Housing Laws

Pet policies must take into account fair housing laws. Under these laws, people whose disabilities require "assistive animals" may live wherever they choose, regardless of a "no pets" policy. However, you can request written verification from an applicant's physician that the animal is an assistive animal. You should also know that assistive animals include more than dogs.

The definition of disability is continually being expanded as discrimination lawsuits are tried in U.S. courts. There is a developing area of medicine that involves the therapeutic effect of having a pet, especially for those who have emotional problems. Prospective or existing residents may be able to claim—with their physicians' support—that their emotional well-being would be improved by having a pet, a situation that could qualify those persons as "disabled" under fair housing laws.

It is a good idea to have an attorney review your pet policies in the context of fair housing requirements before they are implemented.

---

59 million cats and 53 million dogs. This does not count the 13 million birds or 56 million fish—59 percent of U.S. households maintain at least one pet.

While homeowners certainly own more pets than renters do, a recent survey showed that some 23.5 percent of renters maintain a dog or cat. This means that if you have and enforce a "no pets" policy, you are effectively cutting off almost a fourth of your marketplace. It is also the high-income segment of the market—65 percent of pet owners earn $40,000 or more per year.

Establishing a workable pet policy is important for the smooth management of a residential rental property. The key word here is "workable." (Information about pets in rental housing can be obtained from the Humane Society of the United States on the Internet at www.hsus.org.)

Apartment managers should not make the mistake of thinking they can avoid the issue by not having a pet policy. The absence of a policy is an invitation for residents to bring in pets, and the manager has no control. The damage is done when the first dog or cat arrives. You should decide on a policy early, ideally before the property opens. Even if the building has been in existence for a while, a workable pet policy still can be implemented.

You can begin by differentiating the dedicated pet owner from the casual owner. Dedicated owners consider their pets a part of the household and will make sacrifices to meet the animal's needs. Casual owners do not look upon their pets with as much seriousness and usually are not willing to sacrifice personal comfort and convenience for their pets.

One way to separate the dedicated pet owner from the casual one is to charge pet owners more. Some apartment managers charge pet owners additional rent of $10, $15, or $25 a month. Others require a nonrefundable pet deposit in the range of $100 to $300. (According to the survey cited earlier, all of the pet owners paid a separate pet deposit that ranged from $50 to $200.) Both monthly fees and nonrefundable deposits can backfire because, once residents pay the surcharge, they think they have paid for whatever damage their pets may cause. They no longer are concerned with the harm their pets do to doors, carpets, and plants.

A better approach is to ask each pet owner for an additional amount to be held as a *refundable* pet deposit. This way, the pet owner has some hope of recouping the money if the animal behaves. If the pet causes damage, this additional deposit will probably cover it. It is even acceptable to make a portion of the pet deposit nonrefundable (where this is allowed; some states prohibit nonrefundable deposits). For example, you might establish an additional deposit for pet owners of $200, of which $75 is nonrefundable and is earmarked for charges to rid the apartment of fleas and pet odors when the resident leaves. It may also be worthwhile to establish different fees based on the type of pet. Asking for the extra money is a good way of discouraging casual pet owners, who may decide that their pets are not worth the added cost. Those who do decide to keep their pets will probably be more careful with them.

Another way to distinguish between dedicated and casual pet owners is to ask who will take care of the pet when the owner is out of the apartment. This is especially important when dealing with working people. The dedicated pet owner will provide for the animal; the casual owner may not have thought about this problem or care that a barking dog left alone can be a nuisance to others.

However you decide to approach the issue of pets, you should make your pet policy and rules known when a prospect applies for an apartment. By making the policy known early in the rental process and having the policy in writing, there can be no misunderstanding. The following are some of the issues to consider in setting a pet policy along with some policy examples.

- *Numbers and types of pets.* Residents may have no more than one dog or cat; or two lovebirds, canaries, or parakeets; or one myna bird. Tropical fish limited to a 20-gallon tank are permitted. No other mammals, birds, fish, or reptiles are permitted (including monkeys, snakes, turtles, exotic animals, and rodents). No pet offspring are allowed. As a general rule, dangerous animals should be prohibited. This includes certain breeds of dogs.

- *Size of pets.* Dogs must be no taller than 15 inches and cannot weigh more than 30 pounds fully grown.

- *Pet owners' responsibilities.* When outside the apartment, dogs and cats must be kept on leashes at all times. They cannot be staked out or allowed to run loose. Birds must be caged at all times. Animals must be walked in designated areas only. If the pet leaves droppings in other areas, its owner is responsible for their removal. Pets must have all required shots and licenses.

Although difficult to enforce, such rules are needed and should be spelled out along with any other requirements in a *pet agreement* that the prospect signs along with the lease. The agreement amounts to a revocable license that applies to a specific pet. You should ask the prospect to bring in the pet so you can see it and make sure it meets the limitations imposed. It is also wise to keep a picture of the pet on file with the prospect's application.

Besides giving the resident permission to keep the pet, the agreement should also state that: (1) The resident agrees to pay for all damage caused by the pet, and (2) if the agreement is violated or if the animal becomes objectionable, the manager may demand the removal of the pet without affecting the validity of the lease or the resident's responsibility under it.

A pet agreement is an important psychological tool in impressing pet owners with management's seriousness. The pet owners will know what the rules are and that they will pay a penalty if the rules are broken. At the same time, pet owners are not ruled out of the rental market.

People without pets appreciate this kind of policy, too, because they know they will not come home one day to discover that their new neighbors have a Great Dane or a monkey. This protection is an incentive for them to rent in your building.

In short, you have the best of both worlds: A maximized market for your apartments and peaceful relations among your residents.

Possessions.   Pets are not the only potential disruption to the peaceful and orderly operation of an apartment building. Without being negative or confrontational, the leasing agent must try to learn if the prospect has any troublesome possessions, and the manager should have policies to deal with them. Here are some items that should be addressed in specific policies.

- Waterbeds violate most floor-loading regulations. They are messy to fill and empty. If the bed ruptures, the water can damage the resident's apartment and the ones below it. Even if a waterbed remains intact, the chemicals added to the water to keep it from souring could leach through in gaseous form and ruin the carpet. It should be noted that waterbed insurance is available, and you could consider making it a requirement.

- Electronic equipment that requires special outdoor aerials should be discouraged. The resident who installs an antenna on the roof may punch a hole in the roofing membrane or flashing and break the water seal in the roof. Furthermore, a poorly installed antenna could blow off the roof, presenting a danger to people below. Individual television antennas are less and less of a problem now that cable is widely available, but installations of individual satellite dishes present other problems.

- Flammable articles such as torches for glass-blowing and welding equipment for metal sculpture are obvious dangers and should not be allowed.

- Noisy equipment includes drums, stereos played too loudly, hobby tools, and the like. Other residents will object to hearing these sounds through walls and floors.

Lifestyle Choices.   Whether you would rent to unmarried couples or to those who have unconventional lifestyles used to be a matter of choice, and such issues may have been more pressing in some communities than in others. However, if you decide against renting to such people in today's liberated society, you are refusing potential income, and your policy could be interpreted as discrimination. Even if you could establish a policy prohibiting unmarried couples as residents, you will undoubtedly end up with them living in your community. One party would apply for and lease the apartment; in a short time, the second party arrives. You now have two people in residence with only one person responsible under the lease. You would be better advised to rent to the couple and have both parties responsible. The rental policy should not be to judge morality but to determine whether rental applicants can peacefully coexist with other residents and pay the rent.

The Application Process

Your leasing policies have prepared you to welcome rental applicants. Once prospects show up at your property and signal that they want to live there, the application process can begin. This should require completion of a written application form, verification of the applicant's credit and other application information, and collection of an application deposit. As with the other aspects of leasing, the application process should be guided by specific policies.

Application Form.   A rental application form should focus on two types of information—details concerning the prospect and details outlining the terms of occupancy. The applicant should fill out the application form. The leasing agent should check that all the required information has been provided (asking to see a driving license and other identification as appropriate). The leasing agent should then ask the prospect to verify the information and sign the form. The document itself can take many forms, but certain information is needed in order to evaluate applicants properly.

Rental Application Information

- The names of all persons who will reside in the apartment
- The applicant's age
- The applicant's driver's license number
- The applicant's Social Security number
- The applicant's immigration status
- The applicant's nearest living relative
- The applicant's housing record
- Employment information
- Information on checking and savings accounts
- Information on open and closed loans and charge accounts
- Information outlining the terms of occupancy

- *The names of the applicant, his or her spouse, and all others who will reside in the apartment.* All adults who will occupy the particular apartment must be identified to ensure responsibility for the lease. You need to know the total number of prospective occupants in order to prevent overcrowding. Overcrowding is hard on an apartment; too many overcrowded apartments are hard on a building. This condition creates problems in keeping the property clean and providing essential maintenance services. When move-out time arrives, damage to the apartment may be extensive.

  In addition, overcrowding is usually objectionable to other residents. Nevertheless, this varies: There may be no objections if a single person living in a studio takes in a roommate, but expect complaints from neighbors if six people are crowded into a two-bedroom apartment.

  It is important to establish occupancy standards and adhere to them consistently; otherwise you may run the risk of being perceived as discriminatory. It is critical to monitor the interpretations of the *Fair Housing Amendments Act of 1988* that protects families with children because this may affect acceptable occupancy guidelines. You also need to be aware of any state or local occupancy guidelines.

- *The applicant's age.* Check your state law to determine whether age is a protected classification and how old a person must be to sign a non-rescindable contract. If the applicant is underage, get a parent or guardian to sign. A minor can rescind a contract that does not involve one of the primary necessities of life; a person of majority cannot. A minor who is married or orphaned or for whom housing is a necessity is frequently emancipated from the restriction against minors and can execute a binding contract.

- *The applicant's driver's license.* A driver's license, with its ID photo, is one of the most valuable methods of identity verification. The license number should be recorded on the rental application. The full name and address should correspond with those on the application form. Also, the agent can check the birth date on the license to make certain the applicant is of age. The driver's license number may be valuable later in tracking down a resident who leaves without paying rent.

- *The applicant's Social Security number.* Credit bureaus maintain records of people by their Social Security numbers, and this is one of the primary means of personal identification. However, contrary to many managers' beliefs, a resident's Social Security number will have little value in tracking down residents who might later skip out.

  A policy will be needed as to what to do with applicants who do not have a Social Security number. Visitors to this country are a common example. Without a Social Security number, the tenant-screening process becomes considerably more difficult. A policy requiring *all* applicants to have a Social Security number is acceptable so long as it is uniformly applied. It should be noted that almost all individuals who are in the United States lawfully can get a Social Security number.

- *The applicant's immigration status.* Non-U.S. citizens can be grouped as either *legal* or *illegal.* Regardless of status, everyone needs housing, and there is nothing in federal law that prohibits a rental community from accepting either legal or illegal aliens. This becomes a property policy decision. Opting to accept illegal aliens probably means that much of the standard information needed for tenant screening will not be available. Also, illegal aliens are subject to apprehension and deportation.

  A supplemental, non-citizen application form is recommended if the decision is made to accept residents who are not U.S. citizens in your property. This form should be designed to acquire the following information:
  —Name of applicant (including alternative spellings)
  —Birthplace (city, state, region, province, country)
  —Countries of citizenship
  —Passport number and country of origin
  —Names, addresses, and telephone numbers of two references in the United States
  —Alien registration number
  —Immigration status
  —U.S. visa type and date of registration and expiration
  —Length of stay in the United States
  —Driver's license number and state or country of issue

Once this supplemental form is adopted, it must be used uniformly and in a nondiscriminatory manner.

- *The applicant's nearest living relative.* Be sure to get this individual's name, address, and telephone number. Not only is it helpful in emergency situations, the information can be invaluable when you are tracking down a resident who skips out on you.

- *The applicant's housing record.* You need the name, address, and telephone number of the applicant's present landlord or managing agent, together with the size of the apartment, the rent paid, and the length of stay. If the stay has been less than two years, you should obtain information on previous places of residence.

  You should be wary of the applicant who has resided at more than three addresses in the past two years. You do not need a new resident who will move out in a matter of months. However, there may be good reasons for those housing changes, so it is best to take the time to ask. Also, when the rent being applied for is substantially more than the rent currently being paid, it might be an indicator of potential problems ahead. Applicants should be able to explain how they can handle a large increase in rent.

- *Information on the applicant's employment record.* The name, address, and telephone number of the applicant's employer, together with the name of his or her immediate supervisor, should be included. You also want to know the applicant's income, occupation, and number of years on the job. As in the case of residency, you need to know the applicant's employment history for at least two years. If this includes more than three jobs in the past two years, be alert. Determine the reason; it could be quite legitimate. A highly skilled trim carpenter could very well have two or three employers in one year; skilled craftsmen often move from job to job with little or no loss of time. If the applicant does not have this kind of job, you may wish to pass on the applicant rather than risk problems in collecting rent or regaining possession of the apartment.

  The ratio of rent to gross monthly income is a very important factor in determining an applicant's ability to meet rent obligations. Chances of rent collection problems increase proportionately when the rent exceeds 33 percent of the applicant's gross monthly income. Only regular salary should be considered in this test, and by law, you must take into account the full gross income of all adult applicants. Do not include overtime pay—even though it may be very consistent—or income received from a second job. An applicant who needs such income to qualify for an apartment is stretching things and may become a collection problem.

- *Information on checking and savings accounts.* This can be useful in judging the applicant's financial situation and sense of responsibility.

- *Information on both open and closed loans or charge accounts* completes the important credit information on your application.

- *Information needed to draw up the lease.* The application should also include spaces to record information concerning the particular unit for which the applicant is applying. Commonly, the information contained in the application that is needed to draw up the lease document includes:
  —Address and apartment number.
  —Term of the lease, with beginning and ending dates.
  —Monthly rent.
  —Security deposit.
  —Information on pets.
  —List of any optional features or services.
  —Special conditions, including promises of additional improvements, free rent, or special lease provisions.
  All of these special conditions should be not only stated on the application, but also explained to the applicant to avoid later misunderstandings. An applicant becomes wary when these additional items are not stated in writing.

- *Other items to consider.* You may want to ask the applicant for references even though the people listed as references will invariably be primed to give you a positive report. You should also make sure that you know the name, address, and phone number of the person who should be contacted in case of an emergency because that individual will not necessarily be the nearest living relative. Finally, you may want to seek information about the applicant's car(s); asking the year, make, and license number of every vehicle that will be routinely driven or parked on the property is a good place to start. It is also a good idea to include space to indicate that proof of insurance was asked for and obtained.

  Many problems arise from a resident's failure to insure personal belongings. Residents often believe that the building's insurance covers resident possessions. It does not, of course. Including a space in the application form for applicants to indicate whether they have coverage for their personal belongings is one way to avoid this confusion. If the applicant is without insurance, you may wish to provide the names of two or three reliable agencies that can write renters' policies. In any event, the applicant must understand that personal belongings are not covered by the building's insurance.

The final step in the application process is to have the applicant(s) sign the form. The signature area should follow a statement that the applicant(s) grant you permission to investigate their credit background and check out landlord references, employment data, and so on, including any criminal record if that is to be checked.

Application Deposit.   As will be discussed in Chapter 11, a completed application form without an application deposit accomplishes very little. With the deposit comes a decision and a commitment; without a deposit, there is a high probability that the manager could expend a lot of effort and expense with no result.

An effective application deposit can be as small as $25, but it should not exceed $100. A larger deposit will discourage many prospects. Here are three recommended conditions for the deposit:

1. If the application is accepted and the prospect takes the apartment, the deposit is applied toward the security deposit. It is important to first apply money received toward the security deposit and then to the first month's rent. The lease agreement will give you rights and remedies to collect rent but seldom provides for collection of a security deposit that was agreed to but not paid.

2. If the application is not accepted, the entire deposit is refunded.

3. If the application is accepted but the prospect withdraws, the "deposit" is retained to cover the administrative and processing costs. You should avoid terms like "forfeit." People can accept paying a fee for a service, but they do not like forfeiture. The result is the same; the terminology is easier to accept.

Some management companies charge a nonrefundable fee to cover the cost of processing a rental application. Whatever practice you establish, it is a good idea to check with legal counsel; there may be state laws regulating application fees.

Once you have a signed application and a deposit, you can begin checking out the application information in order to decide whether to accept the prospect as a resident. It is essential that every aspect of a background check is applied and conducted uniformly for all prospects.

The Credit Check.   The credit of every applicant should be checked thoroughly. It is foolish not to do this. Credit is an indication of a person's character and is an extremely important tool in evaluating a prospective resident. Without a credit check, you increase your risk of rent loss and costly eviction and collection procedures. Even the best-appearing applicant can turn out to be a poor credit risk, while the seediest-looking person can be as good as gold. A credit check will help you tell the difference.

A credit check is not foolproof. It is difficult to outsmart a professional who can falsify credit references so you do not find out about a problem until it is too late. You want protection against the casual poor credit risk, the person who is not deliberately seeking to bilk you but whose careless financial habits will make rent collection difficult.

The credit reporting industry is making major technological break-throughs. It will not be long before consumers will put their thumbprints on a palette that will instantly identify them and provide a complete credit and background history. In the meantime, all of the national credit data reposi-tories use a form of the Fair Isaac Company (FICO) Credit Scoring System, which is a quasi-scientific way of assessing how likely a borrower is to com-plete his or her responsibilities under a payment contract such as a mort-gage loan or lease. The FICO Score measures the relative degree of risk of a potential borrower. Scores range from approximately 450 to 850 points. Most credit providers are looking for a score of 650 or higher. This is a very important tool in determining a person's credit standing. Landlords and apartment managers are advised to take advantage of credit scoring in eval-uating the creditworthiness of rental prospects. With the amount of data be-ing amassed on virtually the entire U.S. population, these firms will soon be in a position to predict, with great accuracy, the chances of a person be-coming delinquent in making payments or likely to declare bankruptcy.

In many cities, the major credit bureaus can upgrade their service to provide you with the applicant's NSF check writing code. The scale of this code ranges from 1 to 10—one being great and ten being major trouble. You will be looking for people with codes of 3 or lower.

A credit report will include information on bank accounts, outstanding loans, and credit card debt. You should be able to determine how much of an applicant's income is already committed. As noted previously, when the rent is more than 33 percent of someone's gross monthly income, chances of rent collection problems increase. When the total of rent plus monthly payments on installment purchases is greater than 55 percent of a person's monthly gross income, you should not rent to that applicant. There simply will not be enough money left over to meet all normal living expenses.

Leasing decisions based on consumer credit information are regulated under the *Fair Credit Reporting Act* (see accompanying sidebar).

Checking Other Background Information.   The apartment manager or other staff members should make certain inquiries themselves. The first step is to call the owner or agent of the property where the applicant currently lives; if you are dealing with a first-time renter, obviously you will skip this step. Owners and agents who are trying to evict a resident may give him or her a good send-off, so good landlord references may camouflage bad risks. This is a risk you take, and it is to be hoped that honesty will prevail. By contacting the landlord prior to the current one (when applicable), you may be able to obtain a more candid reference.

Next, you should try to verify the applicant's employment record and salary by telephone rather than in writing since correspondence can be

The Fair Credit Reporting Act

In checking an applicant's credit, you must be mindful of the Fair Credit Reporting Act (FCRA) as amended in 1997. Many of its provisions apply to rental apartments, and they are being broadened through "new guidance" as time goes on. Unless the verification of information provided by a prospective tenant is handled directly by the landlord or the landlord's agent or employee, without the aid of an outside service, the tenant is entitled to notice of any adverse action. This means that when a "consumer report," either to check creditworthiness or to screen potential residents, is generated by one of the major credit bureaus or other tenant-screening or reference-checking services or information providers, the requirement of a tenant notice goes into effect. The prospective tenant has the right to know what information was reported and must be given time to correct or modify any inaccurate information.

Another important provision deals with a landlord's *adverse action* that results, even in small part, from information contained in a credit report. Any of the following would constitute an adverse action:

• Refusing to rent
• Requiring a co-signer on the lease
• Requiring a deposit, if deposits are not required of other tenants
• Requiring a larger deposit than would be required of other tenants
• Requiring a higher rental amount than would be required of other tenants

If a landlord takes adverse action, he or she must provide the consumer with a written *adverse action notice*. This notice must:

• Provide the name, address, and phone number of all consumer credit reporting agencies that provided information.
• Make clear that the credit agencies only provided information about credit history, took no part in the decision process, and cannot provide an explanation for the decision.
• Explain the applicant's rights to obtain a free copy of the credit report, dispute its accuracy, and provide a consumer statement describing his or her position.

Individuals may sue for damages, court costs, and fees if their rights are violated, so close attention must be paid to this Federal Trade Commission ruling.

slow. However, you need to be aware that an applicant may give you the name of a fellow worker and set things up so that this friend will give you a positive recommendation. While this is a possibility, you can often detect a problem by the person's hesitant manner. If you are really suspicious, hang up and try again, only this time check with the department head. In any event, using the phone is better than writing to the personnel department because getting an answer may take weeks.

Many local apartment associations or groups of apartment owners and managers maintain a list of people who have given them problems. These difficulties may include a history of slow payments or evictions, troublesome living patterns, or a tendency to cause damage. Joining such a professional organization and sharing information about problems with residents will surely pay dividends. One caveat is necessary: You should make sure any exchange of information you participate in is within the law.

No matter how careful you are, you will occasionally make mistakes in judgment. Your best tactic is to pay close attention to the renter's living and payment habits and to act quickly when something goes awry.

Having a reputable professional firm conduct credit checks and other background reviews is the most-efficient, effective, and economical way to go about the process. Also, it helps to insulate the manager and the management company from claims of discrimination.

Security Deposits.   The subject of security deposits invites opposing reactions. Owners often regard a full month's rent for a security deposit as their right. Without it, they say, there is no protection against the resident who damages the apartment or violates a provision of the lease. The applicant, on the other hand, objects to the security deposit on the grounds that the owner has free use of that month's rent (or other amount) for the full period of tenancy.

Security deposits are in disfavor for another reason: A great many state laws or city ordinances require owners to pay interest on security deposits and to give an accounting to residents whose deposits they hold. Methods of accounting and the rates and frequency of interest payments vary. Some jurisdictions forbid the property owner from using this money, requiring that it be held in escrow for its eventual return to the renter. Owners of property insured under various Federal Housing Administration (FHA) titles are required to invest security deposits in government bonds or with institutions insured by the U.S. government. The laws in some areas exempt interest payments on relatively small security deposits (e.g., $100 or less), and others exempt interest payments on security deposits collected for student-occupied housing and furnished apartments. Security deposit laws vary from one jurisdiction to another, but renters' feelings on the subject do not. Security deposit policies remain a sharp thorn in relationships between owners and residents. In fact, many surveys of residents' opinions indicate that the security deposit is a common grievance.

The biggest reason security deposits are not what they used to be is that they place the property at a marketing disadvantage, particularly when a competing property is being rented without a deposit. If all competing properties require a one-month security deposit, you can gain a marketing advantage by reducing or eliminating your deposit requirement. As an alternative, you might want to ask for a deposit of $100 or an amount substantially below one month's rent.

Given the option, most people would actually prefer to pay more rent and a lower security deposit. We can interpret that as an extension of the American buying principle: How much down? How much a month? For example, if a group of applicants was given a choice of paying $700 monthly rent plus a $700 security deposit or $720 monthly rent plus a $100 security deposit, they would probably compare the $1,400 entry fee to the $820 entry fee and choose the latter, even though it would mean an annual increase in rent of $240 (the $20 per month difference in rent for 12 months). Obviously, this is better for the property. The additional rent adds to revenue while a larger security deposit has little or no financial impact.

Most rental applicants are also paying rent on their present apartments when they sign a lease for a new one. In addition, they are now required to pay a full month's advance rent on the new apartment plus a security deposit equal to another month's rent. While people may be able to afford high monthly rents, not many have savings that will permit them to pay two months' rent in advance in addition to all the other costs of moving. So, given a choice of two apartments whose rents are the same or comparable and which include most of the same features and amenities, renters will typically take the apartment with the lower security deposit requirement—even if it has a somewhat higher rent.

Resident ill will, administrative costs, and marketing disadvantages render the traditional security deposit no longer useful. However, the reasons for requiring a security deposit—to assure the applicant's commitment and to establish a reserve fund to pay for damages—are still valid. To resolve this issue, you may find it useful to adopt a policy of asking for a deposit of substantially less than one month's rent. This accomplishes three things:

1. It provides a marketing advantage over properties that continue to ask for a deposit equal to one month's rent.

2. If the rent and the deposit are not equal, applicants are less likely to consider the deposit as an advance payment of the last month's rent. Properties with this policy have reported a sharp improvement in the number of vacating residents who voluntarily pay their last month's rent.

3. If the deposit is minimal, it may be exempted from controls required by current legislation.

These advantages deserve consideration when you establish your security deposit policy, with one exception. This applies to single-family home rentals. In a building with many occupants, there are people close at hand to report disturbances, undue noise, or situations that appear out of the ordinary. This benefit exists, to a much lesser degree, in a single-family home, and a great deal of damage can be done before you become aware of trouble. A security deposit of two months' rent is recommended when you lease a single-family residence.

The issue of returning the deposit when the resident vacates is very important and will be discussed in Chapter 6, "Polices for Residents."

5

Something you should know:
A lease from 2004 to 2007 is for 3 years
unless it starts in January, in which case it is for 4 years.

The Lease Agreement

Leases traditionally have been written to favor property owners. They were couched in language that is not only hard to understand, but also intimidating. Because many of their provisions are outmoded, leases are becoming harder and harder to enforce in the courts. Lease terms (and omissions) are typically construed against the owner, particularly because they are presumed to have been drafted by the owner.

Nevertheless, written leases are necessary. A written document is needed to serve as a contract and spell out terms and conditions. Owners and residents alike need the psychological value gained from the act of signing a formal agreement.

The lease document can be revised into a more acceptable and workable form, however. For one thing, it does not have to be called a lease. The term *occupancy agreement* or *rental agreement* can be used. This lacks the sting of the word "lease," conveys a more up-to-date approach, and is equally binding. You would be well-advised to work with your attorney in developing a modern-day version of a lease document for use at your properties. It should also be noted that some states require lease terms to be understandable by persons of "common intelligence" (stiff penalties may apply for violators, and preapproval by a governmental agency may be required). By eliminating provisions that are no longer applicable or enforceable and lightening the legal terminology, you can provide a more workable document that will also be valuable in resident relations and as a marketing tool.

In this chapter, we will discuss lease provisions as they fall into several different groupings. These include occupancy terms, special provisions that prospective tenants may ask for, and other common clauses that are typical of residential leases. The discussion here is not intended to be exhaustive but rather to highlight the more common components of a lease. (The issue of residents' rights is discussed in Chapter 6.)

Terms of Occupancy

Certain provisions are more or less standard. The important provisions are outlined here, using the familiar terms *lease* and *tenant* to allow for better understanding.

Parties to the Agreement.   A lease should identify the name of the legal owner of the property; however, when an agent manages the property, it should identify the *agent* of the owner as well as the owner. This establishes that the manager is acting in the capacity of an agent. The owner can be referred to as the owner, lessor, or landlord. Whatever you choose—state law may require specific terminology—you should use it consistently to avoid confusion.

All adults and emancipated minors who are to occupy the apartment should be listed by name on the lease and should sign it, so that all are held responsible for the performance of the agreement. To avoid problems, full legal names should be shown. The law generally holds that there is no such person as "Mrs. John Smith." So, in the case of a married woman who uses her husband's surname, have her sign using her given first name (e.g., Mary Smith).

If you rent an apartment to two or more people and only one person signs the lease and that person later leaves, you may have a hard time collecting from the remaining occupants. This problem can be minimized if you list all adult occupants on the agreement and obtain their signatures. This policy will also protect you in the event of the death of one of the occupants. If a husband and wife occupy the apartment, have them both sign the lease. If one of them dies, the other is still obligated to the lease terms. If the remaining occupant does not pay, you can pursue the remedies provided in the agreement. If the surviving spouse has not signed the lease, you will certainly have more difficulty proving your rights.

If you require a *guarantor* or *cosigner,* this person should execute a guarantee that is either part of the lease or on a separate form attached to and made a part of the document.

Apartment Lease Forms

Real estate management companies and some investor-owners will have their own standard lease forms. Owners and managers wishing to develop a customized lease document for a particular property may find it expedient to follow some of the formatting and language found in standard lease forms generated by local apartment associations and similar organizations. In any case, it is essential that the final document be written with the help of an experienced attorney specializing in lease law. State landlord-tenant laws and local housing ordinances are constantly changing, and the enforceability of your document depends upon getting it right.

Today, the format of choice is a lease form that can reside in the property's computer. The details of the occupancy terms are inserted, and multiple copies are printed, providing the parties with a professional-looking and legally binding contract.

Identification of Premises.   While many apartment communities are known by name, the lease should identify the premises being rented by its apartment number, common postal address, city, state, and zip code.

Rent.   For the most part, rent is in the form of a monthly charge. This is particularly true for unfurnished apartments. Rents are generally due and payable, in advance, on the first day of each month. The lease should state when and where rent is to be paid and require that the first month's rent be paid when the lease is executed and before the apartment is occupied. A few owners make the mistake of dividing the year into 12 periods of 30 days each and charging rent beginning on the day occupancy takes place. This practice is confusing and complicates bookkeeping. If occupancy begins on any other date, the rent should be prorated back to the first of the month, and the lease term should end on the last day of a month to avoid difficulty and confusion at renewal time.

In some situations, such as with furnished units, rents are sometimes quoted on a weekly or semimonthly basis.

In addition to the conventional *fixed monthly rent,* there are other types of rental charges and techniques. These are some examples:

- *Aggregate rent.* Many office and commercial lease agreements provide for an aggregate or gross term rent that is payable in monthly installments. For a time, this practice extended to residential units but it has lost favor with both owners and tenants. Its purpose is to obligate the renter for the full rent amount for the entire lease term rather than for each monthly period as it comes due. This provision permits monthly installments of the rent payments as long as the tenant is not in default. The lease usually contains an acceleration clause that makes the entire sum due if any installment is late or missed. This arrangement saves the manager from having to sue each month as another rent payment becomes due.

There are some states that favor an aggregate rent provision, so legal counsel should advise on its use. Courts take varying stands on such provisions. For apartment leases, the courts tend to disclaim the acceleration provision and to rule on rent claims as if a standard lease with a fixed monthly rent were in effect.

If you use an aggregate rent lease, extra care should be exercised in its preparation. For example, if a lease is written for a two-year term, and an aggregate rent amount for only one year is inadvertently inserted, you have granted two years of occupancy in return for only one year's payment of rent. It is doubtful that the court will give you or the owner much sympathy.

- *Graduated rent.* Use of a graduated rent provision is common in leases, particularly when the term is longer than one year. To avoid confusion and possible later argument, make certain that the beginning and ending dates for each rent rate are stated clearly.

  It is generally easier to negotiate a lease with a rent that steps up periodically. People are usually more concerned with the immediate future and will agree to higher charges at some distant date.

  A different form of graduated rent is often found in apartments in college towns. (Student housing is discussed in detail later in this chapter.)

- *Head rent.* In college towns and in developments trying to attract young single people, you may find rent being charged by the "head" rather than by the dwelling unit. This is used more frequently for furnished than for unfurnished units. In this type of housing, the owner or manager establishes a rent by first determining the number of people who could comfortably occupy the apartment. For example, a two-bedroom, two-bath apartment might accommodate four adults. The apartment is then offered to four adults individually, each of whom might pay $250 per month and sign his or her own lease. The unit can then be rented to four persons who are unrelated or unknown to each other at that $250 per month head rent. One of the roommates can leave without affecting the rent of the remaining three. While these renters enjoy the benefit of low individual rents, they also face the prospect of not knowing their new roommates. There is one thing to remember if you are developing policies for head rent: Apartment layouts that can comfortably accommodate only three individuals should be avoided. Groups of three people are notorious for creating difficulties—invariably two people conspire against the third, who in turn leaves. On the other hand, arrangements to house up to five individuals might be acceptable for a suitable space because additional people seem to defuse the problems of "odd man out."

Generally, when this type of rent program is in effect, the owner may agree to lease the unit to a family or smaller group of people who will accept responsibility for the entire rent payment for an amount that is less than the combined individual rents.

This method of charging rent is unique and is not recommended unless you find yourself in a very difficult or specialized market situation. Bookkeeping and collection problems increase dramatically when head rent is used instead of the standard unit rent.

- *Seasonal rent.* Seasonal rents are common in vacation areas, with the highest rents charged during the period of greatest demand. If you manage an apartment building in Aspen, Colorado, or Palm Beach, Florida, it will be necessary to collect about 80 percent of all rent dollars during a three- or four-month period of the year. During the off-season, demand for these rental units decreases substantially due to the much smaller number of year-round residents.

  Seasonal rents are, for the most part, paid in advance. For example, a person who rents housing for a season that normally lasts three months can be expected to pay the total rent for the season before taking occupancy. Rent for a six-month season would typically be paid one-half at the lease signing and the remainder at the middle point in the term. There are a variety of systems for collecting seasonal rents, but most involve substantial advance payments.

- *Student housing.* Universities and landlords of student-oriented rental housing realize that their "rental season" is nine, not twelve, months long. Most have given up trying to commit students to a full year beginning with the fall term. What happens is that a large number of students pay each month through May of the following year and then move-out, leaving the property without tenants or income. Consequently, it works best to offer leases for the shorter period and simply structure them so that the entire year's rent is paid over the fewer months of occupancy. This also allows management the opportunity of working uninterrupted while making improvements and readying the units for the start of the fall school term.

  This approach creates the bonus opportunity of renting units at a special summer rate—e.g., $350 for each of the three summer months

Escalator Clauses

Leases can be modified so that the rent will increase as the cost of living rises or operating expenses increase. This is accomplished with escalator clauses like those used widely in office buildings. Office buildings typically establish a base year for both real estate taxes and operating expenses. As these costs increase, they are billed to the tenant as *additional rent.* Because office leases are written for longer terms (3–10 years), the rent adjustment protection provided by escalator clauses is necessary.

The same strategy can be applied to apartment rentals, even though their leases are written for only one- or two-year terms at most. The problem is one of applying an automatic device that will let the apartment manager and tenant know that a rent adjustment is necessary to keep pace with changing costs. It should be noted, however, that an escalator provision can be the source of considerable confusion and argument and should be avoided in times of low or moderate inflation.

Apartment managers need an index that reflects price increases, is readily available, and is accepted as reliable. Utility charges and real estate taxes come to mind because they can increase at alarming rates, but they probably are too erratic and too political to meet the test of sustained reliability. The *Consumer Price Index (CPI)* is the most-used yardstick showing changes in prices for a representative basket of goods, including food, clothing, shelter, transportation, health care costs, etc. It reflects changes in the cost of living, not only nationally, but in most major cities as well. The potential for confusion, and therefore argument, exists because the U.S. Department of Labor maintains more than one index. It differentiates between the prices paid by *all* urban consumers *(CPI-U)* and those paid only by urban wage earners and clerical workers *(CPI-W).* Both of these indexes are subject to change when seasonal adjustments are made. The CPI is tracked and reported in the Business Sections in most major newspapers. Anyone can receive these statistics through a monthly subscription that is free for the asking.

on a unit that will be priced at $700 per month during the school term. The big "summer discount" might induce some renters to keep the apartment for the summer rather than move out and have to rent again in the fall.

For both seasonal and student housing, owners must adjust rental rates to produce the required annual rental income over a partial year. Most operating costs go on whether tenants are present or not, so rents are adjusted to recover these costs during times of heaviest market demand. In addition, the rent must reflect the higher incidence of turnover which, of course, increases the operating costs overall. Turnover is very high in seasonal and student housing, frequently twice that found in normal furnished apartments. The level of apartment abuse by the more transient tenants is also higher than normal.

Escalator Clauses *(continued)*

Over the years, the government has made some changes to the types of commodities and their weightings, as well as the base year used for price comparisons. These changes have skewed the index and somewhat distorted its tracking reliability.

Adopting this type of lease provision has its problems with acceptance among renters and the disputes which invariably arise. It is also quite possible that periods of very low inflation will exist at the same time apartment demand is high and larger rent increases are possible.

It is important that renters be told about the presence of an escalator clause at the outset. Managers and owners cannot assume that the clause has been read and understood just because a tenant has signed a lease containing it. Courts no longer assume that everyone reads and understands lease provisions, so you must call the escalator clause to the applicant's attention. One way to do this is to include a legend on the title page of the lease: "This lease contains a rent escalator clause; please read it carefully." Another way is to affix a sticker with similar wording onto the lease. During the application phase and later at lease signing, the staff should carefully explain the presence and ramifications of the escalator clause and then have the applicant(s) initial that part of the lease. In other words, you should do all you can to assure that the renter cannot complain later that he or she did not know about the clause and assumed the lease form was conventional.

- *Other rent.* If rent covers more than just the apartment, say a garage is included, the lease should separate the rent for the apartment from the rent for the garage. Defining what the rent does not cover—for example, utilities, cable TV, use of recreational facilities, or whatever is paid by special fees—is critical, too.

Lease Term. The specific dates on which the lease begins and ends should be stated. The lease period can be any term acceptable to you and the tenant. You can set a term that benefits your rerental needs. For most areas with the typical four seasons, any month-ending date from March 31 to October 31 is a good expiration time. Should you have to rerent, the market is active in these months. Some managers believe that it is usually best to avoid leases that terminate in cold weather months because fewer replacement tenants will be out looking for apartments at those times. Obviously, apartments in warm weather cities would opt for a reverse cycle.

In a new property, leases should be set up so they expire at staggered times rather than all at once. This will minimize rerenting problems. If you are managing an existing property with a tradition of having all the leases come up for renewal at once, you can begin staggering their expiration dates gradually as they are renewed.

Normally, you are under no obligation to renew a lease. You can renew by including the terms of renewal in the current lease or by submitting a new lease document or a lease extension rider.

Suppose you do not renew the lease. The tenant remains and remits another month's rent. If you accept this rent, he or she may become a *holdover tenant* and be entitled to remain in the apartment at the same rent for another year. Local laws vary on this point. You can avoid a lot of trouble and guard against the possibility of holdovers by having your leases run for a specific period "and month-to-month thereafter." Then, if a new lease is not signed and the tenant remains on a monthly basis, you can terminate occupancy at the end of any month with 30 days' notice.

Security Deposit Acknowledgment.   In the body of the lease document, it is advisable to acknowledge receipt of the security deposit and to provide for its escrow, use, and return. This not only helps avoid misunderstandings, but also alerts a prospective buyer of the property that security deposits exist and should be credited to his or her account in any sale prorations. When purchasing an apartment building, an investor is buying both the benefits and burdens accruing from the existing leases—as well as the property itself—and is responsible for performing the landlord's part of all lease obligations. This includes returning security deposits. Unless the security deposit is noted in each lease, a new owner may be unaware of this obligation or its extent.

Special Provisions

Up to now, we have discussed lease provisions that govern the occupancy of a tenant. However, you must also provide for times when the lease term ends prior to its expiration. Examples of some of the more asked-for "escape clauses" follow.

- *Transfer clauses* permit tenants to end their leases by producing a written notice from their employer stating that they have been transferred to a distant city. Generally, that distance must be 35 miles or more. The notice period is typically a minimum of 30 days, with the final day of occupancy ending on the last day of a month. Unfortunately, this policy will prompt some people to forge such a letter, but, for the most part, these notifications will be legitimate.

- *Home purchase clauses* are a favorite request of young couples hoping to buy a house. They provide the right to end the lease, usually with 30 to 60 days' notice and a copy of an accepted purchase contract. When you think about it, the largest group of home buyers is *first time buyers,* and most of those were previously renters. Agreeing to this type of escape clause will broaden your market, but you should be prepared for some premature losses of tenants.

- *Death clauses* may be written for older people who are concerned that leases may complicate the settlement of their estates. This clause provides for cancellation, generally 30 to 60 days after the tenant's death, allowing time to settle matters and vacate the premises.

Of course, you can write a lease with no escape clauses and then try to enforce it. That means if the tenant moves out before the lease is up, you can go to court to collect rent as it becomes due. However, the law in most jurisdictions requires you to mitigate or reduce the tenant's liability. You cannot just let the apartment remain vacant and sue for what the original tenant owes. You must put forth a reasonable effort to rent the apartment to someone else. If you incur expenses in renting it again, usually you can include these costs along with what the former tenant owes you.

Trying to collect on broken leases in court is time-consuming and costly. You need a policy that will be fair to all tenants, giving them the flexibility to move if relocation is required, and at the same time protect you and the owner against rent loss and extra expense.

I recommend that you and the tenant cancel the lease by *mutual agreement* according to one of the following two sets of terms:

1. You both agree to look for a suitable replacement tenant. When one is found and approved by the manager, a new lease is issued, the old one is canceled, and the former tenant pays a fee for administration and advertising.

2. The tenant agrees to pay a set amount, upon receipt of which the manager cancels the old lease and seeks a new tenant on his or her own. The set amount could include forfeiture of part or all of the security deposit.

Care must be taken in handling lease cancellations. There may be specific legal requirements to be followed.

Other special lease provisions may address renewal options and promises made regarding improvements to the apartment. Like escape clauses, these document items may be requested by the applicant and agreed to by the property owner apart from the standard lease terms.

- *Renewal options.* Granting a renewal option gives a tenant the right to continue occupancy for one or more periods at rent levels that are usually preset. As an example, someone might be offered a one-year lease at $700 per month with the right to extend that term for an additional year at $720 per month, followed by another one-year extension at $750 per month. The tenant will take advantage of this provision if it represents a good value at the time the option must be exercised. If the market has softened, however, and the tenant believes that a better deal can be negotiated, the tenant will probably forgo the option. In contracts, terms and conditions should enjoy mutuality. There is little mutuality in an option, and therefore owners and managers should resist including them in leases.

Renewal options make sense when market conditions give the landlord few alternatives or when the tenant is making a considerable investment and the option provision helps ensure the tenant's ability to continue in occupancy. If the option period extends much beyond one year, it is recommended that the rent be tied to the market rent being charged at the time the option is exercised. This way the rent increase does not trail the market in times of high inflation.

- *Promises of improvements.* If you made any promises in the application, they should be written into the lease document to reassure tenants and to avoid future misunderstandings.

Other Common Lease Clauses

A number of other issues are addressed in separate lease clauses and are often referred to as *boilerplate* language.

- *Condition of the premises.* Some printed lease forms state that by signing the lease the applicant acknowledges that the apartment is in a clean and safe condition, even when it may not be; but things are changing. In many localities, there are ordinances stipulating that the execution of a lease by the owner is a form of guarantee that the apartment is in a clean and safe condition and that it conforms to all local codes *(habitability)*. An owner can be held liable if an apartment does not conform to these standards.

- *Use.* The lease should clearly state that the unit's use is restricted to that of a private residence. Any commercial use or illegal activity should be expressly forbidden.

- *Peaceful enjoyment.* Under landlord-tenant law, a tenant has a right to privacy, peace and quiet, and use of the leased space and common areas.

- *Limitations.* A good lease will specify certain restrictions regarding the apartment's occupancy. *It should list all the people who will live there,* with a provision for additions only through birth and adoption. This permits the agent to take action against violators, such as a single person who rents an apartment and then has three or four friends move in later.

- *Repairs and breakdowns.* The lease should specify who is responsible for what. If damage is caused by tenant neglect, the lease should explain how the owner would recover damages.

- *Right of re-entry.* The lease should provide for the owner's right of access and entry. The owner or manager should be permitted to enter an apartment for periodic inspections, repairs, and modernization. The owner should also have the right to show an apartment for rerental during the last 60 days of the lease term, at reasonable hours—which have generally been established to be between 9:00 A.M. and 6:00 P.M. Similarly, the owner should have the right to exhibit the units in the event the building is offered for sale. Without a right of re-entry provision, the landlord may only be able to enter an apartment in the event of an emergency.

  Again, your familiarity with local laws is a necessity. Some laws specify that tenants must be provided with a written notice before anyone enters the apartment. The period of notice is also prescribed in such laws.

- *Repossession.* Included in the lease should be a provision that the owner has the right to repossess the apartment, that the tenant loses the right to possession when he or she fails to pay rent, abandons the apartment, or violates any other lease terms. According to the law, there is a significant difference between the tenant's losing his or her right to possession and the owner's right to seize possession. Awareness of state and local laws on these issues is imperative.

- *Abandonment.* You need to be careful about this one because each jurisdiction has its own definition of abandonment. If you violate it, you may be trespassing.

  The local law should be checked with an attorney. Based on the information you receive, you can specify what constitutes abandonment in each lease. Generally, if a tenant has paid the rent, the apartment is not abandoned—even if the tenant does not live there. Payment of rent usually gives someone the right to use the apartment; nonpayment of rent is one element, but only one, of the test for abandonment.

  Formal abandonment may have to be declared before you can do anything about any personal property that may be left in the apartment. It is important to know your local laws before invoking your rights in the case of an apparent abandonment.

  If you decide to enter the apartment and remove possessions that have been left there, it is advisable to document the appearance of the apartment and to inventory all of its contents in detail. Many managers photograph or videotape the entire apartment to show its condition and contents before removing any articles. Items of value should be stored under lock and key for a period of time. The length of time depends on the value of the articles and, in many jurisdictions, the law. The risk of a claim is great and the advice of the owner's attorney is highly recommended.

Finally, it is critical that staff members do not take items left in an apartment. If such a practice is permitted (or not expressly prohibited), the staff may take items that the resident may return to claim. If left with apartment contents, the manager might decide to donate them to a charitable organization that will provide a receipt and perhaps even indicate a value of the items donated. If the tenant does return sometime later to claim the possessions, the manager can give him or her the receipt and description of the donated items to use for tax purposes. People are often more understanding when they learn that the items were donated to a charity.

- *Fire and casualty.* The lease should state what happens if the apartment becomes uninhabitable as a result of fire, flood, or other disaster. As a rule, the rent stops at that point if the premises become uninhabitable, and the tenant is credited or refunded any unused rent for that month. The owner then has a period of time—90 to 180 days is customary, but the lease should be specific on this—to decide whether to restore the apartment and continue the lease or cancel it.

- *Assignment and subletting.* Virtually all leases contain language prohibiting the tenant from assigning or subletting the premises to another party without the property owner's express written consent. The reason is obvious: The owner or agent must know and approve of the occupants in the property. When this control is lost, serious problems can result.

- *Waivers and exculpation.* Most leases state that the tenants will hold the owner harmless in the event of any property damage and personal injury occurring on the premises. A great many courts have held these clauses null and void (or at least as they apply to bodily injury). A tenant can sue—and generally collect—for damages arising from a personal injury that occurs on the property. While you may want to include this kind of exculpatory clause for it psychological value, be aware that it may not hold up in court.

  Also common are clauses in which tenants waive their rights concerning legal notices, remedies, and procedures. The legality of contract provisions in which the parties waive or lose some of their rights can be expected to be questioned and challenged. You cannot enforce contract provisions that are against the law.

- *Subordination.* This is a common feature in many commercial leases but is much less common in residential leases. A lease gives a tenant a leasehold interest in the property. The subordination clause simply states that the owner can sign on behalf of the tenants and handle certain legal formalities without seeking their approval or acquiescence, so long as these actions do not affect the tenant's right to possession.

- *Condemnation or eminent domain.* This clause generally provides that if an empowered authority takes the property through condemnation proceedings, the lease is automatically canceled without any compensation to the tenant (who is required to leave), but with adequate notice (usually 60 to 90 days).

- *Bankruptcy.* The lease should provide for the eventualities of tenant bankruptcy, insolvency, assignment for the benefit of creditors, and debt reorganization. If any of these problems occur, you may be restrained from pursuing financial claims for monies due prior to the filing date. Your claim might have to wait for a settlement with all of the other creditors.

  Bankruptcy law grants the debtor the right to choose whether to affirm the lease. The decision, as the law stands now, belongs to the tenant and not to the property owner. This is contrary to the language of many residential leases, which read that the owner has the right to terminate the lease in the event of a bankruptcy. An attorney familiar with bankruptcy law should draft this clause.

- *Rules and regulations.* The property's most important rules and regulations should be listed, along with a statement about your rights to change them. The more reasonable and up-to-date these rules are, the better your chances of enforcing them.

- *Signatures and delivery.* Finally, the lease must be signed by all the parties (in the designated *signature block*) and copies delivered to each of them. The validity of a lease is questionable if a tenant does not receive a copy even though all parties have signed it. The owner's signature endorsement should include the ownership title as first indicated on the lease and the capacity of the person executing the lease on behalf of the owner.

With the lease signed, copies delivered, and the first month's rent and security deposit paid, the new resident is ready to take possession. The next chapter will discuss the policies that should be considered to help govern the resident's stay.

6

When a prospect's car stereo shakes the earth,
know that the system at home is even better.

Policies for Residents

Beginning at the point when prospective residents lean toward leasing, your set of resident policies will come into play. Many renters have experienced difficult or unresponsive management, and they will be alert to avoid any repetition. The management staff's answers will telegraph the apartment community's spirit and atmosphere, and your flexibility will be measured carefully.

It is only fair that you communicate to residents what the rules are. What can residents expect if their apartments do not meet their expectations, if something breaks, if they have to leave prematurely, or if an unforeseen problem arises? What is going to happen at renewal time? What is expected when it is time to leave? These are all questions you will need answers to before the first day of occupancy.

Communications

During the looking and leasing process, both the property staff and the new residents are pretty adept at communicating their needs to one another. Once the move-in is accomplished, the exchanges between the office and the renter become much fewer. What few communications do occur often take the form of directives from management or complaints from residents. I believe that management can and should take the initiative and do a better job of communicating what is happening in the apartment community, why, and when. There are events to talk about, get-togethers, property improvements, and service interruptions. Your success with a sustained dialogue will show itself in a noticeably lower turnover rate.

E-Mail. It is becoming more difficult to find a business card that does not provide an e-mail address. E-mail is a quick, efficient, and inexpensive way of communicating with a single party or everyone in a thick address book. The apartment industry received its indoctrination into the e-mail world through its student residents. Virtually all students have e-mail addresses, and it is their communication of choice. Prior to e-mail, managers did not hear too much from their student residents. They were busy with their school and social concerns, and communicating with the office involved time, paper, effort, and stamps. That has all changed. Nowadays, if a student is dissatisfied with some aspect of apartment life, it takes only a few minutes to type out a free e-mail message and transmit it instantly. If these residents want to increase your level of interest, they have learned to send electronic copies to your superiors as well.

While e-mail is a modern and handy method of communication, it also brings an explicit expectation of fast response. A resident who sends you an e-mail is usually looking for a response in minutes or hours. When you invite e-mail communication, you are well-advised to have one or more staff members monitoring incoming messages and sending replies which are responsive and not canned.

With the ready availability of e-mail, the daily volume of messages received by a property manager is probably at least double the combined number of calls and letters. It might sound like e-mail volume might overwhelm a manager's work schedule, but actually it is a very convenient and efficient way of getting things done.

Resident Guidebook. A good way to set the tone of your property and let residents know what they can expect is to publish a Resident Guidebook. It is a smart idea to give each incoming renter this guidebook before the move-in date and certainly no later than the first day of occupancy.

The guidebook should be a simple explanation of all the rules, regulations, and policies of the management, along with some practical and useful information. It should be written in understandable language; a good freelance writer, advertising copywriter, or publicist can write it for you. It is wise to avoid a list of negative dictates: "You can't to this" or "Don't do that." If possible, illustrate the guidebook with professional drawings. If the booklet is lively and interesting, people will read it. It is not a good idea to mail the guidebook or leave it inside the resident's newly rented apartment. Instead, you should hand it to the resident personally with the suggestion to look it over as soon as possible.

Some of the subjects a Resident Guidebook should cover are listed below. Managers should include any additional topics that are pertinent to their properties.

Auto repairs	Occupancy limits
Bicycles, strollers	Parking
Complaints	Pets
Decorating	Recreational facilities
Deliveries	Renewals
Disturbances	Rent Payment
Emergencies	Resident improvements
Keys and lockouts	Security deposit
Laundry room	Stereos, musical instruments
Maintenance service requests	Storage
Motorcycles, campers	Waterbeds

To assist new residents, you may also want to provide some practical information about the neighborhood, such as:

A neighborhood map
Utility companies' names, addresses, and phone numbers
Cable service provider and phone number
Places of worship
Schools, both public and private
Public library
Public transportation stops
Shopping districts
Nearest post office
Telephone numbers of police and fire departments
Voting precinct number and local polling place
Names of government representatives—federal, state, and local

General Resident Policies

It is crucial to establish policies that will guide and influence residents' behavior throughout their period of occupancy. From move-in to move-out, there will be a variety of concerns that need to be addressed. Some of the more important ones are described here.

Move-In.   A move-in policy is necessary to ensure that an orderly procedure will be followed. This is especially important if a number of moves occur in the same building on the same day. A smooth move-in procedure will create a good impression for new residents and guarantee fewer management problems later.

The move-in policy should require each new renter to let you know the date and approximate time of move-in so that you can be on hand to welcome him or her. This notice is also necessary in order to coordinate the use of elevators in high-rise buildings. People moving in become irritated quickly if they arrive to discover another party using the elevator; meanwhile, they are faced with mounting hourly charges as the moving crew stands idle.

Occasionally things do not go according to plan. If the departing residents have not moved out when moving day arrives, you should contact the incoming residents right away and tell them to remain where they are. That is the only thing you can do. If the new residents are already on their way, this can be a real problem. If it seems the delay will be more than a day, you may want to suggest that they make overnight arrangements. You will have to work out some means of pacifying and compensating these people, even though you may not be at fault. (Keeping in touch with departing residents during the days before their scheduled move-out can help you avoid most such close calls. At the least, you might be able to advise incoming residents about a problem with their scheduled move-in before moving day.)

Someone may ask about moving in one or two days early if the apartment is already vacant. Although the resident technically is not on the lease for those few days, it makes some sense to permit an early move-in. Earlier occupancy may allow for easier scheduling, and you will gain some goodwill at little or no cost.

Finally, the manager or a staff member should be present when the new resident moves in to give whatever assistance is needed. It is an opportunity to explain procedures and answer questions, demonstrate how appliances and other apartment features work, make note of any necessary adjustments or shortcomings, and explain to the new resident how and when corrections will be made.

Before the move-in itself, a checklist should be followed to ensure that everything is ready for the incoming resident. The apartment should be given a final inspection; the temperature should be set at a comfortable level; the refrigerator should be turned on; keys, including those for the mailbox, should be ready; and when applicable, the resident's name should be on the mailbox, and the storage locker should be clean and secured. You may choose to go through a formal inspection of the unit with the new occupant on move-in day, noting the condition of the apartment on a standard *inspection report* form. (Having a member of the maintenance staff involved in the inspection is a way to expedite any repairs or other work that needs to be done—a service request can be prepared on the spot.) After the move-in inspection is completed, the new resident should review the inspection report, both of you should sign it, and the resident should be given a copy of the report. This way you have a document on file that verifies your mutual acknowledgment of the condition of the premises. (The move-in inspection also serves as a basis of comparison when the premises are inspected as the resident moves out.)

Resident Improvements.   Some residents may want to improve their apartments with custom painting, built-ins, or new window or floor coverings. They may ask you first or just go ahead and do it, creating a surprise for you later.

As a rule, it is a good idea to encourage residents to invest their own time, money, and energy in upgrading their apartments. By doing this, the resident's sense of commitment to the apartment increases; this adds to the likelihood of developing long-term occupancies.

To understand how this sense of commitment is created, think about your purchase of an automobile. You do not really regard it as your own until you wax it or add some bit of your personality to it. If you buy an antique ring, it does not really feel like yours until you have cleaned and polished it. In the same way, an apartment is not really the renter's home until he or she invests some extra money or special effort in it. Your job is to look for ways to help the resident make that all-important commitment.

When a resident first moves in, there is a period that apartment managers call the "honeymoon." It generally lasts about 90 days. During this time, the new resident, often subconsciously, decides whether the new place is more or less permanent or just "make-do for the moment." When you visit an apartment and you do not see pictures on the walls and little decorator treatments, you can pretty well conclude that the occupancy will be short.

If residents want to have work done in their apartments, on their own, you will need a procedure that minimizes the problems of poor workmanship and restoration costs at a later date. You should develop a policy that addresses resident improvements and places certain restrictions on how they are done. For example:

- Residents must use materials whose installation is readily reversible (strippable wallpaper, light-colored paint).

- Improvements cannot be a danger to others (flower boxes insecurely attached to balcony railings).

- Improvements can be made only after securing management's specific approval.

Some improvements should be prohibited outright. These include any exterior painting; painting any doors, cabinets, or woodwork that have a natural or stained finish; using peel-and-stick papers or shelf-liners; installing permanent, non-slip materials in tubs and on shower floors; and attaching any signs to the property.

Screw and nail holes with a diameter of one-half-inch or less that result from installation of furnishings and decorative items should be tolerated.

Residents may want to install their own refrigerators or add other appliances and fixtures. Here are some things to consider in setting policies regarding such installations.

- *Refrigerators.* Problems arise when a resident uses his or her own refrigerator. What happens to the one belonging in that apartment? A stored refrigerator will deteriorate quickly. You may decide to permit such an installation if the appliance can be utilized in another unit. If you do allow a resident to install and use a privately owned appliance, this change should be marked on your records—and initialed by the resident—so there is no misunderstanding.

- *Plumbing equipment.* Residents should not be allowed to install dishwashers, disposals, washing machines, or dryers in their apartments unless your building is designed to accommodate such equipment. The existence of these appliances can lead to problems with vibration, flooding, noise, and plumbing back-ups. Some will have special power requirements.

  Many residents will substitute their personal showerhead for the standard-issue model. Generally, this will go undetected, as the resident will switch the devices again at move-out. You can just about be assured that the resident's showerhead will consume more water, but usually you are best advised not to make an issue of this.

- *Lighting fixtures.* If residents want to take down your lighting fixtures and put up their own, let them know that the original fixture must be reinstalled at move-out. A qualified workman and not a handy resident should perform both operations.

These are just some of the more common requests you will receive. As others occur, you will need to formulate policies to deal with them.

Apartment Transfers.   A resident may ask to transfer to a different apartment during the lease term to accommodate a change in circumstances. Policies covering apartment transfers should take some variables into account. Ideally, you should not encourage apartment transfers because they create added administrative work and cause premature wear and tear on apartments, but you should also be flexible. A resident who is not satisfied with his or her particular accommodations, and seeks a change, will probably go elsewhere when the lease is up—and you will have lost a resident. This is especially true if there are just a few months left in the lease term.

In determining whether a transfer is a good idea, consider market conditions. For instance, if a resident loses a roommate and wants to move from a two-bedroom unit to a one-bedroom unit, it might benefit you if apartments with two bedrooms are in tight supply and one-bedroom units are plentiful. If that is not the case, you might have the resident agree to pay a prorated share of the redecorating costs for the apartment that is being vacated.

Keys and Lockouts.   Policies on keys and lockouts are needed for several reasons—to reduce replacement costs, to prevent wasted time, and to maintain security.

The renter moving in should receive a fixed number of keys. A fee should be charged for extra keys or for replacement of lost ones. If the resident wants an extra lock on the door or asks to have the lock changed because of a lost key, this work should be done at the resident's expense. However, you should use the property's personnel or a locksmith to do the work to assure the quality of installation and overall compatibility.

Lockouts can be a nuisance. The child of a working resident may be locked out of their apartment after school and come to the management office for the key. There are always adults who occasionally lock themselves out and need keys—sometimes at one o'clock in the morning. To help residents with their forgetfulness, you should have a policy of charging a small fee to let them in—for example, $15 if it happens during the day, $30 or more if it happens after 10:00 P.M. Another approach is to render no help. This forces residents to gain access on their own or pay the locksmith charges. (People who find themselves locked out often do not think as clearly as they normally would and may take to forcing entry to gain access.)

One important precaution should be added to this. You should *never, ever* lend master keys (see the discussion of Locks and Keys in Chapter 3).

Politics and Voting.   Common sense suggests that your property and its management staff should remain politically neutral, but meeting facilities may be made available for political purposes provided they are made available to all recognized political parties on the same terms.

That is where political cooperation should end. Political signs in residents' windows or anywhere else on the premises should be forbidden for reasons of appearance. Displays on bulletin boards should be allowed on an equal basis. Political canvassing or distribution of political literature on the premises should be discouraged.

Some apartment communities are large enough to constitute a voting precinct, and the local election board may ask to rent polling space in your building. This generally is an excellent idea. An on-site polling place is a convenience to residents and encourages their participation in the democratic process.

Door-to-Door Sales and Canvassing.   Rules on these matters pose special problems. Many municipalities have laws governing soliciting. Ideally, you should prohibit commercial salesmen in order to avoid disturbing your residents. There is also the question of your own residents doing the soliciting. Your policy might permit them to invite contributions on behalf of a recognized nonprofit organization but forbid door-to-door sales. Because even charitable solicitations can be a bother to other residents if the person asking for contributions is too aggressive, you may need to set rules for how these activities may be conducted.

Move-Out.   When residents advise you that they intend to move from their apartments, you should spend some time with them reviewing the different move-out procedures so they will know what to expect. It is crucial that the departing residents provide you with their moving date so you know when to begin searching for replacement residents. You should also remind them that a move-out inspection will be conducted so you can determine their security deposit refund and arrange to inspect the premises on the day of move-out—after their furniture and other belongings have been removed. Finally, you should make an honest effort to determine the different reasons that formed the resident's decision to move. Your exit interview should ask pointed questions—you are not looking for whitewashed answers.

Move-Out Inspection and Security Deposit Return.   A resident who is moving out may suspect you of trying to keep the security deposit by finding as much damage as possible. Your policy should be to minimize these fears by establishing a procedure that will be completely objective and fair.

It is to your advantage to have the premises left in the best possible condition so that you can return the security deposit in full and not get into heated discussions about deductions. A well-planned policy will help you meet this goal.

You should let the resident know what the move-out inspection will consist of and explain that a check will be issued promptly. The security deposit refund check should be mailed to the resident within 14 days. It would be hard to justify taking longer. Be aware that local laws often dictate the amount of time you have to return a security deposit. Each year, politicians propose new and more stringent laws to rescue renters who experience difficulty with the return of their security deposits. Penalties of two and three times the amount on deposit are common. Your system should allow for a speedy return of security deposit money as well as a fair evaluation of damages and corresponding charges.

Knowing that their apartments will be inspected on the day they move, renters are likely to take extra care that the premises are in good condition. Without such an inspection, renters may be less careful about the way they leave the apartment. You will find that your costs will be sharply reduced if these inspections are done in the last minutes of the move-out activity while the resident is present.

Another good reason for move-out inspections is that they enable residents to straighten out any misunderstandings about who did what. For instance, you may claim a renter chipped a washbasin. The resident may reply that the washbasin was chipped before he or she moved in, and it has been the same ever since. If you made an inspection when the previous occupant moved out, or if you inspected the apartment with the resident when he or she moved in, you would have a record of this. If the current occupants are right, then you will avoid the unpleasantness of arguing over damage they did not do. Using an inspection form that documents conditions at both move-in and move-out and is signed by both the resident and the manager will help to avoid such disputes.

An inspection may also reveal deficiencies the resident can fix on the spot. You may find that the oven is dirty and say you will have to charge $30 for the cleanup. Rather than pay that, the resident may volunteer to clean it immediately.

When you make the inspection, you should be prepared to make allowances for normal wear and tear. An apartment is a consumable commodity; it wears out like anything else. You should not expect a resident to return it in the exact original condition; nor should you expect a security deposit to pay for whatever you would normally spend to prepare the apartment for the next occupant. The way you deal with any one person quickly becomes common knowledge throughout your property and in the community at large. Fairness is absolutely essential if you are to preserve good resident relations.

After the inspection is completed, you should make note of any repairs or other work that is needed, indicate the necessary deductions, and give the resident a copy of your worksheet. This will avoid disputes over what has to be done, and it also acts as a receipt to assure the resident that the remaining portion of the security deposit will be returned.

The last step in the move-out procedure is to collect all the keys to the apartment and mailbox and obtain a forwarding address so you can mail the refund check. Knowing the forwarding address is a big help if you need to contact this individual later and is very useful information for your marketing people.

Problem-Solving

The apartment manager must be ready for resident-related problems. Having plans to deal with problems can quickly resolve a minor difficulty and keep it from becoming a huge dilemma. A few of the most frequently encountered problems will be examined here.

Complaints.   A complaint that is handled slowly is almost as bad as a complaint that is not handled at all. As a worst-case scenario, you should handle a resident complaint within 24 hours. Most top-quality management companies respond to service requests filed in the morning during the afternoon of that same day. Problems that develop in the afternoon are taken care of the next morning.

It is important to keep track of residents' complaints. Every complaint should be documented in writing. If a complaint is made by telephone, the person taking the call should write everything down and then repeat it so the resident knows the problem is understood. The very fact that the complaint has been acknowledged will help satisfy the resident.

Complaints usually concern three subjects—other residents, the apartment, or the property. Here are some strategies you can use to respond to complaints.

1. *Complaints about others.* "My neighbors play their stereo too loudly." "They're fighting next door." "I think the people down the hall are drug dealers." These are the types of complaints you may get from some residents about others. Some of these are frivolous, but many are not.

   If a complaint deals with an emergency or civil disturbance involving others, find out if the resident has already called the police or fire department. If not, ask him or her to do so immediately. If the resident balks, place the call yourself. Be quick to act if life or property is threatened. Be careful about trying to deal with civil disturbances yourself, particularly fights resulting from domestic quarrels. The police are better trained to handle these.

   If there is a complaint about a nonemergency situation pertaining to others, tell the resident you would like to see his or her experiences presented to you in writing. For every ten telephone calls of this nature, you will get only two or three letters. When you receive the letter, visit the offending resident and tell him or her about the complaint, but do not identify the individual who filed it. After settling the matter, contact the person who made the complaint and explain what action you have taken. This can be done in person or by telephone.

2. *Complaints about the apartment.* Requests for repairs and maintenance should certainly be handled within 24 hours or less. (Response time will vary somewhat according to the severity of the problem and the expectation of the resident.) If you need access to an apartment, let the resident know you will have to enter the apartment during normal business hours, assuming it is not an emergency.

3. *Complaints about the property.* If residents complain about the way the property is maintained ("too much litter," "the grass isn't cut," "the laundry room smells," "recreation hours are too short"), pay careful attention. These criticisms of the property are warning signs of major resident dissatisfaction. They likely extend to many more people than those who actually complain. In fact, your four- and five-star residents may be equally bothered but say nothing; then one day they simply move out. So, if you start hearing general complaints, acknowledge them and begin a prompt investigation.

Emergencies.   Life in an apartment community goes on 24 hours a day, seven days a week, 365 days a year. While your office hours are established to take care of routine business, you need a policy to provide for emergencies in an orderly manner. The first recommendation is that you have a listed *24-hour emergency telephone-answering service.* It should be listed as an emergency number to distinguish it from the regular office number that might be used by prospects calling with questions. You may want to have the number printed on a sticker for residents to put on or near their telephones. Include the emergency number in the Resident Guidebook and post the number at the entrance to the office and on any bulletin boards. The answering service should know whom to call for various emergencies. This might be the site manager, although most properties rotate "on days" among several staff members.

The next recommendation is to *let residents know what constitutes a real emergency.* If a resident needs a replacement light bulb, that can wait; but if a water line breaks in an apartment, that is a real emergency. There are six types of real emergencies:

1. *Flooding caused by a plumbing breakdown.* This must be corrected instantly. The longer repairs are delayed, the more extensive the damage will be.

2. *Lack of heat in winter or air conditioning in summer.*

3. *Damage caused by wind, storm, or fire.* In a disaster, you have to take instant steps to minimize the damage. Residents should call the fire department first in case of fire; if they have not, the answering service should do so immediately before relaying the message to building personnel.

4. *When security has been breached or is threatened by burglary, vandalism, or other disturbances.* Again, residents should call the police first, and the answering service should notify the appropriate staff member.

5. *Back-up of a sewer or other sanitary facility.* This is a health hazard and must be corrected immediately.

6. *Electrical failures or short circuits.* These can threaten the safety of the building and the lives of residents.

The answering service should document nonemergency requests and pass them along when the management office reopens for business. This is an area where e-mail can be used to expedite communications.

The management staff should work together to produce an emergency preparedness manual to outline the steps that should be taken with potential disasters. These are periods of extreme tension for a manager. After the initial shock of the disaster itself, there are physical and emotional pressures caused by injuries, deaths, or loss of possessions. At present, we will limit this discussion to the subject of rent. It is a good policy to discontinue rent charges if an apartment is uninhabitable and to refund or give credit for any unused portion of that month's rent. Then, depending on the terms of the lease, the owner usually has a period of time to determine whether to restore the apartment and continue the lease or cancel it. (Chapter 14, "Insuring the Property," discusses the manager's obligations and responsibilities after a disaster.)

Damage Caused by Residents.   The best protection you have against damage to the apartment caused by the resident is the security deposit. It is very difficult to collect in court for damages that exceed this amount. Your policy should be to try to collect damages at the time of the occurrence, thus preserving the security deposit amount to cover damage revealed when the occupant moves out.

For example, if the toilet overflows because someone has dropped a soap dish or rubber ball into it, let the resident know that this is not a normal malfunction and that payment for the repair is expected. Most reasonable people will accept this; if the resident refuses, you still must make the repair for health reasons.

As for damage caused by resident neglect (e.g., water damage from a bathtub overflow or a window left open during a rainstorm), you should always try to collect—even though you may not succeed. Rarely will you be able to collect anything beyond the security deposit. If a fire is caused by a resident's negligence, you will have to rely on the property's insurance for coverage. The property owner's insurance company probably will not pursue the resident for payment, nor will a court generally rule against a resident in favor of the property owner.

There are several other possibilities to be considered in setting a damage policy. Occasional broken windows, for instance, are generally ongoing maintenance problems; replacing them is a cost of business you should absorb. Property damage caused by a resident's car may be collectible through a claim against the resident's auto insurance carrier.

If you rent furnished apartments, it is advisable to increase the security deposit to cover the added risk of damage. Also, inventory all the furnishings and indicate their condition before anyone moves in so you can use the security deposit to pay for any loss or damage. Photographs and videotape are easy ways to inventory furnishings and document their condition at the time of move-in.

Resident Abuses.   Residents who disregard their fellow residents or the property are a source of many complaints and problems for managers. One resident uses the balcony for storage; another leaves wet clothing in the laundry room washer for hours on end. There may be a family that is extremely noisy or a working resident whose children continually have to be let in after school.

The offending resident may not even be conscious that he or she is causing a problem or is disturbing others. Sometimes, the best way to deal with the situation is simply to show up at the apartment door and discuss it. Most people will agree to correct their ways. On the other hand, if you write a letter, it might be ignored, or the resident might overreact, making the problem worse. A resident will not be able to ignore a face-to-face meeting.

If the offending activity continues, a second visit is in order. On this occasion, you should suggest that perhaps the resident should live elsewhere and offer to cancel the lease by mutual agreement. This tactic demonstrates your seriousness, and the individual may finally reform. If the offer of cancellation is accepted, the problem is solved then and there.

Of course, the resident may reject your offer and continue the offensive behavior. In that case, court action is your next recourse. However, going to court is a long, uncertain process, and the lease will probably expire before the court action is resolved. You may be better off to put up with the nuisance until the end of the lease term, or you can begin the lawsuit in the hope that it will encourage the resident either to change his or her habits or to accept your cancellation offer.

Illegal and Immoral Uses.   How do you deal with a resident who engages in drug abuse, gambling, or prostitution in the apartment? Most leases state that the use of the apartment for illegal or immoral purposes is grounds for eviction, but eviction is a court procedure that is slow, expensive, and open to question. I believe it is better to meet with the resident, cite the objectionable behavior, and offer to cancel the lease and return the security deposit.

Before you take any action, you should consider whether you want to act against the offender at all. He or she rented the apartment for personal use. If what is done within the apartment is not offensive to others or damaging to the property, you may be better off ignoring it. On the other hand, if the problem involves criminal activity, it should be handled by the police.

If you decide to take action yourself, it is best to ask the resident to come to your office. It is not a good idea to write a letter stating the complaint. If the complaint turns out to be unjustified, the resident might use the letter against you in a court action. When you meet with the resident, you can simply say, "I know what's going on here, and I think it would be best for all concerned if you moved."

In most cases, the offender will leave, not so much because of a legal requirement, but because most people want to avoid possible trouble or exposure. You should have the departing resident sign a mutual cancellation agreement, and any prepaid rent or security deposit money you may be holding should be returned to the resident when the apartment is vacated. If the resident is suspicious that you will not refund the money once he or she leaves, you can offer to put it in escrow.

You should also be aware of the legal implications of taking action—or not doing so. Some states impose fines for *not* handling these kinds of situations. An attorney can advise you regarding legal requirements and appropriate actions as well as the need for specific documentation.

Resident Rights.   Renters have demanded their rights, and these rights have been granted through legislation and the courts. When rights are slow in coming, people sometimes use confrontation, the power of numbers, and the media to air their grievances. Landlord and tenant legislation has been enacted in almost every city and state. These laws often require the owner (and/or managing agent) to:

- Deliver and keep apartments in habitable condition.
- Put security deposits into escrow accounts and pay interest to the renter.
- Give specific notice when the owner chooses not to renew the lease.
- Allow the renter to make needed repairs in some cases and deduct costs from rent.
- Allow the renter to withhold rent in certain cases.
- Avoid any retaliatory action against renters who complain.
- Work with housing courts in handling complaints or violations.

It is crucial to know the landlord and tenant code that exists in your municipality. Some states also appoint landlord and tenant commissions to monitor or interpret these laws. Apartment managers must recognize the resident as an equal partner in the relationship between the property owner and those who live at the apartment community.

Tenant Organizations.   Tenant organizations are one outcome of the impact of consumerism on rental housing. They are often the result of both owner and management insensitivity to resident requirements. I believe that the kind of sensitivity needed to provide the products and services residents want should come from management's awareness of existing problems—not from collective bargaining. It is difficult to manage real estate effectively by committee. If you attempt to satisfy every resident through a tenant organization, you may wind up satisfying no one.

Not content to act individually, some renters have realized the power of group action. They have seen what labor unions and civil rights groups have accomplished. So, taking a cue from condominium associations that manage the affairs of buildings, residents may band together in the belief that "the landlord can't throw us all out."

Many tenant organizations are started in response to nonspecific issues. The residents have a general but undefined feeling that it is unsafe to live in the property, or they do not like the way the place is run. Seldom do they focus on specific grievances such as loose carpeting in the second floor corridor. Tenant organizations tend to make decisions solely on the basis of collective emotion and pressure.

Another factor leading to the formation of tenant groups is the idea that democratic principles should rule a community of residents. Participation is the watchword, an idea promoted by the U.S. Department of Housing and Urban Development (HUD) in the housing that it sponsors or assists. In fact, HUD requires the managers of federally assisted housing to support tenant organizations.

Once owners or managers allow tenant organizations to tell them how to run their properties, they forfeit their rights to control and their expectations of maximum net operating income. A manager who becomes too involved with a tenant organization has to deal with the same kinds of problems faced by the manager who socializes with tenants; this softening of the relationship between resident and manager can easily create difficulties.

The best policy is for the manager to deal with tenants as individuals. This means you should not encourage or assist them in the formation of any kind of organization. When a meeting is necessary, you should call it, run it, and adjourn it.

Residents are less likely to feel the need to organize when you adopt the following principles of action.

- *Fair and reasonable policies, uniformly applied.* All of your policies should be founded on sound reasoning, consideration of the residents, and fair and uniform enforcement.

- *Good communication.* If a problem exists, tell residents that you know about it and that you are working toward a solution. You should not be mute or try to ignore a problem. You can communicate with residents through letters, e-mail, or personal visits.

- *Prompt response to service requests and complaints.* Satisfied residents have no reason to band together. By taking care of individual complaints promptly and effectively, you minimize the momentum to organize.

Arbitration.   Arbitration is a viable way to settle serious disputes. By including an arbitration clause in your lease, you and the resident can agree to submit disputes to arbitration. Whatever the arbitrator decides is binding on both of you.

The usual procedure in settling a dispute is to contact one of the 18,000 attorneys, former judges, and industry professionals recognized by the American Arbitration Association. The arbitrator hears both sides and then makes a judgment for one or the other of the parties or recommends a compromise. The fee, moderate when compared to the cost of most lawsuits, is usually divided between the two parties. If residents know their complaints will be settled fairly, they are less likely to resort to group action for satisfaction.

Improving Occupancy Durations

The primary goal is to retain as many residents as possible. The greatest risk of losing residents is at the end of the first lease period. The allure, the excitement, and much of the expectation that existed prior to move-in no longer exists. Residents have now experienced some of the property's shortcomings. Introductory deals, offered initially, may not be repeated at renewal time. Those whose leases are up for renewal may decide that their family budget is "stretched" too thin and decide to find housing with a lower monthly rent. Studies show that as many as three out of four first-time leases are not renewed (Exhibit 6.1, page 131). Subsequent lease anniversaries fare much better, with about one-half or more renewing.

Lease Renewals.   It is standard practice to offer the resident a renewal lease or a *lease extension agreement* prior to the expiration of the current one. Frequently, the new term would be for an additional year. However, this practice actually increases resident turnover. Presenting existing residents with renewal leases has the effect of forcing them to decide what they want to do with their lives for the next one-year period of time. There are many people currently renting their accommodations who have long-range plans to own their own home. By presenting a lease to them, the decision is brought forward. When the renewal lease arrives in the mail, it is common for a couple to set aside the next few weekends to explore other housing opportunities. They owe it to themselves to see if they can improve their situation. Bypassing the formality of a renewal lease does not eliminate the thought of moving, but neither does it force people to action.

You will probably experience the least resident turnover if you use an initial lease term of a year or six months and follow that by an invitation to continue on a month-to-month basis. You should assure residents that rent increases will be limited to once a year, usually timed with the anniversary date of the original lease.

Some building owners fear that residents will opt to move during off-

Length of Stay

In certain businesses, there are dramatic economic advantages to being able to "expand the sale." For example, if a restaurant can encourage you to order a pre-dinner cocktail, an appetizer, or an after-dinner drink or dessert, it increases the average dinner check, and a large percentage of the total goes right to the bottom line. With each change of patrons, there are the added costs of cleanup, linens, and a new setup. When these costs are prorated over larger dinner checks, the restaurant enjoys higher profits. For many of the same reasons, hotels benefit when a guest's stay is extended an additional night or two.

In the rental apartment business, the *average length of stay* is critical to a property's economics. In fact, many property acquisition teams carefully investigate this vital statistic before recommending a purchase. Calculating a property's average length of stay is quite simple. The only number you need is the property's annual *turnover rate* (the percentage of residents who moved out since this time last year). Divide that percentage into 365 days (one year), and the answer is the average length of stay. As an example, suppose the turnover rate is 54%. The calculation would be:

$$\frac{365 \text{ Days in the Year}}{.54 \text{ Turnover Rate}} = 675 \text{ Days Average Length of Stay}$$

If the turnover rate is only 44%, the average length of stay would be 830 days. That means, on average, each resident will stay an additional 154 days longer than in the first example. This equates to far less work and expense. Consider your workweek if you had 20% fewer apartments to prepare for occupancy and go through the whole process of leasing and move-in. The reduction in operating expenses is equally dramatic.

By itself, the turnover rate is just a percentage statistic. However, it can be used to learn each property's average annual length of stay. Then you can set a target for improvement.

season (when there are few replacement prospects available), or they may be concerned that their lender will prefer the security of having annual leases in the file. While the risk exists that people will move out during off-season, the vast majority do not. Also, lenders are coming to the realization that signed residential leases in a file cabinet do not offer the same security as major commercial credit-tenant leases. Hence, they are not as troubled by month-to-month tenancies as they have been in the past.

Renewal Rewards.   One of your most important policy considerations is how you will encourage residents to renew their leases and stay for another year. Existing residents will certainly notice that new renters move into freshly prepared apartments (often with new carpet or appliances). To counter this, you need a specific policy about rewarding existing residents

Exhibit 6.1
Lease Renewal Rates

First Renewal

	10%	20%	30%	40%	50%	60%	70%	80%	90%
Leases Expiring 312	26% Renew			74% Move					

Second Renewal

	10%	20%	30%	40%	50%	60%	70%	80%	90%
Leases Expiring 221	47% Renew				53% Move				

Third Renewal

	10%	20%	30%	40%	50%	60%	70%	80%	90%
Leases Expiring 445	63% Renew					37% Move			

Success depends on first renewal results. In the author's study of seven properties (978 units), renewal rates increased substantially in the second and third years. Overall turnover was 52.45%.

with an apartment improvement at each lease anniversary. Without it, the property will face a constant procession of move-outs, and turnover costs will consume what could be cash flow.

Many apartment operators provide a display showing the various apartment upgrades and improvement packages that can be selected by a resident who continues in occupancy. For example, if the person is just completing one year, the renewal reward might be a fairly inexpensive improvement such as wallpaper for the kitchen or bath, a ceiling fan, new cabinet hardware, or one or more new light fixtures. On the second anniversary, the improvements should have more value. Examples might be a large bathroom mirror, a new medicine cabinet, new kitchen floor covering, or a decorative chair rail. Four- or five-year anniversaries might be rewarded with a new major appliance, new carpeting, or new tile in the bathroom.

The cost of turnover is the highest single expense in the operation of an apartment property (see sidebar). A great deal can be spent making your

Turnover

Without question, frequent tenant turnover is very expensive. In fact, it ranked right up with utilities and real estate taxes in a study of annual operating costs. Over a period of 20 years, national average turnover rates rose from 30% to greater than 50%. In some communities, especially in the southwestern part of the United States, turnover rates regularly approach 100% each year.

A property's *turnover rate* is the number of renters moving out during a one-year period as compared with the total number of units in the property. For example, if 45 residents moved out of a 100-unit property in one year, its turnover rate would be stated as 45%. Resident turnover can be described as occurring in two categories:

• *Natural turnover.* Managers know and should expect that renters will move to increase or reduce their space or to find housing that is closer, newer, nicer, or less expensive. Others will choose to purchase their housing. Some will transfer locations. It is very difficult to slow this type of exodus. People are on their march through life, and housing changes are part of it.

• *Forced turnover.* About one-third of apartment moves fall under this second category, however. These are really *forced moves.* Whether managers are willing to admit it or not, many people move because conditions force them to. Bad neighbors, unrelenting noise, foul smells, air and water leaks, and inadequate parking are some of the more common complaints. Rundown conditions, frequent breakdowns, out-of-date equipment and appointments, and nonresponsive management are others.

It is interesting to study "Monday morning reports" and read the different reasons why renters are moving. Almost all of the reasons for moving fall into the *natural* category. It is extremely rare to find any reference to move-outs that were associated with property or management shortcomings. Over the years, my company has conducted thousands of exit interviews to learn first hand why renters are moving. While they may be bashful at first, they often end up reciting a litany of problems that they endured during their stay. Managers frequently go into denial to protect their jobs, and owners sidestep issues to control costs. Admitting property deficiencies and setting out on a corrective course is one of the surest ways to improve occupancy and profits. When tracking "turnaround" success stories, you will find that management attacked these problems and stopped hiding or denying them.

Many apartment building owners and managers attempt to avoid turnover by maintaining unrealistically low rents. They then work to cut operating expenses in order to deliver acceptable net operating income levels. This can work for a while, as renters hang on to take advantage of the bargain rents, but declining conditions eventually will drive residents away. The best way to minimize turnover is through—

Turnovers *(continued)*

• Careful screening and selection,
• Fair rent pricing,
• A well-run property,
• Constant property updates,
• Cheerful service, and
• Prompt follow-through.

Controlled studies have shown that an apartment community spends two to three times the amount of the monthly rent every time a unit turns over. This figure includes cleanup expenses, decorating and carpet care, window coverings, repairs and replacements, advertising and promotion costs, and utilities and lost rent, as well as concessions and administrative charges. My experience has indicated that the average time between resident move-out and replacement move-in is more than 40 days (as can be seen in the accompanying chart). This does not include periods of free rent that may be allowed or taken. In money terms, if the rent were $800 per month, the associated costs would run between $1,600 and $2,400. Put another way, you could spend up to that amount improving a particular unit if it would make the difference between keeping or losing the occupant. While these figures are averages, they do represent a realistic cost of finding a replacement resident.

44 Days between Residents

12	+	6	+	8	+	18
Before Fixup Period Begins		Fixup Period		Offering Period		Before Rent Begins Again

Many firms have changed their charts of accounts or have added a special control category so that they can keep all the costs associated with turnover in one place. In doing this, they create a constant reminder of the importance of rewarding the existing resident so that the average stay is prolonged.

If you were to reduce the turnover rate in the property that you control by 10%, you would certainly increase operating profits; or you could charge less rent and deliver the same bottom line. Using typical numbers, each 10% reduction in the annual turnover rate, say from 50% to 40%, would allow you the benefit of charging around 3% less rent while maintaining the same net operating income. A 20% reduction in the turnover rate, from 50% to 30%, would double the possible monthly reduction to 6%. I certainly do not recommend chasing a rent reduction. My point is to illustrate that the high cost of turnover is a definite portion of each month's rent. Reduce turnover and you minimize the need for higher rent because your costs have dropped. Every move-out you prevent is one less apartment you have to rent.

current residents more comfortable before you begin to approach the cost of replacing them.

Security Deposit Reduction.   One of the best ways of showing confidence in your residents and expressing appreciation for their tenancy is to return some of the security deposit at given lease anniversary points. If the full security deposit was $150, you might have a policy to return $75 after one year and the remainder after the second. This process certainly acts as a reward and is appreciated by residents. Many of the fix-up costs are already amortized after two years anyway. Returning the security deposit during the term of the lease has the added advantage of partially offsetting rent increases.

Such a policy has an additional benefit: It affects the resident's cash outlay if he or she decides to move to another property. Suppose you decide to hold a resident's full security deposit for the duration of tenancy. When that resident moves, he or she effectively transfers the security deposit from you to the next landlord, and the out-of-pocket cash needed is only the rent on the new apartment. If you have already returned the security deposit, the resident must come up with additional cash to fund the deposit at the next apartment community. An important factor in the decision to move is cost. Managers should adjust their thinking to make it more cost-effective for the resident to stay.

7

*"If a person can't pay one month's rent,
how is he going to pay two?
. . . and he will never pay three."*

Rent Payments

Residents need to understand their obligation under the lease to pay their rent on time. They also need to know what steps management will take to collect rents that are due and unpaid. In this chapter, we will discuss policies regarding rent payment and collections.

Rent Payment Policies

Establishing rent payment policies encompasses aspects of apartment management that should be carefully thought out and thoroughly understood. These first policies concern where, when, and how rents are to be paid.

A Matter of Habit. Traditionally, and by lease contract, rent is due on the first day of each month. Payment of rent is a matter of training and habit. If you do not establish this policy, you will not enjoy prompt or complete payment. You can count on some residents to test you and delay making payments as long as they can.

Many renters spend what they have each month. The majority of workers are paid twice a month, and the typical renter uses most of one paycheck to pay his or her rent obligation. Once a resident falls behind in paying rent, it is most difficult to catch up. Most rent collection problems begin because the manager applied too little pressure in the beginning. Skilled managers know this and constantly apply pressure to keep each rent account current.

Make the Policy Known.   Your rent payment policy should be spelled out when the prospect first completes the lease application. It will not affect your sales presentation because people expect rent to be due on the first of the month. This policy should be stated again when the renter signs the lease. In doing this, you firmly establish the payment policy and eliminate many future problems.

Rent Bills.   Should a resident be billed for rent each month? This is a commonly asked question, and the answer in my mind is "no." Rent is usually a fixed amount. The precise amount is known by the resident; he or she also knows that it is due on or before the first of each month. What, then, is the reason for billing? In a luxury building with variable charges added to the rent, or in a condominium with owners, not renters, monthly billing might be useful. If you lease corporate units, you may be asked to provide invoices for the company's records. For the most part, however, a rental property does not need the extra cost and problems associated with the billing of rent. If the mails are delayed or there is an error in your billing, you have provided an easy excuse for the resident to pay the rent late.

Paying at the Site Office.   You gain maximum control over rent payments when they are collected at an on-site office. Granted, from an efficiency standpoint, more rents can be collected and posted in a single day when they are received by mail at a central location. The loss of control that mailing rather than hand-delivering payments will cause, however, is more than enough to offset this advantage. Convenience to the resident and the benefit of personal contact each month are additional advantages that result from on-site collections.

Lock Boxes.   Some management companies and apartment communities have set up a central cashier or bank lock box system for the collection of rent. These systems often provide the resident with an excuse. The delay in processing information back to the manager is called the "blackout period." During this time, site personnel do not have an up-to-the-minute listing of residents who have and have not paid their rent. Depending on the system, this period can extend to 5 or 7 days. The renter, when approached about overdue rent, learns to reply: "I have sent in my rent payment."

Forms of Payment.   Rent payments can take many forms—electronic funds transfer (direct payment), money orders, cash, personal checks, even third-party checks. You need a firm policy with regard to the form in which rent is paid.

- *Direct payment via electronic funds transfer (EFT) is both automatic and instantaneous.* Probably the majority of the work force now has their paychecks deposited directly into their bank accounts. This process and the direct payment programs offered by utilities are now making electronic funds transfer one of the favored ways of paying rent as well. Tenants have achieved a level of comfort with this payment method, and it saves the chore of writing and mailing checks. The two major drawbacks are remembering to record the transactions in check registers and learning that the money must actually be in the account at the moment the electronic transfer takes effect.

  An alternative for those who use the Internet is to directly "trigger" the rent payment into the property's bank account using one of a number of popular software programs. This method gives the tenant a little more control of the exact time when the money leaves the account.

- *Money orders and cashier's checks are a welcome form of rent payment.* They are convenient to process, recoverable if lost or stolen, and safe in terms of cashability. To a resident, they lack convenience and involve additional expense because they must be purchased. Your policy should be to accept them but not require them.

- *Cash payments present problems.* Managers are often reluctant to accept cash. When it is known that large amounts of cash are kept on the premises, you run an increased risk of theft that can compromise the safety of your site staff. Many managers either discourage cash or refuse to accept cash rent payments (even HUD's policy endorses this). Cash collections require frequent trips to the bank; checks, on the other hand, can be deposited by mail.

  Your policy may state that checks and money orders are the preferred form of payment; but cash is legal tender in the United States, and refusal to accept cash payments of rent may void your right to collection. You certainly can ask residents to pay by check or money order, and most will accommodate you. Most major thefts of rent money result from a failure to make daily bank deposits. With the extra work volume around the first of the month, several days' build-up of deposits makes a robbery an even greater loss. Bank deposits should be made daily.

- *Personal checks still account for a sizeable number of monthly rent payments.* They offer convenience to both the resident and manager and generally can be replaced if lost or stolen. The problem arises with NSF (nonsufficient funds) checks, which frequently are delayed up to two weeks in being returned to the property.

  In my experience, people who write checks when there are not sufficient funds in the bank to cover the amount do not seem to be affected by the increasing charges that the bank levies or the service charges that management imposes. Limit your residents to two NSF checks. After that, you should insist on money orders or cashier's checks.

Post-dated checks are another favorite of people with money problems. The best advice is to refuse a post-dated check. The Fair Debt Collection Practices Act has some rules concerning post-dated checks that will be discussed later in this chapter.

- *Third-party checks should be avoided*. Even though these may be company payroll or Social Security checks and can be termed "good as gold," they present problems. To cash these checks, you may need to make change for the resident if the check exceeds the rent amount. Also, when a third-party check is returned as NSF, it can cause significant problems in identifying the resident, making bookkeeping adjustments, and obtaining a replacement check.

Some may wish to consider accepting credit cards as a method of rent payment. The process is similar to electronic funds transfer, except that the rent amount is charged to the tenant's credit card each month. Some management companies already accept credit cards. However, you should be aware that credit card payments are discounted, and they can disguise renters' inability to make timely rent payments. Also, there are likely to be bank charges for setting up a program and processing these types of payments.

Advance Payments.   Occasionally, a resident will offer to pay rent for a number of months or even a year in advance in return for a discount on the rent. Advance payments may be fine; discounts are not. Even though the additional cash would be helpful in meeting current bills, you would be ill-advised to accept this money if it means discounting the rent.

Rent Collection Policies

To some managers, collecting rent is almost as painful as raising rents. This is not about the rents that show up in your office voluntarily but, rather, the ones that do not. A manager's ability to collect all rent that is due is an important measure of job performance. A poor manager rarely will have a good collection record. Long hard experience suggests that your rent collection policy should contain very little flexibility. I say: "No pay, no stay."

Many managers prefer a more liberal policy regarding rent collections. They quickly point out special circumstances that might be involved, along with the fact that most local laws require a lengthy procedure to dispossess a renter from a unit. Most managers, however, when asked to name the residents whose rent payments will be outstanding on the tenth of the following month, can do so with uncanny accuracy. The point is this: If those residents are so well known, why isn't the manager doing something about them?

Enforce on the First.   If the rent fails to arrive in your office during the very first few days of the month, you must begin enforcement, preferably in person. A telephone call or even a hard-hitting letter is not as effective as a personal visit. Reminder notices and final notices are not worth their paper value, much less the stamp required to mail them. It does not take residents long to discover your complete rent-collecting procedure. They quickly learn the steps you follow—reminder notice, final notice, five-day notice, letter, phone call, attorney. They will make their payments just before the personal letter or phone call. Knowing this, why waste time with the preliminaries?

One thing you have to be mindful of is the *Fair Debt Collection Practices Act (FDCPA)*. This federal law has been on the books for some time, and it includes the collection of rent. The primary points of the law that affect those in the apartment rental business are:

- *Direct collection efforts only to the debtor.* Collection techniques in the past have included advising the employer or the parents of a late-paying resident. While this practice often brought quick results, the rights of the particular consumer were probably violated.

- *Announce the purpose of your communications.* The FDCPA dictates that you clearly announce that the purpose of a telephone call or letter is primarily for the purpose of collecting a debt. This allows the debtor the option to continue listening or reading once you have stated your purpose. Most landlord communiqués are very direct, so this provision should not change your typical collection method.

- *Always notify the resident when a post-dated check is cashed.* The way to eliminate this step is to not accept post-dated checks. Most apartment operators insist that all checks carry the current date. In certain situations you may agree to hold the check for a few days before depositing it, but be sure the check carries the date it was written so that it cannot be construed as post-dated.

- *The debtor has a 30-day period in which to disclaim the debt.* This provision is subject to a number of varying interpretations. Some say that landlord-tenant law effectively provides the debtor with an opportunity to object. Others argue that the contractual agreement of an ongoing lease is different from a consumer debt obligation, and that this provision in the law gives a resident an automatic one-month grace period. Apartment managers should be familiar with this law and how it is interpreted locally.

Spotting Trouble.   Some simple rules will help in spotting potential rent collection problems. When the rent exceeds 33 percent of a renter's gross income, pay attention. The risk of having a collection problem increases dramatically with each rent dollar over that 33-percent mark. Another warning signal should go off when the combination of the rent plus monthly installment payments reaches 55 percent of the renter's gross income. When these two situations occur, there will not be enough income to go around, and somebody will come up short—probably the landlord.

Another early sign of trouble is the NSF check that has been returned. When the first check comes back, that is the time for a personal visit. The resident should be asked to replace the NSF check with either cash or a certified check. You should also make it clear that after two NSF checks, all payments will have to be in the form of money orders or cashier's checks.

Penalty Charges.   When residents become delinquent in paying rent, some managers like to impose a late fee or penalty charge. This is a poor practice. First, it implies that rent can be late as long as a late fee is paid. Residents who pay their rent late and accept the penalty may be inclined to assume that they have paid for the privilege of paying as late as the last day of that month. Such a policy bends what should be an inflexible rule—i.e., that *rent is due on the first.* (By accepting late payments, you may waive your right to collect rent on the first and jeopardize your ability to evict a resident for nonpayment.) Second, courts usually do not lend a hand enforcing penalties. However, by calling the late charge a "service charge," you may be able to collect it; but you will be required to demonstrate how your costs increased because a particular renter was late. While this is preferable to a "penalty," you should not regard it as an alternative to prompt payment.

Discounts.   If you insist on providing flexibility in your rent collection policies, consider this suggestion: Increase rents by the amount you would set as a late or service charge, then allow a discount of that same amount on rents paid *before* the first of the month. Your claim will be for the gross rent once the new month begins. This is both acceptable and enforceable. The advantage of using this system is that you are rewarding residents for making their payments *prior to* the start of the month.

Contests.   Some managers institute contests or incentives to entice residents to live up to their commitment to pay rent on the first of each month. This should not be done! When you offer a prize drawing or some other incentive to pay their rent promptly, you are effectively saying that there is a considerable number of residents who are late with their rent. That admission gives support to the late-paying residents and signals to them that they are not alone, which makes the job of collecting rent even more difficult.

Excuses.   When a resident who is behind in paying rent is confronted by management, a variety of excuses will usually be offered. Seldom will you hear the real reason: "I don't have the money." You will often be told about the deficiencies in the apartment with the explanation that payment is being withheld until the defects are corrected. Repairs or improvements should never be traded for rent. If repairs are needed, they should be made in the normal manner, and you can reiterate your standard procedures for requesting such work. The resident is using this ploy to buy time and save face. After a year or two, managers have heard most of the "standard" resident tales and realize that they are merely flimsy excuses.

Payment Plan.   Once residents admit to being short of the money needed to pay the rent, they may try to negotiate a payment plan. This is something else to avoid. The great majority of these plans fail. The very reason residents are behind is because their expenses exceed their income. If this is true, how can they get ahead again? Usually, they report the promise of a Christmas bonus or an expected tax refund. The question is, how many other creditors are waiting for that same check? Also, the problem is not so easily resolved because there will be a new rent charge with the start of the next month. There are businesses whose existence depends on people who need money temporarily. They are called banks and loan companies. Apartment managers are not, nor should they be, in the business of lending money.

Some will argue that it is better to receive a partial payment than to have an empty unit and no rental income. That theory is totally wrong. You are far better advised to enforce your rent collection policies rigidly. A vacant apartment is far superior to one occupied by someone who has not paid for it. At least you have the potential of leasing it to someone who can and will pay the rent on time. If word gets out that you are "soft" about collecting rent, your problems will increase with each passing month. The weaker the market, the stronger your policy on rent collection should be.

Damage Deductions.   Occasionally, a resident may send in the rent minus deductions for so-called damage: The oven is unreliable; the refrigerator broke and $100 worth of food spoiled; the air conditioner did not work and the family slept in a hotel. Unless applicable laws permit such deductions, they should not be allowed. (Some states recognize the tenant's ability to force repairs by putting the rent in escrow—but not withholding payment—until the repairs are made.) Your policies should insist that reimbursements for damage are a separate matter, and rent is always to be paid in full. If you are responsible for a delay in repairing the stove or refrigerator, pay for the damage separately—not as an offset against the rent. Of course, if repairs are made promptly, such situations will not occur often.

Settle in Court.   It is interesting that some residents will not pay their rent even when threatened with eviction notices, subpoenas, a court date in

---

Checkbook Eviction

One of my favorite techniques for dealing with residents who are falling behind is what I call "checkbook eviction." It works like this: I visit the resident and direct the conversation to his or her inability to keep the rent current. Most renters who are behind in their rent explain that they are going through a troublesome period—job loss, extraordinary expenses, debt overload. By my acting somewhat as a counselor, we find agreement that part of the solution will have to involve a less-expensive place to live. I then offer to end the resident's lease, return any deposits, and forgive any current arrearages. I have even agreed to write the resident a check for an amount equaling about a half-month's rent. No money actually changes hands, of course, until the resident is packed up and ready to drive off the property. Over the years, I have come up with some policies that have rattled owners and managers, but nothing compares to the complaints I receive when I explain checkbook evictions.

The argument is that I am often rewarding a deadbeat who will probably leave the apartment in terrible condition. In addition, the tenant will probably tell neighboring residents, and everyone wishing to leave will wait for me to buy them out of their lease obligations. My answer is rather simple. I have a problem and I want it solved. Going through a lengthy and expensive legal process adds to the problem and often puts the tenant in a worse mood, which may prompt even more damage and greater expense to repair the unit. With my method, I regain possession in weeks, not months. As for broadcasting this settlement, I have not experienced even one such incident. The reason is that even those who have hit rock bottom still try and maintain a degree of pride. Even though they know their neighbors realize that all is not well, they are not about to offer any details about their predicament.

---

front of a judge, and the final humiliation of the eviction process. Sometimes even after the judge has ordered their eviction, they will decide that they want to stay and are willing to pay all back rent plus your legal fees and all court costs. You might be tempted to accept, especially if the market is weak and one additional resident can make the difference between profit and loss. The advice of this writer is: "Pass up the offer and let them go." Experience has shown that you can almost guarantee a recurrence within the year. Use your energy to find a renter who will pay, and let some other landlord waste time chasing the chronic delinquent every month.

Gauging Delinquencies.   In the apartment rental business, you will inevitably lose some money due to delinquencies. People lose jobs; the economy can falter; families get into trouble, and you can misjudge applicants. Just how much rent loss is too much? According to the accepted standard, you are within bounds if you have less than one percent of your total monthly rent outstanding at the end of the month. That is not to say that you should accept one percent as a goal. Many managers achieve a 100 percent rate of collection. I am saying that if your total rent roll is $40,000 per month, you might have as much as $400 remaining to be collected. Outstanding rent between one and two percent signals trouble. The problem may be a softening economy and shorter work hours or layoffs, or it could be the result of a softening rental market. When delinquencies go over the two-percent mark at the end of the month, something is clearly wrong and requires your immediate attention.

Throughout this book, many policies and procedures are recommended. Of all of these, the rent collection policy should be the most inflexible. Adhering to this principle can save thousands of dollars each year.

8

*The goal is to keep water
in the pipes and
out of the building.*

Maintaining the Property

The advice in this chapter is critical to a successful operation. A mistake in adopting a certain office policy, the wrong marketing strategy, or even the wrong rent level will not damage the property's performance to the same degree as will poor preparation and maintenance.

Prospects are looking for more than a place to live. They are seeking a home that reflects their lifestyle and role in life—real or imagined. People do not want to make excuses for their apartments, to themselves or to their friends.

These remarks pertain to both existing and new apartment communities. A new property, if it is to command the premium rent necessary to pay its way, must be presented as a finished product. Prospects who visit new properties should not encounter obstacles that can discourage them, such as construction litter, partially completed buildings, lack of landscaping, half-finished parking lots, mounds of earth and mud, and numerous other construction inconveniences. Most new apartment properties are opened prematurely, a fact that causes permanent damage to their economic potential. It is better to wait until the property is ready; the more complete and perfect a new development is when it is opened, the more successful it will be.

The devil is in the details. They make the difference in a prospect's perceptions of your property. Call it nitpicking, but your prospects often have

144

sharper eyes than you do for things that do not look right or are out of place. Likewise, they are probably keenly aware of the added touches that make a building and grounds more appealing.

You gain an added benefit when a development looks crisp; unqualified applicants automatically filter themselves out as they choose to pass right on by. The nicer the apartment community looks, the more qualified your visiting prospects will be.

In existing properties, declining maintenance and service levels are responsible for more move-outs than any other category of complaints. Residents need a constant show of appreciation. The best way to demonstrate appreciation for residents is to provide them with a well-maintained and improving property together with a high level of personalized resident service.

When you analyze successful rental properties, you will discover that they all have something in common: They look superior, inside and out. Professionals refer to this as *curb appeal* or frosting. This means the property offers more than better architecture; it also has superior housekeeping, which is evident from the moment you walk through the front entryway. Now take a look at properties that have vacancies, and you will almost always find they suffer from poor housekeeping. They may have lower rents, more amenities, and better apartments, but their down-at-the-heels appearance drives prospects away.

If your apartment community is going to attract prospects, you have to do a special job of preparing and presenting it. In other words, make it as attractive as possible. This is essential if you are to capture drive-by traffic, by far the largest single source of rental prospects. Imagine two almost identical apartment communities across the street from each other. The apartments and rents are virtually the same. Manager A invests a lot of money in advertising to draw prospects but ignores product preparation. Manager B does no advertising but takes the same amount of money that Manager A spends on advertising and uses it to improve the property. What happens? The prospects come out to see Manager A's property, but, on the way, they notice Manager B's property across the street. They may go in to see Manager A's apartments, but most of them will rent from Manager B. In short, Manager A hands prospects over to Manager B, who captures them with a better-looking product. Besides having more renters, Manager B is better off in three other ways.

1. The better-looking property will attract a better-qualified resident, who will cause less wear and tear, stay longer, and present fewer problems.

2. Improvements made to a property have a long life and multiple advantages. The benefits derived from advertising expenditures are very short-lived and rarely exceed a few days.

3. The better-looking property can command substantially higher rents.

In short, Manager B's apartment community will rent up faster and attract more qualified residents; and Manager B will be able to charge higher rents, have fewer resident problems, be required to do less policing, and have fewer maintenance and record-keeping problems. All of these factors add up to more net operating income (NOI) for the owner and increase the property's value.

Empty apartments result in money lost forever. When an airplane takes off with empty seats, the revenue from those seats can never be recovered. When a month begins with empty apartments, you cannot go back in time and rent those apartments for the previous month. So, everything you can do to see that apartments are rented when the month begins is money in the bank.

Getting Acquainted with Your Property

When you arrive at a new property, there is so much to learn. First there is the lay-of-the-land—the configuration of the buildings, parking, and support and recreational amenities. You need to acquaint yourself with the unit types, sizes, and layouts, plus learn about apartment equipment and appointments. You will have to investigate the type and quality of construction, the design of the mechanical systems, and current maintenance levels. Finally, you must learn, and adapt to, the resident makeup in this particular community.

There are countless details to grasp, and you rarely get much time to come up to speed. I have found that it is usually best to have staff members give you tours of their respective specialties. During these first tours, I suggest not taking notes; just listen carefully. Later, on your own, you can retrace your steps, making a slow and careful inspection tour of the entire property. It may take parts of several days. You should look into every nook and cranny, trying keys to locked spaces. This time you can make some written notes, but for the most part, you should just jot down questions that arise from your tour. This is not the time to go searching for deficiencies or staff weaknesses. You need to quickly learn everything you can about the property, and you certainly do not want the staff to become alarmed, thinking that you intend big changes. You will find that the learning process is much more effective when you go alone. It is also common for new managers to carefully review the office files, paid bills, residents' rent accounts, service requests, and payroll records as part of their orientation process.

Often through a baptism by fire, the new manager learns the ropes and develops a routine. Most daily activities are a form of reaction. If something breaks, management fixes it. When the grass grows, someone mows it. When there is litter on the grounds, a staff member picks it up. When a bulb burns out, maintenance replaces it. As the seasons change, a different set of reactions is applied. What apartment managers are really saying is that, in most cases, the buildings are managing them rather then their managing the buildings.

Documenting Property Assets

What is interesting about the real estate management industry is that managers typically reinvent the same wheel each and every year. The property being managed is a fixed asset with a finite number of components with a very fixed set of life expectancies. The seasons of the year, for the most part, track along in recurring patterns. Little will happen this year that did not occur last year. So, does it not make sense to take the time up front and document everything you can about this fixed asset?

Here is an example: How many square feet or acres of grass do you have? If you know the coverage rate, you can calculate the number of bags of fertilizer needed for each application. Many managers look up last year's invoices or call the vendors hoping their records will provide the answers.

Sitting at your desk, do you know how many light standards are installed in the property's parking lot? What size and type of bulbs are installed? When were bulbs last installed and when can you expect them to require replacement? You have a fixed number of light standards. You only need to count and record them once. Today, bulbs have very predictable lives. If the bulb is rated for 20,000 hours and you keep the lights on from sunset to sunrise, you can monitor the usage and forecast the time for replacement. Depending on your latitude on the globe, these bulbs will begin approaching the end of their useful life after about 3–4 years. It is much more efficient to change all of the bulbs in one operation (a practice known as *group relamping*) than it is to do each one individually. You also save the time needed to constantly check for burned-out bulbs and the inconvenience to your residents as they find their way in the dark. While you have the fixture apart to replace the bulb, the fixture and lens can be cleaned and the standard straightened and painted. As for parking lot light bulbs, you are now free for another three or four years. Every time you can replace a re-action with a pro-action, you increase the number of available hours in your busy workweek.

Let's try another example: Your property has a fixed number of apartment layouts. How many yards of carpeting are needed for each? How do you want the carpet laid? Where should the installer place the carpet seams for best appearance and longest wear? Doesn't it make sense to work with a carpet provider who will help you answer these questions? Shouldn't you record the amount of carpet needed and develop a permanent seaming diagram for each layout? You need the extra effort only once and you are in control of one more component.

The best time to start making records of what you have now and what you will need to know in the future is when the property is brand-new. At that point, you will most likely have the construction drawings available. Some managers are lucky enough to be on site while the construction superintendent is there, and the architect, engineers, and designers are still monitoring the construction process. They will have many of the answers and paperwork that will be invaluable to you later. The manager and maintenance staff of a brand-new apartment community also have more time available than their counterparts who have been assigned older properties. Fewer things break down, and those that do are typically under warranty. This is the perfect time to begin putting together a binder that will hold all of the property's permanent information. Managers of older properties will need several years to complete the task of inventorying components and systematizing recurring maintenance tasks.

To get started, you will need a ring binder and several, letter-size ($8\frac{1}{2} \times 11$-inch) site plans, printed in color. It may also be desirable to have layouts drawn for certain portions of the property or for some installations. (An example of a site plan is shown in Exhibit 8.1, page 150; use of that site plan to document the type of lighting in the parking lot and the procedure for maintaining it is shown in Exhibit 8.2, page 151.) You should plan on making at least three copies of the binder and preferably more. You may also want to use dividers to separate the various subjects. This book will see a lot of use and abuse so it is best to laminate the sheets as they are produced. The addition of color really helps the reader interpret the information.

Building this book into a comprehensive reference manual is going to be a slow, ongoing effort. If you can complete a section each month, you will be making good progress. The idea is to deal with each maintenance task as thoroughly as possible. When a seasonal task comes up, document everything there is to know about that subject. Next year, about the same time, you will begin enjoying the benefits of your effort. When a major job such as reroofing is required, that will be the time to add the Roofing section to your book. You will soon have an invaluable tool for developing and implementing a program for ongoing maintenance of the property, which will be discussed later in this chapter. The following list briefly describes some common property assets and the types of information that should be recorded about them.

- *Flower beds.* Annuals are commonly planted each spring in flower beds spaced throughout the apartment community. Using one of your site plans, indicate the locations of these beds and identify each with its own number. On the same site plan or on an accompanying matrix, detail the degree of sun each area receives: sunny, partial sun, or shady. Some do this by inserting the number of hours of full sun that can be expected. You will also want to record the number and type of plants that you typically allocate to each bed. Record information about what plants have grown well in the past; soil conditions and fertilizer applications are also very helpful.

- *Parking lots.* How many square feet of paved area do you have? How many regular parking spaces? Handicapped spaces? You will want a record of the widths of spaces, the number of wheel stops, drains and water sources, and the resurfacing and re-coating history.

- *Mechanical equipment.* Over a period of time, every piece of mechanical equipment should be located, identified, and inventoried. What equipment is installed and where? Your building engineer or perhaps the original mechanical engineer can help you document and prepare maintenance schedules for this equipment.

  The equipment to be inventoried includes fans, motors, pumps, ventilators, and valves. You should note anything that has moving parts or needs even occasional maintenance. Identify each piece of equipment by name, location, manufacturer, and model number and assign it a code number using a sticker or tag. With the inventory complete, prepare a series of maintenance schedules for your book detailing what is to be done, when, and by whom. This is an onerous and slow-moving task, but you will have to do it only once.

- *Underground utilities.* You need to know where the utilities and cabling enter the property, their routing through the property, approximate depths, and terminals and shutoffs. Take one of your site plans and mark it with this information.

- *Water supply and sewer lines.* Where does the water enter the property? What size is the piping? How does it branch to the various buildings? Where are the roundway valves to turn off the water and where is the wrench stored and what is its size? Your site plan should detail the flow of waste water, the location of cleanouts and catch basins, and the direction of flow of the storm sewers.

- *Snow and ice control.* Indicate on your site plan where you want the snowplows to push the snow. What areas have a higher priority? How much ice-melting compound or salt is needed for a typical winter?

- *Swimming pool opening and closing.* What is the pool's water capacity? Time to fill? Time to heat? You will need step-by-step details of what needs to be done to have the pool up and going and what is required at the end of the season to close it down. Also needed are the details on the piping system, pumps, filters, and controls and wiring. It is also important to know the size of the deck area, its finish, the pool's shell finish, and sources for coatings, tiles, and water-treatment chemicals.

Exhibit 8.1

Example Site Plan for Recording Property Asset Information

Construction started 1998; 1st occupancies 1999.

Buildings: 82,800 sf; Paved: 88,000 sf; Planted: 147,200 sf

7.3 acres = 318,000 sf = 8.77 density/acre

Bldgs	Units	Type	Size
7	28	1BR, 1B	870 sf
9	36	2BR, 2B	1,072 sf
16	64		

98 parking spaces; clubhouse; pool

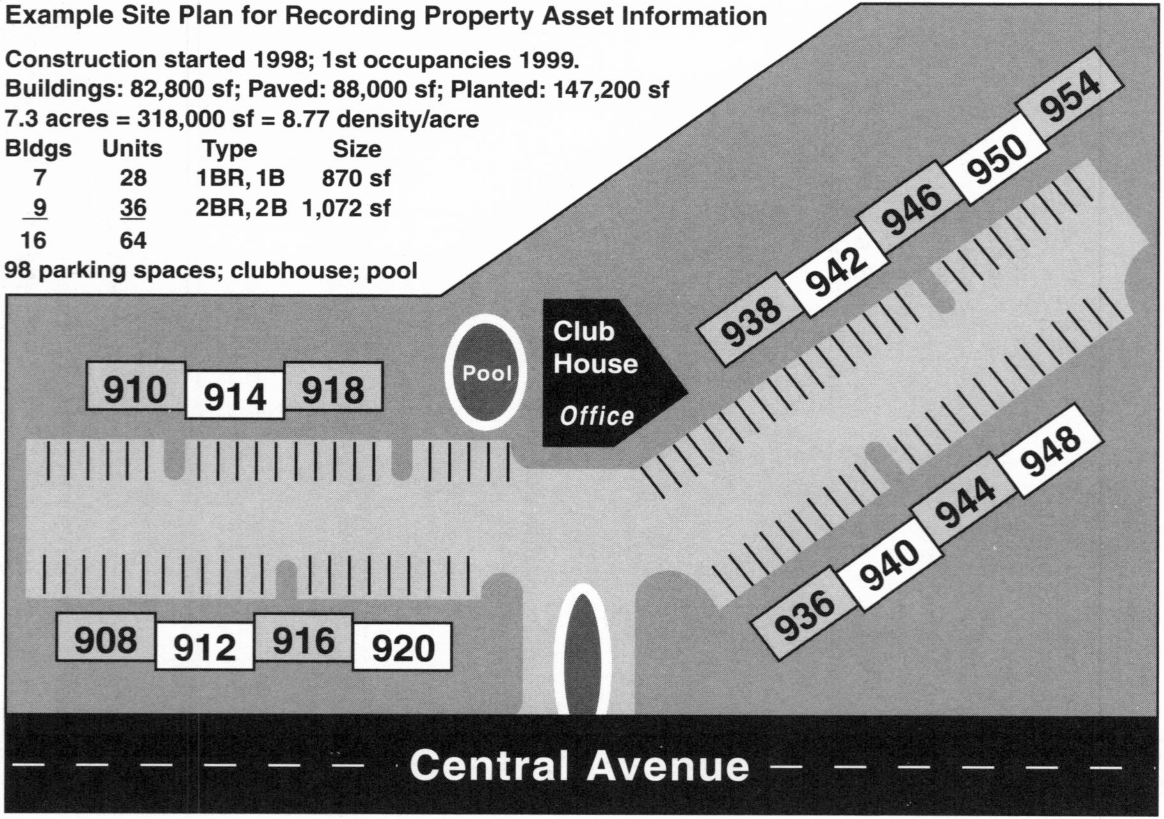

954 950 946 942 938

948 944 940 936

Club House

Office

Pool

910 914 918

908 912 916 920

Central Avenue

Exhibit 8.2
Example Site Plan Including Site Lighting

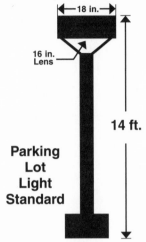

Bulb Life: 20,000 hours
Annual Usage: 4,500 hours
Replacement: Every 4 years
Ballast Life: 10–12 years
Tools: 10 ft <u>step</u> ladder, Phillips screwdriver,
      glass cleaner, cleaning rags.
Staff: 1 person   Skill Level: 4
Time: 20 min/light; 30 min/light + ballast

9 Light Standards on 14-ft 3-in. Poles
Mfr & Model: Hubbel Tube-post, Top-light
Single 250-Watt High-Pressure Sodium Lamp
180° Refractor except #7 & #8, 360°
16-in. Square Lens
Photocell to 2-Pole Contactor
Circuit Breaker: #12 (Clubhouse)

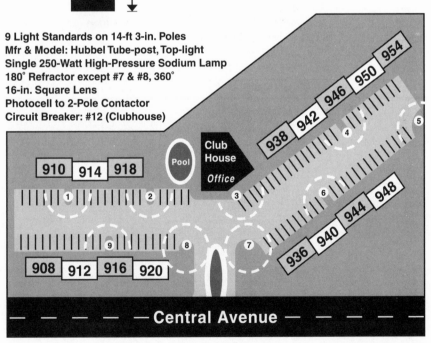

- *Lighting*. This is often broken down into two sections: site lighting and exterior building lights. You should locate this lighting on the map with information about the manufacturer, model number, source, bulbs and ballasts, power requirements, and standards or mounts. (See the example in Exhibit 8.2.)

- *Roofing*. How many roofs? How many *squares* (100 square feet) in each? What is the type and composition of the roofing materials? What type of insulation was used? What is the history of these roofs? First installation? Re-roofing schedule?

In addition, most properties will require sections dealing with locks, plumbing fixtures, windows, hardware, siding/stucco, etc. The idea is to compile every bit of technical data and other information about a particular subject. Squeeze it onto one or both sides of a piece of card stock. This should be your one-stop source of information.

Conducting a Maintenance Inspection

This section will walk you through an imaginary property, pointing out possible maintenance concerns and offering suggestions for dealing with them. Apart from the practical aspects of maintenance, many of the property's components are also important to its curb appeal.

Landscaping. While the building's architecture plays a definite role, a property's landscaping is certainly a major ingredient in creating a favorable or unfavorable first impression. The good news is that, even operating with a tight budget, a manager can have a considerable effect on landscaping.

The best advice is to find the money to commission a landscape architect to prepare an overall scheme. The architect should have experience with rental apartments as opposed to single-family homes, and it should be understood from the start that the plan will be implemented over a period of years as money becomes available. A good architect will typically specify plants that are too small when purchased but in time will grow to the right size. While this is correct, an apartment manager is probably looking for a quick, lush look. You are better served with a few large-sized plants than a number of immature plantings. Ideally, you can budget additional funds on a yearly basis to enhance different areas of the property with major plantings. Here are some landscaping pointers to keep in mind:

- *Don't rely largely on grass to cover acreage*. Grass needs mowing and constant maintenance and can look drab in the slow-growing or dormant seasons. Break up the monotony with beds of plants and clumps of trees. Establishing tiny forests, where there is space to accommodate them, often allows you to use wild plants rather than nursery-grown ones. This way you get plenty of impact for fewer dollars. These forest areas also serve as visual breaks, something that is highly coveted by today's renters.

- *Flower beds or perimeter plantings should be tilled and edged regularly to give the richest appearance.* Ground cover looks good for a few weeks, but it tends to look neglected as the summer progresses. However, this treatment may be essential in areas with very hot summer temperatures because the ground cover helps to cool the earth and hold more moisture.

- *Strive for a pleasing color effect all year.* Use evergreens in addition to trees and plants with gray, yellow, brown, and red coloring.

- *Use concentrated flower beds for accents.* Perennials, including flowering bulbs, provide a welcome note of color at the end of a dreary winter when color is most needed. One note of caution about tulip bulbs: They bloom later and have a more limited life span than other flowering bulbs such as daffodils, leaving you with flowerless plants for an important period in the spring when you would prefer to have annuals in bloom. Many parks and large shopping centers get around this problem by digging up their tulips each year. There is another reason for doing this: Tulips tend to come up crooked in subsequent years, so it is best if they are replanted every fall. The optimal plan would be to keep the flowering bulbs in their own separate flower beds. This way you avoid disturbing the other plants.

- *Plant flowers in masses using lots of the same color.* This maximizes the visual impact. Mixing flowers and colors is a nice treatment in the back yard of a home; but in a rental community, the best results are obtained with large groups of the same flower.

- *Avoid using boulders unnaturally.* Too many owners and managers use boulders as a form of traffic control. Some people coat them with bright white, luminous paint so they can be seen at night. If you need curbs to control cars, then add curbs, not boulders. For a different reason, avoid using stones and gravel as a ground cover. Gravel is dangerous underfoot and to bicyclers, especially when it spreads to your paved surfaces. Also, children will often find egg-size stones tempting ammunition to use against light fixtures and windows.

- *Allow residents to use direct routes.* Universities learned long ago that it is foolish to try to dictate how a person will approach a building or facility. They watch the wear patterns that soon become evident and then construct the walks to accommodate the traffic. Planting bushes and adding barricades rarely blocks shortcuts, and such things end up frustrating the manager. Walks should always be for the convenience of the person using the building or facility.

- *Landscaping and playgrounds do not mix.* Try sand or shredded bark for the playground area. From a safety standpoint, you probably should explore interlocking rubber mats that are made for this purpose.

- *Plan landscaping for easy maintenance.* Lay out lawns, berms, tree clumps, shrubbery, and flower beds so that machines can be used rather than costly hand labor. Avoid narrow strips of grass along buildings and walls, as these usually require hand trimming and special attention.

- *Use water to advantage.* Running or moving water is not only an effective way to deaden obtrusive noise, but also one of the most relaxing sounds. Fountains, decorative pools, streams, and even water from lawn sprinklers help create a quiet and peaceful environment. Utilizing lawn sprinklers in highly visible areas on weekends and other high-traffic periods will pay multiple dividends. Lawns will look greener and fresher, sidewalks and paved surfaces are more attractive when they are wet, and the property will appear cooler. In addition, sprinkling clearly demonstrates that the property is being maintained for the enjoyment of its residents. This, of course, presumes there are no restrictions on water use.

If your budget is too limited for an immediate major improvement, the landscaping can be enhanced gradually. You should also set aside some sort of regular budget to pay for seeds, fertilizers, and replacements for dead or damaged plants. Even with a minimal budget, you can try to maximize the appearance of your landscaping with careful maintenance.

There are few owners who can afford to invest large amounts of capital to make dramatic improvements to an existing rental community's landscape plan. The secret is to have an overall plan and to spend available funds slowly and steadily. You should choose an area to start with and concentrate your efforts until you achieve your intended look. Then, you can expand by shifting your attention to a section immediately adjacent to the finished area. My advice would be: Don't skip around and don't dilute your money or effort by trying to treat too large an area. There will be tomorrow, next month, and next year. Steady progress and an ever-increasing level of quality determine success.

Paved Areas.   Paved areas usually account for the second largest amount of ground coverage. What prospects see and feel provides them with another clue to the level of quality your property offers. Driveways and parking areas should be as smooth as possible. Potholes and puddles caused by poor drainage are discouraging and may make the prospect turn around and leave.

The condition of paved surfaces is often determined when the project is built. The paving may have been inadequate in the first place. The base of gravel may be too thin, or perhaps it was not allowed to settle before the asphalt was applied. Overloaded trucks may have broken down the surface in spots.

Whatever the situation, your job as manager is to do the best possible job of restoring the surface and keeping it in good condition. The site maintenance personnel should be instructed to handle minor patching as the need arises. Inserting hot asphalt materials into a pothole is far superior to using cold materials. Most patches do not last very long and are unsightly because a vertical edge was not cut prior to filling the patch. You will get a better result if you have the maintenance worker use a circular saw with a special blade to cut a square or vertical edge in a rectangular pattern around the hole, remove all materials to a depth of at least four inches, and then pack in the new materials. The patch should be rolled or tamped until it is even with the adjoining surfaces.

As the surface develops cracks, the cracks should be routed and then filled with a hot sealing compound. This work is expensive; but when done correctly and in a timely fashion, it will add many years to the life of an asphalt surface. For help in matters such as these, you can look to your fellow apartment managers or managers of large facilities who deal with this particular problem regularly.

If the surface is worn but still usable, perhaps it should be resealed with a film of liquid driveway coating. When you do this, you will need to alert residents and arrange for cars to be moved so that the coating truck has proper access. Also, *seal coating* can be a messy procedure; people will pick up some puddled coating material on their shoes and track it onto sidewalks and into buildings. For paved surfaces that are beyond surface treatment, a new layer of asphalt (a *lift*) can be applied. This is an expensive process, but it should produce a paved surface that will serve for at least five years.

What does the prospect see first upon driving into the parking lot? Bright parking stripes can make a world of difference; these stripes and any fire lane indications should always look bright and fresh. Concrete *wheel stops* are needed to keep cars in orderly rows and prevent them from running onto lawns. Half-size concrete stops that are intended to halt only one wheel should not be used because a car can miss the stop and run onto the lawn. If snow covers the half-stop, a small plow may miss it entirely and destroy the lawn. You should also stay away from asphalt wheel stops. While these are less expensive than concrete, they deteriorate rapidly and can be gouged by snowplows. Often they have rounded edges that permit car wheels to ride over them. Concrete curbing around the parking lot is no substitute for wheel stops. Without stops, a car's front end, and especially its rear end, can hang over and block the sidewalk. This is annoying to visitors and residents.

Outdoor Lighting.   Lighting provides safety. It is also used to accent and beautify. Lighting standards and fixtures rarely receive any maintenance other than the changing of bulbs or gas mantles. Typical eyesores are parking lot standards that are dented, knocked askew, or broken off altogether. Light poles along sidewalks, set in loose earth or with light concrete ballast, may be leaning over. Fixtures on buildings may be twisted. The glass in many lighting fixtures may be dirty, broken, missing, or filled with insects. If any of these conditions applies to your property, you should correct it. If lights near parking lots are being knocked down repeatedly by cars, guard posts should be installed or the lights should be moved.

Lighting can be attractive as well as functional if it is located properly and maintained well. Landscape lighting, for example, with Bollard fixtures and spotlights around plants and pools can create a pleasant aura. This lighting must be maintained; to reduce breakage problems, plastic panels and globes can be used instead of glass. The plastic costs more initially, but it lasts longer and requires less maintenance.

Parking lots require minimum levels of "moon-bright" illumination. Residents may want the light to be brighter for safety reasons, but it need not be increased to a shopping center level. The higher level will only make your lot look commercial, and safety is not likely to be improved.

Many exterior lighting fixtures are controlled automatically by a timer or a central photoelectric cell. *Photo cells* generally are more practical because they respond to darkness regardless of the time of day or season of the year, as long as they are shielded from the lights they are controlling.

Timers will probably remain the primary method of controlling exterior lighting. This means that clocks must be checked on a regular schedule. It is a basic industry standard to check and adjust timer clocks every other Monday in a pattern that includes the Mondays following the changes to and from daylight saving time. Obviously, your staff must be alert to periodic power outages that will require resetting your timers.

Rubbish and Recycling.   Rubbish handling used to be a pretty straightforward task: The residents generated it, and management contracted to have it hauled away. It is no longer quite that easy. Different items have to be handled differently. Many municipalities insist that trash must be categorized and recycled by type. This adds a whole new dimension to a daily chore. Special containers are needed, and different pickup schedules are common.

Many municipalities contract with one or more firms and determine which ones will be licensed to handle what type of debris. There are many municipal arrangements that make no differentiation in cost between wastes from single-family homes and rental apartments even though homes generate considerably more items for disposal.

Trash receptacles and Dumpsters are typically dirty, streaked with garbage drippings, and dented by the trucks that service them. Some managers put the Dumpsters inside fenced enclosures that are subsequently damaged by the garbage trucks as well as from shifting of the Dumpsters in and out. To try to prevent residents from simply tossing garbage into Dumpsters, a manager may install a wire fence that extends above the enclosure. This rarely stops the problem; and if the garbage hits the wire fence and scatters, the situation is even worse.

There are other problems associated with Dumpsters and enclosures. A manager could install a gate to keep refuse from blowing out, but residents who come to the enclosure laden with two bags of garbage will not appreciate the gate. Neither will the collection crew, who may refuse to make a pickup unless a member of the on-site staff opens the gate and sets the Dumpsters out in the open. A tight enclosure that is closed all the way to the ground will keep refuse inside, but if a resident confronts a scavenging animal, the consequences could be serious. It is better to have an opening at the bottom of the enclosure so animals can escape. Economy or convenience may lead a manager to opt for a large Dumpster. However, a large Dumpster can be a death trap for a child. Furthermore, a large Dumpster requires a large truck to pick it up, and the truck is apt to damage the paved surface.

Whatever size Dumpster you choose, it should be pressure-washed and painted inside and out on a very frequent schedule. The Dumpster should be placed on a concrete pad that is located away from high-traffic areas and general view.

Adding plantings around the Dumpster enclosure may seem like a nice idea, but it only invites other problems. The plants almost certainly will be broken, and they will catch windblown papers. It is much more important to have on-site personnel police the Dumpster area three or four times a day. Dumpsters are never attractive, but people will tolerate them if they are neat.

Directories, Intercoms, and Mailboxes.   While visitors use and depend on directories and intercoms, the building's residents visit their mailbox areas almost daily. Directories need to be current and uniform, with residents' names in alphabetical order. Some managers prefer to set up directories by using a number-code system. A visitor must run down the row of numbers searching for the right party. The code number is linked to the resident's apartment, usually by telephone. This eliminates the task of re-alphabetizing every time there is a change in residents. The problem is that most visitors know whom they are coming to see, and it is a lot more convenient to locate them by an alphabetized name listing. Computer programs control the newer intercom systems, and the reordering of the residents' names is done automatically.

Mailbox faces get dirty with use, residents' nameplates get lost, and hard-to-remove stickers are applied, setting up one more maintenance chore. Only items officially sent through the mail can legally be inserted in mailboxes. This means that handbills will be dumped near the mailboxes. You are not going to have much success eliminating the handbill nuisance, but you can provide a special box, rack, or shelf where handbills can be placed.

It is a good idea, too, to have a waste receptacle and a shelf near your mailboxes. Residents will find the shelf handy when sorting their mail, and the waste receptacle will be convenient for disposing of junk mail. These areas require daily policing.

Entryways, Lobbies, and Corridors.   Properties with a central entrance point require a very high level of maintenance attention. The use factor of doors, locks, floor coverings, furnishings, and elevators in a 100-unit building is often a hundred times that of a garden apartment community whose units are accessed through an open breezeway. The wear and tear on these building components is enormous, and it increases the need for constant maintenance attention.

Just keeping the lobby glass clean becomes a daily chore. Mirrors, a favorite with decorators, are a chronic maintenance problem. Daily spot cleaning and vacuuming is standard practice.

Furnishings, Plants, and Artwork.   Smaller buildings rarely have lobbies spacious enough to accommodate furnishings, but they are more or less standard in the lobbies of larger rental buildings. Furnishings should be built-in or permanently fastened to a wall or the floor to prevent theft. To discourage lounging, chairs are sometimes backless. Contrary to what you might think, furniture should not be arranged in conversational groupings. Lobby seating is installed primarily to provide a homey atmosphere and a place for people to sit while waiting for a ride or a taxi. What you do not want is a regular group of residents arriving, en masse, for their daily visit. A meeting or card room will serve nicely for resident get-togethers.

Plants can add decorative interest along with paintings and sculptures. Like furnishings, however, these decorative items need to be fastened to the floor or a wall to prevent theft.

Elevator Cabs.   Because of close quarters and concentrated use, elevators suffer more wear and tear than almost any other building component. The numbers on the call buttons, especially the lobby level button, quickly show wear. Inspection certificates may be stolen, gum wrappers are often stuck into openings in the walls and ceiling, and graffiti mysteriously appear on the walls. The carpet or other floor covering gets intensive wear.

The elevator shaft acts as a flue, and a layer of dust will build up on the edges of the elevator doors and the outer frames on each floor. If there is no separate freight elevator in the building, passenger elevators have to be used for moving. Many managers hang protective pads in passenger elevator cabs when people move furniture in and out. However, the pads should be taken down when the moving is over, or they are likely to disappear.

Floor Mats.   Well-managed buildings will have runners or mats that are put out during inclement weather, especially in regions that experience periods of ice and snow. A small rectangular mat is better than nothing, but it will do little to protect corridor carpeting. To be effective, the mat or runner has to be about 12 feet long because it takes at least three full strides for shoes or boots to begin drying. These mats also serve a safety function on hard surfaces such as quarry tile, marble, or granite, which can be slippery when wet. Mats should be used only during inclement weather; this means the mats must be picked up and stored when the weather is dry.

Doorway mats may be acceptable outside of apartment doors in buildings with direct entrances to the units or those constructed with breezeways, but they should not be permitted in buildings with inside corridors. The same is true for boxes that might be used for storing boots, rubbers, and umbrellas.

Floor Coverings.   The selection of floor-covering materials involves striking a balance between sustaining a sense of the practical and creating a soft, warm feeling. The front of a single-entry building has the heaviest traffic, so the entry's floor-covering material must be chosen to accommodate this extra wear. As residents and visitors go in different directions inside the building, use and wear diminishes, and softer materials can be introduced.

The use of different materials should be limited: Two are okay, but you should not be able to see three different floor treatments from any vantage point.

Carpet is the standard choice for most residential applications. Carpet is soft underfoot and helps absorb sounds and reduce the glare of lights. Patterns work well in corridors, and the color tone should be a medium value; usually a tight, cut pile gives the best wear. Designers recommend that a contrasting carpet color be used in high-wear areas such as the lobby, the area in front of elevators, or on the floor of the elevator cabs. The carpeting in these areas will require replacement much more often than the materials installed in less-used space. Using a contrasting carpet eliminates the problem of trying to match new to old using the same pattern.

Stair carpeting receives heavy use, especially where the carpet passes over the nosing of the tread. One way to extend the life of stair carpeting is to have the carpet installer leave enough material at the top of each flight of stairs to allow you to shift the carpet down the length of one stair riser. This moves the worn portion into the crevice between step and riser where it cannot be seen easily, thereby doubling the life of the carpet. Stair pads that fit over the nosing of the tread underneath the carpeting are another way to extend carpet life.

The building may have a breezeway or outdoor stairs that you may be tempted to cover with indoor-outdoor carpeting. This material looks fine when first installed but quickly loses its appearance because of weathering, stains, and spills. It is better to leave outdoor stairs and landings in their natural condition or use a heavy-duty formed stair tread.

Indoor Lighting.   Lighting equipment and its efficiency are improving all the time. If the property you are managing is not new, there are probably many innovations you can implement to improve its appearance or energy usage. Bulbs using only 5 or 7 watts of power can produce the light level of those that once consumed 60 watts. Bulbs that will last for 20,000 hours are commonly available, and bulbs with an even longer life span can be expected in the future.

Managers should take the necessary time to study their lighting schemes and search for ways to take advantage of the new light systems that are available. Many apartment communities do not have the funds to change all their lights, but most can afford to schedule replacements in a breezeway or on one floor every other month.

The most important lighting to change is that which would improve building appearance because this has an impact on marketability. The next most important are lights that burn continually because the payback will be the greatest for these. Stairwells, corridors, and basements are among them. Then, work your way to the lighting that is used only a few hours each day. If lights are used in areas that have little or no activity, consider special heat detectors that will quickly turn the light on when they sense the body heat of a human. When the activity passes, there is a period of delay, and the lights then turn off automatically.

Apartment building corridors tend to be either too bright or so dark that visitors have difficulty finding their way. I recommend investing in a light meter and establishing consistent light levels that you find satisfactory.

Exits and Exit Signs.   Some avenues of exit, particularly emergency exits, do not get much use or attention on an everyday basis, but they have a critically important function. Regular inspection patrols must confirm that all of a building's exit pathways are not blocked or constricted in any way. Exit door hardware must work correctly and in no case can these doors be locked or made inoperative. Emergency, battery-pack lighting must also be regularly checked and serviced. These are building areas which do not cry out for attention, but they have a life and death role to play.

Virtually all fire and building codes require lighted, directional exit signs in apartment building corridors and passages. If your exit signs have incandescent bulbs, replace them with long-life fluorescent bulbs. This will minimize bulb burnouts, saving much time and money. Lenses have a way of disappearing from hallway exit signs. There is often a problem of finding a replacement size and style that matches the others. It is best to maintain a supply of replacement lenses for use when needed.

Fire Extinguishers and Hoses.   In the days when water and soda-acid fire extinguishers were common, they were seldom stolen because of their weight and bulky size. The modern, compact, pressurized ABC-type extinguishers can be used in home, car, and boat, and that is why they vanish so quickly from apartment buildings.

Some local ordinances will permit you to place an extinguisher in a cabinet behind a glass door; this discourages theft. Extinguishers that are simply hung on the wall may be stolen and then must be replaced. I have found it a good idea to place each fire extinguisher in a wall recess; this avoids the creation of "shoulder busters" in the hallways. If you follow this advice, make sure each wall recess is kept free of the litter that is almost certain to accumulate.

Fire hoses in corridors or stairwells should be checked to make sure they are hung neatly. Like extinguishers, the brass nozzles on hoses are quickly stolen. Generally, you will be allowed to fit the hoses with replacement nozzles made of plastic.

Odor.   When discussing property maintenance, one cannot ignore the very sensitive subject of odor. Smell (the olfactory sense) is the most easily fatigued of all the senses. This means it is very easy for the apartment manager and the staff to become accustomed to unpleasant odors and, before long, not notice them. However, prospects and residents who notice bad smells are certain to remember them.

Mildew is one of the most common odors, especially in humid areas. The odor from backed-up sewers is another annoyance. These odors are especially common in inexpensively built garden apartments with poor sewer systems and leaky construction. Cooking odors are also prevalent, especially in buildings with kitchens that back up to the corridor walls.

Many corridor odors can be removed by opening exterior doors periodically to air out corridors. If necessary, a window fan can be set in the doorway to speed up the process. If bad odors are a chronic problem, you should consider installing a ventilation system in each corridor. Deodorants should be avoided; they add an odor of their own, which is a sure sign to prospects that you are covering up something.

In a permanently enclosed hall, the easiest way to deal with odors is to install permanent exhaust fans. This advice is not always so easily applied. In a building with pressurized halls, for example, exhaust fans would defeat the purpose of the system. You are best advised to consult a ventilation expert on these matters.

The best approach is to attack the source of the odor if you can. Poorly designed sewer systems should be fixed. Seepage around windows and doors should be diverted. Eaves and overhangs should be vented to provide a constant flow of air.

The odors caused by fire and decay need special treatment. Local exterminators can usually apply foam that will absorb the odor in a few days. The smell caused by water-soaked carpet padding can only be corrected by removing and replacing the padding.

The Apartment

If you have skipped over everything else in getting your product ready, the one place you should never neglect is the apartment you are going to show the prospect. It should be absolutely perfect.

> Picture this: The manager opens the door to show an apartment to a prospect and immediately steps on a stack of literature that has been slipped under the door during the past few days or weeks. The apartment itself is musty, dirty, and either overheated or chilly. The carpet is stained, and the walls are full of holes and marked with dirt where pictures have hung. In the kitchen, the refrigerator has food stains, the stove is encrusted with baked-on debris, the sink shows rust streaks, and powdered insect poison is spread in the cabinets. The bathroom has a tub with dead spiders, a dried-up toilet bowl, and a medicine cabinet with rust stains and a de-silvered mirror. To top it all off, bulbs are missing from the light fixtures or the power is off, so the manager has to show the apartment by flashlight.

This may sound like an exaggeration, but a good many of these conditions are present in many vacant apartments that are being shown. The standard response of the leasing agent is: "We'll fix it before you move in."

This approach seldom works. Prospects judge by first impressions. You can never get the maximum rent for an inferior product. If you ask for and obtain the rent you want for a product that is not in its best shape, then you automatically know you could have received more if the product had been in perfect condition. Prospects respond on the basis of what they see, not on what you promise, and they will predict future service accordingly.

If you do not accept this argument, then ask yourself, "What kind of person will move into an apartment that is not first-rate?" People, changing apartments, generally want to move up in quality and status. If a filthy apartment means moving up, just how bad is the prospect's current apartment? Do you want this kind of person in your building?

Market Ready Means Market Ready

This is the rule: When there is no further reason to enter the apartment to make any improvements, when the apartment is absolutely market-ready, then, and only then, should you show it. More prospects will be lost through violation of this rule than for any other reason.

It is vitally important to make the apartment as perfect as possible before you show it. If you do this, you will get higher rents and attract more-qualified residents. What is more, your property will be ahead of most of its competition. In addition, the closer to perfection your apartment is, the more confident you will be when you ask for the maximum rent.

The rule is: When there is no further reason to enter the apartment to make any improvement, when it is absolutely market-ready, then, and only then, should you show it.

Market-Ready Checklist. There is no need to have all of your vacant apartments ready for showing at the same time. Instead, have an assortment of every type and kind of apartment in what can be called *market-ready condition.* The number of apartments that must be kept in this condition depends on the pace of the market at any particular time and the variety of apartment sizes and floor plans. As a guide, here is a list of twelve items that should be checked to make sure an apartment is market-ready:

1. The apartment power must be on.
2. All walls and ceilings should be freshly painted. Don't overlook closets or shelving.
3. Carpeting should be freshly cleaned. If there are any stains or burns, remove them; otherwise, the carpeting should be replaced.
4. All windows should be washed, both inside and out.
5. Windowsills, the tops of double-hung sashes, ledges, shelves, and all other horizontal surfaces should be wiped clean of dirt and dead insects.
6. Light fixtures and switches should be in working order. Fixtures should be clean, and there should be no dead insects inside the globes.
7. Ceiling fans should be carefully cleaned and free of dust and fuzz.
8. The temperature should be set slightly below what would be appropriate for the season. On moderate days, open the windows to air out the apartment.
9. People pay attention to the condition of faucets and shower heads. After all, these are the source of their drinking and bath water. If

the spout and handles are encrusted with scum or the finishes are pitted and worn, they will certainly contribute to a poor image and slow rentals. These components should look shiny, bright, and new.

10. The kitchen should be immaculate, with all appliances clean and in working order. Make sure the refrigerator and all of its compartments are spotless. Cabinets must be clean and fresh. Pay particular attention to the cabinet under the sink, which can get pretty ugly over time. There should be no stains in the sink.

11. Bathrooms should be spotless. No dripping faucets, stained tubs, or stained and dirty toilets. Don't use epoxy patches to fix chips in enameled sinks and tubs. They never match the color, and they suggest the apartment has had some hard use. Replace the sink bowl and have the tub professionally refinished. The medicine cabinet should look new. If not, replace it; the cost is minor. Tub and tile grout should be tight and clean.

12. Watch out for the typical apartment "starter kit" (i.e., a few clothes hangers in the closet, used bars of soap in the bathroom, and a few sheets of toilet paper left on the roll). Get rid of these.

To help you prepare the apartment, you should make a *market-ready check-list* of all items that need to be inspected. This checklist can be printed on a card that the manager personally signs and posts in the apartment in a prominent position, testifying to its first-rate condition. The card should not be dated; you would not want a prospect who comes in February to see a card dated the previous November.

The supervisor should check to see that only the manager's signature is on the market-ready inspection card and that the card is never placed in an apartment that is not ready to be shown. Following this procedure is critical because it forces the manager to inspect each apartment carefully.

Daily inspection of the market-ready apartments is essential to make sure they stay in top shape until they are rented. Every day, before the start of business, the manager should personally inspect the apartments. The procedure accomplishes several things:

- To visit the apartment, the manager must first obtain the key. This ensures that the key is available. It is surprising how often the key is missing when the manager or leasing agent wants to show an apartment to a prospect.

- Daily inspection lessens the chance of showing an apartment that is not ready.

- Daily inspection also reveals problems that may have developed since the last inspection, such as leaflets slipped under the door, a dead insect that fell into the sink, or a window leak that has stained the carpet.

- The manager is reminded to check the function of lights in the apartment and adjust the heating or cooling.
- Finally, this procedure compels the manager to walk the property, during which time he or she may discover other things that need attention.

In summary, getting an apartment ready means inspecting it to make sure it is in the best condition, and then doing a daily follow-up to make sure it remains an apartment that can be shown to prospects.

Window Coverings.   Draperies, blinds, and other window coverings merit special consideration as part of product preparation.

Draperies are frequently included in suburban garden apartments as a marketing aid. Some city apartments provide them, too. Uniform drapes can give the building a neater appearance from the outside. Residents whose budgets for furnishings are limited also appreciate drapes.

However, drapes can present a problem. Generally, the drapes that come with an apartment are not of the highest quality, and after a while they do not hang properly. Discerning residents realize this and prefer their own drapes. Prospects may even resist renting an apartment because drapes are included; this is an example of negative marketing.

Meanwhile, transient residents who like drapes sometimes neglect them. They may leave windows open, exposing the drapes to dirt, soot, and rain. As a result, the drapes need cleaning too often, certainly every time there is a change in tenancy. Because the drapes are usually poor quality to begin with, they seldom last more than a few years.

Nor do drapes accomplish the uniform outside appearance that many managers want to achieve. Even with drapes, some residents will place aluminum foil against the windows to keep out heat in the summer, and others will put up newspapers, especially on bedroom windows, to make the room darker. In many garden apartment communities, the drapes cannot be seen from the outside because balconies interfere with the view. So the effect on external appearance is negligible.

Vertical blinds are becoming the renters' favorite over the older, horizontal mini-blinds. Vertical blinds, which are often made of a more pliable material, seem to take abuse better. They have a neat and uniform appearance and allow light and ventilation while, at the same time, preserving the resident's privacy. Blinds also divert direct sunlight; this helps hide many imperfections and indentations in the finished walls.

Floor Coverings.   In many rental communities, wall-to-wall carpeting is standard in all living areas (living room, dining room, bedrooms, and hall).

Carpeting is an excellent sound absorber and buffer but only if it is installed wall-to-wall. Some apartments are finished with hardwood or tiled floors, and managers may require residents to install their own carpeting on at least 80 percent of the floor area. This requirement is hard to enforce, and the practice does not adequately reduce noise caused by vibration and furniture being moved.

Carpet styles change with fashion trends, so what is "in" today will probably be "out" tomorrow. Durable sculptured patterns were replaced by shag carpeting. Subsequently, shag carpeting was replaced by "splush" pile, which was replaced by cut pile, and so on. Carpet manufacturers will continue to come up with other new looks. Buying high-priced, long-wearing carpeting for apartments is a mistake; it will show wear patterns and is just as likely as lower-grade carpeting to suffer from stains, burns, and spills. A reasonable life for carpet is five years and rarely more than six.

Many carpet experts say that a manager is better advised to consider using a high grade of carpet padding (say 80-lb. weight) and then cover it with a rather lower grade of carpeting. The denser, more-resilient pad delivers the "cushy" feel of an expensive carpet. When the carpet warrants replacement, new carpeting can be laid over the more-durable, high-quality pad that is already in place.

Carpeting should be cleaned with every resident change and no less often than every two or three years.

Carpeting that is badly stained but not worn, can often be dyed. Expect costs to be about one-half the price of replacing the carpet. You may want to call in a carpet expert before making this decision. Dyeing should be done with the carpet in place. If the carpet has to be taken to a plant, it will undoubtedly shrink. Also, picking up and reinstalling the carpet will add to the total cost, reducing the savings difference. If you have the carpet dyed, the dye may get onto the walls and baseboard woodwork, making repainting necessary. You should also be aware that dyed carpeting will occasionally change color when exposed to sunlight, and the new hues can be undesirable.

A funny, yet not so funny, consequence of dyeing carpet sometimes shows up on the pool deck. Residents whose carpet was recently dyed can often be identified by the stains on the soles of their bare feet when they are sitting in deck chairs.

Less common than carpeting, tiles are an alternative in buildings with concrete floors. Some buildings provide asphalt or vinyl tile as standard; others may have resilient sheet flooring. Hardwood flooring is common in many older buildings and may also be installed in some newer, wood-frame buildings. Oak or ash flooring is expensive to buy and install. Although attractive initially, it can show scratches and stains and must be sanded and varnished to remove these mars. Each sanding removes roughly $\frac{1}{32}$-inch of hardwood floor surface; eventually the flooring nails are exposed, at which point no more sanding is possible. During the life of a hardwood floor, you can expect to be able to sand four or five times. Admittedly, a hardwood floor that has been used carefully by residents can last for years, but carpet is generally a better choice when you compare the cost with that of sanding and eventually replacing hardwood floors.

Ongoing Maintenance of the Property

The sections that follow outline a program of planned maintenance that can be used to avoid a continuing stream of crises and keep your property looking as sharp as possible. You will discover that planned maintenance can be done with fewer people, and this inevitably leads to lower operating and maintenance costs.

Maintenance and Equipment Rooms.   If you are ever asked to judge the caliber of the maintenance in a particular rental community and your time is limited to just a few minutes, you should ask to see the maintenance and equipment rooms. They will reveal the level of organization and cleanliness in the property. A messy, poorly organized maintenance shop is almost always indicative of the condition of the property's equipment. When there is a chaotic accumulation of questionably useful things, there is little hope of ever locating a specific item when it is needed. Also, this practice can create a fire hazard.

Bins and shelving are certainly affordable items, and there is no excuse for not having a specific place for all of the property's tools, equipment, supplies, and replacement parts. The time and money spent setting up a proper maintenance operation will pay dividends for years to come.

Warranties.   In setting up a maintenance program, you should first find out which items are protected by warranties. This may be indicated by labels on the equipment, in the manufacturer's instruction booklets, by separate warranty certificates, and possibly on invoices. Generally, the roof, heating and air-conditioning equipment, pumps, and apartment appliances are protected, at least initially, by warranties.

You need to know about warranties for two reasons: First, a warranty may provide service coverage for an item if it needs repair or replacement; there is no sense in paying for work if the warranty covers it. Second, many warranties are valid only if the manufacturer or an authorized agent performs the service. If you repair the item yourself or have someone unqualified do the work, the warranty may no longer apply.

Purchasing and Job Specifications.   As a manager, you are spending other people's money, and that requires considerable care. Many experienced managers develop a "stable" of dependable contractors who are used for most of the work needed. These managers are comfortable with this arrangement because they know they can rely on these particular firms, and if something goes wrong, the contractors will be there to back up their work. This practice may be acceptable for small, recurring service calls because it does ensure a degree of loyalty when you need it most. However, with larger jobs, you owe it to the owner to seek competitive bids. If you were to have a conversation with one or two of the premier builders in town, you would learn that they work with a list of at least three subcontractors for each trade. They constantly bid one against the other, and they never rig the bids or give one contractor a *last look*. They know that if they do, word will get out quickly, and the benefit of competitive bidding will be lost.

When major work is contemplated, you should first prepare a set of *specifications* detailing exactly what you are expecting the service provider to do. If the work is complicated or specialized, you really should seek the help of an expert in preparing a proper set of specifications. There will be a charge, but that expenditure is insignificant when compared to the cost of a dispute when a job is not done right. Once you have the scope of the work firmly in mind, you may want to visit with a few reputable contractors to get their opinions. More often than not, they will offer suggestions and changes that will save you time, money, and inconvenience. The good ones do this every day of their working lives, and they know what does and does not work.

If you receive widely differing opinions from a number of contractors and are confused about identifying the better solution, seek out practitioners who work with the particular product every day. If your problem has to do with resilient flooring, talk to a facilities manager for a school, hospital, or nursing home where large amounts of that type of floor product are being used. An airport manager probably knows what commercial carpeting gives the best service. The greenskeeper at a country club can fill you in about the pros and cons of lawn mowers. Rarely will you receive the objective opinion you need from the person who is attempting to sell you a particular product. A phone call to another manager or someone who has considerable experience in a given area can save the property owner a great deal of money and save you the embarrassment of making the wrong selection.

With finished specifications in hand, you can send out *requests for proposals (RFPs)*. Big jobs often warrant a *contractor meeting* in which you get together with all the bidders at one time and walk them through the scope and timing of the work. Ideally, the consultant who helped with the specifications will attend to assist in answering questions. Bidders will be expected to meet a precise deadline with their written bids. Normally, the bidders can attend a meeting at which each bid is opened and recorded. If the individual bids vary too widely, something is usually wrong or unclear in the bid documents. You may have to make changes and re-bid the work.

What you do *not* want to do is award work without a written bid or when there is only one bidder.

Periodic Maintenance.   Several areas of maintenance require unfailing, periodic attention. Some of the more important considerations are:

- *Water leaks.* Building water leaks can originate in so many ways. Openings at or around windows, along foundation lines, or through roofs and flashings, sweating and leaking pipes, and overflows and backups are a few examples. Besides damaging the building's components and finishes, water leaks commonly involve damage to residents' possessions. Several days each year should be set aside to hunt for places that water is finding its way into the building. Frequently, these inspections need to be timed to find problems immediately after a major storm, during the melting of an "ice dam," or on hot, humid days when pipes and vents sweat.

- *Plumbing.* Without waiting for leaks to develop, arrange to have faucet washers or valve cartridges replaced periodically. Inspect the flush and flapper valve in each toilet tank. Have spare parts on hand to make quick replacements. The quickest and best way to make plumbing repairs is before a crisis develops, when you can select a time that is convenient for you and the residents. It is better to periodically shut down a tier, a floor, or even the entire building for as long as half a day to replace worn plumbing parts than to shut down repeatedly to handle emergencies. Repairs never get cheaper if you wait; in fact, waiting increases the risk of higher costs and greater damage later.

- *Tub and shower caulking.* As a building settles, the grout between tiles and the caulking at the joint between the tile and the tub or shower floor will work loose. Unless these joints are kept sealed, water will seep into the cracks and damage the walls. Replace caulking or grout as soon as cracks are noticed. These joints often attract unsightly mildew as well.

- *Fans.* Many apartments have ventilator fans in kitchens and bathrooms. These should be kept clean and oiled if they are not permanently lubricated.

- *Filters.* There is no excuse for not changing the filters that serve the heating or air-conditioning ducts at least twice each year. The pleated, fine-pore type of filter (measured in microns) is considerably more expensive but does a much better job of cleaning the air. Dirty filters cause the furnace and air conditioner to work harder while increasing the fuel bill unnecessarily. If the owner is paying the bill, he or she is losing money. If residents are paying the bill, they undoubtedly are disgruntled about paying too much.

- *Smoke and carbon monoxide (CO) detectors.* These may be battery-powered or hard-wired with battery backup. They should be tested—and batteries replaced—on a regular schedule. The same law that mandates installation of these types of alarms typically requires the landlord to check them at set intervals and keep track of these inspections. Some owners and managers have generated lease addendums to transfer the testing and maintenance responsibilities to the resident. My position is that these devices are building equipment and they should be checked periodically to see that they work, that the resident has not disabled it, and that any maintenance such as battery replacement is performed.

Accessing Apartments.   Performing these types of scheduled maintenance tasks or needed repairs will require entering residents' apartments. Residents are entitled to reasonable advance notice before any inspections are done or work is performed; local laws may state specific requirements. Also, if the resident is a pet owner, he or she should be instructed to confine the pet to a separate room.

If maintenance personnel enter an apartment while the resident is out, make sure they

1. Post a sign on the door to alert the resident, who may return while the workers are still inside; and
2. Leave a notice stating what maintenance work was done. This will keep the resident from becoming upset if the workers have left anything behind or something in the apartment is out of place.

If the need for repairs stems from a resident's misuse of the apartment or equipment, the worker should suspend work and notify the office. A decision must then be made about how the cost of repairs will be handled. The law may require that you make the repairs promptly, for health or safety reasons, and seek reimbursement later.

Painting.   The subject of painting deserves some discussion because it is an operation the manager will deal with constantly. Every vacant apartment should be painted before it is placed on the market. In addition, occupied apartments will need redecorating as determined by your policy or the lease renewal terms.

Whether your own personnel do the painting or you hire an outside contractor, experience will help to establish a painting norm for each apartment. This will let you know how much paint is required and how much time is needed. A full-time "house" painter would only be appropriate in unusually large apartment communities. Typically, contract painters can answer an apartment manager's varying needs, even with short notice, and they tend to be more efficient. The following suggestions can help you obtain the best possible results.

- The manager, rather than the painter, should buy the paint or at least supervise the purchase, so brand name, color, and quality can be controlled.

- Acrylic paint is used almost universally. It wears as well as other paints, is easier to clean up, and produces little odor to annoy residents. Application should be accomplished with rollers or brushes.

- Sprayers should not be used in the apartment itself. They are messy, and you risk overspraying and damaging apartment components (e.g., factory finishes, carpeting, appliances). Spray painting doors, cabinets, and shelving produces a much smoother finish when performed by a skilled craftsman. It is best to remove these components to a maintenance room or spray booth and then reinstall them in the apartment when the work is finished.

- Painters must use clean drop cloths and clean up any spilled paint. They should also be responsible for unclogging drains if they clean their brushes and rollers in a sink or tub.

- A low luster or semi-gloss paint should be used in kitchens and bathrooms and on painted doors and woodwork, including window frames. It is more resistant than flat paint to water, dirt, and stains. It is also easier to clean and wears longer. Acrylic paint, in an enamel finish, dries rather fast and it is difficult to keep a "wet edge." This results in a finish that is not particularly smooth and has brush marks. Additives are available to slow the drying time and improve the final sheen.

- The repainting of baked enamel surfaces in the apartment, such as grilles, ventilators, or convectors, should be delayed until it becomes absolutely necessary. These surfaces attract dirt, and, once painted, they cannot be washed as easily. Products such as Soft Scrub cleanser often provide just the right amount of abrasive to clean, but not damage, the component.

- Ceilings that have been sprayed with acoustical coating should not be painted. These surfaces not only soak up vast quantities of paint but, more important, they lose their acoustical properties once painted. Special products and treatments are available if conditions are such that they cannot be left as is.

- Painters should not paint any electrical outlets, telephone jacks, switches, TV cable outlets, window or door frames and hardware, tile, laminated plastic surfaces, or plumbing fixtures. Insist that all switch and outlet plates and window and door hardware be removed before painting and replaced afterwards.

- Natural-finish doors, windows, cabinets, and other woodwork should be oiled or varnished, not painted. You will not need to varnish as often as you paint.

- All closet walls and shelving and the inside of the bathroom vanity should also be painted.

The popularity of paint colors changes with almost the same speed as that of carpet colors and patterns. There was a time when the industry standard was clearly off-white and nothing more. There are still some apartment managers who insist on limiting the color and decorating choices to off-white. They hang on to the old ways hoping for a greater profit based on the savings they think they will achieve in labor and paint costs. Sticking to such habits means missing some of the very best residents who are searching for an apartment that can really be made into a home.

Owners complain that they could make a mistake in the color combination and lose an otherwise acceptable resident because the decor did not suit the prospect's furnishings. The risk exists: You might lose a few prospects when you depart from sterile white. Trends in paint colors and patterns are published widely, and these data will help predict the various color preferences that prospects will be seeking. Also, one prospect may adore the same apartment that another prospect disliked. Imagine if all clothes or automobiles had to meet the exact same set of color specifications. You are interested in finding the discerning prospect who will stay and join your family of residents. These people want choice and variety.

I recommend that you experiment with colors and textures. When you find a combination that works, rather than repeat it, look for an even better solution. This way you will be constantly improving the property's image and attracting more-qualified residents.

Mold and Mildew Control.   Molds are a part of the natural environment; they are everywhere. Problems occur indoors when mold spores land on wet or damp spots and begin growing. Mold spores will not grow if moisture is not present. In apartment properties, the more common places to find mold growth are:

- Shower stalls/bathroom tiles
- Under sink cabinets
- Around leaky or sweating pipes
- Drywall mounted on exterior walls
- Under carpets/padding on concrete slabs
- Ventilation ducts

- Under wallpaper
- Air-conditioning drip pans
- Under indoor-outdoor carpet installed outdoors

The first assignment is to identify and then stop the source of moisture. Find a way to lower the humidity and increase air circulation and ventilation. The next step is to remove all traces of the mold. In my experience, when mold is found on damp drywall, it is best to have the drywall replaced, not just "cleaned off." Painting or caulking over mold does not work. The mold just comes right back. Personnel doing the cleanup will need protection (R-95 respirator, rubber gloves, and goggles without ventilation holes). Infested materials such as drywall and wallpaper should be disposed of properly.

When the area of growth exceeds 10 square feet, EPA cleanup guidelines come into play, and it is usually the time to get in touch with a professional. Mold, if left unchecked, can develop into a nightmare problem that can cost tens of thousands of dollars to remediate. Most insurance companies, stung by large and ongoing claims, have added mold to their growing list of exclusions. Most mold growths, in the early stages, can be minimized or eliminated by just drying up the source of moisture.

Pest Control.   Insects and other vermin are objectionable to prospects and residents alike, and justifiably so. Ants, roaches, and rodents are among the most common invaders and are difficult to eliminate. Ants love carbohydrates. Roaches, rarely in the building to start with, often first arrive in grocery bags or with food products. Rodents need food to survive and prefer darkness. Providing a pest-free environment is the responsibility of management. When problems develop, attack them with a full-scale campaign. Treat the whole building, or at least a major portion of it, not just one apartment. Otherwise, you simply drive the pests from one apartment to another. It is usually advisable to contract for regular pest control, and this work should be performed by a licensed exterminator.

Snow and Ice Control.   This is just a seasonal problem, but one that can turn into a major maintenance headache in many areas of the United States. Most apartment communities are not large enough to justify the cost of a large snowplow, so if there is a chance of any meaningful snow, the best advice is to contract for a plowing service to handle the driveways and parking areas. Maintenance staff can usually take care of the walks and stoops.

There are a number of questions and issues that should be addressed before entering into a snow plowing service contract:

- *Should the snow be pushed or removed?* There is a big difference in the cost so unless the property is very short on space or great accumulations are expected, most will opt to just "push and pile."

- *What snowfall amount triggers the start of plowing?* Usually, a 2-inch accumulation must fall before service begins. There needs to be some flexibility in this because it is very possible to have, say, three snowfalls that are "just under" 2 inches in fairly quick succession, especially at the very beginning of the season. This means that there may be almost 6 inches on the ground, and the plowing has yet to start. Also, your residents will be anxious to see how well the snow control is going to work. The first one or two snowfalls of the season are the ones when everyone is getting their "snow legs," and it helps to "bend" the accumulation rule a bit.

- *Where do you want the snow piled?* This can be answered by a walk-through with the contractor or delineated on a site plan. Generally, you want to clear most snow away from the property entrance and the office and reception areas.

- *How are the charges calculated?* Usually, there is an agreed upon fee for handling accumulations from say 2 inches to up to 6 inches. If the snow keeps coming, that fee might repeat itself for every 6-inch increment. The system and method of charging can vary widely in different locales. Any materials, such as sand or rock salt, are generally billed additionally, by the ton spread.

- *What about reputation, equipment, and insurance?* You want the answer to all three to be an unqualified "good." The snowplowing industry is saturated with would-be entrepreneurs with aging vehicles and little or no insurance. When the big or continuing snows arrive, you need a contractor who will be there, with equipment that works and is up to the task. When there is a foot or more of snow on the ground, it is virtually impossible to find a replacement contractor without paying an enormous premium. Also, when the snow gets deep, parked vehicles get buried and damage claims rise.

Snow-melting materials should be used sparingly and with care. Rock salt is the cheapest and most commonly used; but it can damage pavements and plants severely, and it will not work at all if the temperature falls too low. Also, rock salt can damage carpeting if it is tracked inside. Some localities prohibit its use.

Chemical snow-melting pellets cost more than rock salt but cause less damage and continue to work at very low temperatures. However, these pellets cannot be stored for long periods or they may solidify or lose their effectiveness. If pellets are used, it is best to buy only what can be consumed in a single season.

Shoveling is better than using salt or snow-melting chemicals. Sand works well to provide traction on slippery ice.

Inspection Checklist.   Many of the foregoing maintenance items are contained in standard inspection checklists available from the Institute of Real Estate Management, local apartment associations, or local real estate boards. These checklists are adequate guides; but since every building is unique, you are advised to develop a custom checklist that contains everything you need to know about your property.

There are only two acceptable answers on an inspection and maintenance checklist: "okay" or "not okay." If an item is "okay," then it is in acceptable condition and needs no further explanation. If it is "not okay," then an explanation is required. There should be room on the checklist for a description of items that are "not okay." The person who performs the inspection should write down whatever is wrong; in most cases, the manager should do the inspection personally. Terms such as "good," "fair," or "poor" should not be used; they tell you nothing. The narrative explanation, on the other hand, clearly states what is wrong and what needs to be done about it.

Property Staff versus Outside Personnel.   Once inspections have been made and the maintenance schedule is prepared, you still need to decide who will do the work. Should you use your own maintenance people or outside organizations? This question is hotly debated at practically every gathering of management people. Contracting maintenance work to outside vendors has certain advantages. It

- Augments the work force as needed without adding permanently to the payroll.
- Offers access to specialized skills that members of your staff do not have.
- Provides licensed specialists when required.
- Lessens employee record keeping.
- Minimizes possible pressures from union organizers.

The disadvantages are (1) it often costs more, and (2) you lose an element of control. Given two equally able crews, one your own, and the other belonging to an outside contractor, your crew usually can do the job for less. Also, an outside contractor's reaction time is often slower; you cannot give direct orders because you must work through a designated supervisor. Most contracts provide for specific services to be performed under specific terms, with no provision for extra duties that may arise.

In general, you probably are better off doing the work with your own staff. There is more control this way and, if proper supervision is provided, it is considerably less expensive. However, there are certain maintenance tasks in operating apartment communities where outside service is advisable. We have already discussed the desirability of contracting for painting and pest control. Other examples include:

Staff Communications

Apartment managers promise fast service, and in their efforts to deliver, they find themselves searching for effective ways to communicate quickly with property personnel as well as others. The pager has lost its position of preference. The problems, in part, are transmission delays and the fact that the recipient must still find a telephone to call in, which can be inconvenient. Pagers are often misused or overused. It is commonplace to see office staff paging field personnel constantly throughout the day, for any and all reasons, without any regard for the interruptions they are causing in the normal work-flow process. There seems to be a basic assumption that maintenance personnel are just idly waiting for the next question or work assignment.

The pager does work well for after-hours emergency calls. A common technique is to set up a rotating schedule in which a maintenance person carries the pager at all times for a period of one week. When the office or the answering service receives word of an emergency problem, a page is sent and the on-call staffer responds.

For communications throughout the normal workday, a combination *cell phone plus portable two-way radio* is probably the preferred choice. It permits instantaneous communications with the office, as well as with other staffers who are so equipped, and can be used as a cell phone to make calls as necessary. This system and these communication devices are fairly expensive, but they certainly answer a long-sought need of the apartment industry.

Another alternative is individual cell phones that can be issued to and carried by apartment staffers. The service rates for a variety of monthly packages continue to become more and more affordable.

- *Central air conditioning.* At the very least, an expert is needed to start the system at the beginning of the cooling season and shut it down properly at the end. Failure to do this correctly can mean interruptions and costly repairs during the cooling season. Generally, the building staff can take care of individual apartment air conditioners.

- *Elevators.* Authorized service organizations have the training and equipment to provide the constant maintenance necessary to keep building elevators functioning properly. Never attempt repairs or adjustments yourself; the risk to human life and safety is too great. Managers often disagree when discussing the advantages of full-service contracts as opposed to limited service "grease and oil" contracts. Full-service contracts probably have a slight edge, but they can cost considerably more. Even a full-service contract can involve overtime charges for off-hour emergency calls.

- *Swimming pools.* Like central air-conditioning systems, swimming pools need experts to get them up and operating at the beginning of the season and then again to properly shut them down at the end. Generally, the property staff performs routine, daily pool maintenance unless special licensing is required.

- *Satellite dishes and antennas.* Cable television hookups have replaced most antenna installations as they were previously known, and satellite dishes will be the means of delivering high-definition reception. Virtually all of this gear is solid-state, installed by specialists, and involves very little maintenance at the property level.

- *Recharging fire extinguishers.* Municipalities require annual fire extinguisher tagging. Licensed services will annually recharge and retag these units for a nominal fee.

- *Sewer rodding.* Generally, the site staff can be trained to rod about one hundred feet of sewer length. Anything beyond this requires professionals with special equipment and training.

- *Window washing.* Windows in tall buildings or in places that require special equipment are best cleaned by outside contractors. Your own staff can clean lobby and entryway glass that requires daily attention and windows which can be reached while standing on the ground.

- *Landscaping and snow plowing.* As already mentioned, outside contractors can be employed to reduce seasonal peak demands on staff and large capital outlays to purchase major equipment.

In summary, use of an outside service is often dictated by licensing requirements, the complexity of the machinery to be serviced, and the need for specialized equipment or skills.

Service Contracts. Whether you purchase outside services on an as-needed basis or contract for them on a continuing basis will depend on your analysis of the property's requirements. A good contract that provides for preventive maintenance can help you avoid big expenses later.

Before hiring outside services, shop for a reliable firm and examine the contract to see what is included. Does the fee cover everything, or is there a deductible amount? Does it cover parts and labor? Are overtime emergency calls included? Not surprisingly, the more the contract includes, the more it will cost.

You also have to determine whether to deal with a manufacturer's service organization or an independent contractor. Service from the manufacturer may cost more, but the manufacturer's organization understands the equipment better and has easier access to parts.

Deferred Maintenance

If you set up a maintenance program carefully, most tasks will follow a routine and emergency crises will be minimal. But there is another category of maintenance that lurks in the background. It is called *deferred maintenance*.

The apartment manager should have a budget to cover operating expenses and keep the property looking good and running smoothly. However, you must be mindful that *all properties are in a constant state of decay;* and every property has a degree of deferred maintenance. The key is to continually identify its existence and to keep it under control.

Much of what is labeled as deferred maintenance is really *deficient maintenance* or, more accurately, negligent management. Potholes in the parking lot, dead shrubs and trees, clogged drains, sunken sidewalk sections, broken lights, and leaking gutters are all examples of someone's neglect. These problems are usually highly visible, and lack of attention to them is certainly being monitored by residents and prospects alike.

Our focus in this section is the major building and property components that are steadily wearing out and will need attention in the future.

By monitoring breakdowns and repair orders, you will be alerted to "problems in waiting." For example, if six water heaters fail in one year, you can expect the other eighteen that were installed at the same time to fail shortly. You should be prepared for this eventuality and begin setting aside money in reserve to pay for replacements.

Consider these other examples: After three years, the paved areas in a property are certainly not new anymore, but they still have plenty of life in them. The deterioration process can be forestalled by filling cracks and resealing the surfaces, but there is no reason to embark upon a major resurfacing effort. While the paving is no longer new, it is certainly sound and serviceable. This is a property component with an advancing level of decay that is acknowledged but whose "fix" is *deferred* to a more appropriate time in the future. Roofs and many mechanical devices are other components whose lives can be extended through care, but they will eventually need replacement. Exterior paint has a certain life; repainting too soon just wastes money, but waiting too long rots the siding. Traditionally, appliances go out of fashion before they wear out, so life expectancy does not always determine replacement. Management's job is to recognize the deterioration and decay patterns of each of these major components and be ready to act at the appropriate time. Tracking the aging process and preparing short- and long-range replacement schedules eliminates surprises and painful "cash calls" to the ownership.

Many managers prepare an *issues report* on a quarterly or semiannual basis in which upcoming problems are identified. This type of report goes on to discuss priorities, timing, alternatives, costs, and funding as well as the manager's suggestions and recommendations.

Cannibalization

Sometimes parts are taken from one apartment to make repairs in another. This practice, called *cannibalization,* is very harmful. First, it doubles the work because the working item that was cannibalized will also have to be replaced. Second, a resident feels shortchanged when used parts are installed.

Once you allow cannibalization, it will be difficult to stop. First a fan cover is "borrowed" from a unit; next a thermostat is taken; before long the vanity top has been removed, and soon a major overhaul is needed to reclaim the apartment. When taken to the extreme, the apartment becomes a storeroom, or workers begin taking appliances and other parts home. All of this reduces the chances of that apartment ever being restored to income-producing condition.

Cannibalization should never be permitted. You should maintain an ample stock of frequently used parts or know where they can be obtained quickly.

Supplies and Parts

Having the right parts and supplies on hand is essential to a maintenance program. If you run out of 40-watt bulbs and start using 100-watt replacements, you will create spotty lighting; and bulbs will have to be replaced more often because of heat buildup. Not having the right parts and supplies means the property's maintenance program will not be effective.

The supplies you need will be determined by the property itself. Your walk-through inspection of the property will help you compile a list of what should be on hand. Consider the following recommendations:

- Keep supplies and parts in a central place, not scattered. This will enable you to monitor what is available, what should be ordered, and what may be disappearing because of pilferage.

- Buying in bulk discourages theft. Paint in small containers disappears especially fast. Instead of buying paint in one-gallon cans, buy your commonly used paint in five-gallon containers. Long-lasting chemicals can also be purchased in bulk quantities and dispensed into smaller containers.

- Balance the inventory to take advantage of quantity discounts and, at the same time, avoid having too much on hand. Some chemical supplies deteriorate with time, so it does not always pay to buy in too large a quantity.

- Avoid aerosol sprays. Apart from environmental considerations, they are expensive and easy to steal. You can often buy the same chemicals less expensively in other forms.

- Anticipate needs and schedule purchases to minimize the number of orders placed. Group orders and arrange for a single delivery instead of having your staff waste time making individual trips to the hardware store. Your goal should be to limit hardware store trips to twice a month.

- Use written *purchase orders* for all purchases. Purchase orders should be authorized and signed only by the manager or assistant manager. This reduces the chances of the staff buying too much, buying what is not needed, buying personal items, and getting kickbacks from suppliers.

Maintenance Equipment and Specialized Tools. A complete inventory should be made of all maintenance tools owned by the property, noting the specific location of each item. If an article is assigned to a particular person, list this, too. Tools and equipment also require regular maintenance. This should be scheduled during the off-season when they are not in heavy use and when you can get good service at fair prices.

To reduce pilferage, consider painting equipment a special color or applying a distinctive marking so it can be identified readily and is no longer salable or worth stealing. Proper storage under lock and key will reduce theft, if not eliminate it. Only the manager and the maintenance supervisor should have these keys.

Getting the Right Start

Many apartment managers who attend seminars on property maintenance come away fired up with enthusiasm and the determination to set things right at their properties, but their enthusiasm soon wanes and the maintenance program bogs down. Why? Because in most cases, the manager attacks problems all at once. This seldom works. There are just too many tasks for the staff to accomplish at one time. Resistance builds up, discouragement sets in, and it is soon back to business as usual.

Programmed maintenance can work if each task is divided into manageable segments and each is finished completely before proceeding to the next. Consider this approach: Take a site plan of your property (or a building plan if you have only a single building) and divide it into areas or zones. Label them A, B, C, and so forth. (See the discussion of Documenting Property Assets earlier in this chapter.)

First consider area A. List everything that needs to be done to make area A first-rate. Determine the equipment and staff needed. Gather the staff together and explain what needs to be done in area A. Give each person a calendar and a list of specific tasks. Don't simply say, "Maintain it." Instead, give detailed instructions: "Once every two weeks the grille must be removed; the filter taken out, washed, and replaced; and the grille replaced." These are instructions few will misunderstand. Then put your maintenance personnel to work on area A. Watch them as they work. When they do something right, tell them so. If they do something wrong, correct them. Evaluate the work as they go along. While there may be a supervisor in charge, you must be involved so the supervisor knows what is expected. Work together to set standards of quality, establish schedules, and determine if other tools are needed.

When area A is in first-class condition, walk through it with the entire staff. Make sure that everyone witnesses the changes that were accomplished. Now, when you proceed to area B, the staff knows what is expected of them and how it is to look when finished. Meanwhile, set up a continuing maintenance program for area A so it will not slip again. Proceed through the entire building or development this way. By the time you are finished, the entire property will be in top condition, the staff will know the routine, and you will be on your way to a self-sustaining maintenance program.

This kind of program is only possible if you, the manager, do a thorough job of scheduling, supervising, and evaluating. By doing your homework, you know what has to be done and when, how many people are needed, what kind of supervision in required, and what tools and equipment must be provided. Finally, regular inspections provide the feedback needed to evaluate your system and make corrections.

An ongoing maintenance program will always end up costing less than one based on crisis management. Experience shows there is only a slight difference between the cost of operating a first-class apartment community and one that is run-of-the-mill. The major difference is in daily attention and supervision.

There is also a significant difference in occupancy and turnover rates. A better-maintained property will attract qualified residents faster and keep them longer than a run-down property will.

9

You can't sell from an empty wagon;
keep your vacant apartments ready.

Preparing a
Marketing Campaign

The best leasing agent in the world cannot overcome a product that is substandard. Likewise, a nice property, creatively marketed, can flounder in the hands of an inept sales staff. Patterns of poor service and unfair policies will ultimately result in more move-outs than move-ins.

Successfully renting and rerenting apartments requires an understanding of rental customers, their motivations, and the marketplace—plus some very specialized marketing tools. In this chapter, we will break down and discuss these broad topics and then put them to work in an effective marketing strategy.

Understanding Why People Rent

For a number of years, I have conducted surveys tracking apartment renters who have just made the decision to rent at a particular apartment community. Such studies are very important because they help to pinpoint the "hot button" or primary reason for leasing one apartment as opposed to another. With very little variance, each survey reveals almost the same set of priorities in terms of influences on the final leasing decision (Exhibit 9.1).

Exhibit 9.1
Primary Attraction in Decision to Rent

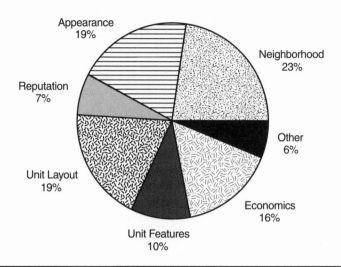

- Appearance 19%
- Neighborhood 23%
- Reputation 7%
- Other 6%
- Unit Layout 19%
- Economics 16%
- Unit Features 10%

Location. The neighborhood where a property is located has always scored as the single most important motivator of renters. People choose the area they want to live in for a number of reasons. Quality of lifestyle is the most common one. Other popular responses to questions regarding location include proximity to the workplace, quality schools, friends, relatives, highway access, and airports.

Property Appearance. Appearance of the apartment community has always been an extremely important deciding factor. The physical condition of a rental community has more to do with the type of resident it attracts than any other factor. After conducting thousands of interviews, I can tell you it is common to hear that prospective renters, who were attracted to an area by the advertisement for an apartment community, lost interest in the property after viewing it. The prospects might have been pleased with the neighborhood, but they were dissatisfied with the property itself. They found alternative accommodations with a more pleasing appearance.

Apartment Condition, Layout, and Features. Apartment layout and features rank next in order of stated importance. It is important to be aware of the means by which people judge an apartment's features. The most critical criterion is the condition of the apartment shown. I have conducted many follow-up interviews of prospective renters who have decided against leasing in an apartment community. The number of prospects who were disappointed with the shoddy condition of the apartment, rather than the neighborhood, appearance, or rent, was alarming. The poor condition of the apartment showed to prospective renters accounts for more lost rentals than any other factor. In fact, in regularly conducted surveys, almost 50 percent of the rental apartments shown were not in market-ready condition.

There is a noticeable difference between rental housing and for-sale housing when it comes to the subject of condition. Renters expect to find an apartment that is in livable and *move-in condition*. Buyers of existing homes, on the other hand, generally expect to make improvements and modifications to personalize and upgrade their new home so the need for pristine conditions is not nearly as critical.

The importance of an apartment's layout or features does not make an impact until the matter of condition first satisfies the prospect. The prospect who finds fault with the condition of a potential rental apartment often cites the layout or the lack of a particular feature as the reason for not renting. When conditions are a turnoff, prospects usually want to make a quick exit, and they prefer to point out missing features as an excuse for not renting. This is a more effective way for prospects to exit because complaints about the apartment's condition will invariably prompt a promise by management to correct the problems.

Reputation. Reputation is also mentioned as a reason that people choose to rent at a particular property. This might include the reputation of the property, the owner, the manager, or a combination of the three. Further questioning of new renters often modifies our interpretation of this response. Properties that appear nice and are well cared for are frequently given credit for a good reputation. The response is based on the assumption that a nice appearance must be the result of the residents who live there as well as responsive and sensitive management. Actually, that is almost always a valid assumption. When questioning prospects about the reputation of a management firm, negative responses are practically nonexistent because prospects would not have visited the property in the first place if they had been aware of problems with management's reputation. When word gets around that a particular apartment manager is unfair or unreasonable, many prospects may never make it to the rental office.

Rent Level. Rent level is rarely stated as a reason for renting or not renting a particular unit. This is not to say that rent is not very important in the overall decision process. Rent is relative. Better neighborhoods command higher rents than do less-desirable neighborhoods. Well-cared-for apartment communities bring higher rents than do poorly maintained ones. Vacant units that are fixed up rent for more than units requiring a great deal of effort and imagination. Rental prospects who do not believe that a particular unit is worth the price rarely bother to discuss "rent versus value," they simply find an excuse to exit.

Market Identification

The apartment manager has an advantage over most other marketing people when it comes to identifying the marketplace. While this benefit is clearly available, few managers make use of it. The best road to future customers can be found by understanding how you gained the customers you have.

Current Residents Tell a Story.   Unfortunately, most marketing efforts begin with a full-scale effort to fill a certain number of vacancies. Even though that is the ultimate marketing goal, dwelling on the vacancy situation will only produce negative results and erode confidence levels. Marketing people who dwell on vacancies are often the very same people who chase the promotional schemes that detract from the property's image. Concentrating on vacancies will produce limited results and make it difficult to stay ahead of the "ten move-in/ten move-out" cycle that plagues so many apartment communities.

A property with 150 units and 25 vacancies has an unacceptable vacancy level, and the property is most likely in financial jeopardy. Given the expense and debt loads of many apartment properties, this vacancy rate (nearly 17 percent) would be near a crisis point. The apartment manager is best advised to ignore this problem in the early stages of creating a marketing program and look to the 125 units with rent-paying customers to find the answers. There are already 125 residents who have accepted what is being offered in terms of location and product and think that it represents fair value. Why did these people perceive this location as more advantageous than that of the competition? When these people were prospects, what features and appointments attracted them? Were they lured by a special concession that could not be beaten by neighboring properties? Obviously something clicked because the property succeeded in attracting the current residents. Understanding these motivations will act as your guide in securing the needed new residents.

In my experience, creating a sort of visual matrix—a *marketing map*— is the best way to identify patterns in the relationship between your residents' *home* (i.e., your property) and their place of *employment*. To begin, you will need a detailed and rather large-scale map of the township that includes your property and a supply of self-adhesive colored dots. (You may also need maps of adjoining townships to complete the display.)

First, locate and mark your property on the map. Next, place a colored dot to mark the approximate location of the place of employment of each of the working adults occupying the rented units. This process is slow because it means looking up each resident's application and then pinpointing one or more job locations on the map. Experience dictates certain procedures. If a number of people work at or near the same location, place the dots close together to display the concentration, but leave enough space around the dots so they can be counted.

If your property is located away from the downtown area and your residents commute there to work, try to find an open area on the map (e.g., a forest preserve area, large park, or lake). Draw a box around this area and label it "downtown." This is done to avoid adding a number of extra maps to the display when the downtown area is far removed from the rest of the market. Place a dot in that box for each current resident who works in the general downtown area. If a few residents travel considerable distances to their workplaces, you can simply exclude them. You are interested in finding a pattern. Chasing a few stray dots will only distract you when you are ready to begin interpreting the results.

If many of your residents are retired, you will need another box, similar to the one created for those who work downtown. The placement of the retirement box should be as close to the subject property as possible, without conflicting with the employment dots. When the number of retired people is meaningful, you may want to select a different colored dot to indicate where these people lived prior to moving to your apartment community. In this case, you are looking for a pattern that signals areas to target in a direct mail campaign. The result will resemble the sample marketing map in Exhibit 9.2.

When you have finished placing the dots, you can sit back and evaluate. The matrix you have created will be an invaluable marketing tool that can be used in a number of ways.

- Establish market boundaries.
- Identify your residents' places of employment.
- Illustrate drive patterns.
- Reveal competition.
- Show public transportation routes.
- Initiate conversations with prospects.
- Help prospects who are new to town.
- Reinforce the decision to move to your apartment community.

Market Boundaries.   The apartment manager can establish the principal boundaries of a particular marketplace easily and accurately. Location is a key ingredient in the decision-making process of most renters. Locations are perceived as desirable because of such things as community prestige, proximity to the workplace, schools, and overall quality of life. As soon as you have 50-percent occupancy, you have enough data to begin to identify your market boundaries. Most renters work, and the travel patterns between their places of employment and your rental community will become apparent. When looking for new residents, direct your marketing efforts within those

Exhibit 9.2
Sample Marketing Map

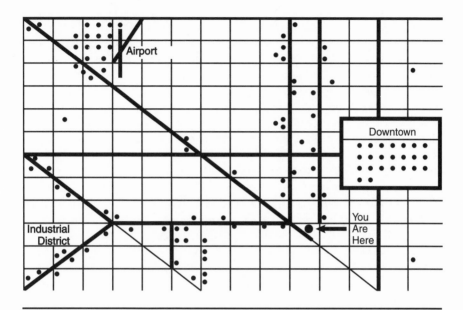

boundaries which are established by your existing residents. This will usually deliver much better results and will conserve your energy and save the expense of blanketing a market area that is simply too broad.

Places of Employment.   As the colored dots are placed on your marketing map, the sources of employment become apparent rather quickly (shopping centers, office complexes, factories, service outlets, eating establishments, schools, airports, etc.). Driving the area will further reveal the identity and scope of these work centers. You will also be able to assess the income level of the people who are employed there. Often you can determine the business climate by noting signs advertising for more workers. Generally, you will add to your list of area employers who can be contacted in the continuing search for qualified residents. Employer names and addresses can be entered into a computer database that will allow you to prepare personalized letters or promotional pieces for use in a direct mail campaign targeted to human resources directors.

Drive Pattern.   When you complete your map, you will see a pattern that indicates the direction most of your existing residents travel to work and what major streets and intersections are most commonly used. It is a simple matter to measure the distance in both miles and minutes to drive. One of the most important ingredients in the decision to move is the proximity to one's place of employment. Preparing a marketing map will help the leasing personnel become more conscious of this concern and equip them with the knowledge to discuss travel times, favored directions, and short cuts with prospects. Drive patterns can also be used to identify potential sites for billboard advertising if that medium is used.

Competition.   Most people follow the same driving pattern—*home to work, work to home*—five or six days a week. People want the nicest place they can comfortably afford within a reasonable travel distance (time) to and from their places of employment. Assuming the workplace is established first, how many apartment communities in the neighborhood offer the same basic level of quality with equally acceptable drive patterns and time requirements? If you determine that the majority of your existing residents travel north or south from your property and that a 20-minute drive time appears to be the norm, you can readily identify your competition because their residents will follow a similar driving pattern.

Public Transportation.   In many households, one or more people do not have access to an automobile. They rely on public transportation to get to work, school, or shopping. The marketing map will point out the major routes used for such travel. It is then up to the apartment manager to learn about the bus routes, train schedules, and fares. Unfortunately, many apartment employees either live on site or depend solely on automobiles for their transportation. Hence, they never have the need to learn about public transportation routes or may not take the time to do so. The marketing map will demonstrate the important public transportation routes that should be investigated by staff members.

Conversations with Prospects.   The marketing map should be placed in a prominent location on one of the walls in the rental center. It is packed with valuable information for the leasing process. For example, it is one of the best ways to initiate a conversation with a prospective renter. Keep in mind the pattern: "home to work, work to home." You should highlight your property's location and ask the prospect to help you find his or her place of employment on the map. In many ways, this is better than filling out a guest card. By the time you have finished preparing the marketing map, you will be familiar with many of the major employers in the area and the favored routes from your property to their places of business. You can give estimates of drive times or mention the shortcuts that people use to avoid areas of traffic congestion. You may very well learn that the prospect's principal reason for moving is to be closer to his or her workplace. This will be helpful when you summarize your benefits at decision time. The marketing map provides you with a highly visible tool that depicts a significant aspect of a leasing agent's daily life—awareness of the importance of proximity between home and work.

People Moving to Town.   About 20 percent of rental prospects are new to the area. The marketing map is even more important to new people than it is to those who have lived in the area for some time. The out-of-towner can easily make a mistake in choosing a place of residence. The leasing agent can be very helpful in explaining the driving distances and patterns that will work the best. Again, your map is a focal point and helps the newcomer understand the relative distances between work and home. It will also show the proximity to shopping, entertainment, and other desired destinations in the area.

The Final Decision.   Even if you have 25 vacancies in a 150-unit apartment community, you will most likely have more than 200 dots on your completed marketing map. This happens because many households have more than one person who works. The impact of hundreds of dots on the map announces that you have lots of residents. Many people choose a restaurant using the same premise: The restaurant crowded with customers is perceived as more likely to be good. The array of dots on your map has the same reassuring effect. Say, for example, that the prospect works at or near the airport, and your map shows that many of your residents also work in that area. This tells the prospect that others who have to make the same basic trip each workday have found this apartment community to fit their needs. It also implies that car pools or an occasional ride might be a possibility. It is especially helpful in the rental process when the prospect learns that a number of current residents also work in the same area. This reinforcement may be all you need to close the deal.

Competing Properties.   Many managers view a competing rental property as a kind of enemy. Because of this, they avoid all but the most essential contact with competitors. This is unwise. It is true that if the property next door did not exist, the job of capturing new residents would be easier. However, the competition does exist and is likely to continue to exist, even if you could succeed in attracting all the prospects. If that were to happen, the present owner of the competing property would probably lose the investment; but the lender or a new owner would surely arrive on the scene armed with an aggressive marketing campaign (and probably capture some of your residents). Apartments are different from other types of businesses. If a shoe store or a grocery store is forced to close because it cannot compete, a different type of business that may have a better chance will probably replace it. An apartment building, however, almost always remains just that. Once competition arrives, it is usually there to stay. So, it is important to learn to coexist.

Many managers have very little first-hand knowledge about their competitors. Typically, the manager will be required to perform a periodic market or comparability study, so he or she will call a few neighboring apartment communities to gather information about rent levels and vacancies. Other than that contact, the only information about the competition is derived from ads and through conversations with prospective renters who have visited other properties.

Your job as a marketer depends on timely and accurate information about your competition. It is critical that you take time each week to update your information about the neighborhood in which your property is located. This certainly includes first-hand knowledge of your competition. This job should not be trusted to others; it must be performed by the person who will be implementing the future marketing plan.

It is best to reserve some time every week, whether an hour or an afternoon, for visiting competing properties. This practice should be followed with absolute regularity. Managers who restrict themselves to their own apartment communities because of a never-ending workload are usually the individuals with the poorest marketing results. These people are also the best candidates for burnout. Visiting other properties and discussing common problems with your fellow managers will do more than a year's worth of seminars to help you come up with new ideas and approaches. Real estate management is a small business, and most apartment managers share a camaraderie that is rarely found in other industries. Take advantage of it.

Choose one of your slow days for visiting (chances are it will also be a slow day for your competitors). Bring each competitor a copy of your complete brochure with all of the inserts and price information, and ask for a copy of their materials in return. The visit should not be an interrogation. Rather, it should be two rental professionals sharing their experiences. Learn what units are renting best, their hours of operation, the best days of the week for showing apartments, and how use of their recreational facilities is scheduled. You should also ask what new technology they are employing. Don't write anything down; seeing this often worries the other manager, who might think an evaluation is taking place.

A visit might take as much as an hour; in one afternoon you can probably meet and talk with three managers. Don't restrict yourself to properties running big ads or buildings that are open every day. In virtually every market, even those suffering high vacancy rates, there are properties that are fully rented and do very little in the way of marketing. While it may prove more difficult to meet the managers or owners of these properties, it is essential that you do. After all, they are doing something right, and you need to learn what that is. I would also caution against letting the negative attitudes of some managers influence you. (This is often a major problem in a difficult market.) Ideally, by observing some of these negative attitudes, you will recognize why those managers are headed for failure, and you can try to avoid following the same path. Visiting your competitors will accomplish at least three things:

1. You will learn exactly what you face in terms of competition, and this will be invaluable in preparing your marketing strategy.
2. You will observe other people's ideas and solutions, which will be helpful in preparing and presenting a superior product.
3. You will build a file of competitors' brochures that will be useful in your rental activity.

Have you ever seen a school or scout program in which everyone was given the same raw materials and guidelines, but the individual participants are challenged to come up with their own unique design? Managers of apartment communities have very much the same challenge. Many start with dull architecture and rooms like sterile white boxes. To these ingredients, the manager adds his or her skills in creating a property personality and the loyal staff to make a difference. Your visits to competitors will uncover many different potential solutions. There will be far more routine solutions than imaginative ones. After you have seen many other rental properties, you will be in a better position to judge the differences and to create changes that will set your apartment community apart.

The benefits of visiting the competition coincide with a great many of the benefits of belonging to a professional association for real estate managers. The savvy professional always seeks opportunities to meet and network with others in the industry and share ideas because he or she knows that the best ideas are never created in a vacuum. In Chapter 11, I will discuss how your relationship with managers of competing properties can produce further benefits.

Learn from the Pros.   Before you get down to the specifics of a marketing program, you should put yourself through one more learning process. In the real estate management business, you are going to lose residents as time goes on. But, it is possible to learn from these losses. As first-time buyers, many renters select a home, condo, coach house, or townhouse in a brand new housing development rather than an existing home offered through a multiple-listing service. When one of your residents gives notice after purchasing a new home, ask him or her about it. Learn the name of the development, the size of the home, the resident's reasons for choosing it over others, and any other pertinent facts such as the cost and the source of financing. You might phrase your interest as if you and your spouse are considering a similar move. Generally, you will find your departing residents to be flattered by your interest in their housing pursuits, and they will fill you in about their different decision milestones.

Your next step is to call that development and inquire about the homes they have for sale. Pay particular attention to the technique that the sales-person uses to get you to commit to an appointment. Make an appointment and visit the development with another person so that the two of you appear as a couple. You might even spend some time preparing so that you look and act like potential buyers. This will enable you to view the complete sales presentation.

When you arrive for your appointment, pay particular attention to every detail. You are about to receive an important lesson in selling. People who sell homes for a living are almost always commission sales agents. Unlike leasing people, who may be paid a salary, these agents must sell, or they will soon be out of the business. Pay attention to the way the salesperson qualifies you according to your needs and the degree of urgency involved with your potential purchase. How were you registered? What did the sales center look like? Were you given a brochure, and when? What did their models look like? Did the salesperson try to match purchase benefits with your needs? Was there an effort made to close the sale? When you said no, did the salesperson try another sales approach?

The selling process, whether for a home or a rental apartment, does not change. The answers to the questions posed above will help you understand how to be a more effective marketer. One of the most common questions asked by people trying to improve their marketing skills is: "What do I say, and when, to obtain the best results?" The answers and techniques are available in a living workshop: Just pretend to be a buyer and study the information you collect. You will need to do this at least six to eight times to gain enough experience to differentiate between good and bad techniques. At that point, all presentations, both good and bad, will contain a valuable lesson for you.

Marketing Tools

The following are some of the elements you can draw upon to promote your property and develop a solid merchandising program.

Selection of a Theme.   If an apartment community is new or undergoing a major change, that is an opportunity to establish a theme to be carried through the entire marketing presentation. If the rental property is well established, the theme may be difficult to change. An established theme should not be regarded as irrevocable, however. If it is out of character with the property, it may need changing.

What is a theme? It is a name and symbol that represent the apartment community and help attract the renting public. The architecture or surroundings of the property may point to an appropriate theme. Perhaps the architecture is Spanish or Western, suggesting a relaxed way of life. A traditional style suggests a more refined lifestyle. There are also nondescript architectural styles that lend themselves to almost any theme.

The presence of lakes, streams, groves of trees, or surrounding farmland provides thematic material. The kinds of amenities on the grounds—swimming pools, tennis courts, playgrounds, sailing, fishing, ice-skating—may suggest ideas, too.

In considering a theme, it might be helpful to consult with the owner and architect who, perhaps, had a theme in mind when the place was built. Also, you should certainly consider the market you are trying to reach. It would be inappropriate to create a relaxed and informal theme for a luxury high-rise apartment in the most exclusive part of town.

Names and Symbols.   Themes are evident in the names of apartment communities and in the symbols chosen to represent them. Most garden apartment communities are identified by distinctive names (e.g., Knollwood Place, Glenfield Springs, Laurel Oaks), whereas in-city apartments are commonly identified by street numbers (e.g., One City Center, 1000 Lake Shore Drive).

It is very important that the name and symbol be presented in a unified manner. Too often a name will be used one way in a newspaper advertisement, another way on a building sign, and still a third way on a brochure. All of this is self-defeating because you are not building a consistent image in the minds of prospects.

Consistency is a key element in marketing and particularly in using a theme. In addition, it conveys a sense of order that is very reassuring to prospects. When they see a clear and uniform theme, prospects gain respect for your operation. Consistency is important for another reason: It helps to reinforce your property's name in the customer's mind.

If prospects see many variations of an apartment community's name (through changes of color, style, placement, etc.), they may not recognize it as the same property. The name is the same but the impression is different. If the name and symbol are always the same, the repeated impressions will leave their imprint.

It is important to develop a unified name and symbol early on so you will be able to use them consistently throughout your presentation. To do this most effectively, work with a competent graphic designer, either an independent studio or someone on the staff of an advertising agency. Select a qualified designer because you will have to live with the results for years.

The significance of a professional design cannot be overstated. Corporations spend millions of dollars to develop trademarks and logos to help identify their products and promote them in the marketplace. Fortunately, with apartments, the task is smaller. Costs are much less, and these costs are incurred only once.

In developing a graphic treatment of the name and symbol, keep things simple. Remember, people need to be able to read your message, often at some distance and while in motion. Avoid curlicues and highly stylized type. Script can be hard to read, and foreign names can be hard to read, remember, spell, and pronounce. Your property's name will be used in a variety of applications—signs, letterheads, brochures, etc.—so keep it simple.

Unified Graphics System.   A professionally designed treatment of the apartment community's name and symbol is just the first step. Also needed is a unified graphics system that spells out the ways the name and symbol are to be used and how you should handle everything else that relates to your property when it appears in print. Ask the graphic designer to prepare a *graphics manual* that shows exactly what is permitted and what is not. The following are items that should be included in this manual.

- *Name and symbol.* Type size and style (typeface), exact ink color.
- *Stationery.* Exact placement of the property's name, symbol, address, telephone and fax numbers, web site and/or e-mail address; specific color of paper and ink; type of paper. (This includes letterheads, envelopes, statements, labels, and so on.)
- *Business cards.* Placement of the property's name and symbol, address and telephone number, together with the individual's name, title (if any), and e-mail address.
- *Signage.* Type size and style, placement of the property's name and symbol, background and other colors for the complete array of sign types that will be needed.
- *Brochures.* Type size and style, placement of the property's name and symbol, ink and paper colors.
- *Advertisements.* Format of ads, type sizes and styles to be used, placement of the property's name and symbol, margins, use of abbreviations and other constant elements.
- *Vehicles.* Color, placement of the property's name and symbol. (This would pertain to company cars and trucks.)

These are just starting points. The graphic designer should examine everything that will bear the name or symbol of the apartment community and include these in the graphics manual. Everyone in the organization who has anything to do with ordering signs, ads, printed materials, or similar items should have a copy of the manual and follow it. It also is a good idea to give copies to your sign painter, printer, newspaper account executive, and advertising agency and insist that they, too, follow the instructions.

Signage.   Once a theme and name have been selected, a symbol designed, and a graphics manual prepared, you are ready to address the all-important challenge of signage. As a general observation, signs are often badly designed and grossly overdone. The average American is exposed to literally tens of thousands of signs every day, and most are totally ignored. When designing signage, you should be mindful of any sign ordinances that may affect the type of sign you are allowed to post or the manner of its display. If signs are going to have any effect at all, they must always be consistent with your graphics system, and they must meet these minimum standards.

- Signs must always look fresh and clean, as if they had been put up that day. Otherwise, they will present a poor image of your apartment community and people will ignore them—or think worse of the quality of your property.
- Signs must be at right angles to traffic, not parallel. Otherwise, they will be hard to see and read. People should be able to read the sign's message through the windshield of a car traveling at the posted speed limit at least 150 feet from the sign.
- Signs should have no more than eight to ten words. If there are too many words, people riding by in autos will not be able to read and interpret the message.

Signs serve four basic purposes: promotion, direction, identification, and information. Promotional signs are primarily off-site billboards, which are discussed and illustrated in Chapter 10. The other three types of signs are discussed here.

Directional Signs.   These signs direct prospects to the apartment community and the rental information center. The number of directional signs needed and where they should be placed depends on how difficult it is to find the property. Generally, if the apartment community is on a well-traveled road in the midst of competing rental properties, a good entry sign is sufficient. If it is in a remote location, directional signs can be helpful. These signs (Exhibits 9.3 and 9.4) are meant to give directions, not to sell.

Another form of directional signage is a *reassurance sign,* sometimes called a trailblazer. It reassures prospects that they have indeed made the proper turn and are on the right track. If you have ever been to a company picnic in a rural location, you have probably seen homemade signs on telephone poles to help lead the way. These are primitive versions of reassurance signs. The apartment community's signs obviously cannot be homemade, but they should be inexpensive because their life span is usually quite short.

As prospects turn into the driveway, they should see a sign directing them to the rental information center. As they proceed along this drive, there should be similar signs at turns or intersections so drivers know exactly how to proceed. Once prospects reach the parking lot, one or more signs should direct them to visitor parking spaces. Signs in the parking area should guide the visitor to the rental information center. If necessary, directional signage should continue into the building so prospects know exactly where to go. All of these signs should conform to the specifications in the graphics manual to reinforce the image you are trying to convey.

Exhibit 9.3
Directional Billboards

These signs are intended to direct, not to sell. The sign illustrated at the top is an example of an off-site directional billboard that might be used on a limited-access highway. The directions are clear but brief. Arrows or additional instructions are not always necessary if the way to proceed is clear.

Identification Signs.   This category includes different sign examples, but one is clearly more important than all of the others. It is referred to by different names: *permanent identification, monument,* or *keystone-entry sign.* The permanent entry sign establishes the character of the property and is both substantial in construction and architectural in design. It usually displays little more than the apartment community's name.

When designed correctly, a permanent identification sign is usually expensive. It should be lighted and made part of a landscaped setting designed for change-of-season or year-round plantings. In the case of a high-rise structure, an engraved plaque that is coordinated with the building can be very attractive. Printing the apartment name on an awning or permanent canopy is another way to identify the high-rise apartment building. The ma-

Exhibit 9.4
Directional Signs

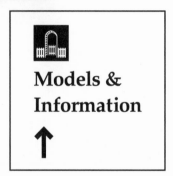

The two signs at the top are examples of reassurance signs, sometimes called trailblazers. They are usually small, inexpensive, and placed on poles along the route. Note the use of reverse colors. This attracts more attention and is easier to read. The models and information sign at the bottom is an on-site, lead-in sign used to direct prospects. These signs should be used sparingly, but enough to avoid confusion.

jority of renters will come as a result of just driving by the property. This sign will be one of their first contacts with your property. If given $10,000 to spend on both an entry sign and a brochure, an apartment manager would be better off spending $9,500 on the sign and only $500 on the brochure. The sign will draw more traffic and have a greater impact than most other promotional activities.

Other identification signs include building address signs and those that identify recreational and supporting amenities, such as swimming pools and laundry rooms. Signs identifying the rental information center, visitor parking, and recreation center are also in this category (Exhibit 9.5). These signs, as well as all other forms of signage, should be used sparingly to avoid cluttering the landscape.

Exhibit 9.5
Identification Signs

Rental
Information
Center

Recreation
Center

386

These signs are used to identify important buildings and locations as well as individual apartment buildings. They can be installed either as plaques affixed to buildings or as free-standing signs on standards. The design and the use of logo, color, and type style should be consistent with the apartment community's graphic plan.

A telephone number with the area code is also an important element on rental signs because people frequently drive through neighborhoods when they are selecting a location. Once a prospect establishes a preferred area, he or she begins to note the best-looking rental communities and will frequently make telephone inquiries as to rent, availability, etc. Cell phones are a preferred mode of communication for rental prospects.

Informational Signs.   These signs have the least value from a marketing standpoint, and their use should be minimized as much as possible. The most common of these are called *command signs*. They include notices put up by apartment managers who like to give commands. Command signs say: "Keep Off the Grass," "Close the Door," "Put Garbage in Dumpster," "Don't Post Messages on the Mailbox," or "No Boots in Hallways."

Often the manager posts such a sign to deal with an immediate problem and then forgets about it. Often the signs are crudely made, and sometimes they can be confusing. One manager posted a "No Hot Water" sign when the plumbing in the laundry room was being repaired and then forgot to take the sign down. You can imagine the bewilderment of residents arriving to do laundry after the plumbing was back in order. Residents quickly learn to ignore such signs if they read them in the first place.

Managers should stay away from these "don't" signs. Instead of posting a "Close the Door" sign, install a door closer. Rather than using a sign telling residents not to put their boots in the hallway, state this rule in a letter sent to residents at the start of the snow season. If there are signs telling people to put their garbage in the Dumpster or not to post notices on the mailboxes, remove them immediately. They only create a negative image for the property.

Some informational signs are necessary and required by law—e.g., swimming pool rule signs. You should comply with the law, but do not add any unnecessary signs or posters (Exhibit 9.6, page 200).

Finally, there is another type of informational sign that finds its way into apartment communities. Contractors, suppliers, and others like to post signs on buildings they serve to advertise themselves. Furniture rental companies and apartment locator services are other examples. Calendars, scratch pads, and ashtrays carrying other firms' advertising have no place in the office or rental area. Managers should establish a policy forbidding the placement of other firms' advertising on the property and enforce it.

Rental Information Center.   Some rental offices look cold, harsh, and commercial. The furnishings are severe and may include a mixture of wood and metal desks and an assortment of uninviting side chairs. The desks are covered with calendars, appointment books, application forms, and five-day notices. Everything shouts: "This is the place where the landlord conducts business!"

Prospects do not necessarily come to rent; they come for information. The appearance of most rental offices makes many prospects feel uncomfortable. They are on guard and antagonistic in an office situation that makes them think they are applying for a loan.

Furnishings for your rental information center should be residential in scale. Choose comfortable chairs and round tables. Create a warm, inviting atmosphere that says, "Welcome!" Use color to liven up the surroundings. Serve coffee in the winter, iced tea or lemonade in the summer, plus cookies. This will help put prospects at ease.

Round tables are especially important. When you and the prospect sit down to discuss the apartment and the lease application, having a desk between you creates a head-to-head selling situation. You want to be on the prospect's side, and a round table accomplishes this automatically.

Exhibit 9.6
Informational Signs

Pool Rules
Hours: 10:00 am to 10:00 pm daily
Children under 12 years of age must
be accompanied by an adult.
No glass in pool area.

Office Hours

Weekdays
10:00 am to 6:30 pm

Weekends
10:00 am to 5:00 pm

Speed

20

Limit

These types of signs should be used sparingly; use them when they are extremely important or required by law. Too often, informational signs are command signs that are hand-lettered on site. They are often graphically inconsistent, rarely obeyed, and irritating to residents.

Providing a place for children to play is a definite asset and well worth the expense. Parents can ask questions without interruption, and the manager does not have to worry about bothersome noise or possible breakage.

Exhibits in the rental information center are important. They are needed to give information about the property and provide a diversion for waiting visitors while you are involved with other prospects. No one wants to stand around gaping at plain walls. People welcome the opportunity to look at something informative. Exhibits also serve another function: They give prospects a semblance of a barrier behind which they can retreat while discussing their decision or their finances.

For exhibits, you can use scale models of the apartment community, a site plan, photos of the building, enlargements of floor plans, photos or sketches of amenities, lists of features, and an area facilities map. One of the best exhibits is a large aerial photograph showing the apartment community in relation to the rest of the city. People enjoy looking at where they are on the photo and identifying familiar sites. Virtual tours and interactive electronic messaging have become very effective marketing tools.

Some apartment communities go so far as to have brochures of competing properties on display (or mounted in a book). This enables the leasing agent to compare the community with other properties and respond to prospects who say they want to see what the competition has to offer before making a decision.

If model apartments are in the same building as the rental information center, you may want to extend the graphics or exhibits into the connecting corridor, so prospects continue to receive a favorable impression as they walk to the model apartments.

Model Apartments. A well-furnished model apartment is an essential part of the marketing program for apartment communities in their initial rent-up periods, for larger properties that must deal with a steady flow of resident turnover, or for those suffering from an undue number of vacancies. An attractive model expresses a lifestyle that cannot be verbalized, only experienced. Observe the following points when you are setting up your models.

- *One model or two?* First you must decide how many models to prepare. The budget will probably dictate the answer to this question. Two models allow you to show two completely different decorating solutions. Taking prospects from one to the other, you can demonstrate the adaptability of the apartment design. Also, furnishing two models allows you to show two different lifestyles, one that appeals to the younger renter, perhaps, and another that caters to a more mature person. Having more than one model makes for a longer tour which, in turn, gives your rental staff more time with the customer. When the models have completely different color and decorating schemes, it allows the leasing agent to ask for an opinion, which can be very helpful when it is time to help the prospect arrive at a decision.

  If you have a full range of unit sizes and they all enjoy about the same market appeal, model the smaller units. Efficiency apartments, in particular, tend to look small when they are empty. A creative furniture layout and decorating scheme can change a one-room apartment into a cozy, functional home. If you have efficiency apartments and choose to prepare a decorated model, you must certainly do a one- or two-bedroom unit as well. A furnished and decorated efficiency apartment will help in the marketing of that type of unit but is of little value to a prospect who is interested in a larger apartment. In fact, a prospect who is shown an efficiency unit after the desire for a one-bedroom apartment has been expressed will probably become irritated, believing that time is being wasted.

When you model a two-bedroom unit, decorate only the master bedroom as a bedroom. (Bedroom decorating is usually boring so there is little to be gained by showing more than one bedroom setting.) Apartments with two bedrooms and one bath are sometimes more difficult to rent. Showing a unit with the second bedroom furnished as a computer room, den, hobby room, or get-away room will do much more to attract renters than decorating another bedroom. If people need the room for a bedroom, they can certainly visualize how it will appear. They probably already have the bedroom furnishings, and most bedroom layouts allow for little variation. Because of this, there is no reason to furnish three- or four-bedroom units; doing so simply increases the overall costs.

- *Select one of the least-desirable units for a model apartment,* not one of the best. Although this may sound backwards, it is really not. Prospects are quick to detect the advantages of an apartment with an exceptional layout and location. Decorated model apartments will help equalize the worst apartment layouts. The poorer layout will gain desirability when creatively decorated. The better layout can stand on its own without the help of sample furnishings. Owners and developers often model only their best layouts. This leads to an unbalanced rent-up: The better layouts, further enhanced with furnishings, rent quickly—and the less-desirable units move even more slowly. Let the model furnishings give those units the needed boost.

  After the initial marketing campaign, and in a strong market, you may find that you need a model to help with re-leasing apartments. It is often difficult or harmful to show an occupied apartment because of poor housekeeping, odors, or similar problems. In these situations, a decorated model quickly pays for itself. When you make the decision to utilize models on an ongoing basis, use a different tack and select one or two units from among your most plentiful layouts.

- *Stay close to the office.* Surveys have shown repeatedly that model apartments are often left out of the rental presentation, usually because the decorated model was too far away and the prospect had a tight schedule. In all likelihood, the leasing agent was trying to shorten the showing time by eliminating the trip to one or more models. When the model is not shown, you negate the expense of having created it and lose all the benefits a model offers to the marketing process.

- *Choose first-floor units.* In walk-up properties, it is important to have your models on the first or ground floor because they offer easy access. Some apartment managers might be afraid that first-floor apartments present too great a risk of break-in or burglary. This is a terrible endorsement, even if the prospect never learns of that fear. The fact that the manager's thinking runs in that direction is an indication of the lifestyle being offered. If the model furnishings are not safe on the first floor, how safe are the possessions of the residents?

Having the models on the lower floors is also important for customer convenience and accessibility. Some prospects have difficulty negotiating stairs, and in those cases, upstairs models will not play a role in the marketing process.

- *Make the decorating and furnishings of the model truly outstanding,* not mediocre, regardless of your market. The more dramatic the approach, the better. While the model may be beyond the average prospect's means, it should not be beyond his or her dreams.

A model apartment is intended to be looked at; it is not for living. Common furnishings, such as a triple dresser in a bedroom or a TV set in the living room, take up space and do little to enhance the atmosphere of a model. Even a shower curtain that is fanned across the bathtub does more damage than one might imagine. Most apartment bathrooms are tiny, maybe five by seven feet, and hanging a shower curtain visually reduces the room size. Instead you can take colorful towels of different sizes, roll them rather than fold them, and stack them in the back inside corner where the bathtub meets the wall (you will need to support the stack, but whatever you use will be hidden).

In the past, apartment managers and developers would hire furniture stores to decorate model apartments. Managers got the job done for little or nothing in return for promoting the store name in the models and in advertising. As a result, most models looked homey and comfortable, but they made little impact on prospects. Too often, this arrangement reflected the inventory of the store rather than the goals of the rental program. The use of rented furniture yields the same results. The style and quality are often mediocre, adding absolutely nothing to the appeal of the apartment.

I recommend hiring a competent *interior designer* and giving this professional license to decorate the apartment and make the most of its advantages. The results may be startling; no doubt they will be memorable as well. One caution, however, is that some decorators tend to use dark colors and heavy finishes that can make prospects feel uncomfortable. You should see some of the decorator's work and have some understanding of it so that the resulting model will not be a surprise.

People will come to see the model apartments and talk about them, and this builds traffic. Prospects may not want to live in a daringly decorated apartment, but they will remember it. High-income prospects will expect to see something innovative in decorating, and moderate-income prospects will be flattered by this approach. Either way, you will impress your prospects and give them something to remember.

You need not worry about recovering the cost of the furnishings if you have used an unusual decor. When the time comes to close the model, chances are that you can recover about 60 percent of their original cost. With mediocre furnishings, you will be lucky to recover 30 percent. The difference is that people are willing to pay more for decorator merchandise, whereas they know they can get conventional furnishings anywhere.

- *Do a complete decorating job.* Decorate right down to the accessories. This includes flowers and place settings on the tables, books on the shelves, guest towels in the bathroom, and interesting utensils in the kitchen.

  However, some managers think it is a good idea to put display food in the refrigerator, towels in the closet, even a half-eaten cookie on a plate to convey the sense that someone lives in the apartment. This is not wise. Prospects will think they are intruders in someone's private home. If they open a closet and find towels inside, they will often shut the door quickly.

  Furnish the apartment like a model, not like a home. This means no magazines or clutter. A weekly magazine is only one week away from being out-of-date. People want new and up-to-date ideas, and they will be less inclined to garner them from models that seem to be stale. Also, clutter is one of the reasons people move. House and garage sales are evidence of this. The opportunity to reorganize possessions and discard things that are no longer needed is one of the few advantages to moving. For best results, your models should look clean and uncluttered.

- *If someone wants it, rent it.* Imagine that you work in a clothing store, and a shopper walks in and wants to buy the outfit on the mannequin. Would you sell it to her? Chances are excellent that you would. Why not? The mannequin is a selling tool. Its purpose is to show off the clothes to their best advantage. In the example it did just that. Obviously, if the store had that same item on the rack, it would be offered before dismantling the display; but if the mannequin displayed the only such merchandise in the store, it would be sold.

  The same rule applies to renting a model apartment, and renting a model offers advantages that compensate for the extra work involved in creating a new one. First of all, you should be able to lease the model with its special decorating for a premium rental rate. Whenever you can improve an apartment so that you can charge a higher rent for it, that is known as *value added*. It is one of the most important things you can do in the operation of rental properties.

Remove the furnishings and use them in your next model with some new pieces and some innovative twists or modifications. You now have the opportunity to create an even better, more-creative model. New and exciting models renew the enthusiasm of the entire staff, especially the leasing agents. After showing the same model for months, maybe even years, agents are certainly bored and often embarrassed about its age and condition. Tired models are said to have "whiskers." When the models are not sharp or interesting, leasing agents begin skipping that part of the tour.

- *Forget mood music.* Background music in a model does not help the rental process. It can actually annoy prospects and often interferes with conversation.

- *Once a model is set up, keep it in first-class condition.* Have the custodial staff vacuum the carpets every day and keep bathroom fixtures sparkling and everything else in good order. Make sure the air is fresh but not "perfumed." You can expect that some accessories will disappear. These should be replaced as soon as the loss is discovered. Don't let the model apartment take on a run-down appearance.

- *Use model apartments only so long as they are useful in the leasing program.* When occupancy reaches 90 to 92 percent, you should consider selling the model furnishings. The remaining apartments can be rented by showing vacant units. At that point, the models probably will show wear and tear as well as age. Despite their innovative good looks when new, styles will change, and your models will begin to look dowdy. This is a good time to close the model(s).

  Some model apartments are shown long past the time when they should have been put back into the income stream. Managers may insist that models are necessary when, in fact, they are maintained as a crutch because the manager is slow to put the vacant apartments in proper market-ready condition.

  In some cases, models are maintained beyond their useful lives because they are used as accommodations for important guests or visiting owners or even supervising managers. This is not recommended. Prospects inspecting these apartments will see partially used bars of soap and rolls of toilet paper, or soiled glassware and utensils, perhaps even a bedside clock radio. It does not take long to deduce that someone lives in the apartment. At this point, prospects feel they are invading someone's privacy and become anxious to leave. Also, as mentioned earlier, an office and model combination should be avoided. Each has its own function and the two do not mix.

In my opinion, there are only a few situations in which it may be necessary to maintain model apartments permanently. One such occasion is prompted by unusually high ceilings. If the normal ceiling height in your apartments is nine feet rather than the more standard eight feet, or the ceiling has a high vault, the extra height can make empty units appear smaller than they actually are. People think that higher ceilings *always* make rooms look more spacious, but that is not the case with an empty apartment. Empty rooms with higher ceilings appear smaller because people are accustomed to eight-foot ceilings. When a room is vacant, prospects will tend to refer to a room's height to gauge its length and width. A furnished model apartment demonstrates that standard furniture, and particularly queen- or king-size beds, will fit nicely. When prospects see a furnished room with higher ceilings, they use the furniture as a gauge. This way the ceiling height works to your advantage and the room appears larger.

Another permanent model situation is in an apartment community with high turnover. Such a property should always have a model unit for showing to prospects. It is especially important that these models are always on the leading edge in order to achieve the maximum impact on rental prospects.

If you are managing an apartment community in which new buildings are being opened in successive years, relocate the models to the newest building. You may reuse some of the old furniture by having it cleaned or re-covered, but you will want to emphasize the newness of the new buildings by having up-to-date models. Doing this creates one unavoidable risk: Renters living in buildings that were opened earlier will be attracted to the new models and may want to transfer to the new building. The risk is worth taking in view of the drawing power that new models will have on prospective renters attracted to the newest phase.

Brochures and Collateral Material. Contrary to what many people think, a brochure has little value in renting apartments. Admittedly, this is not true in the case of for-sale housing. In a campaign to sell houses, the brochure is an important selling tool because the decision to buy is rarely made on the first visit. In the case of renting apartments, however, about half of all rentals are made on first visits. For these people, a brochure is a post-selling tool. It helps reassure people that they have made the right decision, and it covers any questions that may not have been answered.

The rental brochure is primarily intended for the prospects who did not rent on the first visit. Prospects searching for the right apartment often visit five or six apartment communities in a single day and become confused by what they have seen. They cannot remember one property from another and use the brochures they have acquired to help jog their memories.

The brochure should be simple, direct, clear, and inexpensive. A very slick and superlative-packed brochure can work against you. Prospects do not want to be sold; they want to be informed. Give them the facts with a straightforward narrative message that is specific to your property. Don't try to win them over with gimmicky copy. Consider this example:

Four hundred acres of natural beauty. The cool tranquility of a mile-long lake and winding streams. Towering oaks, scented pines, and graceful willows. Brooks, glens, and glades. Wildlife. Flowers. Heavenly Manor offers apartments in the midst of one of the most beautiful settings in our area.

That is a lot of descriptive copy, especially considering that it describes nothing about the property. Such copy says little and is a turnoff to the reader. This copy is more effective:

We're at Lake Drive and Westgate Lane, with easy access to Town Square Mall, the Outer Belt Business Center, and the Jefferson Middle School. Lake Louise, just five minutes away, offers sailing, fishing, golf, a park, and picnic areas. The Municipal Airport and downtown are twenty minutes away. Choose from four large floor plans; one-, two-, and three-bedroom units, each with a den. Washer and dryer in every unit, hi-tech kitchens, and individual climate controls.

When it comes to illustrating the brochure, use actual photographs whenever possible. Stay away from renderings of buildings; people are often suspicious of artwork. I would also offer a word of caution: *Don't illustrate anything in the brochure or write about anything that will not be in your community.* The brochure will likely end up in a drawer, only to be interpreted later as an implied warranty. For example, if you picture a woman with a tennis racquet and there is no tennis court, the prospect may use this to claim that you promised tennis courts. The same is true for any other feature or service that is mentioned, or implied, but not actually provided.

Finally, the brochure should include *the name of your apartment community; complete street address, city, state, and zip code; telephone number with area code; and e-mail address.* This is particularly important for prospects who visit a number of rental properties in different suburbs or cities. Without this information, prospects may have difficulty remembering who you are and how to reach you.

If your property has a web site, include that fact in the brochure. You should also be sure that the contact information is prominently displayed on the web site, along with directions to navigate the site for a virtual tour of the property and models if these capabilities exist. Prospects can then connect to your site and reconfirm your property's features and amenities for themselves.

The same identifying information should be on floor plans and the site plan if these are inserts to the brochure. Floor plans should be as large as possible, preferably letter size (8½×11 inches). People have problems interpreting small floor plans, so make them big. The larger the floor plan, the larger the apartment appears in the prospect's mind. You should also include dimensions on the floor plans for all major rooms. Site plans are good for a multi-building development. A site plan identifies all the amenities and helps orient the prospect to a particular building and its location relative to others.

Besides the brochure, floor plans, and site plan, other items that come under the general heading of collateral sales material include:

- Letters or cards sent to prospects after they leave to thank them for their visit. The leasing agent who helped them should sign these.

- Postcards with a picture of the apartment community. These can be picked up by prospects in the rental information center, or they can be used by new residents to notify friends of their change of address.

- Hard candies wrapped in paper imprinted with the apartment community's name and logo. These might be set out in dishes in the rental office or handed to prospects as they leave.

As you go along, you will discover all sorts of other collateral promotional items. These, too, should tie in with the property's theme and conform to the unified graphics system.

Finding Prospects: Other Sources

Besides drive-by traffic and advertising (which is the focus of Chapter 10), there are several other sources for prospects.

Apartment Locator Services.   Most cities have firms that make a business of assisting prospects in their search for a new apartment home. These firms are usually grouped separately in the Yellow Pages or in the classified section of the newspaper, and they are commonly called apartment locators or apartment finders. Apartment locators offer their services to the prospect by providing a central source for rental listings. The fee, however, is paid by the owner of the apartment community that gains the prospect as a resident. (The fee is typically a percentage of the first month's rent.) Apartment locator services are not offered in every city or town, and the quality of these firms varies widely. A good locator service can be a valuable member of your marketing team. Locator services offer advantages to both rental prospects and the apartment community, among them:

- *Saving time.* Blindly following apartment advertisements can waste a great deal of time for apartment hunters. Ads typically reveal all of the benefits and none of the drawbacks of advertised apartments. A quality locator service will take the time to learn each prospect's criteria for an apartment and will qualify the customer according to price, location, unit availability, etc. Current information about those apartment communities that meet the prospect's requirements is shared to narrow the search and save the prospect time. Many locator services even have videos and exterior and interior color pictures on computer so they can give the prospect a virtual tour of the community and its available units.

- *Identifying special needs.* A number of would-be renters have unusual requirements. Perhaps a prospect has a large dog and has been turned down again and again. Maybe the prospect has a very large family and is experiencing difficulty finding an affordable unit that has enough room. Possibly the prospect requires a short-term lease because he or she is building a house and construction has been delayed.

- *Relocation assistance.* Apartment locator services are most popular among prospects who are relocating from one place to another and have little knowledge of their new city. A locator is often in the best position to provide unbiased assistance in finding just the right accommodations. Corporations with transferees will often work with locator services to help their employees find new living quarters.

- *Market feedback.* Apartment locators are probably the apartment manager's best source of market feedback. Locators typically supply prospects with a number of listings to visit. If the listings do not meet a customer's needs, he or she returns in search of additional listings. The locator is interested in learning what the person did and did not like so that a better apartment "match" can be found. In this process, locators receive some very candid criticism. Maybe the property looked okay in the computer photographs, but set in the context of a declining neighborhood, it proved unsatisfactory. Perhaps the physical condition of the property or the unit itself was not acceptable. Maybe the prospect encountered an unfriendly leasing agent. After a while, apartment locators learn which of the rental communities they are serving are good and which are not.

  Your job is to get these agents to level with you. It will take some convincing that you really want a candid opinion and honest appraisal and not just a few white-washed comments. Locators know if your property is in a neighborhood that is perceived to be bad; or the property has a questionable reputation; or the housekeeping is poor or smells are offensive; or that you are simply asking too much rent.

Cultivating a relationship with a few of the more aggressive locators will pay enormous dividends in understanding your property's true market position.

Many of the better locator services track all sorts of market information on computer databases. They know vacancies, rents, special deals, good properties from bad, market trends, popular upgrades, employment opportunities, and corporate shifts. If asked, many services will share this information with you.

Most companies use locator services to supplement, not replace, their own rental efforts. What you do not want to do is become dependent on the service of locators and exert less effort attracting prospects yourself. In a balanced marketing program, locators should be responsible for about 15 percent of your rentals.

Resident Referrals.   Probably no one is a better prospect than the person who walks into the rental information center after being referred by one of your long-time residents. This prospect is probably the same caliber as the present resident. Moreover, the prospect usually has seen the resident's apartment, likes the property, and is ready to rent. The resident has already done the job of informing and exciting the prospect. Such a prospect is much more desirable than one referred by a locator service or one who merely drives by.

To let residents know that you welcome and reward referrals, periodically send them a letter or flyer announcing this. To qualify, the resident must bring in and introduce the prospect personally, so there is no question of whether a proper referral has been made. You do not want a situation in which a prospect comes in alone and rents an apartment, and later a resident claims to have referred that prospect. A personal introduction eliminates this possibility. When the prospect signs the lease, the resident who made the referral gets a reward.

The reward can take many different forms. The current trend is to make the reward a very nice improvement to the apartment—possibly a new appliance or a special decorator treatment. Townhouse developments sometimes offer to plant a fair-sized tree in the yard outside the referring person's unit or to add some special landscaping. Many properties offer the same reward to both the referring party and the new resident. Knowing that both parties benefit makes it much easier for a person to refer someone.

It should be noted that when rewards are offered, particularly cash rewards, the greatest proliferation of renewal prospects will come from some of your residents whose recommendations you might prefer not to have. Hence, you may want to examine the profile of your current residents beforehand. This problem only seems to occur when the referral prize is cash or a cash equivalent. You can avoid the potential problem by making the reward an improvement to the apartment.

Some states have regulations that limit the use of referral rewards. The restrictions may relate directly to real estate licensing requirements, and the distribution of sizeable cash awards for referrals may be prohibited.

Housing Directors.   Included in this group are housing directors and personnel or human resources managers of nearby corporations, hospitals, military bases, and colleges who seek housing for people transferring into the area. Contacts with these people usually are dominated by full-service real estate firms that offer a variety of services, including home sales and mortgage financing in addition to apartments for rent.

If the location of your apartment community is within easy driving distance of a major employer, it certainly would pay to call on the housing or personnel director and establish a relationship. Your cause will be dramatically improved if you can point to some of their employees who are currently your residents. Don't expect instant results. You should plan to make regular calls, say every two months, to drop off literature and renew acquaintances. It is also worthwhile to inquire about affiliate companies as well as firms that supply or support them. The personnel director will often have advance word of relocations, expansions, or special assignments involving other firms that provide associated services.

You might consider establishing a "preferred employer program," in which you offer special benefits to the employees of select companies. Typically these include no security deposit (or a greatly reduced security deposit), rent discounts up to 10 percent, and the right to cancel without penalty in the event of a company transfer. If you decide to initiate such a program, seek the cooperation of the personnel department to help you promote the plan. It most likely will be your job to prepare the printed materials and posters, but you will need the company's help in distributing these materials. If you choose to go this route, it is really important that you make a full promotional effort. Otherwise, you may find that you have returned security deposits and lowered rents of existing residents who are employed by that firm without gaining any new ones.

Rent-up Specialists.   In many markets, there are firms that will take over the leasing function for your property. Usually they arrive with a team of well-trained leasing specialists who know the techniques of renting and, in particular, the art of asking for a commitment. The fee typically covers their out-of-pocket costs plus a commission for every signed lease they produce. Most firms will tolerate your existing staff, but they almost never share customers or their knowledge of leasing techniques. These firms and their staffs must produce, or they will not be in business long. Most representatives of these firms are much more effective than the typical leasing agent because they have had better training and they are closely supervised.

Employing such a firm might sound like just the ticket. You can hire one of these leasing specialists, fill your property quickly, terminate the relationship, and handle the slower-paced renewals with your own staff. There are major drawbacks to this, however. The cost of the service is high. In very soft markets, the rental progress is often not much better than you were accomplishing on your own, and the prospect bonds with someone who is not your employee. Also, when you utilize outsiders, you are not developing an experienced staff of your own. The most damaging side effect, however, is the high turnover rate of the residents attracted in one of these rental campaigns. I have seen countless examples in which more than 80 percent of the residents who rented under these programs were no longer living in the same apartment after one year. The leasing specialists counter with the argument that they were successful in attracting renters, and if there is any blame for an undue rate of move-outs, it should be directed at the quality of management. Whatever the cause, apartments lease faster with leasing specialists, but the turnover rate increases as well.

10

*Candy and cookies do more
to fatten the staff than
please the customers.*

Advertising and Promotion

More than half of the people who rent apartments do so because they liked what they saw when they drove by the property. Experience shows that advertising attracts only about 20 percent of those prospects who become residents, and most of them come through ads placed in the classified section of a newspaper.

Advertising Media

Many types of advertising media are available to your property, including daily newspapers, apartment guides, the Internet (your web site), radio, television, billboards, direct mail, and telephone directories.

Newspapers.   Advertising apartments for rent in the daily newspaper is not nearly as prevalent or effective as it was in the past. Major dailies throughout the United States have suffered significant losses in their apartment rental classified ad lineage. Some papers have only one-half the lineage that they enjoyed previously. It is interesting to note that many daily newspapers have maintained or increased their advertising rates despite the fact that they have fewer readers and response to their ads is markedly lower.

Some apartment managers believe newspaper advertising is absolutely essential, especially on weekends. They believe that if they run an ad on Saturday or Sunday, prospects will rush in to rent apartments. This is not so. To find out for yourself, you can conduct this test: Discontinue all newspaper advertising for one or two weekends and take note of the difference in traffic count. You probably will see little change in rental traffic.

There are several reasons for this. Drive-bys, apartment guides, locator services, and referrals are responsible for the majority of rental prospect traffic, and these sources of prospects continue whether you advertise in the classifieds or not. Other prospects are drawn to the area by advertisements placed by your competitors; while in the neighborhood, they stop in to visit your apartment community. This also works in reverse when you advertise; your ads will draw traffic that will visit your competition. The best-looking property comes out ahead in this traffic trading. Finally, many prospects are already aware of your property and will not be influenced one way or the other by advertising or a lack of it.

This does not mean that you can skip newspaper advertising altogether. Before you can check the consequences of discontinuing ads, you first have to have an established newspaper advertising program. At a certain point, however, newspaper advertising loses much of its impact, and fewer and fewer prospects can be traced to those ads. Some advertising will always be necessary because of that 20 percent of prospects who are drawn by it and have no other way of learning about you. However, you should not rely on newspaper advertising alone to generate prospects.

Actually, people begin making up their minds to change living quarters six to ten weeks before setting out on their first trip to look at available housing. There is an endless variety of incidents which can prompt people into the process of looking for new living quarters. Their reasons or discontent can be either vague or well-defined. Maybe the neighbors are becoming more and more annoying, or the closets are too small and overstuffed. Perhaps their landlord is not responsive to their requests. Maybe their children are having bad experiences at school, or the long drive home from work is just too stressful. One or more of these dissatisfactions can build up over time.

The "seed to move" might be planted two or three months before the actual apartment hunting begins. During this period, future prospects begin paying attention to newspaper and other advertisements. This might go on for a full six weeks before they actually leave their living room. Just before starting out on their search, prospects begin studying the classified ads. Instinct says that if there are any real bargains, they will be in the smaller classified ads and not in the larger display-classified ads placed by major developments or realty companies.

Then, one weekend, when the weather is nice (but not too nice) or when there has been another incident where they currently reside or they get notice of a rent increase, the actual physical excursions begin. Many of the people who respond to your ads will undoubtedly follow a pattern similar to this.

Their need or desire for a different place to live began months before, followed by weeks of comparing ads, and ending now with actual physical inspections. If your ad appears on the weekend these prospects decide to shop, they might show up at your doorstep in response. This requires a bit of coincidence, the right timing, and some skill in the art of writing an effective ad. Coincidence is pure luck; timing will come with experience, and the skills for preparing an ad can be learned. Consider these points in understanding the three types of newspaper advertising.

- *Classified*. The name comes from the fact that this kind of advertising is classified by subject matter—jobs available, jobs wanted, goods for sale, homes for sale, apartments for rent. The ads are grouped together in one section of the paper, and they are generally set in one-column widths, using the uniform typeface and format of the newspaper (Exhibit 10.1).

  Many newspapers now offer a *customized classified* ad. For an extra charge, a classified ad can be placed in a shaded or outlined box which helps it stand out better in the long columns of ad listings. Also, special graphics can be added as an attention-getter, and small photos can be added to the once staid classified ad.

- *Display*. These ads appear throughout the newspaper. They use photos, art and illustrations, and a variety of type styles (Exhibit 10.2), and the sizes of these ads can vary considerably.

- *Display-classified*. This is a hybrid type of ad that is located in the classified section of the newspaper and utilizes some of the artwork and type style variety that a display ad might have (Exhibit 10.3).

In most cases, you will find that classified advertising is the most productive of the three types. It is recommended for the majority of your promotional advertising.

Regardless of what type of newspaper ad you run, the ad should answer the prospect's three primary questions:

1. *What do I get?* This means describing the important features of the property, beginning with the apartment. Start with the number of bedrooms. That is the first thing prospects want to know. Then specify such things as the number of bathrooms, kitchen equipment, carpeting, window coverings, ceiling heights, method of climate control, utilities, fireplace, washer/dryer connections, and storage space. Go on to list the property's amenities (e.g., swimming pool, relaxation

Exhibit 10.1
Classified Ads

LAKEVIEW AREA—$775
Lg corner 1 bdrm. apt, 2d flr overlooking garden. Great kit., Corian counters; central A/C, washer/dryer hookups, pool.
Call (555) 555-5555

Your Place

1 & 2 Bedroom Apts.
Very large and bright apartments. Natural, wooded setting. 15 minutes to downtown via expressway. Close to schools and shopping.

- Central Air Conditioning
- Self-Cleaning Oven
- Side-by-Side Refrigerator/Freezer
- Fireplace
- Private Patios or Balconies
- Swimming Pool
- Lighted Tennis Courts

From $775

Open daily 10 A.M. to 6 P.M.

Directions: Take SR40 to the Main Street exit and go west 1½ blocks.

200 Place Drive
(555) 555-5555
www.yourplace.com

Equal Housing Opportunity

Classified ads are the most common, and typically most useful, form of promotional advertising for rental apartments. Every ad, regardless of size, must answer the three basic questions prospective residents ask: What do I get? How much does it cost? and, Where do I find it? A series of different ads of varying sizes is recommended to attract maximum readership.

garden, business center, tennis courts, playground, sun deck, lake, putting green).

These features can be set down either in a narrative or paragraph style, or in a bulletin or list style. It is important to vary the form so your ad does not look the same each weekend.

Avoid using too many abbreviations: While BR, Kit., fpl., and TH may be intelligible to you, the reader may not understand them. In any event, abbreviations impede easy reading of the ad. Generally understood abbreviations are permissible (e.g., Apt., A/C, St., Ave.).

To attract different markets and add variety, try switching what

Exhibit 10.2
Display Ad

A place with carefully designed apartments and custom features. A place where you can swim, play tennis, party, or quietly stroll down a wooded path. A place that is meticulously maintained and professionally managed. A special place that will enhance your lifestyle.

Your Place, with 1 and 2 bedroom apartments starting from $775 per month.

During our Grand Opening Celebration we invite you to see for yourself why Your Place is "a place to call home."

Furnished models open daily from 10:00 am to 6:00 pm

Take SR40 to Main Street exit, go west 1½ blocks to

Your Place
200 Place Drive
(555) 555-5555
www.yourplace.com

EQUAL HOUSING
OPPORTUNITY

Display ads create awareness. They are generally used for a grand-opening campaign or on an ongoing basis for a large multi-phase development. The sample ad shown here (obviously reduced in size) might be used as a full-page ad in a magazine or newspaper. Note that this ad answers the three basic questions prospective residents ask.

Exhibit 10.3
Display-Classified Ad

Your Place

1 & 2 Bedroom Apartments

Your Place offers you all you would expect in apartment living and more, "a place to call home." Each apartment is carefully designed to offer you the most in custom features including:

* Central Air Conditioning
* Self-Cleaning Oven
* Fireplace
* Side-by-Side Refrigerator/Freezer
* Solid Surface Counters
* Private Garages Available

For your leisure time, Your Place offers a beautifully decorated club house with a large pool and lighted tennis courts.

$775–$1,080

Your Place is conveniently located only minutes from schools, shopping, and expressways.

Directions: Take SR40 to the Main St. exit—go west 1½ blocks to Your Place.

Furnished models open daily 10 A.M. to 6 P.M.

200 Place Drive
(555) 555-5555
www.yourplace.com

EQUAL HOUSING
OPPORTUNITY

This type of ad is a hybrid of both classified and display ads. It appears in the classified section of the newspaper. Normally, an ad of this type and size is too expensive for weekly use and should be reserved for grand openings or for identity or image advertising programs. A smaller classified ad will generally bring out more prospects than the larger, more-expensive display-classified ad. Use the latter sparingly.

you have to offer from week to week. For example, advertise one- and two-bedroom apartments to attract one segment of the market one week. Then you can advertise three- and four-bedroom units to appeal to the family market the next week. Don't put everything you have to offer in a single ad, or you will confuse the prospect. Each prospect is looking for only one apartment and is not really impressed by your ability to accommodate all family sizes. If you have different-sized apartments to offer, it is better to run separate ads in successive weeks than to promote all of them in one ad.

2. *What does it cost?* Some managers are not sufficiently confident of their rental pricing to list the rent in the ad. They hope that prospects will accept the rent after seeing the apartment. However, for every prospect who is drawn by an ad without a price, the manager will lose about ten others who will not come because the rent is not listed. This is a terrible waste. Make the ad work for you, not against you.

   If you do not want to list a specific price, it is perfectly all right to use a leader price: "From $685." Alternatively, you can give a range of rents: "Apartments from $725 to $880." In fact, listing the top of your rental price range can add to the status of the property. Even if prospects can only afford the lower end of the range, they will enjoy being associated with an apartment community that commands higher rents.

3. *How do I find it?* It is hard to believe, but the directions in many ads for suburban garden apartment communities are incorrect. Often, the person who writes the ad knows the route well and, because of this knowledge, omits a vital step in spelling out the directions. This has been proven to me quite clearly while on consulting assignments in strange cities. Typically, I prefer to find my own way to the subject property and I use the driving instructions as my guide.

   Driving instructions should be crystal clear. They should start from an expressway or a major arterial street, identified by its most commonly known name and route number. Sometimes a major expressway or street is known by different names as it passes through different communities within the same city, making a route number helpful. Make sure the mileage noted in the ad is correct.

   The exit should be identified by name and number. Be sure this name and number are visible to the person on the expressway. You may know the exit as Main Street because you travel this route every day, but all the prospect has to go by is Exit 14. Drive by the exit sign yourself to make sure your driving instructions say what the sign says.

   You should be aware of the renumbering system for Interstate highways that has changed exit numbers so they coincide with mileage markers. Additional routing information will be needed in situations where an exit is available in one direction only.

   Next, tell the prospect whether to turn right or left from the exit (in addition, you might note whether that is east, west, north, or south) then continue to specify all the streets leading to your property. Spell out the instructions carefully. It helps to have your directional signs along the way, too; but as noted earlier, these signs can be removed or knocked down. Make sure the instructions are clear and complete so the prospect can find your property without signs.

There may be a choice of routes to get to your apartment community. However, the most direct route may lead prospects past unattractive scenes or competing properties. Real estate agents who sell homes are careful to take prospects along the most scenic route, even though it may take a little longer. Apartment managers can follow the home sellers' example when writing directions to their apartment communities.

If prospects still have difficulty finding your apartments, the answer may be a display-classified ad that includes a map. The map should be to scale, not distorted, and it should indicate mileage distances so prospects have some indication of how they are proceeding and their location in relation to major landmarks.

It is crucial to keep prospects' three basic questions in mind when developing your ads, but there is much more to learn about the complex subject of newspaper advertising. The following are recommendations regarding the appearance and placement of ads.

- *Headlines.* Avoid catchy headlines. Serious classified ad readers do not want to be entertained. They want to know how many rooms your apartments have and the features, amenities, price, and location. For a headline, it is better to use the number of bedrooms, the name of your property, the area of town if it is very desirable, or the street address if it is well known and follows the established numbering system.

  There are situations in which you can use a headline to call out to a particular grouping of prospects. If you are near a major hospital, you might try "Nurses" as a headline; near a school, "Teachers" or "Students." The readership of your ad by these groupings increases dramatically when you call them out in the headline.

- *Ad size.* Prospects think that the true bargains are in the smaller ads. The one exception to this rule is grand-opening ads which will be discussed later. No matter how small the ad is, just make sure it answers those three important questions.

  The most successful classified ads are the smallest and advertise the fewest units. As stated earlier, try to avoid advertising more than one type of unit. Each prospect will only rent one apartment. By advertising one unit, you create a sense of urgency, which is exactly what you want to do.

  Large ads are self-defeating. The prospect who sees a large ad is apt to think that you have a correspondingly large number of apartments to rent or that the ad is expensive so the rent must be, too.

Apartments in plentiful supply or ones that appear to be moving slowly attract little response. Prospects are looking for the rare find. A small ad helps convey that impression.

Newspapers traditionally arrange classified ads by size, with the large ads at the top of the page and the smaller ones toward the bottom. It is a good idea to vary the size of your ad from week to week so the newspaper will move it around on the page. This way there is a better chance of catching the roving eye of the prospect, and your ad will not be stuck in one position.

- *Type size.* The newspaper ad salesman will tell you that large type is easier to read. Naturally, he or she wants to sell large type because that makes the ad bigger and, thus, more expensive. It is okay to use standard-sized newspaper type for classified ads. When prospects read the classified pages, their eyes adjust to the small type, and they will have little trouble reading your ad.

- *White space.* The newspaper ad salesman also may advise you to use plenty of white space in your ad. This can be overdone. Classified ads call for the judicious use of white space (see large example in Exhibit 10.1). A classified ad that is crowded from corner to corner can be very effective. Display ads, however, may benefit from the relief provided by extra white space.

- *Choice of newspaper.* In most metropolitan areas with more than one daily newspaper, one is usually recognized as the leader in apartment ads. That is the paper to use. You are wasting money advertising in the others.

  Community newspapers can offer a different opportunity. These papers are often published on a weekly basis, cover a smaller geographic area, and have considerably lower advertising rates than the major dailies. A prospect looking for an apartment in a specific area may well check a local paper first.

  If you use both the leading daily and a community paper, alternate your placements so ads do not run in both papers the same week. This will stretch your advertising dollars and allow a better evaluation of the response.

- *Frequency.* Sunday advertising should generally be your first choice. That is the day most prospects look for apartments. In addition to Sunday, one weekday is all that I would recommend. Don't advertise more than twice a week in one newspaper.

  Advertising on one weekday can be effective. This weekday ad can be smaller than the Sunday ad because there generally are fewer weekday ads to compete against. Also, the person who looks for an apartment during the week is a more serious shopper than a Sunday prospect. Many transferees, students, military families, and others who must locate housing quickly shop during the week.

When scheduling ads, take holidays, season of the year, and weather into account. Don't blame the advertising if the weekend offers the first balmy days after a dreary winter. People would rather stroll in the park than visit apartments. Don't expect advertising to attract large numbers of prospects in July and during the first two weeks of August when many people are on vacation. On the other hand, the last two weeks of August and the first part of September are typically good periods for attracting prospects, especially those eager to register their children for the fall term in a nearby school.

The importance of a telephone number cannot be overstated. People have little time to waste these days, and they use the telephone to avoid unnecessary trips. The telephone number is an important ingredient in rental advertisements, even though it would be preferable to have the prospect *come to the property* rather than call. Listing the telephone number is also helpful to prospects who start out for your apartment community but get lost and need additional instructions. Invariably, cell phones will be used for these communications.

Following are a few less-conventional types of newspaper ads and their applications:

- *Grand opening ads.* These are the exception to the rule about the smaller apartment ad being better. You may want to use a large display or display-classified ad for a series of weekends to make your presence known. People expect a large ad in connection with a grand opening, but if the large ad continues to appear long after the grand opening is over, the ad will become stale and lose its effectiveness.

- *Preleasing.* These ads try to attract prospects for apartments that are not yet available. I would advise against them. When you advertise for prospects, you need apartments to show; without apartments, advertising is just wasting money. Rely on drive-by traffic for any preleasing business you hope to do.

- *Shock advertising.* In difficult markets, especially those in which a large number of ads for competing properties crowd the rental section of the popular newspaper, you may be tempted to try shock advertising. This can involve humor, irreverence, a dramatic giveaway, or a next-to-nothing move-in package. The point is to capture the prospect's attention and gain a telephone call or visit. The technique often results in increased prospect traffic, and many people seem to enjoy a little humor in the usually humorless classifieds. However, on average, the prospects attracted by such an advertisement tend to be residents who do not stay very long.

In developing an apartment marketing program, and especially advertising copy, one must be mindful of fair housing laws, which apply to marketing and advertising practices as well as the leasing process and interactions with residents. Advertisements should include the Equal Housing Opportunity statement and/or logo, and ad copy should be written to be nondiscriminatory. Any photos included in ads should show diversity.

Apartment Guides.   Many communities have apartment guides that are published monthly or quarterly. They contain full-page listings of neighborhood apartment properties. Most offer the opportunity for a color ad on the inside and outside of the front and back covers; many offer color on inside pages as well. Apartment guides have become increasingly important in the marketing of rental apartments. It is not uncommon for these publications to outdistance newspapers in attracting potential residents. The guides are available free at many convenient locations. What makes them so popular is that a prospect can find out quickly what is available in a particular neighborhood. Apartment guide ads typically include some or all of the following:

Photograph of the property
Area maps
Sizes and types of units
Rent range and any rent specials
Complete listing of features and amenities
Floor plans
An indication if pets are accepted
Address and directions
Management firm name, telephone number, and web site
Comparison grid summarizing all advertised properties
Important telephone numbers

Apartment guides are very market specific. The people who pick up these guides are potential renters who are actively looking. If you have apartments for rent, you will probably want your property listed.

In some of the larger city markets, there may be two or more apartment guides competing for your advertising dollar. If this is the case, you need to do some research and experimentation. Visit some of the distribution points and evaluate their clienteles. Are the patrons of these establishments the people you are seeking for your apartments? It has been my experience that one guide in a community will deliver a higher-quality renter profile than others. Your job is to find that one.

Web Site.   As discussed in Chapter 3, even small properties can derive benefits from having a web site. There is a fast-growing segment of the population whose members use the Internet to do much of their shopping, including looking for places to live. Color pictures of your property and models can be displayed with the click of a button. Sound and animation are becoming common with broadband hookups and with each new generation of faster and more powerful computers. Apartment sizes and layouts as well as current availabilities, pricing, and even specials are often seen on different web sites. Area maps and specific directions to a given property are becoming a standard feature. The prospect can download this map to take along on the trip. Floor plans and, in fact, the entire brochure can also be downloaded.

Web sites typically monitor and record the number of visitors, their areas of interest, and the time spent. Sites often offer the visitor the opportunity to register, communicate specific requirements, and request additional information; many also provide space for comments. A web site is another avenue of market exposure which definitely warrants your interest. Including your web site in all your other advertising also increases your market exposure.

Radio.   Radio advertising rates are often much lower than people think. Radio can be one of the most-effective traffic builders. There have been cases in which weekend rental traffic built up tremendously minutes after a message was broadcast. Why? Because many radio listeners are in their cars when they hear something interesting, and they respond to it immediately.

While radio can create a lot of traffic, this traffic generally results in few actual rentals. It consists mainly of curiosity-seekers who want to know what is going on and are interested in any premiums being offered. Certainly, teenagers who are drawn by radio messages are not prime rental prospects.

You might try sponsorship of a radio program that plays "beautiful" or "easy-listening" music, or you might choose a classical format. Base your choice on the musical preferences of your target market. Sponsoring weather, traffic, or financial reports is another effective strategy for reaching certain target audiences, as is spot advertising on public radio stations. While it is difficult to track the number of rentals from this kind of advertising, it undoubtedly improves the property's image as well as its rentals— particularly with high-rent apartments.

Radio can be especially effective in connection with grand openings. The heavy traffic built up by radio advertising can help convey an atmosphere of success. A profusion of activity may convince serious prospects that they should rent before all the apartments are taken.

If you decide to use radio, it is a good idea to buy broadcast time in such a way that your spot is aired with increasing frequency from Thursday to Saturday and then stops mid-afternoon on Sunday. Pay particular attention when buying radio time. Many stations have restrictions on when you can buy time. Some popular programs have little or no advertising time available. You may have to buy a package that includes undesirable time periods in order to get the time slots you want. Sometimes the station will schedule your commercials at its convenience, even airing your message several times in an hour or less. Be aware of these possibilities and take them into account when planning your campaign.

Television.   Television is a great selling medium, but it is expensive. Commercials for apartment communities almost always present a message fostering name recognition. Only rarely are they intended to promote the leasing of individual apartments. In most metropolitan areas, the cost of television advertising is prohibitive; the only exception might be the promotion of luxury properties that have large advertising budgets. In smaller cities and towns, television advertising is priced somewhat more reasonably. In many areas, local cable channels have very low rates, and they offer a targeted market. In addition to the cost of broadcast time, there are production expenses. Making a good television commercial costs a lot of money, and it must be done with great care to show your property to its best advantage.

Be wary of certain television traps. One is the low rate for late-night shows that air Friday and Saturday nights. The reason that rates are low during these times is that the audience is small, and chances are your prospect market is not watching.

A second trap is a series of real estate commercials run during the same program. You want to be the only real estate advertiser. You do not want to compete with two or three other rental properties.

A third pitfall is the tendency to purchase advertising time during *your* favorite shows and on *your* favorite stations, without regard for the target market. Don't let personal viewing or listening preferences determine your television or radio advertising strategy. Ask to see an audience profile before committing to a broadcast medium.

Local public broadcasting TV stations may offer promotional opportunities that do not require cash outlays. One such opportunity is a charity benefit auction. Local merchants are asked to contribute goods and services, which are then auctioned to viewers. If you participate, the station will generally prepare a commercial to promote your apartment community. This commercial might be run several times each day leading up to the telecast auction in return for your donation of, say, one year of free rent on a one-bedroom apartment. This can present an opportunity for tremendous television exposure and may also include the production of a taped commercial—all achieved while benefiting a worthwhile charity.

In any case, if you do want to use television, be sure to get competent advice from an advertising agency or other communications professional before making any plans.

Event Programs.   These include printed programs distributed at concerts, operas, and plays. You would be trading on the prestige of the event and associating it with your property. The effect is one of long-term image-building, and you can expect little immediate response. For this kind of advertising to be productive, it must be done on a sustained basis. This type of advertising is quite expensive and is probably most beneficial for new, upscale properties and luxury apartment towers.

Direct Mail.   This is one of the most effective—and most expensive— forms of advertising. Many people are surprised at this, especially when they think of the amount of "junk mail" they receive. However, postage is expensive, whether it is first class or bulk rate. When you add to this the cost of paper, envelopes, printing, addressing, and handling, the cost per person reached is far higher than most other forms of advertising.

The advantage of direct mail is its extreme selectivity: It enables you to reach the people you want to reach. Newspapers, magazines, radio, television, and billboards all present your message to thousands of people, many of whom have absolutely no interest whatever in your property. Direct mail advertising allows you to better target a specific audience.

A direct mail campaign for an apartment community should consist of mailing between 300 and 500 letters. This is an adequate number on which to base an evaluation. A mailing to fewer than 300 people can distort your response evaluation, but more importantly, you are reaching too few prospects. More than 500 risks wasting advertising money if the mailing is unsuccessful; and you may get too much of a response if it does the job. The 300 to 500 range is a safe middle ground.

Offering an incentive such as a road atlas imprinted with the property name, framed art, a houseplant, a clock, or a pen set will increase the response to your direct mail campaign. You will need to experiment with such offers to determine whether the added cost is justified by the addition of qualified prospect traffic and, more importantly, by extra rentals. However, offers that will detract from the quality image of your apartment community should be avoided. Your product is very different from many others regularly promoted with direct mail incentives. People are not going to move their families in order to qualify for free pots and pans or even a microwave oven.

Mailing lists are available from a wide variety of sources, including demographic specialists. You can reach just about any audience profile. You dictate the addressees by zip code, occupation, salary, etc. These lists are rather expensive for the first mailing, but you typically receive a considerable discount when you purchase additional sets of the same mailing list. Note, however, that list sources tend to oversell the specificity of their lists, so check around to find a reliable source.

Do your mailing on a Tuesday for arrival Thursday and definitely no later than Friday. This gives a prospect plenty of time to plan for a visit on the weekend. It is a waste if a letter inviting the recipient to visit an apartment community arrives on a Monday. The invitation is usually forgotten by the next weekend.

A well-planned direct mail campaign should attract a 4 percent response; that is, if you mail to 500 names, 20 prospects should visit. If you score 4 percent or better, mail the same letter to the same list the following week. Most likely, there will be the same response on the second weekend. This is because the second group originally intended to come out the first weekend but for some reason postponed it.

If the response is less than 4 percent, you may want to switch to another list of names or change the approach of your letter. Consider the effect of weather on your weekend traffic, and take this into account when judging the response level.

There is no magic formula for successful direct mail. You will have to work out your own. However, by sticking to the 300 to 500 sample, keeping the letter simple, and experimenting with different approaches, you will find a workable formula.

Yellow Pages (Classified Telephone Directories). People normally do not look in the Yellow Pages for unfurnished apartments. A possible exception to this is if a number of your units have been prepared as corporate apartments. Housing directors, business people, and students who plan rather lengthy stays often use the Yellow Pages to search for furnished apartments. A small ad may attract a number of excellent short-term residents. For most situations, however, the value of a Yellow Pages ad becomes questionable, especially in light of the high cost of a display ad. In large cities, the proliferation of different and competing Yellow Pages publications has generally frustrated the consumer, reducing the value of this advertising medium.

If you do use the Yellow Pages, a simple listing of the apartment community's name in boldface type is adequate. It may be a good idea to include an emergency telephone number for the benefit of residents who may use the Yellow Pages instead of the regular telephone directory.

Handbills and Flyers. Throwaway literature is not highly recommended. Occasionally, handbills or flyers are used successfully in conjunction with grand openings or special promotions, but using them on a regular basis will tend to lower the image of your property. There is an exception to this general rule. If, while completing your marketing (or position) map, you determine that many of your residents work at one of the major businesses or plants nearby, you may want to experiment with placing tasteful flyers under the employees' windshield wipers. The message is that many of their coworkers have chosen your apartment community because of its close-by location. A flyer used in this way should probably be more than a printed piece of paper. A football schedule or a calendar applied to a magnetic backing is a useful item that has a better chance of being retained. It is also a good idea to ask permission to do this so that you do not compromise an important referral source. The firm's human resources director can advise you on the best way to distribute your flyers.

Newsletters.   Desktop publishing programs make it possible to produce professional-quality newsletters for apartment communities—even for rather small ones. The trick is to resist the temptation of letting the piece read as if it were titled "The Landlord Speaks." It should focus on things of interest to your residents: Activities, gatherings, recipes, puzzles, civic events, local restaurant menus and reviews, profiles of residents, or even short stories are fine. It should not be used as a vehicle for announcing your new rules and regulations or other such messages from management. If you violate this principle, you may prompt a resident group to use the same software to produce a newsletter airing their grievances.

Prospects often look at newsletters more as informational pieces than as sales literature. A newsletter tends to create the impression of a viable community. When using the newsletter format, you gain the ability to make periodic updates to reflect the property's changing stages and added facilities. Doing this is much more economical than producing revised brochures. Successive editions of the newsletter can report on construction progress, renters moving in, opening of amenities, the relationship of the property to the surrounding neighborhood, and so on. Additionally, a newsletter can be used for follow-up mailings to prospects who have paid you a visit.

If you choose to publish a newsletter, do it well and make sure it reflects your unified graphics system. If you do not have the publishing resources available, there are newsletter publishing companies that will do the work for you. These "canned" newsletters have a professional appearance, with interesting articles and features and space available for customized information about your property. They are usually printed in color on a quality paper stock. Before choosing this type of service, however, you should compare costs and check to see that your competition is not using the same service.

Billboards.   Billboards can be used to create awareness of your property as part of an overall advertising campaign (Exhibit 10.4). More commonly they are used as *directional signage* near highly traveled roads as explained in Chapter 9. A billboard's primary value is to direct people who already are heading your way.

Billboard advertising has its limitations, however. If a salesperson claims that 10,000 people see the sign every day, it is likely they are the same 10,000 people who are on their way to or from work. A billboard loses its impact almost as soon as it is displayed because people get used to seeing it. Also, the sign needs to be lighted at night to get full value from it. You may have to accept a package of billboard placements on a rotating basis, which can mean poor locations as well as good ones. Finally, billboard ad-

Exhibit 10.4
Promotional Billboards

Not intended to direct or to inform, promotional billboards help reinforce awareness and identify. They must be large, properly placed, and contain few enough words to be read and understood quickly. The use of "reverse" color combinations, as shown on the lower sign, will attract more attention from a greater distance. Remember to keep the message brief.

vertising is expensive. The number of billboards is constantly being reduced because of pressures exerted by environmentalists and others, and that increases the rates for the remaining billboards. All of this suggests that billboards have limited value for renting apartments. What is a powerful vehicle for selling soft drinks is not necessarily right for marketing apartments.

Airport Displays.   These displays reach one of the most active and affluent segments of the housing market, including executives being transferred. In large metropolitan airports, the cost of this advertising is prohibitive. In smaller cities, airport displays, including kiosks in airport lobbies, are reasonable in cost and effective as part of a major advertising program.

Benches.   Advertising on benches at bus stops provides an accommodation to riders and others and puts your apartment community's name in front of the public at large. An ad on a bench at a key corner close to your apartment community might draw some prospect traffic. If you can afford to erect a bench and bus-stop shelter, with architecture and landscaping that matches the character of your property, so much the better. However, bench advertising can be damaging when the inferior condition of the bench or its surroundings reflects poorly on the property's image.

Banners.   When leasing becomes difficult, some apartment owners and managers seem compelled to put up banners on one or more buildings to attract the attention of potential renters. "Now Renting," "One Month Free," and "Win A Trip" are common messages. The community next door, not to be outdone, soon hangs out its own banner with a message that is even more urgent. Business rarely increases, at least in terms of qualified applicants, but a signal is sent to all renters announcing the fact that deal time is here. Your existing residents may begin to wonder if they can achieve a better housing deal by moving. Even if they do not move, they will demand more from you because they sense that new residents are receiving special benefits. Many of your long-term residents will be embarrassed by these banners. They certainly will be upset with the less-qualified residents who seem to be attracted by this form of last-ditch advertising. The biggest and best "banner" should be the property itself. Put your effort into making the property look better, and you will stand out among the rest.

Human Directionals.   One of the most desperate marketing strategies is to hire someone to dress up in a trendy or eye-catching costume and direct prospect traffic to your apartment community. People have used clowns, giant rabbits, and even an imitation Pope. Common sense should tell most apartment managers that very few prospective renters will be encouraged to visit a property and possibly lease an apartment just because a clown standing in the street suggested they do so. Managers who simply do not understand the sensitive nature of the housing business usually make these attempts. Because apartment managers deal with one of the most personal of commodities, marketing techniques must be chosen carefully. Using human directionals insults virtually all housing customers.

Transit Ads.   Like billboards, the same people are generally exposed to the same transit ads on each trip. Many of the people who use public transportation are not in the market for apartments at your property, especially if it is a suburban garden apartment community and the transit line is operating in an urban location. Transit ads on the outsides of buses get dirty quickly and reflect poorly on the property's image. The person stuck in a traffic jam behind a noisy bus spewing exhaust fumes is not likely to react favorably to your ad. Also, you may not be able to get the routes you want for the best advertising exposure. For all of these reasons, transit advertising is not recommended for renting apartments.

Miscellaneous Advertising.   This category includes skywriting, sponsorship of baseball and soccer teams, sponsoring a float in a holiday parade, and similar practices. Their value is limited, however. This is strictly for creating name recognition. You cannot expect prospects to come out to rent an apartment just because they saw your property's name on a float in a parade.

Traffic Builders

Other strategies and techniques can be used to draw traffic and prospects. These things can work well alone or as part of an advertising program.

- *Premiums.* To get people to visit your apartment community, you may consider offering a premium in your newspaper advertising or direct mail promotion. Premiums have been used successfully by savings and loan associations, banks, gasoline stations, and appliance dealers to attract customers. However, no one will move for the sake of a premium. All premiums will do is help increase traffic. If that is your goal, fine. However, premiums should not be used as an enticement for people to sign a lease application. Nothing will be an inducement if the apartment does not fit their needs. If they do sign, they probably would have signed without the premium incentive.

- *Giveaways.* While premiums are relatively high-quality gifts, giveaways are harmless attention-getters. Included here are buttons, balloons, and T-shirts imprinted with the property name or logo or both. People accept them as token gestures, but if done excessively, such commercialism can damage your property's image.

- *Celebrity appearances.* These are successful traffic builders for grand openings. They also may be good if the celebrity lives in the building and is willing to appear for the benefit of the other residents. Otherwise, a constant stream of celebrity appearances gives your building a Las Vegas atmosphere, which many prospects and residents will not like.

- *Charitable and public service activities.* If your apartment community is conveniently located, you may be asked to make it accessible for various public service activities. The local public health service may ask if it can set up a trailer to conduct blood pressure or cholesterol tests on your premises, or the Red Cross chapter may need a room to hold a blood donor drive, either of which would draw outsiders as well. Perhaps your property might be considered a donation spot during an annual holiday drive to collect toys for underprivileged children or the starting point for a charity run or bicycle ride.

All of these are legitimate activities to stimulate public awareness of your property and increase the number of visitors. It may be difficult to attribute rentals to such activities, but if there is little cost involved and they do not downgrade your image; you should permit them.

One thing to be very cautious of is any activity that draws large crowds of people (e.g., a rock concert). This will drive away prospects, irritate residents, and probably do some serious physical damage to your property.

- *Trips and contests.* The basic rental strategy here is this: The greater the prospect traffic, the greater the number of renters. It would appear that in weak market situations, whatever it takes to increase traffic is acceptable. Offering a wonderful trip as an inducement to lease would seem to be an effective way to attract additional renters. You will probably get a discount on these trips because of a special arrangement for volume, but they are expensive. Improving the property as a whole or upgrading individual apartment units would certainly be a better use of the money. It will also avoid the negative feelings harbored by existing residents who have seen the advertisement offering new, untried residents a vacation. I have seen these programs backfire when the travel arrangements went awry or the trips did not include all that was implied. There have even been situations in which resident organizations were formed by groups of residents who first became acquainted during a less-than-perfect trip.

  Running a contest for a nice prize is a less-expensive approach, but it has little influence on rental results. The prize might be a year's free rent, a luxury trip, or a new automobile. Unfortunately, contests rarely produce any measurable increase in prospect traffic or rentals. After all, the majority of states offer the chance to win millions of dollars with the purchase of a one-dollar lottery ticket. Such contests are public and highly regulated. Why would someone wish to participate in your contest?

Public Relations

When applied to a merchandising campaign, public relations (PR) refers to *publicity* used to call attention to an apartment community, establish its image and theme, and keep it in the news. Public relations is much more than merchandising. It includes policy-making, product design, personal relations with prospects and residents, complaint handling, and community relations. It involves finding opportunities for you and your property to make a good impression; it is positive image building. Because the focus of this chapter is on merchandising the product and attracting prospects, only the merchandising role of public relations will be addressed here.

The power of public relations is in its believability. People often believe what they read in the newspaper or hear from a friend, but claims made in an advertisement are regarded with some skepticism. For public relations to have this believability, it must be divorced from advertising. If people know that a newspaper regularly trades off editorial space in exchange for advertising, they view the publicity as advertising and discount it accordingly.

To a great extent, the success of a PR program for an apartment community depends on the manager's ability to produce stories and photo opportunities for local newspapers and for radio and television stations as well. This is no job for an amateur. Just as apartment managers should not design a property's symbol and graphics, they should not dabble in PR either. To be effective, you should have the best talent available.

Public relations and publicity campaigns are not free. True, newspapers do not charge you when they mention your property in an article, but someone must be paid to create the publicity that led to your inclusion in that article. If you try to save money in this area, you will have only poor or unsatisfactory results.

Once the right PR talent has been hired, make it clear that you want publicity to build rental traffic, not to feed someone's ego. You want publicity that focuses on the apartment community and its features and appears in newspapers where the public can see it. Ego-building publicity focuses on the developer, manager, and owner and is restricted to real estate news corners or trade publications that the general public does not even read.

Beyond local publicity, a PR counselor may be able to interest a national magazine in doing a story about your property. While these magazines reach a far larger audience than the target market, the prestige will boost the image of the apartment community. In addition, reprints of national magazine stories can be distributed as information pieces in the rental information center and included in direct mail campaigns.

11

*Great closers offer choices
of something or something,
not something or nothing.*

Converting Prospects
to Residents

The preceding chapters have dealt with marketing aspects that do not involve direct contact with the customer. Now, we are ready to discuss the practices that will come into play when you are actually in contact with the rental prospect. This human interaction will be the least-controllable part of the rental effort. Hopefully, the physical product and the warm atmosphere you have created will overcome any miscues in the face-to-face sales presentation.

The finished apartment product is the culmination of months and often years of planning, thought, and revisions by highly trained experts. Choosing and decorating models, creating ads, outfitting rental centers, and preparing colorful collateral materials are also the result of specialists working at a measured pace with a carefully planned goal in mind. What follows when the customer appears, either by telephone or in person, will be unrehearsed.

Customers come in about every size, shape, mood, and background. An endless variety of wants, needs, limitations, and abilities drive them. The property's staff must match each customer's needs to the rental community using knowledge of the area, the product, alternative choices, and basic selling techniques. This can be difficult to do, but apartment managers do have a distinct advantage. When a potential renter makes contact with you, that person has indicated a possible desire for a change in his or her housing arrangements. This means at least one level of "market sorting" has been accomplished. Imagine how much more difficult apartment marketing would be if it was necessary to start from scratch, as is often the case with people who sell life insurance or do cold-call telemarketing. They must search out an audience, plant the idea of need for their type of product, and then proceed to sell their particular product to fill that need. The rental apartment business enjoys two selling benefits up front—housing is a necessity, and, more often than not, the customer initiates the first contact.

The apartment-hunting process is time-consuming because of the distances between rental communities and the number of options that are usually available to a prospective renter. The telephone is often used to save time during the initial scouting efforts. The prospect has usually established a set of criteria that arises from his or her particular situation. This list includes *requirements* as well as *desires* and frequently reflects a "stretch" in actual needs.

This is no different from the way people shop for automobiles. The car-shopping process starts with gathering information about the latest features; it includes a plan to avoid the problems inherent in inexpensive models and extends to ultimate resale values. After a period of investigation, a decision will be made, but the buyer's initial expectations will surely be compromised. The brutal reality of affordability will eventually play its role in the decision.

Similarly, the point at which the rental prospect's call is received will determine the degree of compromise in his or her original wants and needs. For example, the first or second weekend into exploring the rental market, a prospect will stick pretty close to the mental or written list of needs and desires. Keep in mind that the prospect's wish list is being justified and buoyed by all of the advertising specials listed in newspapers and on banners. It will be some time before the customer fully understands just what the rent dollar will actually buy in the marketplace. Eventually, the prospect will begin to set priorities.

Leasing agents must be trained to understand the evolution of this notion in the prospect's mind—the idea of "wanting everything"—and be patient while the market's realities take effect. Otherwise, agents can become disillusioned quickly by some of the negative responses they receive. Chances are that the prospect has not yet stepped outside of his or her living room, and the limitations imposed by the market are yet to be learned. It is tempting to start selling the apartment community during these exploratory telephone calls. It may make the leasing agent feel that he or she is contributing to the sales effort, but it will not do much to increase the rate of rentals. The telephone is a valuable tool, but its usefulness at this point is in helping to secure a face-to-face appointment.

The Telephone Inquiry

It should be understood that a rental prospect who telephones wants to shorten the shopping time by garnering as much information as possible about the property. The prospect will want a very nice apartment with a long list of amenities, all at a very special price. The job of the staff member who answers the telephone is to make an appointment for the prospect to come and see the apartment community. To do this, it is necessary to engage in a conversation that answers some, but not all, of the prospect's questions while at the same time probing for the answers to certain critical questions to help in *qualifying* the prospect. The following topics represent the information that the leasing agent should get from the prospect (though not necessarily in the order stated) as well as the appropriate follow-up activities.

- *Introductions.* When taking calls, the leasing agent should ask for the prospect's name, and the caller should be given the agent's name. Prospects might be hesitant about giving their names or, more importantly, their telephone numbers or addresses, until they can determine at least a certain level of interest. The agent should not dwell too much on learning the caller's name or current address at this point in the conversation. The information will be requested again later.

- *Requirements and needs.* The question to be asked is, "How might I help you find your next home?" The response will rarely describe what the prospect will actually accept, so the leasing agent should not be too concerned if the property or apartment does not appear to be an "exact fit." Rather than allowing the prospect to ask all of the questions, the leasing agent should interject questions to learn about the caller's requirements and needs. The conversation should be one of give-and-take, with both the prospect and the agent making inquiries and responses. This is the start of the qualifying process.

- *Timing and situation.* The leasing agent can often break up a recitation of needs by asking about the prospect's intended moving date or interjecting a question about what prompted the need for a move. The answers to these questions will usually be honest and will help to "flesh out" a profile of this particular prospect. Such information will become very valuable as the rental process advances.

- *Budget.* The leasing agent should ask the caller for an acceptable rental range, knowing that the estimate will probably be conservative. Prospects do not want to miss any bargains or specials, and they want to pressure the leasing person to come up with the very best deal. Actually, the prospect's strategy is reasonable, and it is probably much the same approach you would take.

- *How to contact the prospect.* If there is even a semblance of a "fit," the leasing agent should learn how to contact the caller. At first, it is important to establish rapport and begin an exchange of information with the caller. If it appears that the leasing agent can help the caller find a new home, the questions "Where can you be contacted during the day?" or, "Is it better to contact you during work hours or at home?" can be inserted into the conversation. These inquiries might work better as part of the appointment process that follows. It is natural to ask for a phone number when people make appointments in case an emergency would force a postponement. Caller ID will give you the phone numbers of many prospects. This is a feature that is well worth its nominal cost.

- *The appointment.* All that anyone can do on the telephone is "sell an appointment." Renting an apartment simply cannot be done by phone. In order to get almost anything today, you must ask for it. This certainly includes getting rental prospects to visit your property. Skilled leasing agents often ask for an appointment using a compound question: "Is one day of the week better than another and, is there a time of day that works better for you?" With the answer to one or both of these questions, the leasing agent can suggest a specific time and day for an appointment. If the prospect avoids making a specific appointment, it is a good idea to ask for a general appointment. In other words, you want to get the caller to commit to coming out on a particular weekend or one evening during a given week. An effective way to get a commitment from a prospect is to promise to set aside the necessary time to familiarize him or her with the general rental market as well as all that your rental community has to offer. A willingness to share time and knowledge often produces a corresponding commitment.

  The importance of asking for an appointment cannot be overstated. In fact, at apartment marketing seminars, the presenter will invariably spend considerable time discussing its importance. Yet, a simple survey will prove that rental personnel seldom ask for an appointment. You can prove this to yourself: On a slow afternoon, when phones are not ringing and there are few prospects, pick up your apartment guide and call your competitors. Inquire about an apartment for yourself or a "friend who is moving to town." Record how many make a point of introducing themselves and how many actually try to "sell you an appointment." You will also learn other telephone techniques that you may want to adopt or avoid.

- *Directions to the property.* After making an appointment, the leasing agent should confirm that the prospect knows how to get to the apart-

---

Tracking Prospect Telephone Calls

There are some important tools available to apartment managers for tracking rental prospects who call the property. Two of them are described here.

Prospect Tracking Software. Real estate brokers use special computer software to keep track of prospective home buyers. The same software can be used to track rental prospects. The information acquired during a telephone interview can be entered as it is being given or immediately after the caller hangs up. These programs will give you an electronic form to record names, housing needs, family or household information, budget limitations, timing, etc. It will record and remind you of any appointment and will print out a reminder sheet containing everything you know about the prospect. You will be amazed by the warm response you receive when prospects realize that you remember them and their particular situations. This software will go on to prepare follow-up communications as well. What used to take hours now involves nothing more than a few keystrokes. This is another tool that pays for itself by increasing staff efficiency and rental results.

Telephone Tracking. There are services available to the apartment industry that will provide some extremely important telephone information. By using different telephone numbers or assigned codes in your advertisements, these services will track your property's telephone calls. It will record how many calls were received, what times they occurred, their duration, the area from which they originated, and the telephone number of the person calling. You will learn the best days and the peak hours. If the record shows that the majority of calls lasted less than a minute or two, you will know that the leasing person on duty did not do much in the way of creating interest in the property. You can also cross-check callers with the prospects who later show up at the property. Most of these services provide periodic summaries using colored graphs and charts to help demonstrate what is happening via the telephone at your property.

---

ment community. The agent should ask where the prospect will be coming from and summarize the appropriate directions. Computer programs are readily available to prepare a customized map that will lead the prospect to your property's doorstep with step-by-step instructions. These maps can be faxed to the prospect or downloaded to the prospect's computer.

- *Re-introduction.* At the end of the call, the leasing agent should state his or her name again. Many callers will have forgotten the name of the person at the other end of the line, but they will not admit to this memory lapse and ask for the name. A rental prospect is much more likely to keep an appointment if he or she knows the agent's name.

- *Record prospect information.* Leasing personnel must develop the discipline to record the information gathered during a telephone inquiry. Preprinted forms (similar to a *guest card,* discussed later in this chapter) or blank cards can be used to record the information derived from telephone inquiries; specialized software and telephone tracking services are other ways to document prospect information (see sidebar). Later, this will save time and often the embarrassment of repeating what has already been said when the prospect arrives in your office. The leasing agent can pick up from that point and get started helping the prospect find a suitable home.

This brings up the issue of one of the disadvantages of paying leasing people a salary rather than a commission. Leasing people who are paid only if they play a role in producing renters will record and register everyone they meet or talk with on the phone. These people are simply not going to take the chance that a person whom they have worked with on the telephone might arrive at the office without knowing the leasing agent's name. Leasing agents paid a salary will often do a creditable job of getting a prospect to commit to an appointment, but they will not always record the information that was learned about the prospect during the telephone inquiry. This omission is worse than starting over. One of the forces that motivated the prospect's arrival at the property had to do with a feeling or relationship that developed during the telephone conversation. If the leasing agent fails to record the information obtained during a telephone conversation with a prospect, the relationship is reset to zero when that customer walks through the door.

Preparing for the Visit

When the door opens and a rental prospect walks in, the "selling" job is almost half over. This is so because his or her very presence indicates that a number of benchmarks have been satisfied. The neighborhood must be acceptable, or the prospect would not have visited. The person's opinion of your apartment community's appearance and condition must be favorable, or the prospect would be on the way to his or her next stop. Obviously, the prospect has not heard anything negative about the reputation of the property and its manager, otherwise he or she would not have bothered to visit. What remains to be discovered by the prospect is the actual apartment(s)—layout, functionality, availability, and price; the atmosphere of the community; and the leasing agent's dedication to solving housing problems. Assuming you have done your homework in preparing the product and putting the available units into marketable condition, much of your success will come from the relationship formed between the leasing agent and the prospect.

Seller or Helper.   After working with many leasing people over the years, certain trends have become evident to me. Those agents who consistently achieve the greatest results present themselves more as helpers than as sellers. Their approach is to find out why the prospect wants a different place to live, identify any special needs and restrictions, and then make an effort to meet the established requirements.

Think about the salespeople you have dealt with who took the extra time and interest to see that you chose the right product, style, or size. In addition to assisting in your initial purchase, the salesperson may have gone the additional step and offered suggestions to further enhance or accessorize the purchase. This has become so rare an event in today's high-speed world that one is amazed and flattered by any interest or concern. Some novices may call this kind of approach high-pressure selling, but how can that be so if the customer does not feel pressured? A true salesperson who becomes involved in helping the customer satisfy a need or desire will always perform better than one who simply offers a product or service without putting forth any helpful sales effort.

It is not uncommon for top leasing agents to suggest competing rental communities when the units in their property do not match the prospect's requirements. These agents do not stop helping a client at that point; instead, they make some telephone calls. The prospect's knowledge of the neighborhood is no match for that of the professional leasing agent. The leasing person's assistance can save this prospect many hours of fruitless apartment hunting. Taking the time to help a prospect locate housing that will satisfy his or her current needs will pay dividends in the future. First of all, the prospect will probably tell others about the way he or she was treated and helped. This will not be the last time the prospect will need housing; next time one of your units may be just right. Also, the competitors you call will be grateful for the referrals, and that may earn you referrals in return. The goodwill generated from this action is immeasurable. I have seen leasing people disciplined and even dismissed because they sent prospects to competing apartment communities. Their supervisors just did not understand that "when an apartment doesn't 'fit,' it doesn't 'fit,'" and the relationship with the prospect will be destroyed if the agent attempts to force the issue.

Knowledge of the Product.   Leasing agents cannot be much help to prospects if they have limited knowledge of both the property they are renting and the neighborhood in which it is situated. It often appears that the more information given to the leasing agent at the time of initial employment, the less that person seems to learn about the property. When details are available in neat packages, information does not always register in a person's memory bank.

The best results are usually obtained when leasing agents are chal-

lenged to prepare their own database about the property and the neighborhood. They should measure and record room sizes, ceiling heights, square
footages of cabinet space, and lineal footages of closets; assess the attributes
and limitations of the various unit types; and judge which ones will rent
most easily. Leasing people must know the property from their own thorough study, not merely as a result of their many tours with rental prospects.

The same is true of knowing the neighborhood. The agent must actually ride the bus downtown and to the shopping areas. Agents should walk
into the schools and inquire about the grade levels, courses and curriculum,
reputation, school district boundaries, and school bus routes. They need to
know about the businesses, churches, and organizations in the neighborhood, as well as the local government. As noted in Chapter 9, agents must
also visit competitors. If they are not allowed time for this orientation, the
rental results will be limited to what can be achieved by a desk-bound clerk.

The Tour.   Product and neighborhood information will be used throughout the presentation, much of which will take place during a tour of the
property. The routes and the features to be included in a particular tour will
vary with each rental prospect, but the agent must plan for a number of
combinations well in advance.

Ideally, the leasing agent hopes to have the opportunity to pause a moment with the prospect, become acquainted, and determine the prospect's
housing needs. Unfortunately, many prospects are hurried at first because
they want to assure themselves that there is a "possible fit" before taking the
full tour and hearing the entire sales pitch. Prospects come to view apartment units, not support amenities or routine recreational facilities. It is
sometimes difficult to slow the process sufficiently to allow prospects to feel
the sense of the apartment community. Respect the prospect's sense of urgency: The leasing agent cannot afford to waste time searching for keys or
deciding what units are available. That work must take place daily, before
the doors are opened for business.

There should be few surprises during the course of the prospect tours,
and the surprises encountered should be truly beyond the realm of the leasing agent's control. Each agent should make a habit of walking the grounds
and following the various routes available for showing the property to a
prospect. This includes recreational facilities, parking areas, laundry rooms,
sidewalks, steps and landings, model units, and, of course, the units that are
for rent. Obviously, the apartments should be in market-ready condition.
This bit of advice has that textbook sound. Few people will argue with the
premise that a preliminary tour should be made each day, but few managers
and leasing agents put this into practice.

Sometimes the apartment to be leased is still occupied, and this requires
even more advance planning. Usually, the best plan is to meet with the current resident and explain the need for his or her cooperation when the

apartment is shown to potential renters. Many residents feel that this is an imposition, and some may have to be reminded that the lease clearly provides this right of access. Residents would much prefer that you wait until after they have moved to begin your re-leasing process. More time should be taken to qualify prospects when the tour involves occupied units. With luck, a match will be found after just a few showings, and residents can be spared further intrusions. The more advance notice, the better the reception will be. Choose reasonable hours to call for permission to show an apartment, and do your best not to schedule showings during a child's nap time or during mealtimes.

What happens in the case of an existing resident who is a poor housekeeper, or one who has proved to be unsatisfactory, perhaps even subject to an eviction suit? You have to forget about showing that apartment. If the housekeeping is terrible, it will surely offend most prospects. If there is even a hint of odor, do not show the apartment to a prospective renter. Wait, clean it thoroughly, air it out, and allow time to eliminate the problem. Granted, taking an apartment out of the income stream is expensive; but it must be understood that prospective renters simply will not choose an unpleasant apartment. When prospects see a completely unacceptable unit, they are not likely to rent anything at that property. If you are successful in leasing such an apartment before its problems are corrected, the chances are excellent that the incoming resident will present an even greater problem than the previous one.

If models are available, show them first. This accomplishes two things. Prospects are eager to find out what the units look like. Showing the models satisfies that need and gives the agent some time to promote the amenity package and get better acquainted with the prospect before deciding which available units should be shown. Usually, the choice should be limited to two units, so it is essential that the agent determines the prospect's needs quickly. The agent should not be carrying a long list of available units or a handful of keys because this would indicate a number of vacant units. People want what is in demand; the leasing agent is less likely to be successful when a prospect learns that there is considerable inventory. Of the two apartments to be shown, the best should be saved for last. Actually, the first apartment is often a trial. The prospect's reaction to it will signal what to show next. A third unit should be shown only when the agent learns of additional criteria during the first two showings. In most cases, confusion will set in after two showings, making it difficult for the prospect to come to a decision. When prospects go away to think over all of their housing options, they rarely return. Also, revealing the availability of several units weakens your bargaining position and undermines the property's appeal.

Showing an apartment demands a blend of enthusiasm, feature demonstration, and the ability to allow the prospect some freedom to look around. Virtually everyone can identify the primary rooms, so statements such as, "This is the kitchen," either insult the prospect or guarantee that he or she will not listen to additional comments. Prospective residents usually appreciate an agent who directs attention to an energy-saving furnace, insulated windows, an electronic intercom, an ice-maker, or a flat-surface cooktop. Reports about easy maintenance and creative room uses will also be appreciated. People are not particularly interested in knowing the total area of an apartment, but room dimensions are always of interest. If a prospect begins to point out features on his or her own, the agent should take note and slow down the presentation. Prospects can sell themselves on apartments more effectively than a leasing agent could ever hope to do. This frequently occurs when one person does the scouting and returns with the other decision-maker in a semi-final round of looking. If you listen carefully, the prospects will identify their favorite features as well as their reservations.

Collateral Package.   If there is printed material available to hand out, brochure sets should be prepared in advance and ready to hand to the customer. There are mixed opinions about the timing of handing out materials. Some agents want customers to have the material in hand, so they can refer to it or make notes about apartment features, unit numbers, rent, and other details. Others believe brochures distract the prospect and eliminate the reason to return to the rental center after viewing the units. You may want to experiment to see what works best at your property.

Guest Cards.   When customers walk in the door, you are going to need a method of recording their names and other particulars. It is standard practice to use a printed *guest card* with spaces for information about the prospect and his or her rental needs (e.g., name, address, phone number, employer, apartment size, preferred rent, moving date). You may also want to record how the prospect learned about the development (advertising, drive-by, direct mail campaign) because this enables you to track the success of your promotional efforts. You have to determine who completes these cards and when it should be done. In some cases the agent completes the card shortly after the initial introductions. The true pros never go through the formality of filling out the guest card, though they may jot down information as they talk. It is not uncommon for the agent to delay completing the card until the prospect leaves. This requires much more concentration on the part of the agent, but it makes the sales presentation smoother and eliminates the interruption of completing such a form.

The Prospect's Arrival

Now that we have addressed the different aspects of dealing with a prospect, let's consider what happens when one walks through the door. The entry of the rental prospect triggers an opportunity to demonstrate your rental community. The leasing agent must be quick to act and ready to learn the answers to a number of very important questions. The following are the key points of a leasing presentation.

- *Introductions*—Unlike introductions over the telephone, the exchange of introductions during a visit to the rental center must be handled immediately and completely. The longer one delays getting the customer's name, the more awkward it becomes. If the prospect's name is difficult to say, or is not pronounced clearly, the leasing agent must take the time to learn the name and know its spelling. A person with a difficult name is no doubt accustomed to helping others learn it and will take the necessary time to do so. While the importance of knowing and using a prospect's name may seem too rudimentary in a discussion directed toward professional leasing people, you should know that many surveys reveal that leasing agents do not learn the prospect's name until after the application is completed. It is difficult to demonstrate a sincere interest in the prospect and his or her housing situation on a nameless basis.

- *Ready or looking?*—Early in the presentation, the leasing agent should ask the prospects if they are ready to make a commitment if the right apartment comes along. If the answer is "yes," the leasing agent will know how to handle the response when the prospect is asked for the order—in the apartment business, a deposit and a completed rental application. The "yes" response indicates the need for a change in housing. So, when the leasing agent asks for the order and the prospect resists, the problem is that the benefits demonstrated thus far have missed the mark in some way. On the other hand, if the answer to the question about commitment is "no" because the prospects will not need an apartment until next spring, there is little reason to even ask for the order. In this case, the leasing agent should be helpful and polite, but the fact that a decision will not be made immediately makes the approach somewhat different. When prospects' timing is just too early, you should gather information about what type of accommodations they will be looking for, when they will begin looking in earnest, and their price range. Then ask if you can stay in touch and alert them about new availabilities and any specials that might be offered. Follow-up in these situations will often produce a new resident in the months ahead.

- *The prospect's rent budget*—The leasing agent should ask about the prospect's price range in the first few moments of the presentation. If the answer is $600 and your units start at $850, that issue should be dealt with immediately. The longer the matter of price is delayed, the more difficult it is for the prospect to admit that an apartment is beyond his or her means. People recognize that time is valuable and that the leasing agent is putting forth a lot of effort to help them find suitable housing. If the presentation proceeds too far, prospects who simply cannot afford the product have a difficult time admitting they are not rental candidates. When the price issue is delayed too long, the prospect often listens to the whole presentation and begs off with a statement like: "I am very interested, but I just need some time to look at what other properties have to offer." Too many of these responses and the leasing agent's confidence begins to erode.

If the prospect's budget falls within, say, 20 percent of your published rent, it usually pays for the leasing agent to continue with the full marketing effort. Most people are conservative when announcing their budget limitations, and the leasing agent may be able to help with a little creative rent structuring. When prospects cannot afford your apartments, the leasing agent should suggest they visit neighboring properties that are within their means. As I said earlier, a leasing agent should do even more than that: He or she should ask customers for permission to make some calls to help them find quality rental housing at a price they can afford. This will take some tact, because people are very sensitive about their inability to afford something other people consider popularly priced.

- *Motivating force*—Moving is expensive, time-consuming, tiring, and unpleasant. So, when someone arrives at your door looking for an apartment, you can believe that there is an important force at work. It is critical that the leasing agent knows and understands the reasons for the move and the major benefits being sought. It is not enough to know that the customer wants or needs a change in living quarters. In workshops with experienced leasing agents, I have counted more than 200 possible reasons for moving. The sales approach the leasing agent takes with a prospect who is about to be married is very different from the method employed when a person is beginning divorce proceedings. A couple hoping for a home of their own some day will not have the same "hot buttons" as a retired couple who just sold their large house. The leasing agent's job is to demonstrate the benefits of an apartment. Knowing the motivating force behind a move enables the agent to emphasize those benefits that might be of interest to the customer.

- *Urgency*—The leasing agent's approach must have a sense of urgency. A change in housing is a big, sometimes painful, decision, one that can easily be postponed if there are not sufficient reasons or benefits to justify the move. When there is just one available apartment, the level of urgency is obvious and can be very effective. When there is a "desperation banner" hanging on the side of the building and the newspapers are loaded with ads offering every possible incentive, it is far more difficult to convey such a sense of urgency. In fact, this is one of the primary reasons I recommend spending money to give each of your apartments its own personality (this is discussed in Chapter 13, "Upgrading and Renovation"). Then, even though there are other apartments available, the apartment being shown will be viewed as something special.

- *Surprise*—As the relationship between the leasing agent and the customer develops, the agent should be thinking about announcing some kind of personalized "surprise." For example, let's say that the prospect has indicated that he or she hates to waste anything, especially money. A skilled agent may respond by explaining the benefits of the energy-efficient heating plant. Later in the presentation, the agent might add the surprise of an unusually high "R" rating of wall and ceiling insulation. Maybe the agent surprises the customer by offering to provide some wallpaper or allow the prospect to move in a little early. There are dozens of possible surprises. These should be planned in advance and introduced at the moment the prospect is deciding whether to sign an application or keep looking.

- *Questions and objections*—If a prospect begins asking questions and raising objections, this is a positive sign. Questions and objections are often used as a ploy to avoid making a decision. They signal that the prospect wants to say "yes" but can't quite make a decision. Most people display hesitancy when faced with major decisions such as choosing housing, automobiles, and expensive clothing. Often, rental agents will misinterpret a prospect's objections or negative comments as a dislike of the property or apartment. When prospects take the time to spell out objections, they are actually interested but they need help making a decision. An uninterested prospect simply listens to your presentation without comments, objections, or interruptions.

  Most leasing agents can recite all their competitor's special features and all the negative aspects of their own property. This results from absorbing prospect objections. Leasing agents must learn the most fundamental principle of marketing: People need help in making decisions. When objections and questions are raised, the prospect is ready. Knowledge of the prospect, the neighborhood, and the competition will now all come into play. The ability to overcome objections and to answer the prospect's questions depends on product knowledge. The better prepared you are, the easier the task. Each case will be somewhat different, and experimentation is necessary. In time, experience will help point the way. You do not have to overcome each and every objection. Rental prospects commonly express objections just to create a smoke screen to postpone the act of making a decision.

- *The closing*—The two most frequent reasons for a disappointing leasing performance are the condition of the apartment being shown and failure on the part of the leasing agent to ask for the order. I mentioned earlier that success in getting an appointment depends on a willingness to ask for one. The same principle applies to the conclusion of the leasing agent's presentation—i.e., getting the prospect to fill out a rental application. A customer has walked in the door, driven by a need for a change in housing accommodations; the leasing agent acts as an assistant in solving the prospect's housing predicament. The leasing agent has qualified the prospect in terms of the immediacy of his or her needs, budget parameters, and the benefits to be gained by the move. Assuming the product is worthy of the prospect's consideration, shouldn't the leasing agent ask him or her to join the community? If the prospect is hesitant, is it because the agent has failed to answer a question or satisfy an objection? Will the prospect volunteer or identify the reason behind his or her reluctance, or must the agent initiate a probe? Unfortunately, many leasing people complete their tour of the models and an apartment or two and, if the customer doesn't say "I'll take it," the presentation is over. This stems from a lack of training and the fear of rejection.

    The best way to help a novice leasing agent is to have him or her visit new housing developments to observe the selling pros at work. Have the leasing agent note the "close attempts" and the words and phrases that are used. Equipped with a dozen or so of these techniques, the leasing agent should be able to modify them for use in closing apartment rentals.

    There is a period of nervousness that affects most leasing people when asking for the order, but this must be overcome if the individual is to be successful. Hopefully sooner, rather than later, the agent is going to strike the right relationship with the prospect and summon the courage to ask for a deposit and a commitment; and the customer's answer is going to be "yes." The best time to make a deal is immediately after wrapping one up—thus the pattern of success begins.

    The main message here is that the leasing agent must ask for the order. Most apartments do not rent themselves.

- *Application deposit*—Making a commitment to rent and placing a deposit are closely related. If the customer says yes to the "close question" but departs without leaving a deposit, little has been accomplished. The amount of the deposit is not particularly important, although a substantial figure certainly demonstrates a strong degree of commitment. A chronic deficiency revealed in many apartment shopper reports is the fact that the customer was not asked for a deposit. That means that the prospect remains just that, a prospect. The prospect may come back and rent; or he or she might make one more stop and discover a better deal. When a person puts down a deposit, there is an element of closure or finality.

When it is difficult to get a commitment from prospects because the rent is too high or they want a series of improvements to the unit, many experienced leasing agents will ask for a deposit and an application, making acceptance contingent on the prospects getting "their deal." This accomplishes some important things. First, the prospects go home and discontinue apartment hunting for the moment. That means they are not going to be lost to a competing property—at least not today. Also, if the prospects will entertain the idea of putting down a deposit, it indicates serious interest. However, if the prospects bring up objections, yet refuse to write a deposit check that is fully refundable if their requests are not met, they may just be looking for a way to say goodbye. Finally, once people have put down a deposit on an apartment or, for that matter, almost any other commodity, there is a sense of relief that comes with making a decision. These prospects begin to "live" the advantages and benefits of the new apartment even though it is necessary to wait for the acceptance of their terms and application. After a few days, a compromise between the offer on the table and a middle-ground counteroffer is much more likely to be achieved.

- *New appointment*—When it becomes obvious to a skilled leasing agent that the customers are not going to make an immediate decision to rent, the agent should do his or her best to make a new appointment for the prospects to visit the property again. The prospects might say that they want time to visit some other properties for comparison purposes or that they want a friend or relative to have a chance to see the unit. The agent should then try to fix a specific time or at least a day for a return visit.

Over the years, I have noticed that the very best leasing agents go through a personal debriefing session after their presentation to a serious prospect. Usually within minutes of their visit with a customer, they will sit down and review the person's needs, timing, and budget constraints. They will briefly record the prospect's housing situation and try to summarize the customer's primary and secondary reasons for seeking new accommodations. In going through this process, they are evaluating their skills and abilities in understanding the customer's needs and making sure they listened to what was being said—how the customer answered specific questions.

Next they will review the benefits they presented to help the customer

Exhibit 11.1
Sample Presentation Record

Name:		Intro: ☐
Timing:	Budget:	
Ready:	Looking:	
Situation:		
Motivating Force:		
Benefits:	Surprise:	Close:
Urgency:		Deposit: ☐
Comments:		
Date:	New Appointment: ☐ When:	

This is an example of a form that would be filled in by the leasing agent during or after the presentation.

make a decision. They ask themselves: Did I ask for the order? Did I think of a "surprise" or special inducement to help the customer choose our property? Did I create a sense of urgency? The answers to these questions are not for others to see. They are intended to help the leasing agent candidly appraise the completed presentation and make mental notes for improving future presentations.

Finally, the agent might record any other comments that would either help with any follow-up commitments that were promised to the customer or be useful in making future presentations. This might include other approaches that can be used in follow-up contacts or during a second appointment that will help convert this prospect to a resident.

This type of *personal presentation evaluation* is usually made when someone who appeared to be a serious prospect leaves without committing to a lease or an application deposit. Usually an agent can skip this process if the customer commits to becoming a new resident. That outcome means the agent has been successful.

Leasing personnel should be strongly encouraged to go through this type of debriefing process to help them hone their skills. An example of a form that can be used for such an evaluation is presented in Exhibit 11.1.

Follow-up Action.   When a prospective renter heads for the door, you will often hear a promise to return at a later time. Chances are that is not what they mean. House sellers call these "be-backs." When a prospect leaves without renting, you face an uphill, but not impossible, task.

Knowing that a substantial number of prospects are not going to commit during their first visit, it is advisable to do some planning in advance. There will be questions that come up during most interviews for which you might not have a ready answer. Make a mental note of any inquires that have even a minor bearing on the decision-making process. Of course, if they are essential to a lease decision that day, you will follow through on the spot and get the appropriate answers. Many inquiries are just part of the conversation process—incidental, but not critical, to a decision. Make a record of these concerns anyway, as they will be used later.

During the "farewell" part of the interview, ask prospects if it would be all right if you follow up with them. Most prospects will simply agree. You now have your invitation to call back to thank them for their interest in your community and to provide the answers to those unanswered questions. The fact that you remembered their inquiry and took the time to research an answer will impress most people. Most likely, you will learn how their apartment search is coming along and if they have made a decision yet. If they have found the right apartment, wish them well and ask them to remember you to any of their acquaintances who might also be in the market for an apartment. If they are still looking, you have the opportunity to reintroduce your community and, perhaps, "sweeten the pot" with the offer of a bonus of one kind or another.

The traditional "thank you" note is a nice gesture, but you should not expect a lot of "saves" as a result of your mailing out this handwritten card. It is really more of a courtesy than anything else. Lately, there has been a tendency to use e-mail both for answering pending questions and for the follow-up thank you. This technique is expedient, but it does not really provide the personal touch necessary to rekindle interest in your community.

In the final analysis, the conversion rate of prospects who have visited and not rented is not very good. Out of 100 prospects you follow through with, you may get 40 to agree to a return visit. Expect only about one-half to actually show up. You can congratulate yourself if you convert five or six of those to the status of residents. Prospect follow-up is a painstaking process that is filled with rejection, but in my opinion, the extra rentals are worth the effort.

Waiting List.   Having and maintaining a waiting list is a nice talking point and certainly adds to the status and appeal of your property. The staff will enjoy a moment of pride in being able to report that you have people waiting for certain units. However, unless an apartment becomes available within, say, a week or so of a prospect signing up on your waiting list, you should understand that his or her apartment search will not remain static. As I stated earlier in this book, there are one or more influences spurring the desire for new quarters. Unless one of those influences happens to be the securing of *that particular apartment,* the prospect will most likely continue scouting alternatives.

Evaluating Results

Having made appointments, shown apartments, and closed on some leases, you will need methods to track and evaluate rental progress. Is there a nice, steady flow of prospect traffic, or are there more "slow" days than busy ones? Do prospects seem impressed with the property and the units being offered? Are vacancies stuck at the same level for months? Is the staff losing their enthusiasm? Answers can often be found by doing some reevaluation in these areas.

- *Prospect traffic.* When traffic slows, take stock of each point in the marketing program. A new advertising message often helps. You can almost count on the fact that your advertising has become stale. Scrap what you have and work on a new approach. Don't lose your image by adopting a shock approach or getting caught up in give-away mania.

  Most importantly, check the product. The vast majority of apartment lookers start as drive-bys who were impressed enough to park their car and come in. When fewer and fewer prospects show up in the office, be slow to blame the market—more than likely the property is losing its edge.

  In soft market periods, it may be very difficult to get more people through the door each week without a fire sale approach, but you can improve your sales performance with the traffic you have.

- *Value for the money.* When prospects choose not to rent, it is because they believe that they can get more for their money somewhere else. Managers and leasing people often get trapped by the notion that everyone wants to pay less. There are actually many more people in the marketplace willing to pay more if they can just get more. They want a nicer place to live with a higher level of care and maintenance. If you have money for trips, gifts, or free rent, try a different approach: Spend it on the vacant apartments, giving each unit an extra degree of quality and appointments.

- *Persuasion.* Is the staff showing or selling? Is an effort being made to learn each prospect's motive for moving? Are the agents skilled and practiced at the art of matching the property's benefits with the prospect's needs and desires? Is the prospect "asked for the order"? Maybe not.

Selling is not simply being nice, it is an art that must be practiced over and over. The problems of daily rejection must be put in perspective. Time must be spent working on sales presentations, and when business is slow, there ought to be sufficient time.

Prospect Conversion Ratio.   Many property owners and some market analysts choose to dwell on the *conversion ratio*—the number of rental presentations that are made as compared to the number of new leases signed. Over a period of some time, this ratio can prove beneficial in spotting a problem or sorting out ineffective leasing agents, but it should be used with caution.

New properties have a much higher ratio of lookers to renters. It is common to record as many as ten to fifteen lookers for every deal made in a new, high-profile development. In a property that has stabilized, the conversion ratio will be something more like five or six prospects for each lease signed. The secret to utilizing these ratios as an evaluation tool lies in not broadcasting them to the staff. Some owners and supervisory managers announce their opinion of what the proper conversion ratio should be. Once the leasing agents learn the magic number, they simply adjust the weekly traffic figures to generate the desired ratio.

Work with the conversion ratios as a tool, but do not force them. If you are truly achieving a rental for every three or four people who walk through the door, study the competition and your rent levels. There is a good chance your rents are too low. If, on the other hand, you only rent one apartment for every nine or ten showings, it is a pretty good bet that the property has some serious flaws. Either would indicate the need for some major changes.

Shop the Property.   Most leasing agents dislike the use of *shoppers*. Let your leasing agents know in advance that you plan to use shoppers to spot mistakes for the sake of correcting them, not to punish anyone.

As a matter of fact, it is a smart idea to use shoppers even if leasing agents are converting prospects to residents at a ratio of five- or six-to-one. A shopper might discover that if the agents were doing everything they are supposed to do, they would be converting at an even better ratio. In that case, the rents may be too low and you can raise them safely. Have your apartment community shopped three or four times a year just to make sure agents are doing their best.

The shoppers might be young couples who look like prospects. If they have a baby or small child with them, so much the better. The point is to select shoppers who closely match your resident profile. Also, have two or three teams of shoppers who can visit the apartment community on the same day but at different times. The reason for this is that it will help to substantiate the existence of selling patterns that need attention or correction. This will also help to counteract the denials that can be expected when a leasing agent is confronted with a negative report. If the same report is made by more than one shopper, the agent has less of an argument.

The shopper should note the date and time of the visit and the name of the leasing agent. The shopper's report should be a strict narrative with no subjective comments. You will be amazed at what the shopper's report can reveal. Here are some actual examples. In one case, shoppers were denied their request for a tour of the models. In another case, an agent walked around without shoes. One agent told shoppers that if it started to rain, the tour would end. At one property, the rental information center was closed during the middle of the day.

The written reports should be reviewed with your leasing agents individually and privately so each understands what he or she is doing correctly or incorrectly. Don't let the agent adopt a defensive or negative posture. Explain what was done wrong and point out the correct techniques.

Setting Goals.   After you are satisfied that the rental staff is doing a good job, have them set their own performance goals. Ask them *how many apartments they would like to rent this month.* Chances are the staff will set a goal much higher than you would set for them. However, if you rephrase the question to *how many they actually expect to rent,* you will get a somewhat lower number. That is because the latter question is asking for a specific commitment. People generally will do everything they can to meet their own commitments. If they miss the goal, help them analyze the reasons why.

To improve the productivity of your rental staff, consider various methods that may not include the payment of money. As a motivator, money loses much of its effectiveness in a comparatively short time span. An ongoing program of paying bonuses for rental results loses its punch very quickly.

Contests, with rewards and recognition to the top performers, foster a spirit of competition. They almost always spur the staff to higher levels of achievement. A contest raises the achievement bar, and there will be a flurry of activity to avoid ending up near the bottom of the list.

A Final Check.   If, after doing all of the above, you are still not happy with the prospect traffic numbers and conversion ratio, check every link in the leasing chain step-by-step—policies, rents, product preparation, merchandising, even the property's design. When you find something that can be improved, begin making changes.

12

Managers are crazed when rents are raised;
tenants bemoan, but don't need a loan;
owners smile paying bills for awhile.

Setting and Raising Rents

The business of renting apartments is not much different from most other enterprises. Capital is needed to fund construction of the building, and there will be operating expenses. A promise of profit must be added—or why get involved? The question then becomes: Are there enough people in the area who are willing to rent their living quarters at rates sufficient to pay the bills and return that profit? Finding venture capital, figuring out expected costs, and determining a level of profit are fairly straightforward steps. The stickler is the customer. What will be expected in terms of location and facilities? How can customers be attracted? Most importantly, can enough rent be charged to make everything work out? It is this last question—and finding an answer to it—that we will explore in this chapter.

Cash-on-Cash Return

The best way to begin is to learn where it all must end. Real estate investors make it pretty clear that they want a cash-on-cash return for their invested dollars:

$$\frac{\text{Annual Cash Flow}}{\text{Total Cash Invested}} = \text{Cash-on-Cash Return (\%)}$$

Exhibit 12.1
Income Groups

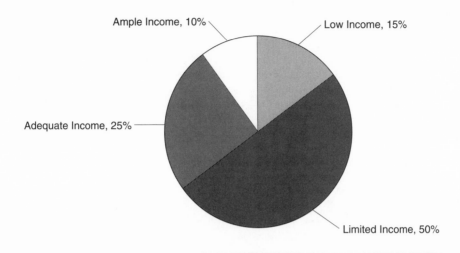

Ample Income, 10%   Low Income, 15%

Adequate Income, 25%

Limited Income, 50%

Investors will make some allowances for real estate's tradition of being a hedge on inflation and the fact that real estate, unlike most other investment vehicles, allows for a considerable degree of control. Also, many investors will forgo some immediate return for the promise of a higher return at the point of eventual sale. Today, however, the prime goal is "cash return"; and it is important to remember that return cannot be realized until after all other bills and obligations are satisfied. Any mistakes in the purchase cost, financing fees, or operating expenses, or any shortfalls on the income side, have a direct effect on the cash return. When there is not enough money to satisfy everything, the owner's return is the first to be affected. When this occurs, rent levels are studied closely in hopes of finding financial relief. The last move in this balancing act is to begin trimming or delaying expenses which can set the property on the wrong course.

So many of these financial missteps are avoidable through a better understanding of the housing marketplace. This requires a look at who your customers are going to be and just how much they are willing to pay.

Income Groups

There is no single process for determining the proper rent level and direction. Among residents there are at least four, and probably more, income groups (Exhibit 12.1) that must be identified and dealt with separately because they each require a different approach. Some groups present severe restrictions when it comes to the subject of rent. The financial position of each group must be examined as well as the housing alternatives available to them.

Low-Income Group.   A house is a house and there are few differences between the costs of producing and operating one housing unit versus another. Basic building components are the same regardless of where they are placed. Amenities and larger rooms might add a 30-percent premium between the cost of producing a rental unit that is part of a low-income development and one that is targeted to the middle- to upper-middle-income group. Unless and until there is an amazing breakthrough in construction technology, there is little probability of creating low-income rental housing that is self-supporting. This means subsidization of one sort or another will be needed. Subsidies mean controls, and controls mean rules, delays, and added expense. Many developers prefer to sidestep the problems of dealing with the government and restrict their activities to market-rate, conventional housing. This forces the government to "sweeten the pie" to attract investors back to the business of housing those needing a degree of financial assistance.

It is a given that additional housing programs will be forthcoming to attempt to find a fair, manageable, and effective way of housing people with limited financial resources. My estimate is that about 15 percent of the nation's households fall into the *low-income* group, which needs help in paying their monthly rent. Assistance can be in the form of government rent subsidies, grants, tax credits, or below-market interest rates. All of these involve an understanding of complex governmental procedures. The need for low-cost housing will probably always outstrip the supply side because of these restrictions and the limited potential for profit.

Limited-Income Group.   Many apartment buildings have been around for a long time or were built during a time when "cheap" was the operative word. Today, these buildings struggle for survival. Without a major infusion of cash to make increasingly needed repairs, these properties face an uphill battle in attracting residents who will move in and stay. The feasibility of investing large sums of cash in these properties may very well be questionable. The alternative is to accept just anyone, and many of these new residents can be counted on to cause more damage. Such properties become homes to those who do not have a lot of income or, for that matter, much of a choice. New rent levels must be closely tied to increases in the residents' effective spendable income because there is little room for increases in their household budgets.

Residents in the *limited-income* group (about 50 percent of current households by my estimate) are extremely price sensitive: A $30 increase in the monthly rent can force them to seek housing elsewhere. This puts the manager in a very awkward position. Say, for example, he or she knows that operating costs have risen to such a point that a $40 per unit per month increase is needed. The manager also knows that this is more than most of the current residents can afford. An increase of this size will force a number of them to move to an apartment community with lower rents, or at least to one that is offering a move-in discount or rent holiday (concession). In addition to the laws of supply and demand, there is another force at work— *ability to pay.*

Anything but the most modest rent increase can cause undue move-outs. The move-out usually entails a loss of revenue between residents plus the added costs to prepare the vacated unit. This can further reduce what little bottom line there may be. An operating cash shortage does not have much of an effect on the utility bills, recurring services, insurance, or real estate taxes because if they are not paid, the property faces some negative consequences. Delaying the property's general upkeep and needed repairs may avert some financial problems, but it definitely puts the properties serving this income group into a downward spiral.

Adequate-Income Group. People in this group do not have money to waste, but they have some discretionary income in their monthly budgets. Depending on individual priorities, people in the adequate-income group usually opt to spend those extra dollars on one or more indulgences. A fancier car, a nicer place to live, better home furnishings, and extended vacations are a few of those options. In terms of housing, people in the adequate-income group may opt for homeownership, or they may choose to rent and save the additional worry and work of having a place of their own.

It is common for owners and managers of less-desirable properties to make an attempt to attract people in this adequate-income grouping, but most of these efforts fail because of the group's high sensitivity to location, neighborhood, and property appearance and condition. On the other hand, there is fierce competition from developers of for-sale housing such as condominiums, townhouses, and coach and manor homes. This housing is priced to compete closely with upscale rentals, especially when tax deductions and potential appreciation are considered.

The people who make up the *adequate-income* group (about 25 percent of the market) can and often do pay rent amounts that not only cover expenses and debt service, but also return a profit to the investor. These renters stay longer and cause less damage. Their incomes are such that they can keep pace with cost-of-living rent increases.

Most of the profit-minded apartment developers are at work to serve this group. They strive to deliver fresh housing concepts with the latest in innovations. They are crowded by competitors so their livelihood depends on presenting an exceptional product and value. Their staffs are highly professional with a wide variety of skills. If the value of the product they offer is not in balance with the rent being asked, they know the people in this group will quickly choose one of their many other housing alternatives. This is the industry's prime market—it is the most intensely competitive because the laws of supply and demand govern it.

Ample-Income Group.   The people in the *ample-income* group (approximately 10 percent of the market) do not concern themselves with questions of owning or renting. They do whatever suits their needs and desires. If they decide to rent, these people will surely make the necessary modifications to fit the apartment to their lifestyle and furnishings. The developer of the high-end rental housing that attracts the ample-income group must concentrate on an exceptional location, a well-built structure, and some generous and interesting apartment layouts. Some of the finish appointments are not as critical because many of these residents, with their teams of designers and decorators, will work together to customize their homes. They are not fools when it comes to spending, but money is not their primary concern. In this group, more prospects and residents are lost through skimping than overcharging. "Elegant," "quiet," "gracious," and "secure" are their buzzwords. These people do not choose housing that is trendy, and, when satisfied, they move infrequently. People of means understand and can afford rising prices. Unfortunately, the ample-income group represents only a small segment of the rental market.

Setting Rents for the First Time

As a manager, you may be asked to participate in the job of establishing rents for a property that is being constructed or one that has undergone a major renovation and is now targeted to a different rental audience. If the property is designed to house the low- or limited-income group, there is probably little for you to do in terms of establishing rent levels except to acquire an understanding of the rules and limitations imposed by any regulating authorities. The main rent-setting activity takes place in housing built for those enjoying adequate and ample incomes.

Cost versus What the Market Will Bear.   When establishing a schedule of rents for the first time, the object is to produce enough income to cover costs and return a profit. This need has to be balanced with the fear that if rents are set too high, an unacceptable number of vacancies will linger on the market. The process for doing this is fairly simple: Find a point in between what you know you *can get* and what you *cannot get.*

In the past, rent projections—or *pro formas,* as they are commonly called—were often made in the quiet of an office, where the addition of an extra $40 or $50 to an apartment's rent level involved only a few keystrokes. Rents are often just numbers "plugged in" to balance the owner's projections. If cost estimates exceed income projections, some "stretch" in rents is usually possible, but one should not get carried away. Sometimes the manager is ostensibly "asked," but in reality is told, to endorse a rent schedule that has no relationship to the actual marketplace. This happens because housing entrepreneurs "want to build," and they are willing to take their chances down the road.

When a new property comes into the market, there is a degree of the unknown regarding the amount of rent that can be achieved. The rents that the manager uses for comparison usually belong to properties that are older, even if by only a few months. When a property is brand-new, it should have features and appointments that have not yet been seen in the marketplace. If nothing else, "brand-new," by itself, typically commands a higher price. Managers tend to be conservative (too low) in their estimates of rent levels while owners err on the high side. The right answer is usually somewhere in the middle. Finally, there is a force called the *nerve factor*—simply having the nerve to ask for more rent.

Pattern Pricing.   Many developers and managers search for a pattern of rents that is easy to remember while delivering the needed revenue. This usually produces two or perhaps three levels of rent for each of the apartment types. Let's use an example of a two-story, garden apartment property that has both one- and two-bedroom apartments. A decision is made to establish a rent differential of $125 between the one- and two-bedroom units. There is agreement that units on the second floor are more desirable than those on the first floor, so a premium of $25 is added to all upper floor units. Then a further surcharge is added to adjust for the greater desirability of units facing the relaxation garden as opposed to those overlooking the parking lot. The process is simple and fast, and it is hoped that the customers will accept the logic.

Unfortunately, there is a problem with pricing schemes this simple. Rental customers are keen shoppers, and they will quickly discover any flaws in a pricing system. Those flaws take the form of bargains when prospects spot advantages while comparing different units in the building. The prospect might notice that all of the one-bedroom apartments are not equal. Some may have better layouts than others, or better views; or some units might have larger windows or extra closet space. When there is no price differential to equalize desirability, the better units will be taken first, while the now over-priced, less-desirable units remain vacant. *Pricing must reflect differences* unless you are marketing a development with units of identical layout, features, view, and access, a situation which I don't think happens to exist. So, we will continue exploring other rent pricing systems.

Total Square Feet.   Another common method used to set rent is to divide the total rent dollars needed by the sum of the square feet of all the units. That gives the rent-pricing practitioner the necessary rent per square foot.

Exhibit 12.2
Sample Comparison Grid

Unit Type: _____

	Subject	Comparable #1		Comparable #2		Comparable #3	
	Description	Description	+ (−) Adj.	Description	+ (−) Adj.	Description	+ (−) Adj.
Property							
Current Rent							
Item							
Location							
Age and Condition							
Appearance							
Parking							
Amenities							
Area of Unit							
Carpeting							
Appliances							
Drapes or Blinds							
Storage or Deck							
Utilities							
Net Adj. (Tot.)							
Adj. Rent	$						
Per Sq Ft							

After that, it is an easy matter to calculate the rent levels of each apartment size rounded to the nearest $5 or $10. The thought behind this is that people are really renting space, so the rents should reflect only the amount of space rented. However, the square-foot method will get owners and managers into a good bit of trouble. While people do rent space for money, the many other variables that come into play make this system almost worthless. Apartments that are smaller in terms of number of rooms as well as square feet carry a disproportionately higher share of the rent burden. The difference in square footage between a two-bedroom, two-bath split and a two-bedroom, one-bathroom apartment can be small, but the rent levels are likely to be significantly different. This is because certain layouts are in favor and, as a result, command more rent regardless of size. Also, considering only apartment size does not take two important things into account—utilization of space and the fact that in every marketplace there is a maximum rent that residents will pay. There are computer programs that can make mathematical adjustments between unit types, but the weighting process for different features depends on empirical data that must be constantly updated to reflect current market trends.

Comparison Grid Analysis.   Comparison grid analysis is one of the techniques used by real estate managers to help assure that a competitive schedule of rental rates is developed. The idea is this: By making adjustments to the rental rates of comparable properties, allowing for varying features, sizes, and appointments, the analyst tries to simulate a typical prospect's application of value (see Exhibit 12.2). For example, the manager may decide that an extra 150 square feet in an apartment is worth $25 per month, or that a dishwasher is worth $5 per month. The evaluation process differs with the person completing the comparison(s) and, more particularly, the style preferred by the person who trained that individual. The more common approach is to subtract allowances in categories in which the comparable units are better than the subject apartment and to add an allowance when the comparable properties are less desirable than the subject.

There are some important drawbacks to this system that should be discussed. The most obvious is the weighting of the endless possible differences that exist among apartment properties. Furthermore, for the analysis to have any degree of accuracy, it should be performed individually for each apartment style and size. For example, the weighting for a dishwasher in a two-bedroom apartment might carry a value of $7, while the same appliance may only be given a value of $4 in an efficiency apartment. Setting the dollar amount of the adjustments poses an even bigger problem. Many people who use this system limit their adjustments to $5 or $10 increments. This almost always produces an incorrect indication of the proper rent level. The schedule of charges and credits must not only be broad, but also deal with some rather finite estimates of the value of different features and appointments. An extra foot or two of closet space is probably not worth $5 per month, but it is worth something to a prospect who has a lot of clothes. Added counter space, a side-by-side refrigerator-freezer, gas versus electricity for cooking and heating, a good layout versus a marginal one—all of these features are worth something. Sometimes differences should be valued in dollars, sometimes in fractions of a dollar. The estimates are almost always arbitrary and usually reflect only the opinion of the manager who is making the schedule. The system also depends on the ability of the competition to set rents properly because the rents being developed are based on those of the competition. Finally, it is important to remember that your rents are being set for the future while the comparisons are based on rents that were set some time ago.

While comparison grid analysis calls attention to the importance and value of different features and appointments, it is most difficult to implement properly. This method is widely taught but little used in practice because it is so difficult to document and quantify the myriad differences.

Best-of-Type Pricing. As with setting any price, the most fundamental ingredient in setting rent is a thorough understanding of the marketplace and the rates being charged by competitors. Once equipped with this information, the practitioner can do a creditable job of setting rent, regardless of the exact name of the method. Best-of-type pricing involves breaking down the units into groups of like kind. In other words, all of the one-bedroom units with an alcove would make up one group, and one-bedroom units with a den would constitute another.

Once these groups are identified, the person responsible for setting the rents should visit each and every unit. It is necessary to identify the *best* individual unit in each group. The units are basically the same; that is how they came to be in the particular group. However, there will be differences in their access or view, or they will have some subtle feature or benefit. Perhaps only a limited number of the units in the grouping have an extra window, closet, or niche. After carefully reviewing each unit, the manager should determine which apartment is the most desirable. It is also important to consider the total number of units in each size category. For example, in a development of 100 units, 10 units of a certain type should produce a more aggressive rent than 50 units of a given type. Unless the unit layout is completely unacceptable, a shortage of supply usually increases a unit's desirability and thus adds to the rent. After taking the supply of a unit type into consideration, a rent amount should be set for the best apartment of that type. Do this by asking yourself: What is the most rent I can reasonably expect to get from my best unit of this type? Then the runner-up should be revisited to determine how much it is worth relative to the absolute best. The answer might very well be that there is too little difference to quantify. If that is the case, then it should carry the same rent as the very best unit in this group. Continuing to the second runner-up, deductions should be made to balance its desirability against that of the best in its grouping. Again, the deductions can and should be small if the differences are small. The system should not be compromised to gain a rhythm or to establish an easily remembered pattern. Computers are available to do the arithmetic; one should concentrate on simulating what the customer will do in terms of weighting the difference. Moving in descending order of desirability to the worst unit in the group, appropriate deductions should be made along the way. The process is then repeated for each apartment type.

The major problem with best-of-type pricing is that it is slow, requires repeated trips to the apartment units, and cannot be done sitting in the office. If done correctly, it will almost always produce the largest total rent amount, and it will contribute to a more balanced rent-up of the property. This happens because the rent-setter is doing exactly what the renting public does. *You want to regulate desirability with different rent levels.* This should prevent renters from snapping up bargain-priced units while the less-desirable units remain vacant because they are priced at a rent that is unacceptable to the renting public. Best-of-type pricing takes into consideration such issues as status, views, and the absorption rate.

Status and Rent. In setting apartment rents, there are a number of valuable lessons to be learned. First of all, housing is very much a status symbol. It is one of the principal ways to display personal achievement. Luxury high-rise buildings satisfy the desire for status identification with their impressive entryways and lobbies and with such amenities as doormen and concierges. Garden apartment properties offer gatehouses, private clubs, and elaborate recreational facilities. These extras receive the most attention when residents boast about the facilities to their friends; actual use by residents is less significant than their status appeal. If there was no desire for status identification, housing requirements could be met with functional, sterile cubes. Apartment managers should recognize this fact before they begin setting rents for their properties.

The American buying public believes that if something costs more, it must be better. This method of determining value is based partly on national tradition and partly on status appeal. If rents are competitive (i.e., the same as or less expensive than most other developments), the property may lose more than needed revenue: Status appeal is also lost. This loss is crucial because status appeal is often factored into the decision-making process, consciously or unconsciously.

An example, something that has been used successfully for a number of years, proves the importance of these principles. The manager of a high-rise building has only to redecorate the common areas of the top floor or even the top two floors—e.g., install superior carpeting and wall covering in the public corridors, add some costly and dramatic improvements such as a marble accent wall or rich woodwork around the elevator area, maybe install some expensive-looking corridor lighting, and install new wood-grained apartment entry doors with high-quality hardware that includes a distinctive door-knocker. Even though these improvements are only in the common corridor, the manager can charge 3 to 6 percent more rent per month for each of these apartments. The apartments themselves are identical to those on the lower floors. Nevertheless, the premier floors will not only command exceptional rent, but also be in the greatest demand. Why? Status identification—a person's need to show superiority. Friends who visit the residents on your specially decorated floors will appreciate the extravagance and understand that there is an associated cost. This is the essence of status appeal.

Garden apartment properties often capitalize on the status principle by creating a special area of *limited-edition units*. Usually the manager will choose a secluded location or one that has a better natural setting than the rest of the property. This area may be fenced off or separated in some way from most of the other units. Additions might include special landscaping, individualized entryways, jumbo patios, wooden decks, screened-in porches, bay windows, and private gardens. Interior upgrades can also increase the variety and value of such apartments.

The desire to impress others is demonstrated in many ways. You do not have to work in apartment management very long to know about the proliferation of requests for service around major holidays. During these times, residents want problems corrected and improvements made to their apartments because friends and relatives will be visiting. Your residents want everything to look just right. People's homes reflect their achievements, and your residents will not appear very successful if they are living in a broken-down apartment. A manager's sensitivity to these preferences will prove effective in setting and achieving maximum rents.

Views.   People place considerable value on the views from their apartments. There is more to this subject, however, than you might expect. Where they exist, lake, ocean, or mountain views are very important during the day and even more so at times of sunrise and sunset. Yet these views often have little value after dark when most people return from work. Hence, it is important to visit each of the units at night during the rent-setting process, to see the evening view and determine its appropriate value. In urban environments, a city view with its endless patterns of light has as much appeal as a lake or mountain view does elsewhere.

It has long been assumed that a person who rents an apartment on a higher floor gets a better view. However, as one proceeds above the midpoint in a high-rise building, the improvement in the view is negligible. You can test this theory yourself by taking someone to the fifteenth floor of a high-rise building to look out the window and note the view. The next step is to blindfold your companion and go up and down in the elevator to confuse his or her sense of location. Finally, go to the eighteenth floor and remove the blindfold so your companion can look out the window. Without the help of a relatively significant landmark, chances are it will be impossible for that individual to detect the additional three floors of height.

Fifteenth floor views and eighteenth floor views on the same side of the same building are essentially the same. The only way to discern the difference in location is by the apartment number on the door. Therefore, any rent differences between two such units should be slight. There should be little or no discount for loss of view and only a small discount to account for the loss of status appeal that result from not being higher in the building.

Absorption Rate and Rent Level. It is essential to have a good sense of the number of units that can be absorbed into the marketplace at your initial rent levels. In addition to introducing new units at an acceptable level, rents must be set so they represent good value and, as a result, produce a well-paced rent-up. What must be avoided is a problem known as "biting your tail." You do not want to bring too many units "on stream," nor do you want to price apartments so high that you find yourself with units that have never been rented at the same time you face the problem of dealing with lease renewals on units rented earlier in the leasing campaign.

When you are in the rent-up stage for more than one year (with a single phase), it is usually a sure sign that your development is at odds with the forces of supply and demand. The problems are considerable when you are trying to rent the last of the units and you must begin negotiating renewals with those early renters. Chances are that if the initial rent-up has taken almost a year to complete, you have offered bonuses, specials, or concessions; the existing residents will want their share as part of their renewal requirements. Ideally, you want to select a schedule of rents that represents enough of a bargain so that the units are all rented before the renewal cycle begins. This can make the difference between a successful development and one that is constantly fighting a vacancy problem.

Comparing Pattern Pricing with Best-of-Type Pricing. Let's look at an example of a building 25 stories tall, with 24 floors of 12 apartments each—a total of 288 units. The residential floors are numbered 1 through 24, and the four corner units on each floor are one-bedroom-plus-den apartments. The remainder are efficiencies and two-bedroom units. For convenience, I'll discuss only the one-bedroom-plus-den units on the front corners of the building. The front of the building faces a row of similar buildings across a wide boulevard. Twenty-five feet away from one side of the building is an aging nine-story apartment residence. On the other side, there is a large, picturesque park.

Pricing by floor (pattern pricing) results in the rent structure for these

Exhibit 12.3
Pattern for Floor Pricing

Floor	Tier Facing Park	Tier Facing Building
24	895	887
23	885	877
22	875	867
21	869	861
20	863	855
19	857	849
18	851	843
17	845	837
16	839	831
15	833	825
14	827	819
13	821	813
12	815	807
11	809	801
10	803	795
9	797	789
8	791	783
7	785	777
6	779	771
5	773	765
4	767	759
3	761	753
2	755	747
1	745	737

	Tier Facing Park	Tier Facing Building
Monthly total	$19,640	$19,448
Average monthly rent		$814.33

two tiers of one-bedroom-plus-den units as shown in Exhibit 12.3. Rents increase floor-by-floor in $6 increments, moving upward from the midpoint of the building, with a $10 increment for the top two floors. Descending from the midpoint, rents decrease floor-by-floor by the same $6 increment used in the escalation of rent, with a $10 reduction in rent for the bottom floor. The starting point or *base rent* is slightly higher on the side of the building facing the park than it is on the side facing the old building.

This rent schedule was simple to put together, and it follows a pattern that is easy to remember. The benefits stop there, however. For purposes of comparison, let's use some of the principles we discussed earlier and apply the best-of-type pricing method to the same building.

Exhibit 12.4

Matching Price to Value (Best-of-Type Pricing)

Floor	Tier Facing Park	Tier Facing Building
27	920	920
26	920	920
25	890	890
24	890	890
23	890	890
22	878	878
21	878	878
20	878	878
19	865	865
18	865	865
17	865	865
16	865	865
15	852	855
14	852	845
12	852	835
11	852	825
10	842	815
9	842	805
8	835	795
7	830	785
6	825	775
5	820	765
4	810	755
3	800	745

Monthly total	$20,616	$20,204
Average monthly rent		$850.42
Percentage increase over pattern pricing		4.43 percent

The *best-of-type pricing* method achieves the closest correlation between price and value. Let's apply this to the two tiers of one-bedroom-plus-den apartments in the previous example. First of all, we will change the floor numbering system. Apartments on higher floors have greater status appeal, and that means more rent dollars. Because the lobby level is about one and a half stories in height, the numbering sequence can logically begin with the third floor. The thirteenth floor can be omitted because superstitious people avoid it. The resulting top floor number is 27 rather than 24, as was the case in the earlier example.

After thoroughly studying the competition, the manager identifies the best one-bedroom-plus-den apartments in the building—the top apartments overlooking the park. Based on complete knowledge of the market, the rent for those apartments is estimated at the highest rate the market will bear. Before setting the rent, however, improvements are made to the top two floors to create special penthouse-type units. When the improvements have been made, the manager assesses their market value. After comparing both floors and finding virtually no difference in view, the manager establishes identical rents for all of the one-bedroom-plus-den penthouse-type units. Moving downward, the corner units on the next three floors are found to share the same view as the top floors, so their rent is reduced by the market value of the penthouse upgrades only. Continuing the inspection, the manager discovers that the view suffers slightly on the next three floors and the rent is lowered accordingly. Further rent reductions are applied to blocks of units to adjust for loss of view and the reduced status appeal of lower floors as the middle of the building is approached (see Exhibit 12.4).

So far the principal difference between this pricing technique and pattern pricing relates to diverging view and status adjustments that translate into different levels of desirability. Best-of-type pricing produces a higher average rent. I have not mentioned any rent realignment to account for the different views from the two sides of the building. Why? Because in the inspection, it was discovered that the older building does not impede views or have a negative influence above the fifteenth floor. On the fifteenth floor and below, the presence of the older building is obvious, and the rent adjustments begin to reflect this.

Pattern pricing established a difference between the two sides that was maintained throughout the building. This was unnecessary on the higher floors because the view and appeal would not be affected by a nine-story building. On the floors with a view of the adjacent building's roof, careful consideration reveals that a small rent deduction is not adequate compensation for the undesirable view. Because rents for apartments above the fifteenth floor on this side of the building are not reduced, apartment rents on the lower floors can be discounted substantially to compensate for the loss of view.

Once again, the manager does not want to make the mistake of allowing bargain-rent apartments to exist. The bargains will be snapped up, leaving behind the most difficult-to-rent apartments.

In the best-of-type pricing method, substantial adjustments were made for the less-desirable units, and at the same time the rents were higher overall than those determined by pattern pricing. Even more important is the fact that the building will undoubtedly rent up faster using the best-of-type rent schedule. While pattern pricing looks good on paper, the best-of-type method simulates what prospects do—namely, match price to value.

You may wonder if maintaining different rates for units of similar size will confuse prospects. The answer is yes. Most developments have little variance in their pricing structure, so there will be some resistance to establishing a proper pricing system. Leasing agents may also be confused. However, prospects are not shown every unit in the building, and discussion of rents should be in the context of a specific unit. When you prepare rent schedules detailing the rent for each unit, much of the confusion is eliminated. At the same time, prospects can be assured that your rents are firmly established and not subject to negotiation.

The same principles that are used in setting rents in large high-rise buildings will also work for smaller buildings or garden-type housing. There are differences in virtually every housing unit for the same reasons—i.e., view, layout, access, size, and floor level. The pricing procedure remains essentially the same.

Making Adjustments

No matter how much care is taken in the initial pricing of a property, mistakes will be made. It is quite possible to misjudge the desirability of certain units. Constant review and adjustment is necessary to prevent such a mistake from becoming a costly problem. Unfortunately, the unskilled apartment manager does not always recognize mistakes. To illustrate this point, ask a manager which units are in the greatest demand. Often the quick response will be that one specific type of unit is always full. The manager should realize that when units rent too quickly, or if demand is extremely heavy, those apartments are underpriced.

Assuming you have a good product and you present it well, the pace of the rent-up program will be controlled by the rent schedule. If certain unit types lease overnight, the best units have been given away at bargain prices. Prospective residents have discovered something in that particular unit type that makes it more desirable than the other apartments of the same size—i.e., the rent is too low. The renting public may be willing to spend more than the manager thought for larger kitchens, extra closets, and so forth. Maybe renters know from experience that city views from a high-rise are often more pleasing than the lake view—something the manager failed to take into account.

While it is important to rent as many apartments as quickly as possible, it is equally important to ensure a relatively even rent-up pace. Admittedly, the state of the economy nationally and locally will play a role in the amount of demand for different unit sizes, and this should be taken into account. Generally speaking, each unit type should rent at approximately the same pace. A rapid rent-up of a particular layout or unit type usually indicates a problem with the rent schedule.

Upward Adjustments.   The easiest way to make fast-renting units less desirable is to raise the rent. This makes the slower-renting units more desir-

---

When to Adjust Rents Upward

If certain apartments are renting much faster than others, raising the rents of the fast movers will increase the desirability of the slow movers and produce a more even flow of rentals.

If the entire property is renting much faster than the competition, consider increasing all rents until you begin to experience some resistance. The apartment manager's task is not only to rent all the units, but also to achieve maximum rental income.

---

able because of the wider gap between specific rents. Reaction time is most important. If the manager reacts slowly, the fast-moving units will be completely rented before the rents can be raised. On the other hand, there must be enough time to identify a genuine trend.

If the manager cannot determine why one type of unit is renting faster than the others, the rent for the fast-moving unit should be increased in small amounts—for example, $4 and $8 increments—until the proper balance is reached. The reasons some units are more popular and rent up faster can often be determined by asking applicants why they made their choices. People will usually provide a ready answer. Typically, apartments with layouts similar to those in the decorated models rent faster than others. Prospects choose such layouts hoping to duplicate the decorating ideas seen in the model. Generally, the manager should anticipate this extra demand and set higher rents for the apartments similar to the models. These increases should be made after the initial rent schedule has been created. Normally, a premium of $6 or $7 per month can be safely added to the rents for these units. You may be puzzled by this idea in light of my recommendation that you use less-desirable units for your models; truly, I am not contradicting myself. Units with the same layout as the model will command higher rent because the exciting decorating possibilities of that particular layout are immediately apparent to prospects. This, of course, will not be the case later on when the model is closed down. Rents for these units will then have to be "eased back" to offset that loss in desirability.

Leasing progress and rental rates should be reviewed each week. If rent-up is progressing rapidly, a daily review is not unreasonable. The manager's job is to maximize rental income, and constant attention and review are needed in order to ensure that outcome.

There are comparatively few problems with rent adjustments when you are implementing rent increases. The difficulties occur when downward adjustments are indicated. There is little complaint from existing residents when new residents pay more rent for the same unit type, but residents will definitely raise objections when they discover that new renters are paying less.

Downward Adjustments.   Just as upward rent adjustments are made in response to market changes, certain conditions may dictate the need for downward adjustments. If the product is in top-notch shape and is being presented properly, yet some or all of the apartments are renting slowly, a downward rent adjustment may be in order. Rent reductions are generally appropriate only in situations of substantial vacancies when an over-ambitious rent schedule is interfering with a steady rent-up.

Assume, for example, that a manager has a total of 240 apartments, 80 of which are one-bedroom units with a den. The manager believes that this unit type is more desirable and therefore worth more rent. Initial rent-up of this unit type is slow, and, of the 80 units, only 10 have been rented. A check of the market reveals that the competition is experiencing pretty much the same problem. Rent levels determine how quickly a residential property rents. In our example, assume that the manager had been successful in leasing the regular one-bedroom units at a lower rent. It is only in attempting to rent the one-bedroom-plus-den apartments that resistance is encountered. The manager knows there are people who need only a single bedroom but would like the luxury of a separate den. What is not known is how much more rent the prospect will pay for a den. Pricing the one-bedroom apartments with a den the same as the one-bedroom apartments without a den will produce a flurry of rentals for the larger units. So you know they are worth something more, but the question is, how much more?

When errors are detected, the rent schedule should be adjusted accordingly. In our example of a building in which only 10 of 80 apartments were rented, a rent reduction is obviously necessary. Once the nature of the problem is identified, the manager must determine the extent of any adjustment.

Adjustments do not necessarily have to be in the form of rent reductions. Rent reductions have a negative effect on the value of the property and should be used *only* when other choices are not available. Before making a downward adjustment in rent, the manager should ask one question: "Is there a way I can improve the apartment so it is worth the rent I am asking?" If the answer to this question is "yes," the manager should make the improvement rather than reduce the rent.

Sometimes a rent reduction may prove to be the manager's only alternative. This is particularly true in new developments where it is difficult to further improve the property. In a new development, rent reductions should be extended to those people who rented earlier at the higher rents. Using the previous example, the 10 people who initially rented the one-bedroom-plus-den apartments should now receive a rent adjustment so their rent equals the new, lower rate. Ideally, they should also receive a refund for the excess rent they have already paid. The manager may choose to handle the refund by issuing rent credits or rent coupons. Again, retroactive refunds are necessary if the development has been open for only a few months. They are not recommended when rents are lowered in established properties.

Failure to pass rent reductions along to existing residents may cause many problems. In particular, it guarantees poor resident relations. Ultimately, resident dissatisfaction will cost you more than the money you forfeit through the reduction in rents. If the need for the reduction is due to an initial pricing error, early residents should not have to suffer as a result of your faulty pricing policy.

Concessions.   When the rental market begins to soften, the banners and advertisements offering free rent appear. This is certainly the oldest and most commonly used method to attract new renters while preserving the basic rent structure. Owners who have an unusual number of vacancies are willing to give up one or more months' rent for the security of a lease and the knowledge that the rent loss will stop soon. The concession has both its good and bad points.

The concession enjoys its day in the sun when times are tough and vacancies are numerous. That is the same time that a rental property owner is struggling to keep his or her development and pay the bills. It is exactly the wrong time to be giving away rent. The whole idea behind concessions is to use them as a means to attract new rent-paying residents and stop the losses. This presents a dilemma: How do you get the word out to potential new residents without rubbing it in to your existing residents that they do not qualify for the same treatment that is now being offered to perfect strangers? Some owners and managers just ignore their existing residents and hang a banner or insert an advertisement announcing the concession. Some even add words that specifically exclude present residents in case they should try to claim the same deal for themselves. It is very difficult to explain why an existing resident is not entitled to the same benefit offered to the public at large. This often drives residents into a decision to move when their leases expire, thereby exacting a bit of revenge while gaining the advantage being offered by competitors. There is no way to promote a concession to the public while keeping it a secret from your existing residents.

The concession can, however, bridge a short-lived downturn in rental activity, thus protecting the integrity of an established rent roll. When concessions are offered, it is better to sacrifice the first month's rent rather than reduce the monthly rent by a prorated one-twelfth each month. First of all, people need "chunks" of money, not "dribbles." In other words, a single saving of $900 is much better than twelve $75 reductions. The money will come in handy to cover the costs of the move or perhaps some new furnishings. Small amounts over time have a way of getting lost with the everyday bills, so the advantage has much less impact. Meanwhile, the manager hopes the market will strengthen quickly so that when the lease comes up for renewal, further concessions will not be necessary. Knowing that he or she must give up a month's rent, the smart manager opts to get it over with immediately. While twelve months of a smaller prorated amount might be more helpful

Concessions Have a History

Concessions, or "rent holidays" as they were called in the past, became particularly prevalent in the 1930s during the Depression. Several months of free rent served as an enticement to gain extra rentals in a highly competitive marketplace. Most owners were eager to sell their property and recoup what they could after the stock market crash. There was little market for half-empty buildings, so owners and managers did what they could to fill their properties, including granting concessions. Many buyers were hurt during this period, having based their investments on artificially inflated rent rolls. These buyers did their purchase arithmetic using twelve months of the listed rent when, in fact, considering the concessions that were granted to attract new residents, the effective annual rent only included eleven or in some cases ten months' rent or less. The problem became so severe, laws were commonly enacted that required owners to mark the face of the lease in large letters indicating that a concession was granted. The words "concession granted" were to alert the buyer to investigate the amount and extent of the concessions and to act as a warning to use extra care when calculating the purchase price and terms. Most of these laws are still on the books. During a downturn in the economy, it would not take too long for buyers who thought they had been duped to initiate another round of litigation.

in the ongoing cash crunch, it is much better to miss the first month's rent and get the resident accustomed to paying the higher monthly amount. When residents ask what their new neighbors are paying, it is clearly better to have them quote the "retail" rent rather than the net discounted rent. If an increase is achievable at renewal time, the manager wants the increase to be added to the base rent, not to the discounted figure.

The concession is an extremely effective closing tool. While it probably should not be used to get more people to walk in the door, it can have quite an impact on a prospect who is debating whether to rent or keep on looking. However, it is rare indeed to find a leasing agent who truly knows how and when to use the concession as a leasing tool. Given the authority to offer a prospect a month's free rent, leasing agents often blurt out the offer in the first few moments of the leasing interview, and this naturally has an adverse effect on the closing process. When people shop, they want what is in demand, not what must be given away. The offer of a month's free rent in the early part of the interview leads the prospect to conclude that the available apartments have not been very well accepted. It serves as a signal to the prospect that he or she should look for reasons why the apartments are not renting.

The leasing agent must continue with the basics of renting—developing a rapport, determining the prospect's motivating force and timing, demonstrating the benefits, and asking for the order. In order to be effective, the offer of free rent must be presented as a *personal accommodation* to that particular prospect: "We would really like to have you join our community. Would it help your decision if I can get the manager to approve a break for the first month?" It should appear as a gesture of goodwill to help the new resident get started. Try to avoid the term "free rent" or the word "concession" if possible.

Another form of concession is frequently granted but not thought of as such. An example of this occurs when a prospect arrives and announces that he or she does not need the apartment for another two months. If the manager is willing to commit a particular apartment to that individual today, for a move-in date in the future, he or she is effectively granting a concession. The manager is giving up the hope of rent during the interim months in return for the prospect's commitment to lease. This is a business decision, and there is certainly nothing wrong with doing this. The problems often develop after the decision has been made.

Let's say that the prospect subsequently asks for permission to move in early or to take possession of the apartment and begin making some improvements before the actual starting date on the lease. Many managers answer with a loud "no," or they ask for a prorated rent for the extra days of occupancy. It is my opinion that the rent is lost once you have made the business decision to give it up by agreeing to a later move-in date, so why not allow the early occupancy? Doing so will cost you absolutely nothing and may very well save the property the utility charges on that unit for the time in question. It will also strengthen your hand with renewals because it precludes existing residents from bringing up the fact that units around them have been vacant for extended periods of time. This situation is much the same as going to a hotel that has your room made up and available at 9:00 A.M. on the day of check-in. The management can demand that you wait until the posted check-in time of 3:00 P.M., but to what advantage? They might as well extend the courtesy of early occupancy to you. Shouldn't apartment managers do the same?

Coupons. These are merely concessions in a prepackaged form. They range from very primitive "rent dollars" printed at a local quick-print shop to elaborately engraved certificates that are numbered and bear the name of the recipient. There are many situations in the operation of an apartment community where dollar-value coupons can be used effectively. You might choose to offer a renewal reward to an existing resident for his or her commitment to a lease renewal. You may find yourself at a competitive disadvantage because you have electric heat, and residents serve notice that they intend to move when they receive a high bill in January or February. Coupons that can be applied toward rent would certainly help residents balance their budgets during those months and possibly prevent a number of move-outs. Residents may be rewarded with a dollar-value coupon when they pay their rent before the beginning of the month. New residents can be awarded coupons as a method of concession. This maintains the rent roll while letting the resident pick the months in which the discount will have the most favorable effect on their budgets. Referral bonuses to both the existing resident and the person being referred can be readily paid in the form of coupons. Discounts offered through an arrangement with local employers is another way coupons can be used. Some apartment communities even allow holders of coupons to purchase improvements or upgrades for their units.

A coupon program is most effective when the production and distribution of the coupons is done with the same care that would be given to real currency, treating them like traveler's checks, for example. Spend the money necessary to produce a coupon with an engraved appearance on the best quality paper. Apply serial numbers and designate space for the signatures of both issuer and recipient. Denominations of $20, $50, and $100 are usually sufficient for most transactions. The coupons are often bound in an inexpensive wallet or binder, again like traveler's checks. Typical limitations would be that no more than two coupons can be redeemed in any one month and that the coupons are not transferable.

Deficiency Discount.   A deficiency discount is a different form of concession in which the resident's rent is reduced in return for accepting an apartment with a real or imagined deficiency. The thought is that a resident willing to move into an apartment that has not been redecorated or is in poor condition should get a break. The rationale: The owner saves money on repairs and gains a resident who is not quite so fussy. In a perfect world, a deficiency discount is probably the wrong way to go, as it lowers rent and property values while sometimes attracting a less-qualified resident.

Bruised Apartments.   Used creatively, the concept of a "bruised apartment" can be an effective leasing tool. Imagine that you have taken prospective renters through your property, and they now appear ready to leave without making a decision to rent. They seemed to like the property and the apartment layouts and appointments, but they sidestep your attempts to "close" them. They say that they want to look around some more and take some time to consider what they have seen. Assume that you have been offering them units that rent for about $820 per month. This might be the perfect time to say something like: "I don't know if you would be interested, but we do have one unit, very much like those you have seen, that is going to be offered at a discount because it has a couple of bruises. This apartment is going to be priced at $750 because it has a small burn on the kitchen counter and a slight tear in the kitchen floor covering." These prospects were ready to leave just moments before. If they change course and express an interest, you have learned a very valuable bit of information: They do not want to spend $820, or they cannot handle that amount of rent. People are often reluctant to announce that they cannot afford something. Instead, they just keep looking. Have you ever gone car shopping only to be floored by the prices? Occasionally, the sales agent will suggest that you can have a demo, a dealer car, or a model that is being replaced at a considerable discount. Those savings can make the car affordable, and within a few weeks, you will forget the fact that it came with 5,000 miles on the odometer. People flock to factory outlet stores for much the same reason. They will overlook a scuff or minor defect in return for a good price.

If you are going to make a deal with these prospects, you are going to have to find a way to lower their monthly housing costs. Maybe it will be the bruised apartment or one that does not have quite the size or view or one you have in excess. This technique has helped you learn that price is the issue. Your job now is to find a way to create a financial fit.

Rent Level and Property Value.   Rental property is an investment, and its value as an investment is directly related to the amount of rental income it generates. That is why any increases or reductions in rent have such wide-reaching effects.

We learned back in Chapter 1 that apartment buildings are typically valued by using the *income capitalization approach,* which is a fancy name for a simple method of estimating the value of income-producing real estate. The formula again is:

$$\frac{\text{Net Operating Income (I)}}{\text{Capitalization Rate (R)}} = \text{Value (V)}$$

If rents can be raised, or expenses cut—or a combination of the two—the NOI will increase. Assume for the moment that, currently, a typical capitalization rate is 8 percent. Using that 8 percent "cap" rate, every dollar of increase in the monthly NOI has the effect of increasing a property's potential value by $150 ($1.00 × 12 months = $12.00 ÷ .08 = $150). Of course the opposite is true if NOI decreases by that same $1.00. Things are not quite that automatic—the investor does not receive any gain until an actual sale takes place—but the relationship of income to value is very real.

Raising Rents in Established Properties

The discussion so far has dealt with structuring rents in a new development and the up-and-down adjustments necessary to achieve proper pricing. Now let's turn our attention to the methods and timing for increasing existing rents in established properties. This is an unpopular subject but probably one of the most important concerns managers have in the operation of multifamily housing. It is unpopular from residents' standpoint, of course, because they do not want their housing costs to increase. Apartment managers also find the idea of raising rents unpleasant because of the extra work involved and the need to explain to residents the reasons for the increase.

Raising rent is necessary to offset increases in operating expenses, to help absorb higher debt service costs, and to maintain a fair margin of profit in an inflationary economy. All of these are valid points, but they are not operative if certain market indicators say otherwise. In other words, additional rent may be warranted; but if the market signals read "stop" or "caution," the property owner and the manager must respect the indicators or face an even greater loss through increased vacancy.

Basically, there are four indicators to tell the manager whether or not the time is right to raise rent—vacancies, concessions, delinquencies, and new construction. They work together to tell you the time to proceed with a rent increase, when to proceed with caution and some degree of restraint, and when to forgo an increase altogether. Note that this discussion of raising rents assumes there are no rent control laws governing the amount one is allowed to charge for space; rent increases for rent-controlled properties must be considered within the guidelines of the law.

Vacancies.   Empirical data over a number of years indicate that the vacancy level of a property is the most important single indicator when considering a rent increase. The ratio of vacant units to the total number of units reveals the state of the market, the management and condition of the property, and the acceptability of the current rent levels.

The references to vacancy here are to physical vacancy rather than economic vacancy. The difference between the two is as follows:

Physical vacancy is the percentage of the total number of units that are vacant and available for rent. For example, if there are five units vacant and available for rent in an apartment community with a total of 100 units, it is said that the physical vacancy is 5 percent.

Economic vacancy indicates the number of units that are out of the income stream. Using the same example, in addition to the five vacant units, there might be two units that have been rented for the month after next: These units are vacant but no longer available. They are not producing any income at this point in time, so their lost revenue is part of the economic loss. Other components of economic vacancy are units being used as models, offices, or staff apartments; units that are damaged or unrentable; and units occupied by residents who are delinquent in paying their rent.

The decision whether to proceed with rent increases should follow the guidelines below:

Less than 5% (physical vacancy)	Proceed with rent increase
Between 5% and 8%	Proceed with caution
More than 8%	Wait for improved market (review again in 3 months)

Vacancies or, more specifically, excess vacancies, carry the strongest weighting of the four market signals. Generally, it is advisable to defer the implementation of a rent increase when physical vacancies exceed 8 percent. This level of vacancy is signaling that something is wrong in the marketplace, the property, or both. To push for higher rents at this time will only work to exacerbate an already difficult situation. A rent increase could very well lead to an easing of resident selectivity, increased move-outs, loss of image, higher operating costs, and a lengthened economic recovery. When vacancies are above 8 percent, work to improve your present position before proceeding with a rent increase.

Concessions.   When concessions are being granted, there is a reason: They usually signal a weak market. A specific examination of concessions may reveal that vacancies are low because the manager has been granting extensive concessions. In such cases, the occupancy level does not reflect the true state of the market. Earlier in this chapter, we talked about one type of concession—renting an apartment for an agreed date in the future. Anything over 40 days (the typical lead-time in renting an apartment) would indicate a market weakness and should be acknowledged as a concession. The guidelines in this category are these:

No concessions	Proceed with rent increase
One month concession	Proceed with caution
More than one month	Do not proceed if there are any other "stop" indicators

Delinquencies.   When times are tough, most managers ease up their collection efforts, and that quickly increases the amount of collection losses. Rental delinquencies provide one of the surest and fastest feedback signals of a weakening market. Any sign of increased delinquencies should be monitored very carefully.

The percentages listed below refer to the amount of money that is outstanding at the end of a given month. For example, if the gross potential rental income totals $40,000, and $400 is outstanding at the end of the month, it is said that the delinquency rate is 1 percent. In the same example, $800 outstanding would indicate a delinquency rate of 2 percent. If there is an ongoing legal problem with one or two residents who owe considerable amounts, these amounts can be deducted from the monthly total. The same is true if your accounting system continues to build up monthly balances of residents who have skipped out and there are only minimal chances of re-covery. Guidelines for increasing rent when there are delinquencies are:

Less than 1% delinquency	Proceed with rent increase
Between 1% and 2%	Proceed with caution
More than 2%	Do not proceed if there are any other "stop" indicators

New Construction.   This guideline exists to prevent the manager from making a judgment about the current marketplace without looking at what is in the "pipeline." The absorption rate of new apartments is painfully slow, and just a few new developments can create havoc with the occupancy level of many existing properties. If a new 100-unit development opens nearby, it can reduce the occupancy level of 20 similar-sized properties from a cash-flowing 95 percent to a money-losing 90 percent almost overnight. The new property has several built-in advantages. Its interest payments during the rent-up period are probably included as part of the construction loan (mean-ing that many new properties are not saddled with monthly mortgage pay-ments during the first months of operation). This allows a more liberal grant-ing of free rent allowances and/or construction discounts. The manager of a new development can also be more cavalier because operating ex-penses—especially real estate taxes, make-ready expenses, and repairs—are only a fraction of those of an established property. New developments are blessed with all move-ins and virtually no move-outs, so their weekly rental progress appears as net revenue gains without any offsets.

I have termed the amounts of new construction in any community "little," "some," and "lots." Quantifying these terms depends on the size of the rental community and the absorption rate of new rental units. In a city the size of Des Moines, Iowa, "little" might be 200 units, while in a city the size of Atlanta, Georgia, "little" might refer to 2,000 units. The "some" cate-gory might be 300 units in Des Moines and 4,000 units in Atlanta. It will take some experience in a particular rental environment to quantify these three classifications. Absorption rates for new rental properties are much lower than most people think, so if you err, make sure it is on the conservative side. The final set of market signal guidelines for rent increases is as follows:

Little (new construction)	Proceed with rent increase
Some	Proceed with caution
Lots	Do not proceed if there are any other "stop" indicators

Evaluating the Rent Increase Climate.   If the answer to each of these guidelines is "proceed," then a rent increase is not only possible, it should be rather aggressive. The percentage of the increase should diminish as the number of "proceed" responses is replaced by "proceed with caution" indicators. One "stop" indicator is usually the absolute maximum when deciding whether to raise rents. If that one stop indicator is for vacancies, you are usually best advised to postpone a rent increase until the overall occupancy level improves. Ignoring these market signals can cause irreparable damage to an apartment community.

Once an analysis has been made and you have established the indications for market acceptance of a rent increase, the next step is to determine the amount of the increase.

Determining Rent Increases

In addition to the above four market indicators, there are other benchmarks that can act as guides when determining the proper amount of a rent increase. These restrictions work in concert with one another, and the new rent amount should be the lowest figure after first applying each of the following tests.

First Increase.   This test is provided more for precautionary reasons than as a guide. A great many developments get off to the wrong start because they ignore this principle. When considering a rent increase on the first lease anniversary of either a new property or one that has undergone a complete renovation and is now back in service, the amount of the increase must be twice the amount of what is necessary. In other words, if you determine that an increase of $30 per month is needed, you should double that figure and ask for $60. Why? Because a $30 increase will only produce the desired $30 revenue if all of the leases are renewed at the beginning of the new year. This is highly unlikely because very few residential leases expire on the first of January. Expirations are typically spaced throughout the year, with the largest concentration occurring during the late spring and early fall. On average, the amount of increased revenue derived from the first round of rent increases is only one-half of what is sought. Doubling the needed increase, however, might very well be too much in a competitive market.

The "need to double" exists only when leases are renewed for the first time following the property's introduction or re-introduction into the marketplace. With subsequent increases, the added revenue of the previous year's rental increase fills in the missing gaps as the year progresses. For example, if the rent for a specific unit is set to increase by $20 on the mid-year lease anniversary—say, July 1—the property will receive only $120 of additional revenue this year (July through December = 6 months $\times$ $20 = $120). If the rent for that unit was also increased $20 per month on the previous anniversary, the prior year's increase will continue to produce added income.

Income Group Influence.   Income group classification will play a critical role in determining how much rents can be increased. In the low-income (subsidized) classification, your decision will typically depend on the governing body's regulations. Normally, rent increases involve an increase in the resident subsidy, and they are most often tied to either an index or some degree of proof that the property's operating expenses have increased. Some authorities declare that rents can be raised using an annually adjusted percentage basis. The manager's job is really one of understanding the amount allowable as well as the timing and implementation process.

Residents in the limited- and adequate-income groups are subject to forces of supply and demand that have different limitations, depending on the particular classification. As I have said, the people who fall into the limited-income classification are struggling and very price sensitive. The demands on their income are considerable, so potential for rent increases will tend to be meager. An increase in rent for a resident in this grouping means something else must be compromised. In past years, the limited-income group has barely been able to keep pace with the Consumer Price Index (CPI). Pushing rents beyond this indicator will result in resistance and an undue level of move-outs. The safest level of rent increase appears to be about 1 to 2 percent *less* than the current rate of increase indicated by the CPI for that locale. During periods of very low inflation, this could compute to a negative amount. When this occurs, it is probably best to forgo any rent adjustment.

Those in the adequate-income group can better afford a rent increase, and experience shows that they can tolerate increases that equal about 1 to 2 percent *more* than the current increase in the CPI. However, there are other indicators that must also be recognized before a final determination can be made as to the exact amount of a renewal rent increase.

The people in the ample-income group follow much the same pattern evidenced by those in the adequate-income group, but the daily lifestyle of those of ample means is less affected by the rate of increase in the CPI. These people are not as likely to move because of a rent increase that exceeds the index. People of adequate income do, however, possess the wherewithal to move at their pleasure, if they should decide that their rent dollars are not being well spent.

I should offer a word of caution when discussing rent increases that are related to the CPI or some other index. During periods of high inflation, the media will present stories tracking the pattern of rent increases and comparing rent increases to other items in the CPI. Of course, these stories are directed to a wide audience and usually earn a prominent position in the newspaper. The problem is that the information, while statistically correct, may present a deceptive picture. To illustrate this, let's assume a small city used to have a total rental housing stock of 20,000 apartments. These units were renting at an average rate of $700 per month. Now, after a building boom that has taken place over the past three years, an additional supply of 4,000 very upscale apartments has come into the market. These units are brand-new and are clearly superior to anything built in prior years. These new units, on average, rent for $1,050 per month. The addition of these higher-priced units has the effect of increasing the overall rent average from the old $700 to $758. This raises the average rent in this sample town by almost 8.3 percent, and that is without any rent increase for the existing rental units. The headline, "Rents Up 8.3%!" will certainly stir up the rental community. Even worse, some apartment managers may be tempted to try for the "average increase" and suffer major move-outs in the process.

Amount of Last Increase.   Regardless of the other indicators, you must establish limits on the amount of a rent increase based on your pattern of previous increases. For example, if you have set a pattern of $20 increases in the last round or two of rent increases, you will have difficulty getting more than 125 percent of the past increase, or in this case, $25. When you push for a larger amount, even though some of the other indicators appear to allow for more, you will most likely face an undue level of turnover.

Typical Rent versus Street Rent.   This is one of the best all-around indicators to help a manager determine the proper rent level. It works on the principle that there should always be a margin between the *typical rent*— the most common rent currently being collected for each unit type—and the street rent being asked of prospects walking in the door today. The range that delivers the best results for me is 105 percent. The calculation works as follows. Assume that most one-bedroom units in your apartment community are generating $775 per month. There may be a sprinkling of units going for as little as $715 per month and some recent rentals that range above $800, but the mode (most frequent entry) is that $775 figure. To determine the street rent, the rent that you should be asking of today's rental prospects, multiply the $775 base rent by 1.05. A rent of $814 is indicated by this calculation. If this amount strikes you as too high and you worry about market acceptance, it might be your signal to ease up. If, on the other hand, you have been successful in obtaining rents from incoming residents at a higher level, say $825, you should assume a more aggressive posture with your next round of renewal rent increases. The idea is to maintain a differential of about 5 percent between your typical rent and your street rent.

These tests are designed to help you strike the right balance between achieving the greatest possible increase in annual revenue while avoiding the losses from an undo number of move-outs. The following are some strategies to consider when you are planning to raise rents.

- *Limit increases to once a year.* Wage and salary increases tend to happen once a year, and the renting public thinks rent increases should follow the same pattern. Housing is a long-term commodity, and residents have come to expect annual rent adjustments. Some apartment managers believe that a series of closely spaced, smaller increases will result in lower resident turnover. The suggestion of a rent increase carries with it a certain irritation factor, regardless of the amount. Presenting this news twice in a period of one year almost guarantees a negative reaction, and that means needlessly high move-outs. Studies continually show that one increase of, say, $34, results in far fewer moves than two semiannual increases of, say, $14 each.

- *Allow a long lead-time.* At least 60 days is the right amount of notice to give when a rent increase is one of the changes in the lease renewal contract (unless the lease or applicable laws state otherwise). This runs contrary to the thinking of some apartment managers who believe that the shortest possible notice results in the fewest move-outs. The thought is that if people do not have much time to react, they will sign a lease rather than scurry around to look for a new home. Too many housing alternatives exist for that tactic to work. Also, some residents may not be that satisfied with their current relationship with management, and they will react negatively to the "rush act."

  Most people spend what they make, and they need time to adjust their budgets to accommodate a rent increase. Many residents become irate, at least initially, when faced with a rent increase. This mood will mellow as they see their neighbors accept the same increase and brand-new residents, who have obviously shopped around for the best value, move in at similar rent levels. A long lead-time prior to the start of a rent increase will help, not hurt.

- *Use odd dollar amounts.* You might get the idea that rent increases in $10 and $25 increments are nice because they are more easily remembered, and the bookkeeping department will have an easier time with them. Unfortunately, rent increases, and for that matter initial rent amounts, cause an adverse reaction when they are in nicely bracketed amounts. People interpret a $25 rent increase as an example of the owner getting richer and the resident getting poorer. At the same time, an increase of $26 is often perceived as an amount to answer a specific need, probably to cover increased operating costs of the same amount. Round or bracketed amounts ($20, $30, $50) are associated with the owner wanting more money at the resident's expense. Odd numbers, both in the amount of the increase and the resulting rent, suggest a closely calculated operating budget. So use $27 instead of $25, $41 instead of $40, etc. If you use a computer, you will have little trouble handling the odd amounts.

- *Adjust for desirability.* The popularity of different unit types and prime locations changes from time to time and you, as manager, should be ready to adjust the rent levels accordingly. One year the two-bedroom, two-bath split apartment may be the most popular. A few years later the two-bedroom, 2½ bathroom units with a den may be the "hot" apartments, and the rent levels should be adjusted to reflect this shift in favor. Sometimes second-floor units are more popular than first-floor units. If your experience bears this out, adjust the rent at renewal time to compensate for anticipated increases and decreases in demand. If you have a lot of vacancies in one type of unit and virtually no availability in another, increase the latter's rent at a higher rate and go easy on the increase for the hard-to-rent unit. It is a rare occurrence when the market and your pricing are so in balance that you can apply a percentage increase uniformly to all unit types. If you fail to make yearly adjustments for ever-changing desirability, the imbalance will only get worse.

- *Use graduated rents.* If you think what is needed in the way of a rent increase will pose a hardship for the residents and cause a high rate of move-outs, consider a graduated rent increase. This will involve a letter explaining that costs have risen at such a rate that a substantial rent increase is needed. The letter should state that rent will be raised in two stages because you are mindful of residents' budget restrictions. For example, you might explain that during the first seven months an additional $18 will be due each month, and during the last five months an extra $13 will be due (in other words, for the last five months of the year the total rent increase will be $31). This does not violate the one increase per year rule because the increase is announced at one time, even though it is implemented in two stages. Note the use of an odd break in the number of months and the odd rent increase amounts. Finally, the graduated rent increase should not be used two years in a row. It should be reserved for inflationary times or just after a major renovation or upgrade program has taken place.

- *Test the increases on vacancies first.* The place to test the acceptability of a higher rent is with the vacant units. After all, the people who shape the market are those who are out shopping and looking to find a different home. The person moving is exposed to much higher costs than the residents who remain where they are. If, in spite of the extra costs of moving, prospects are choosing your apartment community—even with the new higher rent level—it is an indication that you are offering good value. This, of course, assumes that you have not lowered your resident selection criteria. Try several units at the new price to be sure it was not an anomaly and determine whether you can sustain the new rate. People with leases coming up for renewal are actively following the classified ads, and they will quickly become aware of your new rent levels. When they see new high-caliber residents moving in at regular intervals, they will be reassured that your rental community and, more specifically, their apartment size and type represent good value for the money.

- *Fix up before the increase.* One of the reasons for raising rents is that rising costs erode the budget and prevent you from properly operating the property. A property's shortage of funds almost always becomes apparent in the general maintenance level and the "showy extras." The problem is that you need the money from the rent increase to put things right. It is tempting to raise the rent first, and then, with money in hand, begin the fix-up and upgrade work. That absolutely will not work. Beg or borrow the money, but the fix-up program must take place *before* the increase is announced. While you are in the fix-up mode, making things nice again, residents will often stop to ask— "how much is the increase going to be?"

- *Charge for apartment improvements.* When preparing a vacant apartment for the next renter, it is both common and recommended practice to make improvements to the unit that will help it rent quicker and attract a high caliber of new resident. That is fine, but with each improvement, there should be a corresponding increase in the rent. For example, if you replace the floor covering in the kitchen, you might increase the monthly rent by, say, $4. A new carpet might necessitate an increase of $15; crown moldings, $12; new kitchen counter tops, $13; and so forth. This is done because existing residents see virtually everything that goes on in the rental community, and they certainly will learn what you have done to improve the nearby vacant unit. Your residents may just stick their heads in and look around while the work is underway, or they may be invited as visitors to the new neighbor's apartment. You, as manager, must be in a position to offer current residents the same improvements if they inquire why their apartments do not have the same updated appointments as those of the new residents. Even with the offer of a discount, most residents will likely decline when they learn that the improvements are available at an added cost. It is important for the existing residents to know that the improvements being offered to new residents are available to everyone. Most people will make do with what they have and continue to pay less rent. An occasional few will opt for something new. The trouble begins when the rent remains the same for the new resident getting a made-over apartment.

- *Drafting.* This is a process that offered some help with raising rent in the past but, unfortunately, is not always effective. To describe the process, imagine that units in a certain vintage property rent for, say, $700. A newer property is constructed in the neighborhood and it has all of the latest "bells and whistles." This, plus the fact that it is new, might be enough for its units to command rents of $950. At the next round of renewals, the older property might normally be entitled to a 4 percent or $28 rent increase, but now, because of the higher rent threshold in the neighborhood, it may be possible to achieve a $38 rent increase. Drafting has proved helpful to many properties where rents have fallen behind the pace of operating cost increases.

Drafting works best when there is little difference between the older product and the new property being built. For a long period of time, the typical rental property was comprised of stacks of "cookie-cutter" white cubes. The carpet changed colors and patterns, the plastic laminate on the kitchen counters differed, and so did the color of the appliances. Some developers added more common area amenities, but the differences between an older property and a new one usually involved the fact that one had a fresh new appearance. As renters became more discerning and developers began to understand that they must offer features closer to those of the homebuilder, the differences between old and new properties became noticeably greater. Fifteen-panel French doors are replacing sliding doors, so typical in the older product. Bay windows, vaulted ceilings, arched doorways, island kitchens, great rooms, giant bathrooms, bedroom retreats, and private verandas have all been introduced. These features damage the value and appeal of the older, second- or third-generation "standard" rental properties. Drafting does not work when the differences between yesterday's and today's product are just too striking.

- *Timing.* Managers need to properly time the implementation of a rent increase. The industry standard points to annual increases timed to take effect on the anniversary of the original move-in date. This assumes that the move-in occurred on the first day of the month. If it did not, the date should reflect the first full month of occupancy.

  If your residents are currently on a month-to-month basis, you may elect a common date each year for a general rent increase. This is not normally advisable. While it gets the extra work connected with a rent increase out of the way in one operation, the risks are considerable. The biggest risk is the chance of a rent protest if the increase is interpreted as too high. Choosing a single date for a general rent increase consolidates your yearly move-outs into one period. This "bunches" up vacancies and strips you of the *urgency factor* that is so critical when closing deals. The extra workload also taxes the entire staff.

Universities and college-town landlords usually make their rent changes coincide with the start of the fall term. Operators of seasonal rentals usually adjust their rates at the beginning of the new season. Properties with garage rentals, especially those in colder climates, set their new rents in the fall of the year when the demand is at its highest.

- *Offer an improvement package.* One of the reasons that renters have a difficult time accepting a rent increase is that they are being asked to pay more for an apartment that is now a year or two older. Consumers are accustomed to commodities costing less as they become older (used cars, second-hand clothing, etc.).

  A way to help offset this feeling is to package one or more improvements into your lease renewal and rent adjustment offer. You might offer a ceiling fan, a full length mirror, an ice-cube maker, and some new under-cabinet lighting. A lease renewal with an accompanying rent increase is more easily accepted when you add some improvements. At the same time, you are upgrading the property and lessening its slide into old age.

- *Create a back door.* Let's say that you are renewing a lease and have tacked on a $34 rent increase. As part of your program, you are also offering two rather nice improvements. While visiting one of your long-time residents, you are told that she cannot afford the extra rent and must look for a less-expensive apartment. You really hate to lose such a good, long-standing resident, so you offer a compromise. You agree to halve the rent increase and she agrees to forgo the apartment improvements. She saves moving and you save a move-out.

Any rent-raising strategies you implement will have to be tailored to your apartment community based on your resident profile and the local marketplace. In a down economy, extra creativity will be required, and these suggestions should give you a place to start.

13

When a building is ugly,
lipstick and perfume won't help.

Upgrading and Renovation

There is a saying in real estate that advises, "Don't buy a ten to twelve-year-old house." Those who have done so know how true this warning is. At first glance, things look pretty good, but there are some surprises waiting. This is just about the time that problems with the water heater, air conditioner, appliances, plumbing, roofs and gutters, and other fixtures can be expected to begin failing. The buyers of these houses will get to know their new purchase intimately during the next few years.

Rental apartments follow a similar pattern, but they run on a faster track. (The age of the multifamily rental housing stock in the United States is shown in Exhibit 13.1.) At the five- to seven-year mark, the honeymoon is over, and the problems begin mushrooming. They are the result of both general building decay and the damage caused by multiple tenancies. Additional obsolescence is attributed to advancing technology and changes in fashion. Owners and managers often have a difficult time recognizing this process and remain steadfastly convinced that their real estate is frozen in time.

Too many property owners believe "renters won't notice." These owners may have every imaginable feature and convenience in their own homes, but they have trouble understanding why renters are not satisfied with basic, Spartan living. Some owners even want extra rent when they replace a component that has worn out.

Exhibit 13.1
Age of U.S. Multifamily Housing Stock

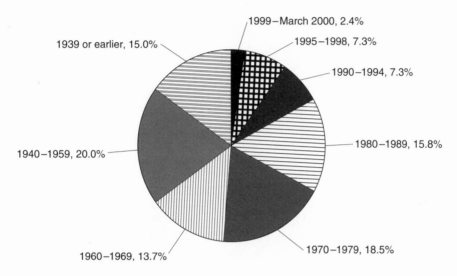

1999–March 2000, 2.4%
1995–1998, 7.3%
1990–1994, 7.3%
1939 or earlier, 15.0%
1980–1989, 15.8%
1940–1959, 20.0%
1970–1979, 18.5%
1960–1969, 13.7%

Source: U.S. Census Bureau "2000 Census of Population and Housing."

There is one major difference between the home that is owned and the one that is rented. When an owner wants to replace outdated components, remodeling is a common option. When an apartment dweller wants something better, he or she usually ends up moving.

Planning Ahead

As fixtures and appliances wear out, either physically or through a change in fashion, the property owner must keep pace. Every owner should be saving for that day in the future when these things begin to fail, but most do not. This was less of a problem in the past for a number of reasons. First of all, innovations and technology moved at a slower pace. Back then, the differences between brand-new and ten years old were comparatively minor. These days, just a two-year difference is significant. Traditionally, owners and managers of rental apartments do not put money aside in a reserve fund for major updates. Owners look to refinancing as the way to raise money for major replacements and improvements. Raising cash through refinancing depends largely on an increase in the property's value. When the property has a rundown appearance and does not measure up to others in the marketplace, that increase may not exist.

Owners are faced with choices relating to the property's age and condition which include upgrading, renovation, modernization, or demolition and a whole new start. Property improvements can be broken down into three distinct categories—*must-do, should-do,* and *could-do.*

Must-Do.   This category includes the required replacements or repairs to the structure. For the most part, these are big-ticket items that are essential to the property's continued operation, and they are typically not discretionary. Examples include roof replacements, new heating or cooling plants, replacement windows, settling foundations, plumbing or electrical upgrades, and health and safety compliance. Their costs can be in the tens of thousands of dollars.

The unfortunate aspect of a must-do investment is that there is almost never an associated increase in the rent. A renter expects the roof to be watertight and is not willing to pay more because the property owner had to spend money to ensure that this is the case. The same is true for plumbing and the heating and air-conditioning system. When you put out a "for rent" sign, it is implied that the major components of the building function normally. This disturbs some owners because they like to measure their return on how much cash they have had to invest, including the money spent just to bring the property to a livable standard. They often ignore the fact that money was not set aside from operations and placed into a reserve fund. If the property was recently purchased, the must-do items really have the effect of raising the purchase price.

In the final analysis, managers are graded by their ability to achieve better occupancy levels and higher rents by making changes in the property and its operation. Money, usually the limiting factor, often leads managers to play down must-do improvements in favor of the should-do and could-do expenditures that have a much greater effect on the manager's scorecard. If the available dollars are invested in a roof that brings no additional income, there is a corresponding reduction in money for lush landscaping, new carpet, better decorating, and upgraded apartment layouts. Your reputation as manager will quickly suffer if you direct a property turnaround in which most of the money is invested in visible upgrades, but your residents live under a leaky roof or with old corroded pipes just waiting to ruin all of the new improvements. Must-do items form a foundation for the rest of the work you are planning. You cannot ignore these critical items even though they will not produce an immediate payback.

Should-Do.   Items in this category help bring the property up to modern-day standards. They include new carpeting and appliances in the apartment units; upgrading of entries, stairways, or corridors; resurfacing of parking lots; and a general renewal of the landscaping.

Performing should-do work will help to keep existing residents and attract qualified new ones. The money spent in this category can be meaningful but, unfortunately, the return on investment (ROI) is generally less than the owner might realize from alternative investments. Money spent on these improvements simply protects the money already invested. Without this periodic reinvestment, the decline in resident profile and property value will accelerate.

Most people have seen the need for should-do items in hotels or motels. The lobby begins to look seedy and so do the corridors. The carpeting in the guest rooms is matted and stained. The furniture shows signs of hard wear. The bathrooms are out of date. If you are a regular traveler, you know this is about the time that you begin searching for new accommodations. Money must constantly be funneled back into a property if it is to maintain its position in the market. If this does not happen, you will witness the beginning of the end. As an apartment manager, you will expend considerable energy explaining this transition process to ownership.

When considering the purchase of new kitchen appliances, examine the feasibility of buying refrigerators with one or more special features rather than the stripped down models. You need to ask yourself if the more-expensive refrigerators will give you an edge in the marketplace, and you need to know if you can charge additional rent for it. If the answer to either question is "yes," the best advice usually is to opt for the fancier product. This advice runs contrary to some past practices. Back then, owners and managers often opted for stripped-down equipment because of their fewer parts and lower prices. This strategy only downgrades the rental unit and prompts prospects to look elsewhere. Renters are very aware of the modern conveniences available in the market, and they want to enjoy these conveniences themselves. This recommendation is not intended as a license to go overboard and purchase ovens and dishwashers with every conceivable button and function. Increased purchase and service costs cannot be forgotten.

Light fixtures, faucets, shower heads, medicine cabinets, mirrors, woodwork, hardware, windows and windowsills, paint, floor coverings, even bathtubs and vanities in an apartment community have often been the cheapest products available. This fact does not go unnoticed by prospective renters. When one of these components fails or requires replacement, rather than search out an item of equal quality, spend the extra money necessary to begin a systematic upgrade program. Investigate better alternatives and begin to replace these poor-quality components with the latest and most-durable designs.

Could-Do. Items in this category are purely optional. These improvements might include enlarging a small bathroom, converting a bedroom to a "get-away room," or adding a private patio off the living room. Adding wallpaper, changing wall colors, installing new cabinet hardware and locksets, and revamping the bath or kitchen layout are just a few more possibilities in the category of could-do.

Unlike the must-do and should-do categories, money spent on could-do items brings substantial rewards. Returns on invested capital can range as high as 30 percent. Anything that is done to set an apartment apart from the run-of-the-mill or gives a unit a special personality pays quick rewards in both added profits and a better clientele. Could-do improvements almost always include the updated housing fashions and trend-setting conveniences. Unfortunately, could-do improvements must wait until the first two categories are addressed and satisfied.

Wear It Out or Upgrade.   Location is often the primary factor in determining whether an apartment community is allowed to run out its natural life or undergo a major rejuvenation. The former is called *use it up, wear it out*. In other words, rental properties in so-so neighborhoods have little upside potential and can only continue to cycle residents through their apartments. As the years pass, these apartments will show wear on an exponentially increasing basis.

Making a decision to initiate a major upgrade and renovation program is extremely difficult, especially when residents are already struggling with their current rents. The issue is not whether people will appreciate newer and nicer features or not—too often they simply cannot afford them. Undertaking a major renewal program will most likely involve wholesale changes in tenancy as well as a keen understanding of location and demographic considerations.

Neighborhoods with a concentration and preponderance of large apartment buildings have the least chance of undergoing a renewal process. When renters are overwhelmingly in the majority, there is less permanence, commitment, and deep-seated community interest. Many owners of large apartment properties do not live in or near their investments, so they never quite understand the pulse or the needs of the local community.

Areas with groupings of dated single-family homes and small rental properties have a much better chance of undergoing gentrification. It follows that their ratio of owner-occupant to renter is much higher. The resident profile is often dominated by younger people who invest their energy and imagination. There is frequently a spirit of competition as the residents strive to outdo one another. Their real estate purchase is often a stretch, and they recognize that they are at risk, so they put their all into making it a success. All of these positive forces contribute to a neighborhood momentum that increases values, and soon the word begins to spread.

There are countless examples of neighborhood turnarounds where old, really worn out buildings have been given new life. There is always a risk in the early stages as to whether or not a particular neighborhood will take off. When an area is on the skids, it is a hard call to know which ones will actually succeed in a rebirth.

Remodel or Demolish.   What happens to the existing rental stock that does not begin to qualify as modern? You can look to for-sale housing for the answer. Surely you have noticed that, in prime housing locations, it is common for a buyer to pay a substantial price for a house only to send a bulldozer over to demolish it in a single afternoon. There once were and still are situations in which an existing dwelling can be completely remodeled and made to deliver the functions and features of new construction. However, property owners (and managers) are learning more and more that it is often best to destroy the building and start again. Remodeling within the confines of existing support walls, recognizing existing plumbing and mechanical limitations, and complying with updated building codes and environmental regulations often produces a compromised product at a cost that approaches or exceeds the cost to build new.

Changes in Housing Styles.   When I was first getting started in apartment management, I attended a series of real estate classes. It was common for the instructors to explain how housing designs were conceived and the rationale for space allocations. Back then, the thought was to allocate space according to its degree of use. For example, the average person spends the least time in the bathrooms and closets, so they were given a minimal amount of space. Kitchens were off by themselves and generally only large enough to hold the equipment of the day. Bedrooms were sized to accommodate a bed(s), a dresser, one or two nightstands, and no more. Ceilings were kept to a height of eight feet or less to minimize the number of stairs to climb and to deliver the smallest number of cubic feet requiring heat and maintenance.

What is happening in the way of style changes in the newer rental developments is more than dramatic, it is revolutionary. The old line apartment builders who continue to resist change are being pushed aside. Actually, the rental apartment industry has suffered a significant outflow of its best and most well-heeled residents because of its snail-like pace in recognizing what has been happening. Large numbers of would-be renters have gone out and purchased new townhouses, condominiums, and coach and manor homes that include the latest in designs, layouts, features, and appointments.

The apartment industry has always lagged behind in coming up with innovative housing ideas, but that gap is showing some signs of closing. The new apartments coming on stream are totally different from those that were built just a few years ago. Volume ceilings add an importance to living spaces. Great rooms are replacing the combination of living, dining, and food preparation (kitchen) areas. Bedrooms are referred to as "retreats" and are large enough to hold lounge-style furniture. Bathrooms, while not as obscenely large as in some single-family homes, have grown by at least 150 percent as compared to the old standby of 5 feet by 7 feet. Nowadays, you walk into closets that are organized to hold three and four times the apparel as before. Computers now rate their own defined spaces with special wiring and connections. Kitchen equipment is loaded with updated features, and most of the textures and finishes are improved and certainly more durable.

Comparatively, only a handful of these modern-day apartments are up and renting. If you keep a close eye on what the home-building industry brings to the market, you will be in an excellent position to forecast the future of rental housing. You will have the distinct advantage of hindsight in determining which ideas will be accepted versus short-lived fads, as the rental industry generally trails by about five to seven years.

Variety and Change.   In approaching the subject of apartment upgrading, it is important to consider the degree of variety and change to be introduced. Variety is one of the most important ways to increase a property's appeal as well as its rent levels. What no longer works is offering and reoffering the same old product which happens to be exactly what most apartment properties do. Apartments with routine layouts and everyday appointments will be forced to accept a lesser tier of tenancy.

When you take a ride down a street with rows of single-family homes, you will see, firsthand, how people establish their identity and implement their needs and desires. Even though many of these homes began as cookie-cutter versions of the same plan, the owners have made their own special modifications. Renters also want variety in their housing, but they must look to the property owner to do the customizing.

Starting with the structures themselves, you should avoid having fifteen identical buildings: Vary the color schemes, alter the landscaping, add different treatments to the stairways or corridors. When striving to achieve variety, you need to exercise caution in the addition of new materials and textures. It does not take long to create a carnival atmosphere. Vary the combination of colors, but maintain a common thread that ties the separate buildings together.

In the individual units, find ways to get away from the standards (i.e., one-bedroom, two-bedroom). You will always have enough of them. Remove a wall, if you can, to create one great room. Perhaps you can expand the kitchen by eliminating the dining area or double the size of the bathroom by borrowing space from a closet or hallway. A bedroom without an accompanying bathroom can be transformed into a den, library, or get-away room. Maybe the layout can be improved by relocating a doorway or shortening a hallway. End units offer opportunities to add an extra bank of windows. These alterations can work to improve the exterior appearance of the building as well as the look and function of the apartment itself. Even though a building was originally constructed with sliding glass doors, these need not remain forever. Sliding glass doors have a tendency to leak; they can be a security problem, and they dictate furniture arrangements. A new set of windows that incorporates a swinging door to the patio or balcony can remedy these problems as well as modernize the look, both inside and out.

When the design permits, extending the balcony deck to stretch between the apartment's living and sleeping areas will pay for itself in just months. The top floor apartments can sometimes be modified to include volume ceilings or skylights or both. Converting three so-so units into two dynamite units will pay dividends for years to come. Connecting a first- and second-story unit together into one with its own staircase is another way of adding variety and value. With any of these changes, you will also reap the benefit of attracting top-caliber residents.

Many managers have had the opportunity to visit major rehab projects where creative architects and designers have taken old apartment buildings and even vacant factories and converted them into very special apartments. Most cookie-cutter apartments have potential. Break away from the routine. Give your apartments a different look and layout. *Give them a personality.* Start slowly and become more creative and aggressive as you move forward and gain a feel for the market. Most managers do not have the training or the skills to conceive major changes on their own. Seek help from people with training and talent. A good way to begin is with a progressive professor and his or her class of architectural or design students. Provide them with a tour plus pictures, plans, and layouts of your property. Offer prizes to the students and a gift to the school. Students are not intimidated by the past, and their minds bubble with fresh ideas and approaches. Tell them what people want today in the way of living spaces, bathrooms, and kitchens.

You should make a yearly trek to the "Parade of Homes" in your area to understand the lifestyle changes taking place and the things people perceive as desirable. Once you take the time to understand what people want, it is fairly easy to scale down a version to fit the space and pocketbook of an apartment community.

Rather than serve up the same old tired apartment layout month after month, take each apartment as it becomes available, study it, and then begin to make changes. Soon, you will have the start of a varied apartment inventory that will increase prospect interest and resident longevity.

At this point, a word of caution is appropriate. Few will argue with the premise that most people want to enjoy a better lifestyle and improved living conditions; but you, as manager, cannot ignore the issue of affordability. Many renters have some, but not unlimited, flexibility to pay additional rent. It is unwise to go overboard with expensive improvements. One way to avoid this problem and stretch your upgrade budget is to limit the number of improvements in each apartment. In the past, my company conducted an annual contest in which we would form teams among our employees to see who could come up with the most exciting renovations. At first, we assigned each team an apartment and gave them a fund of $5,000 to pay for improvements. This resulted in some dynamite changes, but we ended up over-improving one apartment. We learned that we were far better off with an improvement allocation of $1,500 to $2,000 per unit. Our money went further, and we did not end up with monthly rent that was completely atypical.

Test Your Rents.   Updating and upgrading apartments does many things. Besides the variety aspect just discussed, it helps managers better understand rent level limitations. Whenever you make these improvements, you should also make an upward rent adjustment. As people opt for these upgraded apartments and agree to pay more rent, the staff's confidence in their product and pricing strengthens.

There was an unexpected advantage to our team contests that searched for ways to make apartment improvements. At the point of judging, the teams were asked to suggest a rent for the improved apartments. Invariably, the property supervisors had to "tone down" the rent increase. Partly because of pride and personal commitment, the teams typically went overboard with the rent premium for their masterpieces.

Morale Booster.   One of the greatest benefits of upgrading apartments has nothing to do with the physical property. It is a great morale booster. The routine of preparing and leasing the same apartments day in and day out wearies apartment employees. When they get the opportunity to become involved with making changes and adding extras, their energy levels soar. They talk about what is happening and how it can be done differently. They become students of the rental market and begin offering new ideas.

When the leasing staff is out on their tours with prospects, they have an excitement in their voices when they present the upgraded apartment. They are more alert to customer reaction, and they bring that input back to the strategy sessions. When these apartments rent quickly, and they do, the entire staff can share in the accomplishment. The transformation in attitudes is difficult to explain, but it is fun to see. It easily beats employee parties and almost beats pay raises.

Four Levels of Rehab

Apartment rehabs can take many forms. They range from getting your feet wet with a single apartment to a major remodeling that changes both architecture and apartment layouts. Most endeavors will be at one of the following four levels.

One Unit at a Time.   The easiest and most common rehab undertaking is a one-at-a-time approach. This involves selecting a single apartment and making a series of changes and improvements to it. These might be modest changes to the layout, a careful redecorating job, new appliances and equipment, bathroom upgrades, or changes in hardware and appointments. Substantial rent increases are sought and generally accepted. This approach has several important advantages. It extends the useful life of the rental investment. It attracts an audience of more-qualified prospective renters while helping to extend the stay of existing residents. It may take up to two months to make the changes, and the cost can be equal to two to four months' rent. Generally, these improvements are paid for with operating funds, eliminating the need for a capital infusion.

Facelift. Often referred to as a "perfume job," the facelift is just what its name implies. It refreshes the exterior with some landscaping improvements, exterior painting, and resurfacing of some of the paved areas. In addition, there are often modest improvements to some of the common areas and limited improvements made to some or all of the apartment units. This work could cost $1,000 to $5,000 per unit. Frequently, such work is undertaken by an incoming new owner and is accompanied by a general rent increase. The major problem with this approach is that it provides the property with a very short-lived benefit. A year or so later the luster of the improvements will have faded, often to the point of being unrecognizable.

Overall Upgrade. These improvements are more comprehensive and address more of the property's components. A general renewal of the exterior surfaces such as siding, paint, landscaping, paving, and concrete are undertaken. Common spaces leading to the apartments are typically redone. All or most of the apartments get a makeover as well. This includes new paint, carpeting, and appliances. This work requires an enormous outlay of money—$10,000 to $15,000 per unit is not unusual.

The problem with this level of rehab is that you end up with a property that has been totally freshened but is still old. From the street it has not changed much, and the apartment layouts still reflect those of yesteryear. In four or five years, it will be difficult to pinpoint just what was improved. At first, the apartments will command more rent, but that advantage will be neutralized as the newness wears off.

Major Renewal. This level of rehab has garnered the interest of some of the best-known apartment specialists. They spend their full time searching for well-located apartment communities with the right combination of attributes. Per unit budgets can be $30,000 or more. This work is anything but mere cosmetics. Roof lines are often raised. The exterior look is completely changed. Architects ignore old apartment boundaries and come up with exciting new layouts that incorporate all of the latest features and appointments.

If you were to go on a one-year sabbatical, you would certainly believe that someone came along and tore down the old building and constructed something brand-new.

Rehab Examples

A few examples might help to illustrate what can be accomplished by offering something a little special or out of the ordinary. The first has a cost of less than $500 and can be done in less than a week. It is a great introduction to the fun and profit of apartment rehabbing. The last two involve much more daring and expense.

Quick and Simple. Over the years, I have had the opportunity to address real estate management personnel in training sessions and seminars. The subject of upgrades and improvements is almost always included to alert management professionals to the importance of maximizing a property's potential. For the most part, however, those attending are the properties' managers and not the decision-making holders of the purse strings. To get the managers started in the upgrade process and to give them the confidence to "sell" the ideas to the property owners, I ask them to follow these steps, and, at least during the first try, not to detour from the steps in my plan.

Start by selecting a vacant apartment with a popular floor plan. Have a staff member or carpenter install 3½-inch colonial crown molding between the walls and ceilings of the entryway area and the living and dining areas. Next, use Benjamin Moore flat ceiling white to paint the ceilings. (I chose Benjamin Moore because it can be found in most areas of the United States, and it saves me trying to describe a color.) Then, do a careful job of painting the walls using Benjamin Moore #910 in a flat finish. Now comes the important step: Paint the new crown molding using Benjamin Moore Super White in a pearl finish. Complete all of your other apartment preparation steps. Increase the monthly rent $18 and begin offering the apartment to prospects.

Assuming a period of normal rental activity, expect the apartment to rent to a highly qualified prospect within two or three weeks. I have offered this suggestion to thousands of managers over the years and have received countless letters and calls telling me about their success.

Actually, there are several forces at work when you implement this plan. If you followed my instructions, the chances are the walls in your demo apartment have a little more color than the typical "vanilla" paint job. Whether you like the color or not, it does add variety, and that's good. The crown molding adds a degree of elegance and has the visual effect of the ceilings appearing higher. Introducing different colors and paint finishes further distinguishes the apartment. The thought might occur to you to continue this treatment down the hall and into the bedrooms. That should *not* be done. Managers need to stretch their upgrade dollars, and the extra work will not have enough additional customer impact to warrant the expense.

There will be little problem securing the higher rent because the unit is different—and partially because you had the nerve to ask for it. Why not try it? There is little risk, and the rewards will amaze you.

Rehab Examples *(continued)*

Daring, Expensive, and Long-Lasting. I was called out on a consulting assignment to help the owner of a 96-unit apartment community solve serious vacancy and stagnant rent problems. The property enjoyed a very special "downtown" location in a popular suburb that had express commuter train service to the big city's business center. Because of the close proximity to the train service, the original developer talked the village board into a variance that reduced the number of parking spaces to less than one per apartment. This proved to be a terrible mistake, and it was not uncommon to find some cars parked on the lawn and others double- and triple-parked. Residents found themselves "parked-in," and they would lean on their horns hoping the violators would show up. The facade of the building had a Tudor look, with stucco, imitation half-timbers, and a fake mansard roof. My advice was to remove two of the six-unit buildings in order to open up the land plan and correct the parking dilemma. I also recommended that the buildings be given a "new skin," using a brick and stone treatment and removing the fake mansard roof.

This approach shocked the owner who was really looking for a much simpler and cheaper solution. He carried on for some weeks about destroying 12% of his units. Finally, after considerable resistance, the owner agreed that a major fix was required. It took a solid eight months to get the permits, do the demolition, and make the improvements. The work was expensive and there were several cost overruns. However, the rehabbed property stays fully leased with a select cadre of residents and delivers a greater cash flow, this even after servicing the debt that was added to pay for the improvements. The lesson here is: *Less is sometimes more.*

An Enlightened Developer. This example is not about a property rehab, but it illustrates an approach that can be used in a major renovation. A developer purchased a tract of land and commissioned a builder to construct three five-story, semi-luxury, elevator buildings. The developer's architect was also told to create an elaborate entryway for the development. When completed, this entryway included a gatehouse, expensive planting, and a large rock formation complete with a spectacular waterfall, which fed meandering creeks that ran through the property. The cost of the waterfall was estimated at more than $750,000. The builder dutifully constructed the buildings and the waterfall, but openly ridiculed the developer for wasting so much money on the pretty, but useless, waterfall.

Later, the builder, who had a parcel of land across from this property, decided to construct a similar three-building development for his own account. However, he chose to save money by omitting the waterfall and, instead, installed a better line of appliances and an expensive grade of carpeting. The units were offered at a lower rent, even though the project was nearly two years newer than the one across the street.

Less than three years later, the average apartment rent differential between the two developments was more than $60 per month. To this day, the development with the waterfall continues to maintain its market superiority. Its owner collects $125,000 per year more than the competitor across the street; it has first choice of incoming residents, and it usually has a waiting list. What conclusion can be drawn from this? People want housing that makes a statement, and they are willing to pay a premium for it.

The economics of this level of rehab are extremely inviting. Major renewal works best when a property enjoys an ideal location but its apartments have lost their attraction. The winning formula is when the combination of purchase cost and major rehab cost does not exceed the cost of building a brand-new structure. When it is done right, the ROI for this level of rehab exceeds that of most other real estate investments.

A major renewal program can and usually does involve not renewing leases or relocating residents. Sometimes actual evictions become necessary. It is just possible that the current residents will not fit into the picture when the new rents are announced. Some developers prefer to tackle the entire property all at once while others work in phases. A timetable of a year or more is not uncommon.

Adding Amenities and Upgrades

The danger in spotlighting a few of the newer and more popular amenities and upgrades, as I do in the following sections, is that the pace of change is very rapid. I can only hope that, when this book is being read, these ideas will not have been totally eclipsed by new technology and changing fashions.

Business Centers.   A fully equipped business center is a common inclusion in many apartment community clubhouses. When done right, these centers are well-equipped, with multiple high-powered computers sporting DVD drives and flat screen monitors. They connect to the Internet through high-speed cabling or using wireless technology. High-resolution color printers, scanners, and fax machines are available for the residents' use. In addition, an array of other popular office equipment and accessories is provided to help residents with their office chores. This type of facility is one of the best draws for attracting high-profile renters such as career professionals. Residents will ask that this facility be kept open for extended hours.

Relaxation Gardens.   The swimming pool was once the central outdoor gathering place for apartment residents, but with the passage of time, its popularity has waned. Also, in many parts of the United States, bathing suit and suntan weather passes all too quickly. The desire to be outdoors and enjoy the sun and fresh air still remains, however. This is what prompted the introduction of the relaxation garden. This space is usually cordoned off with high bushes, and it is landscaped with beautiful plants and flowers, reflecting pools, and a fountain or two. Comfortable lounge chairs and small tables are set about for use by the residents. People gather in the garden to visit, read, or just sit back and relax. Hours of operation are not normally a concern. Incidentally, the apartments that overlook the garden area are typically offered at a rental premium.

Private Garages. A great motivator for people to leave rental housing and purchase a home of their own is their desire to gain a garage. Rental developments have resisted this market demand for years, but not any longer. The better apartment developments now offer private garages. This does not mean carports or shared garages. People want their own garage space with an individual garage door opener.

Garage buildings with a row of four to six garages are often placed along property lines to provide a buffer between neighboring properties. A creative land planner can position small groups of garages advantageously around the property.

The profit margins in renting garage space far exceed those that can be achieved by renting apartments. Private garages, especially in the colder northern climates, rent for about 10 percent of the apartment community's average rent for a two-bedroom unit. The particular marketplace will determine just how many private garages should be offered. You are certainly safe with about 5 percent of the apartment total for starters. Generally, it is best to stop when the total number of private garages reaches 15 percent.

Gated Setback Entries. The gated apartment community enjoys a strong drawing power. People like the extra level of security and exclusivity in spite of the added construction and labor costs that translate into higher rent. Apartment managers should pay attention to the newer developments to see how they incorporate the gate system. It is more than just installing a gate at your main entry. The better developments set their whole entryway back from the roadway. This, when coupled with a careful landscape design, increases the status and privacy of the community.

Apartment Changes. People want the feeling of space. This means volume ceilings and fewer walls that delineate rooms. The contemporary kitchen is often part of the living space, separated only by an island. The entry to the second bedroom is often positioned to serve as an expansion of the living area. Alternatively, this room might be used as a den or computer room. Hallway space is kept to an absolute minimum. There are fewer closets, but they can store a great deal more. The master bathroom is stunning when compared to what has been offered to renters in the past.

Built-in bookcases, niches, framed mirrors, and decorative moldings are some of the little, but expensive, extras being offered. Hard-surface countertops continue making inroads on plastic laminates. The apartment industry is finally recognizing the importance of quality hardware because there are very few components that prospective renters actually touch. One of those items is a change to door levers (note that levers are replacing knobs, in part to comply with code requirements). Inferior materials send all sorts of negative signals about the quality of the property.

Property upgrading should be a constant concern of owners and managers alike. The trap is that it is so easy to get in the rhythm of simply re-renting the exact same apartment over and over again. Unless you are staying in step with the times, you can be assured that your resident profile is slipping.

14

Three questions about fires:
Where? How Bad? Insurance?

Insuring the Property

At this writing, the insurance industry is undergoing significant changes which are having a major impact on the rental apartment industry. Insurance carriers and reinsurers are being negatively affected by higher than expected losses, litigation over coverage issues, and diminishing returns on their reserve fund investments This has led to the decision of several primary carriers and reinsurers to exit the multifamily market entirely. Coverages that have been widely and competitively available are becoming more and more difficult to secure. In addition to rising premiums, deductibles are higher, coverages are being limited and the list of exclusions is growing. The government has been petitioned to step in to "backstop" certain casualties and to place limits on some types of claim awards. Be aware that the business of insurance is in a major state of flux and the topics covered in this chapter are most definitely subject to change.

In every hour of every day, more than 275 fires will occur in the United States, and rental apartments are certainly involved in a good number of them. Common causes of fires include kitchen accidents, smoking in bed, grilling on a patio or balcony, overloaded electrical circuits, and malfunctioning heating equipment. As a property's concentration of residents increases, so do the chances of a serious fire. The added risk of loss from a variety of other causes is also very real. Sooner or later, the apartment manager will be confronted with insurance issues and the need for a working knowledge of how to deal with a loss.

You, as the manager, will almost surely be the one to maintain the actual policies for the apartment property. Even if you do not hold the policies and pay the premiums, it is imperative that you understand the property's coverage in the event of a loss because many insurance questions will be directed to you. For example, if an unidentified truck knocks over a light standard in the parking lot of a property you manage, you will need to know which policy covers such damage, the insurance carrier, the agent, the policy number, the policy expiration date, any deductibles that apply, and the method or form for reporting the incident. Similar information will be needed in the case of injuries to people (employees, residents, or guests) or damage to other people's property from any one of a number of possible causes. Operating without insurance information makes things far more difficult. Most managers readily appreciate the need for insurance knowledge and are rather quickly appointed keeper of the policies. It is implied that the manager will not only keep these policies in an orderly and safe manner, but also assume the responsibility of monitoring expiration dates and, perhaps, coverage amounts. What starts out as someone else's concern quickly becomes a rather considerable obligation.

Insurance for an apartment property breaks down into three basic forms of coverage:

1. Casualty losses involving the physical assets of the property.
2. Liability claims brought against ownership or management.
3. Medical and disability costs relating to injured employees.

The *mortgagee* (the lender) is most interested in the insurance protection for the property or physical plant. The property, in most cases, represents the lender's *collateral*. If a loss occurs, the lender must be assured that the money necessary to put the property back into rentable condition will be forthcoming. On the other hand, the manager, employees, residents, and the general public are more concerned about the liability aspects of the property's insurance coverage. The discussion that follows will address the different types of coverage within these three major classifications of apartment community insurance.

In years past, insurance coverage was available for a number of basic losses or casualties that could disrupt or destroy the property or the well-being of it occupants or the financial status of the owner or mortgagee. This coverage often took the form of individual policies with specifically chosen limits, and these policies were obtained from one or more carriers. Nowadays, insurance companies offer an *all risk* (or *special property*) policy form.

All Risk Coverage

This type of policy includes most of the property and liability coverages that in the past were offered as separate policies. Several types of coverage are built into a single policy, and only special needs are accommodated as extra-cost add-ons. The fundamental difference with the all risk policy is that everything is covered unless it is specifically excluded. In other words, losses that might otherwise be questionable are covered because they are not excluded. The onus is on the insurance company to clearly state the exclusion on which denial of a claim is based. The more or less standard exclusions are riot, war, and nuclear disasters.

Recently, mold has been added to the list of common exclusions. This is not particularly surprising when you consider that mold is really preventable and its spread and damage is generally within the control of the property's ownership.

Other exclusions fall into the category of yard fixtures, and these include fences, detached retaining walls, swimming pools, and paved surfaces (e.g., walks, roadways, aprons, and parking lots). Piers, wharves, docks, and beach areas or diving platforms are examples of improvements that are excluded from many policies. Similarly, foundations, underground pilings, sewers, or drainage systems are often not covered. Outdoor signs, lawns, trees, and plants are also commonly excluded from coverage. When these things are covered, the policy may contain limits as to the amount that can be recovered.

In addition, some coverage may be lost after a building remains vacant or is unoccupied for a period of time, commonly in excess of 30 days. Special *endorsements* can be added to the policy to continue such coverage when needed.

Insuring Against Property Loss

Losses from perils such as fire, storm, or vandalism are the first to come to mind in this category. Property coverage also includes losses due to wind, hail, lightning, collapse, explosion, smoke, aircraft, and broken pipes and fire hoses. The vandalism portion insures against damage caused by vandals and burglars. Examples of other coverages that can be added, with an increase in premium, are theft and water damage, including sewer backup.

The amount of coverage required is usually determined by the insurance company's underwriting department and is provided in an *agreed amount endorsement* or *agreed value* amount. The underwriters make certain that the limit granted is representative of the 100-percent value of the building and its contents. Today, limits are almost always stated on a *replacement cost* basis instead of the *actual cash value (ACV)* basis used in the past. The limit of insurance is then adjusted annually using an *inflation guard provision* that establishes a percentage of increase.

Generally, the agreed amount provision replaces a long-used system called *coinsurance,* which resulted in many settlement disputes and misunderstandings. Coinsurance is still used in some high-risk situations with losses due to flooding or windstorm (as from a hurricane) or even losses involving terrorism.

Optional Coverage.   With the seemingly endless combination of building types, locations, climates, inclusions, and values, there is a corresponding number of insurance option combinations. The insurance industry has measured the risks of many of these exposures, and underwriters have calculated extra premiums and customized special coverages for almost any situation—most, of course, at an additional cost. The following are some examples of the more commonly requested options.

Boiler and Machinery.   This coverage protects against losses sustained in connection with damage to a building's boiler, pressure vessels, and mechanical systems. Any added premiums are established by the insurance carrier's underwriting department and are related to the cost of such apparatus and the exposure to damage.

Plate Glass.   Exterior plate glass insurance is commonly an add-on. Coverage is usually limited to a fixed dollar amount per lite (pane) of glass or to a total loss amount per occurrence or during the term of the policy.

Contents.   This coverage might be needed to insure lobby furniture, recreation building furnishings, exercise equipment, office or model furnishings, apartment furnishings (should you have any furnished units), and the like. A value is usually established, and coverage frequently involves a deductible amount to eliminate small claims. The policy may also be endorsed to include *fine arts coverage* for paintings or sculptures that are used to decorate the lobby or common areas. Contents coverage is typically written on a replacement cost basis.

Computers and Printers.   Computers are the focus of many apartment office break-ins because they are light, highly portable, and can produce instant dollars for thieves. This kind of equipment is usually named in a schedule provided by the insured in which a description, serial number, and model number identify each piece of equipment. Coverage can be added to include software programs and the time required for restoring lost data.

Natural Disasters.   Hurricanes, floods, earthquakes, volcanic eruptions, mud slides, and the like were once referred to as "acts of God." Now they are referred to as "causes of loss" and individually identified in the policy. Losses involving these types of hazards may be included under a "difference in condition" (DIC) endorsement. Insurance covering natural disasters often involves very high deductibles.

Flood insurance is unique because qualifying for coverage means that the insured property must be in an area that is prone to flooding and in compliance with government guidelines for flood prevention. Insurance can be provided by the National Flood Insurance Program or by private companies.

Improvements and Betterments.   This coverage is carried by occupants to insure any special improvements they have made to their housing units. These treatments can include anything that becomes a part of the real estate such as floor covering, paneling, built-ins, climate-control devices, upgraded bathrooms or kitchens, and more. This type of coverage is seen more often in common interest properties such as town homes and condominiums than in rental apartments.

Rent Loss.   This type of coverage is almost standard for rental properties. Lenders invariably require rent loss insurance as a condition of their making a loan on the property. A great many loans on rental property are termed *nonrecourse,* which means the lender's sole recourse to satisfy the debt is the property that is pledged as collateral; the lender has no claim on the borrower's other assets. If the property has been damaged by a casualty and is left partially or totally uninhabitable, rental income will be interrupted, and the funds for making mortgage payments will be reduced or discontinued altogether. The rent loss coverage substitutes for the lost rental revenue after the damage is sustained and until the building can be readied for occupancy again. Frequently, this coverage applies for up to 12 months, although it should be noted that there are many differences among rent loss coverages.

Deductibles.   Claims processing is expensive, and the number of comparatively small losses far exceeds the number of major incidents. If an insurance company can avoid the processing expense and the payment of the smaller claims, it is in a position to offer coverage at a lower premium. This is accomplished by setting a minimum dollar amount for claims called a *deductible.* Deductibles can range from $100 to more than $1,000,000. Some property owners and institutions can set aside adequate amounts and choose to effectively self-insure against all but the most catastrophic losses. Others set up a loss pool among several properties and cover them as a group using a blanket policy with a substantial deductible. This drives down their annual premiums and the loss pool funds losses up to the deductible amount.

Volume Purchases.   As with most commodities, greater volume results in lower prices. Insurance companies are no different: They prefer volume and will discount premiums to attract bulk business. Many owners of multiple properties have elected to group their properties together under one *blanket policy* to obtain the lowest annual premium. Such an owner might also be able to include one or two higher risk properties in the package at a much lower rate than that which should be expected.

Insuring Against Other Claims

Everything discussed thus far has involved possible loss or damage to the property itself, but there are many more risks. Rental property is a business, and in the course of operating that business, owners and managers are exposed to a myriad of potential financial losses—often very serious ones.

Liability Coverage.   Liability insurance protects the property owner and those involved with the property's operation (e.g., the managing agent) from claims of bodily injury and damage to property belonging to a third party which an insured person becomes legally obligated to pay. If someone were to slip and fall on a walk or stairway in the property, it is the liability insurance that would provide financial protection. It would also defend the owner as well as any other insured person in the event of a lawsuit arising from such an accident.

Anyone acting as a manager of real property is automatically included as a *named insured* as part of general liability coverage, but it does not hurt to confirm that the apartment manager is specifically listed as a named insured on all of the property policies. (Usually this is addressed specifically in the management agreement.) The manager is actually better off if not categorized as an *additional insured,* as this classification carries some additional restrictions. It is not uncommon for the managing company to possess a greater net worth than the owner of the property being managed. Lawsuits tend to include everyone associated with the property, even those with the most remote connection, and especially those individuals and entities with some degree of wealth. For that reason, the manager as well as his or her employer needs liability insurance protection. On the other hand, liability coverage is not normally extended to financial institutions.

American society is increasingly litigious. Awards resulting from claims of people sustaining bodily injury can range into the millions of dollars for damages in addition to those directly related to the injury. This exceeds the limits of most basic liability policies.

Umbrella Protection.   There is always the possibility of a major liability claim exceeding the basic liability coverage. To protect against this, the property should have additional umbrella coverage, which is available from either the basic policy carrier or a second one. This coverage, which is its own separate policy, would undertake the payment of claims that exceed the basic liability coverage. The limits of umbrella protection can be as high as, or even higher than, $20 million. The premium is usually quoted as a specific dollar amount per million dollars of added liability coverage. Because personal injury losses can reach such enormous amounts, even the insurance companies will reinsure themselves against a major claim.

Employment Practices Liability.   This is a relatively new policy form that is designed to cover judgments arising out of employee claims of sexual harassment, wrongful discharge, discrimination, and disability that result in lawsuits. This insurance is fairly expensive, and an employer might have to accept a high deductible in order to afford the coverage.

Tenant Discrimination Liability.   This is a new form of liability protection which has grown out of the increasing numbers of fair housing lawsuits and awards. The uncertainties of provable fault and jury reactions result in high deductible levels, conservative coverage limits, and very high premiums. Coverage is voided, of course, if the insured acted in a willful manner.

Directors and Officers.   The elected representatives of common interest real estate need a form of protection called *directors and officers liability* insurance. The insurance company will defend the directors and officers from all manner of claims and lawsuits.

Errors and Omissions.   Managing real estate is a complicated business with a great many responsibilities. As a managing agent, you are very definitely exposed to financial risks if you should make an error or fail to perform a crucial function within the scope of your authority. As is the case with most risks, there are insurance carriers willing to protect you against such losses—for a price. This coverage is called *errors and omissions (E&O) insurance,* and it is typically purchased and paid for by the managing agent. Because of the substantial awards made by juries in liability cases—especially those awarded in decisions against the medical profession—errors and omissions coverage is expensive and offered by only a handful of insurance companies. This coverage usually involves a large deductible to eliminate smaller claims. The policy carefully defines what constitutes an error or an omission. Gross negligence on the part of the agent is often excluded—as, of course, is fraud.

Non-Owned and Hired Auto.   This is a rather special form of third-party liability and property damage insurance that allows an employer to buy insurance coverage as protection from claims arising out of accidents involving vehicles that are not owned by the property (e.g., an employee's automobile). It is commonplace in the operation of an apartment property to send one of the maintenance people to the hardware store or to the gas station. The manager might ask the bookkeeper to make a bank deposit at lunchtime. Examples of "hired auto" also include asking a person to borrow or rent a vehicle to perform a particular task. If any of these people is involved in an accident while performing a work-related duty, the liability can quickly shift to the employer.

Coverage for these risks is comparatively inexpensive, but the potential for loss is substantial. This is particularly true when the employee has inadequate coverage or none at all. You should also know that if your firm, the managing agent, is involved in sending your people on such errands, you will also need protection either as a named insured on the apartment community's non-owned auto policy or through separate coverage.

Insurance to protect vehicles owned by an apartment property as well as those who drive these vehicles is a separate policy and not often part of the non-owned auto coverage.

Host Liquor Liability.   Another common occurrence, and hence a liability exposure, is the accident that results from the consumption of alcoholic beverages. Perhaps alcohol is served in your development's clubhouse or during the social activities offered by the property. If an accident causing injury or death occurs—and it can be proved that the responsible party was consuming alcohol on your property prior to the accident—you can be sure that those involved, including the managing agent, will be included in any resulting lawsuits. Host liquor liability insurance protects those involved only when the beverages are given away, not sold. To sell liquor, you need not only a license, but also a completely different kind of coverage called *dram shop* insurance. If you do not plan to host parties as part of your resident activities but choose to host a single event, you are advised to contact your insurance agent to purchase host liquor liability insurance for that single event rather than run the risk of catastrophic loss.

Fire Legal Liability.   What if your property suffers a major fire, and the dense, black soot discolors the white building next door? The fire damage to your building would be covered by the property's fire insurance, but what about the adjacent building? Your insurance carrier did not agree to repair all of the buildings in the neighborhood. Fire legal liability, which is an optional coverage, can be obtained to handle such situations.

Crime Coverage.   Depending on the types of coverage included in your policy, this insurance protects the apartment owner from some twelve to fourteen different risks, the most common of which are employee dishonesty and burglary, plus destruction, theft, and disappearance of currency. A *fidelity bond* is another way to insure against dishonesty of individual employees.

Workers' Compensation

This coverage is the third in our list of basic insurance forms and it is somewhat unique. First of all, workers' compensation is always a separate policy. It is also one of the only types of insurance that cannot be assigned to a new owner. The managing agent should be named as an *alternate employer*. This insurance is required by state law. In some states, however, an employer may be allowed to carry the risk independently if sufficient financial ability is demonstrated. This insurance protects employees who are injured during the course of their work-related activities by paying the medical costs and providing salary (short-term disability) benefits while the employee is recovering—or continuing (long-term disability) benefits if the employee is partially or permanently disabled.

The premium is determined by the job hazards inherent in the work being performed and the amount of money paid in wages. For example, the rate per $100 of salary for a building engineer might be $15 while that for a leasing agent might be less than $2. The engineer's job involves whirling machines and pumps and a host of potential sources of injury, while the leasing agent's greatest risk might be the possibility of falling down some steps. The initial or deposit premium is determined by listing the different classes of worker exposure and estimating your workers' annual wages during the upcoming year. At the end of each year, the insurance company audits the payroll records to arrive at an adjusted premium. Either this is invoiced to make up any difference owed, or a credit memo is issued for an overpayment.

It is not uncommon for properties with no employees to maintain workers' compensation insurance. The likelihood exists that a manager might hire a student or other casual laborer to help out with a particular project, which might result in an injury and a workers' compensation claim. It is also possible that a contractor may not have proper insurance or adequate coverage, and the liability transfers back to the property owner or the managing agent or both. Workers' compensation insurance, in these examples, will defend the managers' positions.

It is absolutely essential that you *secure current certificates of insurance from all contractors and subcontractors who perform work on the properties you manage.* There are several situations in which the liability of an independent contractor can be transferred to the owner and operator of the property. Some states have laws stating that a contractor without a license and insurance is deemed to be an employee of the property. During the workers' compensation audit, some insurance carriers include the value of work performed by individuals and contractors as if they were direct employees when these people show no evidence of insurance. If you do not constantly verify the existence of current policies and sufficient coverage for each tradesperson who works at your properties, you may well find yourself providing that insurance or, at least, undertaking the associated risks. You will also be expected to use a fair amount of due diligence and reasonable judgment when accepting a subcontractor's workers' compensation certificate. For example, tree trimming and removal is a very risky occupation which means a high workers' compensation insurance rate. On the other hand, firms that just mow the grass have a considerably lower rate. Some tree service companies may try to masquerade as a landscaping company to save on premiums.

Handling Insured Losses

Knowing what to expect and how to proceed in the event of a loss is one of the most important aspects of real estate management. Managers have some very definite responsibilities in this area, and the failure to handle them correctly can shift much of the liability to the management firm. In most cases, a period of learning and an allowance for mistakes are part of the process of becoming a manager. However, mistakes in handling an insurance claim can result in huge economic losses to both the property owner and the management company.

Report All Incidents.   The advice to report all incidents or losses may seem self-evident, but this first procedure following a loss is omitted regularly in the operation of rental property. Suppose one of your groundskeepers sustains a cut on the hand while using a hedge trimmer. A common response might be to administer a little first aid and hope that the healing process is quick and pain-free. Perhaps you hear about a person who fell on a slippery spot in the parking lot. You do not know the time the accident occurred, the exact location, or even the identity of the individual involved. What can you report? The simple answer is, report everything you know and everything you heard. When insurance is purchased, the burden of responsibility shifts to the insurance carrier with three very important exceptions:

1. The premium must be paid;
2. All incidents must be reported promptly; and
3. Action must be taken to lessen any damage if a loss should occur.

The reluctance to report claims may stem from a general optimism that everything will work out, fear that insurance rates will be increased, or unwillingness to assume the burden of additional paperwork and investigation. Wishing it so will not help. Insurance has been purchased, and a manager's job requires that potential claims be handled in a responsible manner. The failure to report a claim happens when incidents appear to be minor or information about them is vague or incomplete, not when major incidents occur. The law gives injured parties considerable time to register any claims for damages. If it is discovered that you had knowledge of an incident involving an injury and failed to report it to the insurance company, it may be determined that you breached an important condition of your insurance agreement. You can avoid such problems by reporting all incidents to the insurance carrier immediately. It is all right if you lack much of the background data, such as the person's name, time of occurrence, or extent of injuries. The insurance company has people capable of securing the missing information. Your job is to report all incidents.

Do Not Volunteer.   When a catastrophe such as fire, windstorm, or tornado results in a casualty loss (i.e., loss of property), there is usually a great deal of commotion. The scene is anything but pretty. The weather may be inclement, and such incidents frequently occur at night. As you would expect, emotions run high in a situation involving the loss of furnishings and other personal possessions. Some people may have been injured trying to escape from the peril. People may be homeless and without proper clothes to wear.

There are plenty of opportunities to volunteer, but in my opinion, apartment managers should not do so. You may have vacant apartments that could be used to house those of your residents who have lost their homes, but that is not one of the provisions in your lease document. There are legal implications and ongoing consequences when you begin to go beyond the bounds of a normal landlord-tenant relationship. As a manager, you do not have the authority to commit and obligate the property's owner to these added burdens.

I would also add these words of caution: Television crews may want pictures and answers to questions ranging from "What happened and why did it happen?" to "Who is responsible?" Reporters sometimes try to address all the issues in one telecast. As for the media, it is best to let someone else do the talking. In the minutes immediately following a disaster, it is likely that your grasp of the situation will be incomplete. When the statement is aired publicly, you may regret your attempt to make a coherent statement from limited knowledge, so it is best to hold off making any comments.

Do Not Admit Liability.   As a manager, you are best advised not to admit liability. Immediately following an incident, you can almost be assured that you do not really know exactly what happened or why. Guessing is wrong and may later jeopardize the position of the property or the insurance carrier. Let the experts do their investigation.

Know Your Public Adjuster.   When you are called to the scene of an apartment property that has been damaged by fire or some other force, you will often be approached by an individual who hands you an impressive-looking business card with a generic name involving insurance or insurance adjustments. This person will typically act calmly and be very knowledgeable about what steps should be taken next. This can be very comforting to a manager who has not experienced the emotions associated with a property loss. Unfortunately, many managers might begin to work with this stranger under the assumption that he or she is an agent of the insurance carrier. You should be aware that the adjusters who arrive at the scene are most likely public adjusters and do *not* represent *your* insurance company. Once they have secured an obligation from you, they gain a foothold in the loss settlement and restoration work, and their fee is commonly a percentage of the monetary loss. These public adjusters have numerous contacts. With just a few phone calls, the public adjuster can begin getting results. Workers begin to arrive to take care of necessary chores: A tarpaulin is placed over a hole in the roof; doors and windows are boarded up to secure the building, and emergency electrical lines and portable boilers are installed to furnish heat to the damaged structure. Seeing a public adjuster seize the authority and order this repair work, the manager often becomes convinced that things could not be better when, in reality, the adjuster's actions may be obligating the management company or the property owner to substantial fees. I strongly advise you not to become involved with these people.

This is not to say that all public adjusters are "fire truck chasers." There are many public adjusters who perform a very valuable service in interacting with the insurance company's adjuster. They know the rules and the settlement process. The insurance company's adjusters know these people, and they share a mutual respect for each other's positions. Before a casualty occurs, network with other apartment managers to learn the names of two or three public adjusters so that you have them recorded in your address book.

Protect the Property.   The work that the public adjuster authorizes is classified as protecting the property from further damage. That is the remaining obligation of the insured. There will be a time gap between the occurrence of the casualty and the moment the insurance company's representative arrives on the scene. Until then, you are not only authorized to act but also responsible to mitigate any further damage to the property. You should always maintain an address book in your car and at home containing the home telephone numbers of various tradespeople or contractors whom you can call during emergencies. That list should surely include a board-up service, electrician, plumber, carpenter, heating contractor, and a locksmith. Talk with them in advance so that you know they will respond. You should also have alternate firms or individuals available. There are no advance warnings for emergencies. Your job as manager requires that you act quickly and decisively, so you must always be prepared. The cost of this emergency work will be added to your insurance claim on a dollar-for-dollar basis.

Insurance Adjustment and Restoration. Adjusting an insurance loss is a very detailed and complicated process. It is absolutely no place for a beginner. Even for experienced managers who have been through many fire or casualty losses, the adjustment procedure can be troublesome. The authorized insurance adjuster who is assigned to the loss is the employee or agent of the insurance company, not the property. The insurance company is anxious to settle the matter and see that the restoration process is begun, but it is not going to provide funds without evaluating the situation. The adjuster appointed by your insurance carrier will go through each and every component of the building methodically and decide whether it needs to be cleaned, repaired, or replaced. Insurance companies have a schedule of allowances that may or may not be sufficient to complete the work. The adjuster's estimation of what is acceptable may not be what you know to be necessary in the marketplace. Under certain policies, some items are subject to depreciation deductions (actual cash value basis), which can present a rude surprise when the final settlement amount is announced. The adjuster does this every working day; you do not. Managers should seek outside help.

Most cities have a "fire-builder" or *restoration contractor* who is very experienced in both the adjustment of insurance casualty claims and the actual restoration work. A few calls to your colleagues will give you the names of these people and some background information. The good ones are expensive, but they know this very specialized business. They know the rules that the insurance company will follow, and they know what you are entitled to. Their chances of achieving a proper settlement are far better than yours unless you have considerable experience in insurance settlements. The good ones are very efficient at the dirty and dangerous business of fire restoration. There is a big difference between building a new building and restoring one that has been damaged in a major fire or natural disaster. The method of compensation is often a percentage of the money needed to restore the property. Some managers choose to pay a consulting fee for the help in adjusting the loss, and then they do the actual restoration with their own cadre of contractors or personnel.

With luck, the properties you manage will suffer very few losses requiring the services of an insurance adjuster. When the occasion does arise, you should take the time to learn more about this very important subject.

Risk Management

Institutions and very large real estate management companies maintain a risk management department to seek out and minimize potential hazards. During periodic inspections of the property, they identify problem areas and prepare a written listing of recommendations for the manager to consider and implement. Many of these take the form of housekeeping practices such as the storage of flammable products, slippery floors, clogged aisle-ways or blocked exits. Others may center on emergency procedures or evacuation drills. Occasionally, these recommendations will involve major structural or mechanical modifications with costs running into the tens of thousands of dollars.

Many insurance companies offer a form of risk management to their policyholders. Frequently, just after a new policy is issued, the insurance carrier sends a risk management specialist to the property. This person prepares a rather extensive list of the potential problem areas. Some of these reports contain several pages of recommendations. This is the very same property with the same existing conditions that the insurance company agreed to insure just a few weeks earlier. Now, they seek to minimize their exposure by having you modify and update the property. If the property fails to undertake some of the suggested corrections and a casualty occurs, will that have an effect on a subsequent claim? Only time will tell.

15

*Delay budgeting long enough and
real numbers begin falling into place.*

Budgeting and Planning

I have several acquaintances who operate many millions of dollars worth of rental property without using any budgets. When challenged about this practice, they respond, "What if a large compressor burns out and needs to be replaced but isn't budgeted?" or "What if we get twice the normal amount of snowfall—what would you do, consult a budget?" These same people are famous for not wasting money; rather, they spend what is necessary to properly operate their properties.

Many managers would champion this "no budget" approach and skip the arduous task of putting together comprehensive operating budgets. Developing and using a budget is time-consuming and potentially restraining, but a budget is a valuable tool that demands forethought, goal-setting, and control. Budgets also provide a means to monitor progress. Unfortunately, too many budgets are prepared in haste, and their relationship to reality is weak from the very beginning. Other budgets are realistic initially but later cut back by an overly optimistic owner or superior wanting to show a better result on paper. This practice destroys the budget as a working tool within weeks of beginning the new year. Sometimes budgets are created indicating expectations of high rent revenues and low expenditures while the person who is actually responsible for increasing rental income or holding back on expenses makes no contribution to the budget's development. This practice ends up frustrating everyone involved. Another problem with budgets is the short tenure of some managers; it is not unusual to find a manager trying to live within the bounds of a poorly conceived budget made by his or her predecessor. These difficulties contribute to the appeal of operating without the burden and constraints of a budget.

However, when put together carefully, using projections that are not forced, the budget will provide you with a map to guide you through the next fiscal year.

Types of Budgets

September and October are known as "budget time" in the apartment management business. In areas of the country with four distinct seasons, the high point of rental occupancy and income usually occurs in mid-October. By this time of year, rent increases have been put to the test, and most discretionary expenditures have been made. Utility, seasonal, and apartment make-ready costs are winding down to their lowest levels of the year. At this point, the manager has nine to ten months of year-to-date operating data in hand to guide next year's projections. Still, preparing an accurate budget is an all-consuming project that will involve significant time commitments from several staff members.

A variety of budget types are commonly used in the management of rental apartments. More than one type of budget may be needed to effectively plan for your specific property.

Net Operating Income (NOI) Budget.   This type of budget reflects the gross potential rental income, vacancy and collection losses, sundry income projections, resulting collection expectations (effective gross income), and a listing of proposed operating expenses (see Exhibit 15.1). In actual practice, each line item is broken out by month and totaled for the year.

In a budget of this type, the monthly debt service is omitted or dealt with in a separate accounting. All inclusions up to and including the calculation of the NOI are matters of concern to the manager, a potential buyer, an appraiser, or others interested in the earning capability of the investment. Including the mortgage with its associated debt-service payments adds an ownership variable to the budget and does not, or at least it should not, affect the proper operation of the property.

Cash Flow Budget.   Most budgets for rental properties fall into this category. They follow the same pattern as the NOI budget except the cash flow budget does track the payment of mortgage principal and interest each month. The final budget line is referred to as cash flow. This is the spendable cash that constitutes the return on investment (ROI) or the periodic

Exhibit 15.1

Sample Annual Budget (NOI Format)

	Estimate	%	Estimate	%
Income				
Gross Potential Rental Income			$990,000	100.0
Vacancy Loss	−49,000	−4.9		
Collection Losses	−10,500	−1.1		
Model and Staff Discount	−12,400	−1.3		
Total Rent Loss			−71,900	−7.3
Laundry Receipts	7,200	0.7		
Other	500	0.1		
Total Ancillary Income			7,700	0.8
Effective Gross Income			**$925,800**	**93.5**
Expenses				
Payroll and Related Costs			$74,000	7.5
Electricity	16,500	1.7		
Water and Sewer	25,000	2.5		
Heating Fuel	8,000	0.8		
Utilities Total			49,500	5.0
Pest Control	3,500	0.4		
Trash Removal	9,900	1.0		
Snow and Ice Control	4,500	0.5		
Services Total			17,900	1.8
Supplies			6,500	0.7
Maintenance and Repairs			34,300	3.4
Office Operations			6,800	0.7
Management Fee			41,700	4.2
Advertising and Promotion			9,500	1.0
Legal and Accounting			4,500	0.5
Real Estate Taxes			148,500	15.0
Insurance			35,000	3.5
Miscellaneous			2,200	0.2
Estimated Operating Expenses			**$430,400**	**43.5**
Net Operating Income			**$495,400**	**50.0**

This example represents a budget for a full year. As noted in the text, allocations would be broken out on a monthly basis for tracking purposes. Note that percentages shown here have been calculated based on gross potential rental income. In actual practice, the management fee is calculated as a percentage of effective gross income (revenue collected) and so stated in the management agreement.

income that is so critical in attracting investors. It is important that managers see this monthly expenditure requirement, but adding the debt-service payments to a basic operating budget presents some problems.

An owner who has been aggressive, or even unrealistic, in acquiring one or more levels of debt can effectively destroy the proper operation of the investment. The ability of an owner to acquire debt is not an automatic indicator that a property's income can support the accompanying payments. This problem may eventually influence the budget because most managers adhere to an unwritten rule of payment priority. It goes something like this: Pay the mortgage first, or there won't be any property to manage; pay the employees next, or they won't come to work; then pay the utilities so that you have light, heat, and water; and finally, pay the insurance and real estate taxes so the lender won't take the property back. These are must-pay items, and they also represent the most significant portion of the budget. If there is going to be a cash shortfall, its impact will almost certainly show up in the maintenance, upkeep, and repair expense categories.

Budgets with negative cash flows are usually unsatisfactory to owners. They often turn up the pressure on the manager to increase income and cut back on maintenance-related expenditures in order to balance accounts. This sometimes results in less care checking prospects' references in an effort to fill more vacancies and the postponement of needed and scheduled maintenance projects. Properties suffer when burdened with servicing an unreasonable debt load.

Annual Budget.   Most budgets detail income and expense projections for each of the months in the upcoming year. Nevertheless, there are situations when a total of annual income and expense items is sufficient. Usually an annual budget is prepared for submission to lenders, appraisers, investment partners, tax assessors, or others who do not need or should not be concerned with the monthly details of income or expenses. An annual budget is far less revealing and more difficult to track than a monthly budget schedule. For that same reason, an annual budget is not very valuable to either the manager or someone closely monitoring ongoing property performance.

Quarterly Budget.   This budget, prepared in advance for each of the four business quarters, has become quite popular. There are several reasons for this:

- Budget numbers correlate to both weather cycles and changing rental activity during each of the four quarters;
- Managers can forecast income and expenses much more accurately using the smaller blocks of time; and
- Budget optimism is more likely to be kept in check.

People who develop a quarterly budget are often more accountable for their predictions than are those whose budgets culminate a year from now. Shorter budget periods are also more effective in stimulating achievement. When quarterly budgets are used, there is usually an annual companion budget that includes far less detail. The conservative annual budget is used for longer-range planning, while the shorter quarterly budgets function more as goal-setting targets and learning tools. Utilizing this combination is the budgeting method I favor.

Rent-Up Budget.   Some situations call for "special purpose" budgets. During a rent-up campaign, even a month is too long an interval between budget reports. Most rent-up budgets are prepared on a weekly schedule for periods of thirteen weeks. These budgets typically break out all of the various unit types and track week-to-week rental progress.

The expenses during a rent-up campaign are much different than those that will occur after the property stabilizes. Initially, the major costs will be advertising, public relations, collateral materials, rental personnel, incentives, and promotions. Real estate taxes, repairs, make-ready costs, and even mortgage payments will not become meaningful amounts for some months. The primary purpose of the rent-up budget is to monitor rental progress and to regulate the use of advertising and promotional funds.

Major Expenditure Budget.   This is a budget that is used to consolidate the major expenditures planned in a given period. For example, major expenditures might include new siding, a complete exterior paint job, redesigned courtyard landscaping, or the replacement of ten sets of appliances. By maintaining a separate budget for these items, they can be separated from the budget items that recur every year, making budget planning and analysis easier. This budget is frequently made before the actual operating budget is prepared because the decision to do certain work should be influenced by the need for the work rather than the availability of funds. The major expenditure projects can be assigned priorities and later re-evaluated, after the operating budget is prepared, to determine which items can be accommodated with the projected availability of cash.

Major expenditures are often kept in a separate expense category to make year-to-year budget comparisons easier. Consider the repainting of all exterior wood surfaces, expected to cost $30,000. This expenditure should not be combined with the ongoing painting and decorating that must be done each year. In this way, the manager can follow the spending pattern for each category and recognize the difference between recurring annual maintenance items and special projects.

I prefer to draw a distinction between major and capital expenditures and treat them separately during the budgeting process. Because the two are often confused, it is important to differentiate between them: A *capital expenditure* represents a true improvement to the property; *major expenditures* are replacements and repairs. Hence, that $30,000 bill you incurred repainting the siding and trim constitutes a major expenditure; the $50,000 you spend installing tennis courts is a capital expenditure.

Replacement Reserves. This is different from the major expenditure budget. Think of replacement reserves as something like a lay-away plan. Major expense items such as the roof, heating and air-conditioning plants, appliances, and carpeting are assigned a life expectancy. Money is set aside, often earning interest, and remains available to pay for replacements when necessary. The money put away each month or year for this purpose is called a *sinking fund.*

Properties that are insured under federal or state housing programs are required to make periodic deposits into a replacement reserve. The payments are allocated to different component categories and tracked on a reserve schedule. When a replacement becomes necessary, funds are deducted from that category and used to pay for the required item. Occasionally, permission is granted to shift money between categories to cover an unexpected replacement expense.

While replacement reserves are carefully structured and regulated in government-assisted housing, they are far less formal in the case of conventional rental properties although some lenders may require replacement reserves as part of conventional financing. Owners frequently set aside funds over a much shorter period of time in anticipation of a planned major expenditure. The owner may choose to set aside $1,000 per month for a year and a half to pay for an $18,000 reroofing job. The money is budgeted on its own reserve schedule and is not included with the listing of other operating expenses. Reserve expense items are usually detailed after arriving at the property's NOI. The money paid into the reserve fund is taxed just as if it had been earned and paid out in cash. In the year that the major expenditure occurs, reserve funds are transferred to the operating account to handle payments. At that point, the money spent is recognized and may be treated either as an expense or a depreciable asset, depending on the accounting method chosen. The Internal Revenue Service requires the value of capital items to be depreciated for tax purposes over a set period of time *(cost recovery),* which may or may not coincide with the actual useful life of a particular improvement.

Contingency. In any upgrading or remodeling budget, the last line item should be one labeled contingency. All budgets, and most particularly budgets detailing rent-up or major improvement expenditures, should provide an allowance for unknown items. This amount is often a percentage of the total budget. If the cost outcome is easy to predict or the work being budgeted is routine, a contingency of less than 5 percent may be more than adequate. When undertaking remodeling that involves opening walls, shoring up structures, or otherwise venturing into the unknown, prudent contingency allowances may approach or even exceed 15 percent. The answer to the question, "What is it for?" is simply, "I don't know." What you do know is that there are going to be hidden costs in this project. If you can specify one or more possible expenditures such as higher labor costs, additional drywall patching, or rotten pipes, you should increase that budget amount or add a line item to cover that category of expense. The *contingency* category is for items that you cannot reasonably foresee.

Preparing a Budget

There is a series of important considerations in the process of preparing an operating budget for a rental apartment property. Obviously, the more experience a manager has operating a particular property or type of property, the more accurate and useful the budget will be. Without the benefit of past records, the budget preparation process will require much more time and reveal greater variances and outright distortions. Some useful guidelines follow.

Realistic Figures.   Starting with income, there is a tendency to make calculations using current rent levels and to ignore the aging of the leases. It is also very easy to project rentals and fail to account for free rent allowances. Experienced managers have learned to be conservative with their income projections. Owners are never upset when their managers report more income than was anticipated in the budget; the problems arise when the situation is reversed. Being conservative is even more important regarding projections of unscheduled income.

When budgeting expenses, managers should not skimp or ignore the price increases that will surely occur. This does not mean they should not search for ways to operate a property more efficiently or investigate new trends or techniques. Utilities, services, insurance, and real estate taxes follow a pattern and can be tracked fairly easily, but it is worth making some phone calls and doing some investigation to avoid surprises. Payroll and related expenses often create a major problem. It is easy to account for existing salaries, but there is a tendency to forget to allow for overtime, salary increases, seasonal workers, vacation replacements, incentives, and benefits. My experience indicates that this category is typically the most underbudgeted and overspent. Supplies, repairs, and maintenance are the other expense categories that are most frequently misjudged during budget preparation. Budgeting errors do not always show up, as some managers spot potential budget shortfalls and either reclassify expenses to other categories or reduce expenditures for needed advertising, repairs, or supplies. This can harm the property in many other ways.

Again, the best advice is to develop a workable budget with realistic projections. If you are pressured into creating an unrealistic budget in November, you will only be forced to apologize and make excuses all next year.

Acceptable Variances.   Just how far off can you be and still be within an acceptable variance? The apartment industry has some practical guidelines to help answer that question. Normally, you control the degree of acceptable variance by your use of budget amounts. In other words, by estimating the water bill to be $3,434, one is effectively expressing a high degree of confidence in the projection. Anyone reading the budget might assume that the water bill will be very close to that figure, plus or minus a few dollars. Had the projection been $3,400, the reader might expect actual expenses to vary within the range of $3,300 to $3,500. With "big number" expenditures, it is usually best to insert numbers rounded up to the nearest thousand (000).

Budgets are estimates and a lot can happen in one year; leave a little room for the unknown. A pro's budget is filled with lots of triple zeros and double zeros. Apartment managers should not try to predict income or expenses to the dollar.

Budget Categories.   There is little to be gained by establishing a great number of income or expense categories. The more categories you have, the more likely things are to be misclassified; analysis is also made more difficult. This problem is exacerbated when overspending occurs in certain budget categories, and the manager begins changing expense classifications to minimize budget forecast miscalculations. The following are the basic income categories:

Apartment income (rents)
Other scheduled income (parking, commercial, etc.)
Concession income (laundry, vending, etc.)
Unscheduled income (clubroom rentals, late charges, NSF charges, forfeited security deposits, etc.)

The list of operating expenses can be considerably longer, but many major investors choose to limit the display of expenses to these six major categories:

1. Utilities
2. Services and supplies
3. Payroll and related expenses
4. Management, administrative, and promotion
5. Real estate taxes and insurance
6. Maintenance and repairs

Grouping expenses in these broad categories eliminates most of the confusion concerning category identification and provides the budget reader with a quick method of monitoring expense performance. Unfortunately, when too few categories are listed, the budget is not as great a help to an apartment manager. The typical breakdown for tracking and comparison is contained in these categories:

- Utilities
- Services
- Supplies
- Payroll and related expenses
- Advertising and promotion
- Management and administrative
- Legal and audit
- Insurance
- Real estate taxes
- Repairs and maintenance
- Miscellaneous

These are often referred to as *control categories*. When the budget is created and subsequently monitored, there may be a series of subcategories that make up the components of a particular control category. For example, the control category Utilities might look like this when the complete budget is printed out:

3000	**Utilities**	**32,200**
3010	Electricity	16,000
3020	Natural Gas	11,000
3030	Water and Sewer	3,200
3040	Telephone	2,000

When preparing the budget, it often makes things easier to break down expense categories into even smaller and more precise groupings: control category, subcategory, sub-subcategory. These extra sublevels help the budget's author compile and organize types of expenditures, but they should not be published in this fashion. When budgets are tracked with these myriad entries, they are time-consuming to read through, confusing, and a constant irritant.

Seasonality. For each category of expense, it must be decided whether projections should reflect the trends observed in the previous months or in the same period during the preceding year. The latter focus is called *seasonality*. For example, when preparing a budget for heating expense, one should be more interested in what happened a year ago January than in the "lead-up" months of November and December (months that are typically warmer than January). Lease-up expenditures, yard maintenance, exterior repairs, and utilities are a few examples of expenses that correlate more to a season than to the previous month's pattern. Even expenses such as insurance and real estate taxes have seasonality because these charges are not paid monthly. Laundry income is something else that follows a definite seasonal pattern. In cold weather locations, January usually shows the smallest laundry collections because heavier winter clothing tends to be less washable, and many people receive new clothing over the holidays. July is one of the most lucrative laundry months because people change their washable summer clothing much more frequently. These patterns are well-established and can and should be accounted for in monthly budget projections.

On the other hand, services, supplies, and many maintenance expenditures follow a monthly pattern. Income items follow their own patterns as well. Renewals and inflation often have a way of increasing rent each month; this makes a month-to-month progression much more indicative of current trends than the amount collected at this time last year.

In most areas of the United States, the fuel consumed to heat a property during the first ninety days of the year is more than one-half of the annual total, with January's fuel expense being the highest. In order to be a useful planning and tracking tool, the budget must reflect consumption expectations rather than the annual heating costs divided evenly by six cold months, or, even worse, by twelve. The same is true of air-conditioning expenses during the warm months. Managers estimate monthly heating expenses with the help of "heating degree-day" statistics that are recorded by several governmental agencies, most notably the U.S. National Weather Service, part of the National Oceanic and Atmospheric Administration (NOAA). These records have been collected for more than 100 years for most communities. Similarly, "cooling degree-day" statistics may be used to estimate air-conditioning costs (see sidebar).

Daily temperatures and heating degree-days are recorded and reported at airports and many other locations. Many major newspapers report degree-days every day and often print temperature variances from a normal or average year. Subscription services are also available to provide wind and moisture information as well as very specific degree-day data for each hour of the day. While this is interesting, it is much more than anyone needs for budgeting purposes.

As an alternative, you can analyze monthly heating and air-conditioning costs from past years, thereby developing a history and pattern to guide your budget projections.

Property Size.   You might expect this section to address the issue of economy of size, and to some extent it does. Nevertheless, there are limits to the advantage of size. The per-apartment costs of operating a large property tend to be higher than those of operating a mid-size property, except that

Calculating Heating and Cooling Degree-Days

Heating degree-days are calculated for the heating season as follows: Starting with the base temperature of 65 degrees Fahrenheit, subtract the average temperature for a given day to produce that particular day's heating degree-days. Assume today is the 28th of February and the average temperature for the day was 45 degrees. To find the heating degree-days for that day, subtract 45 from 65 (65 − 45 = 20). If you have been keeping a running total of the amounts for each day during February, you can now add the final 20 heating degree-days to arrive at the February total.

Knowing the average heating degree-days for each month makes it easier to estimate heating costs. To begin, we need to know how much it costs to satisfy one heating degree-day. For example, if you know that your total gas cost is $22,000, including fuel adjustments, taxes, meter charges, etc., and the average number of heating degree-days in your location is 4,900, you can calculate that about $4.50 is required to satisfy a single degree-day. If February's total is 850 heating degree-days, you can expect that month's gas bill to approximate $3,825. In the example, we did not break out the gas used for cooking, heating water, and operating clothes dryers. You can approximate these costs by monitoring your gas bills during the summer months.

Cooling degree-days are calculated in much the same way, except that the base temperature of 65 degrees is subtracted from the average daily summer temperature to calculate that day's number of degree-days—e.g., a day with an average temperature of 90 degrees would have 25 cooling degree-days (90 − 65 = 25).

those with fewer than 50 rental units tend to have very high per-unit operating expenses because of inefficiencies inherent in their very small size.

In a multi-year study, differences were more pronounced as the size of the properties being compared increased. These differences occurred in six distinct areas—vacancies, payroll, repairs, supplies, advertising, and legal expenses. Exhibit 15.2 shows a stacked bar chart containing the six categories grouped by property size. The sample contained 104 properties with a total of almost 36,000 apartments. The properties were separated and placed into four size groupings: 125, 250, 500, and 750 units. The annual total of the six operating expense categories increased by almost $600 per year when the 125-unit and 750-unit groupings were compared. Some of the findings of this study are detailed in the following sections along with some analytical commentary.

Vacancies. The average number of lost-rent days between the departure of an old resident and arrival of a new one ranged from 22 days in the 125-unit group to 51 days in the 750-unit group. The time required to make a

Exhibit 15.2
Inefficiency of Scale

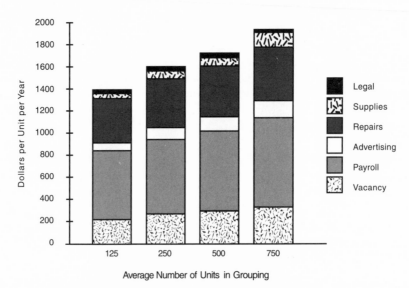

Comparison of Operating Expenses (36,000 Unit Study)

This chart represents the operating expenses—6 specific expense categories—that were analyzed and compared across 104 properties with a total of 36,000 apartment units. Properties were grouped by size for comparison.

vacant unit market-ready was 12 days for the smaller properties and 35 days for the larger ones.

Managers of the smaller apartment communities learned about move-outs several days sooner than their counterparts managing larger properties. Interviews with managers confirmed that those handling the smaller rental communities appeared to have a more personal relationship with the residents. Consequently, the manager of the smaller property was alerted to potential move-outs sooner, giving that manager a head start. This adds to the advantage of the manager of a small property who has fewer units to prepare each month. The difference in preparation time eats away at the larger properties' earnings.

Payroll.   You might expect the number of apartments per staff member to increase in the case of larger properties, but in fact the opposite is more typical. Staff members with highly specialized responsibilities are basically non-existent in the smaller properties but become commonplace as the size of the apartment community increases. In the large properties, there are often staff members who only handle a single task. Even during slow or busy times of the month, jobs such as bookkeeping or leasing are rarely shared or augmented by other staffers.

Repairs.   At smaller properties, the tendency is to make repairs, while at larger properties, owners are more likely to replace components. Perhaps the maintenance staff of smaller properties learn to fix components in place because they have little or no room to store replacements. Also, managers of larger properties spend considerably more in hiring outside mechanics and tradespeople than do those who manage the smaller 125-unit properties.

Supplies.   You might expect the manager of a large apartment community to attract the attention of a wholesale supplier offering considerable discounts from the prices charged at the local hardware store. Though savings may exist in terms of price per item purchased, the study found that larger properties purchased larger quantities on an apartment-per-year basis. Waste, over-ordering, and subsequent pilferage was far more prevalent at the large properties.

Advertising.   During the comparative examination of advertising, it was discovered that the 750-unit apartment communities purchased more than three times the number of lines of print space per vacant apartment as the smaller 125-unit properties did. Ads for the smaller properties typically highlighted a particular unit and usually ran in weekend newspaper editions only. These ads were small, rarely over ten lines in length. It would seem that the size of the community dictated the size of the advertisement. Ad size did appear to have a relationship to the number of prospects who responded—more prospects responded to the larger ads—but the prospect-to-resident conversion ratio was clearly better in the smaller properties.

Legal Expense.   Although legal fees make up a very small percentage of an apartment community's overall expenditures, the pattern of higher legal costs followed the increase in the size of the properties being studied. It is interesting to note that, in the five years of the study, there were very few evictions in the smaller apartment communities. During the same five years, there was an almost monthly procession of court cases and evictions in the larger properties. This is certainly attributable to the more personal relationship that exists between residents and managers in the smaller properties.

Rent Revenue.   An additional observation from this study is worth sharing. The smaller apartment communities were more successful in achieving higher rents per apartment, probably because smaller properties offer more identity than do large ones.

Time and training can diminish the expense imbalance between smaller and larger properties, but the person putting together an operating budget must take a property's size into account. The budgeting method cannot be as simple as developing a set of per-unit expense figures for each category and multiplying them by the number of units in the apartment community. I believe owners and managers should consider breaking down the very large properties into smaller, more economical sections. This is much easier to accomplish, of course, when there is a geographical boundary such as a corner lot with entrances on two major streets, or if architecture varies from one section of the property to another.

Property Age and the Budget.   There is a tendency to budget expenses for apartment communities the same each year, regardless of their age. When it comes to repairs and maintenance, however, there are significant differences between newer and older properties. Budgeting for repairs and maintenance for years two through four is fairly simple. Most equipment and components still function almost like new, and those items that do malfunction are often under warranty. Parts are readily available and repairs usually involve only a part or two rather than complete systems. Ceiling and closet painting can often be skipped; carpets need shampooing rather than replacement.

After the first four years, however, the repair and maintenance pace picks up considerably in continuing four-year cycles. Assuming constant dollars (in other words, ignoring any inflationary effect), these two expense categories, considered together, increase about 6 percent per year. That means in five years, repairs and maintenance costs will have risen 30 percent—before any cost-of-living increases are taken into account. Over ten years, plan on a 60-percent increase in the costs of repairs and general maintenance. Older buildings simply cost more to maintain, and an accurate budget will reflect that fact. Unfortunately, just about the time this becomes obvious, another trend becomes clear: Achieving rent increases also becomes correspondingly more difficult as a building ages.

Budget Analysis

Once a budget is prepared, there is still the job of comparing it to actual results and learning ways to analyze budget variances. Some variances occur because the budget does not account for the natural lag between the month in which an expense is expected and the month when the bill for that expense is actually received and paid. The utility bill paid this month usually covers the preceding month's charges. This is true of many bills. The exceptions are payroll, management fees, real estate taxes, and debt-service payments. This effect levels out when analyzing the entire year because, at that point, you have accounted for all twelve months. Variances arise when the budget is examined a month at a time. It is usually better to adjust the budget to reflect the month when a charge or invoice will be received or paid rather than the time the commodity or service is delivered or performed. Select a method that will be used consistently. If the estimate of income and expenses does not reflect reality, the budget loses much of its month-to-month usefulness as a tracking tool.

Budget Slippage. If certain categories start to "slip" as the actual expenses begin to accumulate each month, it may be necessary to revise the budget. The budget is not etched in stone and should not be used to demonstrate just how far actual figures can vary from budget estimates. A budget is not worth much as a tool when it fails to project what is actually occurring. Sticking to a budget that is not working is a waste of time.

Last Year Comparisons. In addition to the item-by-item tracking of budget to actual income and expenses, the most widely watched variable is a comparison of this year's figures to the amounts recorded for the same period, one year ago. This provides the budget analyst with a point of reference and is invaluable in spotting trends.

Percentage of Income. Tracking the percentage of gross potential rental income is useful because it indicates trends in the larger and more important categories (e.g., real estate taxes may equal 15 percent of gross potential income). This method is best used when comparing the year-to-year changes that occur for a single property or for properties with close similarities. When applied to properties with a wide disparity in rent levels, however, the comparison loses much of its value.

It should be noted that most computer programs that generate financial analyses provide a column to express both income and expense breakdowns as a percentage of gross potential income. However, some software programs produce calculations showing the percentage of *collections;* this can be very misleading and may cause considerable confusion.

Studies of garden apartment properties indicate that the total operating expenses expressed as a percentage of the gross potential income can vary by as much as 20 percent, depending on the average rent level. Properties serving residents with limited incomes tend to be older, need more repair, and, more importantly, have a lower rent schedule than do some of the newer, more up-to-date apartment communities. While the rent may be only half that of the more-expensive and more-luxurious developments, certain expenses remain virtually the same. The charges for services such as rubbish removal or pest control are probably much the same throughout a municipality, and the utility companies charge standard rates for heat, light, and water. Owners who have several properties with a wide range of rent levels often have trouble understanding why one property requires 45 percent of its income for operating expenses while another property in the same town requires 60 percent or more. The answer is, the percentage of gross potential income that is required to cover expenses goes down as the average rent level goes up.

High-rise buildings are not only much more expensive to build, they also frequently add expensive amenities such as door attendants, parking garages, and a host of specialized services. These properties are usually analyzed individually and not by comparison to others.

Dollars per Room.   One of the standby indicators for comparing the operating results of one property to those of another is dollars per room per year. This is not nearly as popular a method as percentage of gross potential income. Though less affected by differences in rent levels, this method does not take size of rooms into consideration, nor does it consider bathrooms (a meaningful source of problems and expense). It requires uniformity in preparing the count of rooms, or much of its analytical value is lost. (Chapter 1 includes a discussion recommending a room-counting method.)

Cents (or Dollars) per Square Foot.   Appraisers commonly use cents— or dollars—per square foot as another method of comparing operating expenses. It should be emphasized that square foot references in real estate are made on a yearly basis with one major exception, apartment rents, which are expressed monthly. When displayed in a square-foot format, apartment rents are detailed in cents (or dollars) per *rentable square foot.* In other words, the rent is calculated using only the space that is contained in the occupied unit, and no allowance is made for the areas that feed and support the living space—often referred to as common area or nonyield space.

While the residential manager receives rent for only the rentable square feet, he or she must operate and maintain the entire property. Hence, operating expenses are expressed on a gross square foot basis. This is probably one of the most popular methods of examining operating expenses and is especially useful when comparing different properties. Breaking expenses down to rentable square feet can lead to problems because of the constant adjustments necessary to compensate for differences in architectural styles and varying proportions of nonyield space. I am not aware of any database collecting apartment expense information on a rentable-square-foot basis.

Cost per Apartment.   Analyzing a property's operating expenses based on the cost per apartment per year might appear too simplistic, but it does produce surprisingly accurate results. The key to this method is expressing all of the property's expenses as a single total. Within a single apartment community, the cost to operate a smaller apartment is about the same as the cost to operate a larger one. Because turnover rates are higher in smaller units, make-ready expenses are incurred more frequently. This offsets the higher per-unit preparation cost for a larger apartment. Repairs to mechanical systems and appliances do not vary much between apartments of different sizes, making these costs fairly similar. Significant differences in operating expenses will be revealed if comparisons are made by line item, but these expenses have a tendency to equalize when treated as a total.

Cost per Plumbing Fixture.   In my opinion, analyzing operating expenses on a cost-per-plumbing-fixture basis produces some very reliable results for a number of reasons. This method involves looking at the number of plumbing fixtures per unit, a figure that will be closely related to both the size of an apartment and the rent level. In addition to adjusting for the extra damage and breakdown exposure of additional plumbing connections, the relationship of plumbing fixtures to costs is a real one.

A count of plumbing connections would include the obvious, such as the kitchen sink, bathroom vanity, tub, and water closet as well as those connections necessary for disposals, dishwashers, hot water dispensers, icemakers, washers, bar sinks, bidets, hot tubs, fountains, and other fixtures. Larger bathrooms often have multiple sinks or bathing facilities, and each one should be counted as a plumbing connection. Most of these items require additional apartment area, and this signals increased operating costs. As the number of these fixtures increases, your residents are likely to be more affluent, and your rent level—the prime indicator of a property's quality of operation—is apt to be higher. I believe that this method of budget analysis will become more popular.

As you can see from the foregoing discussions, budgets and budget analysis can take many forms. The point to be made is that budgets are necessary to plan the financial future of investment real estate. Preparing and adhering to a well-thought-out budget is admittedly a burden, but without one, there will surely be some unpleasant surprises.

Business Plan

Those in the forefront of real estate management are lessening their focus on annual budgeting and concentrating more on three- and five-year business plans. Knowing what is going to happen in the next twelve months just is not enough to prudently guide a multimillion dollar investment. Goal-setting and planning frequently encompass five years or more.

These business plans may be initiated and developed by an experienced real estate manager, but they absolutely must be in concert with the owner's needs and wishes. A multi-year business plan is extremely helpful in directing the financial and physical focus of the property's ownership and management. The following summarizes some of the more important issues that need to be addressed.

Assessment of Local Area Trends.   Usually the first step in creating a business plan is to candidly assess the state of the neighborhood and identify any apparent trends. Neighborhoods are usually going through one of four broad phases:

1. Development and growth
2. Maturity
3. Decline
4. Rebirth

Virtually all of the business planning discussions and decisions will use this information as a primary premise. It will answer questions related to overall economic and demographic patterns and trends, employment opportunities, housing and its affordability, and a wide range of issues contributing to the health and viability of the area.

Property Description, Condition, and Status.   This starts with a complete description and inventory of the subject property and a breakdown of its assets. Just about everything that describes and pertains to the property is listed or presented in a matrix form. A sample list includes: lot size, zoning, tax number, date and type of construction, building and parking areas, site and floor plans, number of units, unit sizes and floor areas, mechanical systems, and features and amenities.

This is followed by a narrative description of the present condition and estimates of the remaining useful life of the physical plant and its components. Generally, this section provides commentary about the subject property's condition as it relates to the neighborhood and competing properties.

Current vacancies and vacancy history are typically charted to highlight unit popularity and resistance points in rents. Apartment demand levels, neighborhood vacancies, and absorption rates are also researched and documented.

Comprehensive Resident Profile.   Generally, much of this information is gleaned from individual apartment application forms. Ages, marital status, population counts of adults and children, occupations and income estimates, and length of stay are a sampling of the more important items that make up the property's resident profile.

Exploration of Alternatives.   The owner's goals and financial wherewithal will help decide the depth and extent of exploring alternatives. The property's construction and configuration often become limiting factors as well. However, all properties have a *highest and best use,* and it is important to search out what is the most advantageous course for the subject property.

Financial Consequences.   Often, in a recitation of trial and error, various approaches are explored with a description of proposed strategies that might have a beneficial effect on the property or its operation. Potential problems and risks are identified, including estimates of any need for the infusion of new capital. Potential profits and eventual rewards are then forecast for each scenario.

Summary, Conclusion, Recommendation, and Implementation. While last in our listing, this segment of the business plan is actually presented first in the finished document. It briefly summarizes the marketplace, the property, and its situation and reviews options and financial considerations. It then explains the conclusion process and clearly sets forth a recommendation for action. This section concludes with a form of mission statement outlining the purpose, goals, timing, and progress benchmarks.

Management Plan

Formal real estate management training classes put considerable emphasis on the *management plan* and the process for preparing one. A management plan contains much of the data and information gathered in the creation of a business plan but in a largely expanded format. With the business plan, there is an underlying assumption that the subject property is under ownership and a program is being sought to maximize and perpetuate operations and value. The management plan starts with a much broader approach. It goes into considerable detail describing and analyzing the "health and welfare" of a geographical region. This, of course, would be very important to, say, a large institutional or out-of-town investor looking for a potential purchase. It is a much more intensive analysis of all of the factors related to the property's location, condition, competitive position, and highest and best use. It is written to thoroughly acclimate the reader to all aspects of the property. Management plans can also delve heavily into financing variables and options as well as different tax-delaying techniques.

A thorough and comprehensive management plan can take a month to research and prepare and consume 150 or more pages of photos, text, charts, and exhibits. When done right, it is a valuable work product and can cost many thousands of dollars.

16

Your file is your friend.
Find time to write often.

Computers, Accounting, and Record Keeping

The job of monitoring the property, administering the paperwork, and handling the accounting tasks is formidable. Managing or owning an apartment property, even a small one, without enlisting the help of a computer, makes very little sense. The computer greatly simplifies virtually every aspect of apartment management.

Computers

What makes the computer so important is its ability to handle repetitive tasks using only the tiniest fraction of the time required to do the work manually. As one might gather through reading this book, there is a lot to the apartment management business, and most managers need more time on the property to see that everything is being done correctly. That is difficult to do when you are saddled with paperwork, schedules, lists, letters, and basic record keeping.

Equipment and Programs. The technology of most computer equipment is obsolete before it even leaves the store. Basic accounting and record keeping can easily be handled by most of the equipment that is already available and in use. However, additional speed, memory, and graphics capability are required to handle photographs, virtual tours, 3-D representations, customer tracking, map and floor plan generation, rent forecasting, and computerized maintenance and staff scheduling, just to name some of the more obvious uses.

Sophisticated networking connections, high-speed cabling, and wireless Internet access are common in the offices of even small properties. Inexpensive color printers enhance the look and readability of management reports, proposals, budgets, etc. Compact discs (CDs) and digital video discs (DVDs) are used to hold and retrieve almost limitless files and data. Scanners are becoming as numerous as copiers; in addition to photographs and charts, they allow text documents to be captured as manipulatable graphic images.

There are software programs that will do just about anything you want to accomplish with words, numbers, and pictures. Even now, leases and most formal documents or notices start out as blank sheets of paper in the printer. Customized color brochures and sales literature can be generated in minutes. Most management offices have collections of letter formats and other written communiqués on their computers all cataloged and ready to be personalized with the push of a button. Cross-referencing residents and addresses, once a laborious task, now happens instantaneously.

I would offer this caution about computers, however: Some managers will go overboard learning about the computer and its endless potential. Hiding behind a computer while producing reams of reports cannot replace on-the-job common sense. Apartment management is a business of people contact. Apartment managers should use computers to provide more time to spend with their customers.

Accounting

Personal computers can make your accounting work easier, but they cannot think for you. To begin to put your machine(s) to work, you must consider all the aspects of accounting for the income and expenses of your property.

Types of Income. In the process of managing rental apartments, you will collect and spend a great deal of money belonging to other people. The collections fall into two basic categories—scheduled income (the rent roll) and unscheduled income (any income received other than rent). The design of any accounting system for tracking scheduled income should be based on tracking the fixed factor (which is, in this case, the apartment units) and not the variable factor (in this case, the residents). If there are 120 units, the system must account each year for 1,440 unit months (43,800 days) of potential income. It is to be hoped that most units will be occupied by rent-paying residents, but all units—vacant ones, those used as offices, models, unrentable units, those used for storage—must be accounted for each month. A system that does not maintain a running financial history of each and every rental unit can be easily compromised.

The second form of income, unscheduled receipts, presents more problems and accounting risks. More money is misappropriated, "lost," or stolen in this category than all others.

Unscheduled revenues come from several sources—resident payments to cover damages, fees from concessionaires, charges for use of a hospitality or recreation room, lease settlements or related charges, back-rent payments on accounts that have been written off, and income from building-owned laundry equipment, among others. Much of this money comes in the form of cash. It can amount to many thousands of dollars over a one-year period. Because of this, and the fact that collection cannot always be anticipated, the opportunity for loss through theft or misuse is great. Managers need to be alert and to devise systems to prevent loss or disappearance of these funds. No system is foolproof, but steps can be taken to at least minimize the risk. Remember, when money is discovered missing, the property loses two ways—the money itself and the employee who took it and must now be discharged.

Security Deposit Funds.   Security deposit funds are a daily part of a manager's work. The manager starts by issuing a receipt for this money to the individual resident. The money is then typically deposited into the property's operating account or, in some jurisdictions, it must be maintained in a separate *escrow account.* Some laws now require that the entity collecting the security deposit (e.g., the management firm) remain responsible for the reimbursement at the time of move-out. Such laws are a response to complaints by renters who have lost their security deposit money because the property was sold or the owner became insolvent. Failure to properly escrow funds and promptly return deposits results in some rather stiff penalties.

More and more municipalities have passed laws requiring the owner to pay interest on security deposit funds. Usually, this means actually preparing a check each year, not just crediting the security deposit account with the earned interest. Either way, if the interest exceeds $10, the owner—or more commonly the agent—must issue a Form 1099-INT signaling to the Internal Revenue Service (IRS) that interest has been paid.

Owner's Custodial Account.   All monies collected on behalf of the owner should be placed in a custodial or trust account separate from the funds of the managing agent. There should be no *commingling* of the property owner's and the management company's funds. Separate custodial accounts for a property owner's funds are required by most state laws and ethics codes and by the U.S. Department of Housing and Urban Development (HUD) for all federally insured or assisted apartment properties.

Accrual versus Cash Accounting.   For the most part, accrual accounting has replaced cash-basis accounting, because the IRS requires it in most cases, and it is the preferred general accounting practice. It certainly provides a truer financial picture than cash-basis accounting. Accrual accounting is also essential if the accounting records are to be audited. Many computerized management programs are a mixture of the two forms of accounting. These systems track rents on an accrual basis but account for many expenses on a cash basis or when paid. It becomes the job of the owner's accountant to sort out the differences at income tax time.

Purchase Orders.   In order to provide true accrual accounting, the accounting of expenditures should begin at the time a product or service is ordered or a commitment is made. Without such information, the owner or his or her accounting consultant does not have a realistic picture of the property's financial position at any given point in time. Many computer programs require that purchases be made with a purchase order system that begins tracking a potential obligation from the time the order is issued—not when the invoice is received or the bill is actually paid.

It is important to make all purchases with a written and numbered purchase order. This is essential if you are to keep track of what is ordered, what orders are outstanding, and whether the invoice amounts reflect the quoted prices. If you have a file of such orders and a building is sold, you can easily contact vendors whose shipments have not been delivered and cancel the orders. Otherwise, vendors may fill the orders and then bill you or the former owner, a situation that could lead to disputes. The new owner may refuse to pay the bill, claiming not to have authorized the order; the vendor might then put a lien on the building, further complicating matters. This unpleasantness can be avoided if you cancel unfilled orders. Without an integral purchase order system, you will have trouble remembering what orders are open. The remedy is to put everything in writing.

Every purchase order placed by a managing agent should contain a notice to the effect that *the management company is acting as an agent, not as the principal, and that it will disclose the identity of the principal if requested*. This signals to the supplier that your company is an agent and that the principal, not the managing agent, is responsible for payment of the invoice. (Obviously, the notice is not necessary if the manager is a direct employee of the owner.) Without this notice, the supplier can assume that the managing agent is acting on his or her own behalf and will look to the agent for collection if the invoice is not paid. It is very rare that a supplier will ask the identity of the principal, but if you are asked, you should be allowed to disclose this information.

Bill Payments.   As managing agent, you need policies and procedures for paying bills. The major points to be considered follow.

Tips for Handling Bill Payments

- Choose a period to pay bills when money is available and when you have the time to do the paperwork.
- Inform all vendors of your bill-paying procedures.
- Be aware of discounts and gross versus net billings so you can take advantage of discounts.
- Avoid paying bills that are cash on delivery (COD).
- Don't use petty cash funds to pay vendors.
- Have bills approved by the site manager who ordered the work *before* they are processed for payment.

The approval process should include comparison of the invoice to the purchase order to verify the product(s) and/or service(s) purchased and the agreed-upon price. The total amount and applied taxes should also be verified.

- *Choose a period to pay bills when money is available and when you have the time to do the paperwork.* Do not have suppliers submit bills by the tenth of the month for payment on the first of the following month. While it is true that bank balances are highest in the beginning days of the month, this is also the manager's busiest time because he or she is handling move-ins, collecting rents, taking complaints, and doing extra paperwork. It would be better to select a time that is less hectic—perhaps the middle of the month—for bill payments.

  In the same regard, it is unfortunate that most mortgage payments are due on the first of each month. Invariably, there is not enough money collected and in the bank to meet the first-of-the-month payment date. At the time the mortgage was originally made, it would have been an easy matter to arrange for payments to be due later in the month. Even if the mortgage is established, it is worth a try to have the payment date set forward. By setting the date at the fifteenth, there will be more money on hand, and the payment can be handled more comfortably.

- *Inform all vendors of your bill-paying procedures.* This will discourage calls from vendors who want to know when they will be paid.

- *Be aware of discounts and gross versus net billings.* The manager should take advantage of these discounts merely as good business. If you cannot take discounts because of a short turnaround period or because of a lack of funds, notify owners of this right away. Otherwise, if they find out that you are not taking advantage of discounts, they may put in a claim for the money because you were negligent.

Negotiating discounts and payment terms is frequently part of the apartment manager's responsibility.

To take advantage of discounts, you may have to deviate from your established bill-paying schedule. For example, many discounts are only available if payment is made within 10 days of the invoice date; if you pay in 15 days, the discount will not be granted. Some vendors, however, will honor a discount even if payment is made 30 days later because money is money. Others will strictly observe the discount period.

Utility companies may bill on a gross versus net basis. The lower net amount must be paid by the stated due date; the higher gross amount is due some days later. If your operation is large enough, the utility company may extend the net period.

You also need to be aware that you may be billed for utilities in a vacant apartment even though it is leased to a new resident. The same thing may happen if a resident moves in early. To avoid this, have the resident sign the utility application and turn-on card when the lease is signed, so his or her utility service and charges will begin with the date the lease is in effect or the move-in date, whichever is earlier. It is to your advantage to have utility company forms in your office and mail the signed forms to the utility company yourself. Residents will appreciate the fact that you have saved them some time, while you ensure that the chore will be addressed immediately.

- *Avoid paying bills that are cash on delivery (COD).* Some vendors insist on COD payment, especially if they have had bad experiences with apartment owners and managers. Once you are in the habit of paying COD, vendors will insist on it because it is the quickest way to get cash. There is no incentive for them to change. However, COD payments will complicate your record-keeping and bill-paying procedures.

    If necessary, change vendors in order to avoid COD billings. With a new vendor, allow time for the vendor to run a credit check and approve the account. This is recommended for purchases of all supplies, materials, and services. The only exceptions would be payments for one-time items, such as emergency, non-contract snowplowing for which the driver demands cash.

- *Don't use petty cash funds to pay vendors.* If you do, you will need a large amount of cash on hand to pay all the vendors who will soon demand cash. These funds are subject to theft and misuse. It also leads to poor record keeping. Petty cash is for incidental purchases such as postage stamps and postage due, small shipping charges, gasoline for lawn mowers, and minor office expenses. A revolving fund of $200 should be adequate for most properties.

- *Have bills approved by the site manager who ordered the work before they are processed for payment.* If checks are prepared centrally, they should not be sent to the site manager for review prior to being forwarded to the vendor. Some firms do this, claiming that it enables the site manager to know who is being paid and to hold back a check if there is a last-minute question about performance. This should have been determined *before* the bill was approved for payment.

    The danger of letting the site manager approve the check or forward it to the vendor is that it provides the chance to extract a kickback from the vendor, even if it is nothing more than a free lunch. By simply calling the vendor and saying, "I've got your check," the site manager exerts some pressure on the vendor. This leads to a poor business relationship, which in turn will cost the owner money.

Form 1099.   Vendors who are not corporations must be issued a Form 1099-MISC (miscellaneous income), detailing the amount of money that was paid to them in the year. This form must be in their hands shortly after the end of the calendar year. Many computer programs can prepare these forms to be sent to vendors, the IRS, and state authorities (where applicable). The IRS does exempt minor amounts from this accounting of miscellaneous income. Managers should always be aware of the *current* IRS definition of a "minor amount." The IRS rigidly enforces its regulations, and there are penalties for noncompliance.

As stated earlier in this chapter, the management office is responsible for issuing 1099-INT forms to residents who have been paid interest on their security deposit money.

Taxes and Reporting Forms.   As managing agent, you will most likely prepare payroll checks, and this will involve making regular deposits of monies withheld for federal and state income taxes, as well as accounting for both employer and employee Social Security and Medicare contributions (FICA), employer contributions to federal unemployment insurance (FUTA), and other payroll taxes. Most management firms are also responsible for filing Form 941, Employer's Quarterly Payroll Tax Return, which reconciles tax liability. Shortly after the end of each calendar year, every employee is entitled to receive a Form W-2, Wage and Tax Statement, detailing gross wages earned as well as the total amount of taxes withheld and contributions made into his or her Social Security and Medicare accounts. Where applicable, money withheld for state and local taxes must also be accounted and reported.

Sales taxes on rents have been discussed in many locales, and, in some cases, levied. The accounting and reporting for these taxes can be a laborious process.

Management Statement.   Basically, managing agents produce a monthly statement of receipts and disbursements for the owner. It is not intended to replace all other accounting documents or procedures. The problem is settling upon an accounting format that will provide the necessary information and satisfy most clients. A large percentage of management business is with large institutional owners who have hundreds of properties in cities and towns across the country. The asset managers who work for these institutions want your reports to conform to their company's style and format of accounting so they can be seamlessly consolidated with the reports from all of the other properties in the portfolio.

Many computerized accounting systems do not offer the flexibility of making major modifications to meet a client's specialized formatting needs. In these cases, managers often must deviate from their system and manually produce a special report in order to secure an institution's management business. Alternatively, a management firm may acquire additional software to be compatible with the institutional owner's system; when there are several institutional owner-clients, the management company may have to run different software programs to meet their reporting needs.

Some information management systems can extract data and rearrange the output display to meet specific requirements. With advancements in technology, some managers are in a race to see how many different reports and report variations can be conceived to dazzle owners. It is not uncommon to find monthly management reports for a 150-unit apartment property that are over one-half inch thick. Many owners are not impressed; they are overwhelmed. The opposite, a one- or two-page statement packed with color graphs and charts that gives the client a quick, understandable review of the property's operations, is becoming popular as a technique for presenting an overview. Most owners and asset managers will still want detailed reports on specific activities at the property in order to prepare consolidated financial reports.

The management statement is actually a collection of reports, usually starting with a narrative or *executive summary* (or an *issues report*) that explains the month's activities to the owner. This is followed by separate reports detailing the rent roll, miscellaneous receipts and disbursements, reserve account transactions, and other activities. Management statements are typically prepared and sent to the owner shortly after the end of each monthly reporting period. Many firms end their accounting month before the last calendar day so that the management report can be prepared during the slow business days rather than the busy first few days of the month. Once the pattern is established, however, it is critical that it be maintained because owners will become accustomed to that schedule. This monthly package typically includes the original paid invoices and a check for any payment due the owner.

The basic components of the monthly management statement (excluding the introductory narrative) are explained below.

- *Rent roll with monthly activity.* Each apartment and all other rental spaces should be listed in numerical sequence, regardless of whether the unit is leased. Once this order has been adopted, it should not vary much from month to month. Listed with each apartment or entry should be all other fixed information, such as unit and floor number, building name and/or address, and unit type and size.

  Following on the same line is the variable information, including resident's name, amount of security deposit, term of lease, rent, and rent status. If a particular unit is vacant, this portion would be blank. The more sophisticated programs often detail the amount of rent lost since the unit was last occupied. Possibly, under a single apartment unit, information would be given for more than one resident in the same month (e.g., residents moving in the current month or in future months, collection from a delinquent former resident).

  The information concerning the resident is a running history. It should show the status listed at the end of the previous month, all transactions during the current month, and the ending status. Without such a detailed description, an owner cannot properly monitor the activities of the property; nor can he or she evaluate the managing agent's performance.

  Some agents do not list the entire rent roll but instead report by exception. This type of report is easier for an agent to prepare and easier for an owner to read, but it lacks the unit-by-unit detail necessary to really explain what is happening.

- *Miscellaneous receipts and monthly disbursements.* This is a chronological listing of all monies received from sources other than rental units (e.g., collections from vending equipment and recreation room fees). This list details the name of the payer and the amount paid.

  The statement will go on to detail monthly disbursements, with check numbers, in the order paid. In addition to ongoing operating expenses, there commonly are debt-service payments, payments for capital expenditures, and distributions to owners. Most managing agents will utilize a chart of accounts to classify different items of income and expense, thereby organizing and bundling similar or like items.

  The disbursements listed are often only those actually paid, and amounts owed but unpaid are not reflected. This procedure can give an owner the false impression that all bills are paid and accounted for. One way to avoid this is to include a listing of any unpaid bills at the end of the statement period so the owner is alerted to the property's actual financial situation.

Monthly Management Reporting

- Narrative or executive summary; issues report
- Current rent roll with monthly activity
- Miscellaneous receipts and monthly disbursements
- Escrow and reserve account transactions
- Summary of all financial transactions

The following additional reports may also be included to provide a more complete picture of the property's fiscal and market positions.

- Complete general ledger
- Security deposit liability report
- Separate delinquency report with monthly aging
- Listing of accounts payable
- Bank account reconciliation
- Balance sheet (statement of financial assets and liabilities)
- Square foot income-expense analysis
- Occupancy report
- Vacancy analysis
- Comparability analysis (details rents and features of competitors)
- Prospect traffic and conversion report

- *Escrow and reserve account transactions.* Items on this list might include a monthly deposit into the owner's real estate tax fund with an indication of the current balance. Regular monthly deposits into an established reserve-for-replacement fund are frequently recorded in a separate section of the management statement. This keeps the owner informed of the reserve account balance and any interest earned on the accumulating funds. When expenditures are needed for "reserved-for" building components, the money is usually transferred into the operating account to pay the particular invoices. Many owners do not maintain a formal reserve-for-replacement fund as such. When a major expenditure is contemplated, they typically begin setting money aside for a period of months to build up the necessary cash fund. This accumulation of funds is likewise documented in the monthly management statement.

- *Running summary of all financial transactions.* This summary usually contains a beginning balance for the month, total of collections, total of disbursements, an updating of the escrow and reserve accounts, remittances to owners, and the ending balance. While it is the summary of everything that has happened financially during the month, this schedule is usually positioned first, ahead of all of the more detailed reports. Frequently, this summary will contain a series of charts to illustrate important statistics about a property's operation.

When things are going well, this may be the only schedule that attracts the attention of the owner.

Records

As an apartment manager, you become the keeper of the records, and there is no shortage of items that need to be maintained, filed, stored, protected, and rotated. When you first become manager, the owner usually entrusts you with many of the records that have been accumulated in the course of the ownership and operation of the particular property. These files might include leases, contracts, insurance policies, warranties, payment books, real estate tax information, correspondence, etc. As time goes by, many of these files and documents will be moved to storage boxes after being replaced by more current paperwork. All of these materials must be maintained in a manner that ensures their safekeeping and ease of retrieval. The following sections describe the more important records and offer some suggestions about the maintenance of these files.

Leases.   Documents dealing with the occupancy of the apartments (and perhaps parking or commercial enterprises such as laundry facilities) are important legal papers. They represent the income potential of the property. As such, they are valuable and should be carefully protected. If the leases were to be lost, stolen, or destroyed, you would have difficulty duplicating these records; and the job of enforcement and tracking would become much more onerous. Daily references to lease information are usually handled via computer without the need to retrieve the actual document. Managers generally maintain the original leases in locked, fire-resistant cabinets. The permanent, active-lease file is usually set up by building, and then by unit number within that building, not by an alphabetized resident list. Files are organized in this fashion to provide a complete and permanent record for each unit. A cross-index file is usually generated to facilitate locating a particular person's lease. As leases expire and are replaced with new ones, the outdated leases are kept in a less-secure fashion in alphabetical order. Inquiries involving expired leases are almost always initiated with the name of the resident rather than the unit identification. The lease documents are the property of the owner, and they must be turned over to the owner when they are requested. Laws vary regarding the length of time one must hold leases; it is common to hold them for at least five years after expiration.

Warranties and Owner's Manuals.   Property managers and, more specifically, site managers, end up with sizeable collections of warranties and owner's manuals. These documents may not be needed for many years, but they are valuable and must be protected. For example, a new roof may carry a 10- or even a 20-year warranty. Many air-conditioning compressors or refrigeration units come with a 5-year or longer warranty; and sealed window units frequently have long warranty periods. Virtually every pump, motor, and appliance comes with some sort of factory warranty. Sometimes the manufacturer can determine age by the model or serial number, but you should not count on that always working. Frequently, the warranty period is extended when delays are incurred in finishing construction, but you will need the paperwork to help prove a claim.

When you buy a new device, it is expected to work, or you will quickly demand repair or replacement. When a problem develops shortly after purchase it is easy to remember where you bought it and who the sales representative was. As time passes, memories fade, and the process of securing a repair or replacement becomes increasingly complicated. When a breakdown occurs and you have the warranty and owner's manual filed in a safe place, you will be several steps ahead of the game. Top managers guard these reference materials carefully and make sure they are transferred with the property if there is a sale or management transition.

Plans and Occupancy Certificates.   When a building is under construction, almost everyone seems to have a set of plans *(working* or *construction drawings)* and specifications. As the years slip by, the sets of plans become more and more tattered as they are moved to different locations. A complete set of plans is often heavy, certainly bulky, and rarely fits in a standard file cabinet. It is, however, very valuable; and it should be protected and not stored behind a door or sent to the maintenance area. The need for plans will become apparent later in the building's life when renovation, retrofitting, or replacement of some hidden, but major, mechanical item must be undertaken. As the manager, you should do your part to protect the original drawings.

Occupancy certificates or zoning documents are other examples of papers that have a way of getting lost. Preserving these papers in a permanent file can save countless hours in later years.

Contracts.   Operating an apartment building means removing trash, exterminating bugs, cleaning windows, keeping up the grounds, and maintaining complicated machinery. These activities usually involve outside vendors, and that means contracts and letters of agreement. Having access to these documents can avoid misunderstandings. They have legal significance, and they are binding on the owner of the property. Contracts need to be filed for safekeeping, even after the contract period has passed. They belong to the owner and should be turned over to the owner if there is a transition in the property's management.

Correspondence and Memos to the File.   Apartment management involves a great deal of letter writing to a wide audience, including owners, residents (future, present, and past), neighbors, bankers, insurance carriers, governmental agencies, and vendors. Most agents choose to file correspondence by property. You should use a system that is consistent and will facilitate retrieval of the documents you file.

Memos to the file are an important part of record keeping. The society we live in is litigious, and our minds are simply not capable of recalling exactly what was said or agreed upon during a discussion. Whenever a situation shows any potential for developing a misunderstanding in the future, write a memo that records your understanding of the circumstances; then file the memo away for future reference. You will never have a clearer understanding of a conversation or negotiation than you do in the moments immediately following it. Memos to the file require an additional time commitment—a burden considering the number of activities that you must pack into each day—but such memos are essential if you are to be in a position to defend yourself if a problem does occur. In fact, many top professionals make a regular habit of recording the highlights of virtually every discussion they have in a chronological diary maintained in a binder or steno pad. These diaries are then labeled with the starting and ending dates and filed for future reference. Without such a record, you may find yourself defenseless in a situation that develops years after the fact.

Insurance Policies.   As noted in Chapter 14, the managing agent will probably inherit the job of maintaining the property's insurance policies. Most managers keep insurance documents under lock and key in fire-resistant cabinets. This includes the policies that are in effect as well as those that have recently expired. The responsibility that goes with keeping the policies includes tracking policy expirations and alerting the owner to upcoming renewals. The manager who maintains the insurance records will have a difficult time dodging some level of liability in the event that a loss occurs and the applicable policy has been allowed to go unrenewed. *Tickler files* used to remind you of crucial dates must be unfailing when it comes to insurance policy expirations.

Certificates of insurance collected from contractors should also be retained in a file, and a tickler file of expiration dates should be maintained.

Property Taxes.   Real estate and personal property taxes are commonly called ad valorem taxes. An *ad valorem* tax means "according to value" or "according to worth" (of the property), as opposed to an income tax, which is "according to income."

In some cases, real estate taxes are the largest single item of expense for the buildings being managed. Proper record keeping requires the maintenance of a separate tax file for each property. This file should contain the following information:

- A legal description of the property.
- The permanent tax identification number.
- Information concerning the valuation of the land and the building.
- Timetables and procedures for handling assessments.
- History of the tax rate to the present day.
- Name, address, and telephone number of the tax attorney assigned to the property.
- Copies of paid tax bills.
- Special assessments and other taxes.
- Correspondence regarding protests, appeals, and complaints.

In addition to the permanent tax file, a tickler file is also needed as a reminder of approaching payment and protest dates. As managing agent, you are obligated to make sure that real estate taxes are paid whether or not you receive a bill. If you do not get a bill, it is your obligation to find out what is wrong. When you do receive the tax bill, check carefully to see that it applies to your property.

Some localities also collect personal property tax and sales tax on rents. If this is true in your area, you must set up and maintain a record of payments made and returns filed.

Employee Time Records. As explained in Chapter 2, property employees (including most managerial help) are entitled to at least the minimum hourly wage for the first 40 hours of the workweek and time-and-a-half for overtime. In effect, this makes all building personnel hourly employees, whether they are paid a salary or an hourly wage. Therefore, it is important to keep records of all time worked and to pay overtime when necessary.

A record system is initiated by giving each person a timecard each week. Have your employees fill in the hours worked each day, and then collect the cards at the end of the workweek (the cards should also be signed by the employees). Be sure to keep these cards on file and inspect the times before issuing payroll checks. If an employee works more than 40 hours in one workweek, overtime must be paid.

Actual time records are essential in any investigative hearings. The vast majority of Wage and Hour Law settlements are made on "proof of the record"—that is, what the timecards show. Without a card, it is your word against an employee's.

Canceled Checks, Deposit Receipts, and Copies of Paid Invoices. You should provide space and develop a system to preserve and retrieve records of rent payments, bank deposits, and invoices that you have paid on your clients' behalf. Five years is the minimum holding period. In a well-run management operation, there is little need to fall back on these records, but there will be situations when the recovery of these documents is crucial to solving a dispute or claim.

Backing Up Computer Records.   Almost all management records are generated and saved using computers. Because computers are so reliable, little thought is given to protecting the data stored in them. Every manual written about the business applications of computers stresses the importance of backing up your stored data. Most management operations arrange for remote backup and file storage, using private services and Internet hookups. As a minimum, you need to make regular data backups using high-capacity CDs or DVDs. These should *not* be stored near the machine that holds the original data. Owners, employees, residents, and vendors will usually have some patience with you after learning about a major breakdown, but that grace period rarely exceeds a day or two.

A Final Word

Apartment managers are expected to handle and be accountable for thousands of tasks each year and that includes processing large sums of other people's money. They need to do this predictably, efficiently, and accurately. Failing to do so can result in a shortened management career. You should take the time to think through and set up systems that will provide the needed paper trail while freeing you to take charge of the properties you manage.

Glossary

abandonment   A relinquishment of leased premises by the tenant before the lease expires without consent of the owner.

abatement   A reduction of rent, interest, or an amount due; also, any reduction in amount or intensity.

absorption rate   The amount of space of a particular property type that is leased compared to the amount of that same type of space available for lease within a certain geographic area over a given period of time, accounting for both construction of new space and demolition or removal from the market of existing space. Also, the rate at which a market can absorb space designed for a specific use. Absorption rate for rental apartments can be computed as follows:

	Units vacant at the beginning of the period
plus	units constructed new during the period
minus	units demolished during the period
minus	units vacant at the end of the period
equals	units absorbed during the period.

access control systems   Security measures designed to limit access to buildings and leased premises and to parking lots and garages. Specifically, electronic locks on doors that are released by entering a code using pushbuttons or a numeric keypad or by presenting a magnetic encoded card to a reading device. Keypads or card readers are installed in the door or adjacent to the door jamb.

accessibility   The quality or state of being reached, easily approached, or used as an entrance. An important component of the Americans with Disabilities Act is removal of barriers that limit or complicate access to buildings and areas of public accommodation by people with physical disabilities. More broadly, the law also requires accommodation to make facilities accessible for those who are hearing and vision impaired. See *Americans with Disabilities Act (ADA)*.

ACCREDITED MANAGEMENT ORGANIZATION® (AMO®)   An accreditation conferred by the Institute of Real Estate Management on real estate management firms that are

351

under the direction of a CERTIFIED PROPERTY MANAGER® and comply with stipulated requirements as to accounting procedures, performance, and protection of funds entrusted to them.

ACCREDITED RESIDENTIAL MANAGER® (ARM®)   A professional certification conferred by the Institute of Real Estate Management on individuals who meet specific standards of experience, ethics, and education. See also *CERTIFIED PROPERTY MANAGER®*.

accrual accounting   The method of accounting that involves entering amounts of income when they are earned and amounts of expense when they are incurred—even though the cash may not be received or paid. Compare *cash accounting*. In real estate management, it is common to account for items that repeat at regular intervals on a cash basis and those requiring accumulation of funds toward a large dollar payout (e.g., real estate taxes) on an accrual basis. This is referred to as *modified accrual accounting* or *modified cash-accrual accounting*.

actual cash value (ACV)   Insurance that pays a claim based on the purchase price of the item, usually allowing for depreciation because of age and use. Compare *replacement cost*.

addendum   A legal document that adds to or amends the terms of a written agreement, as a lease or management agreement; also called *amendment* or *rider*.

additional insured endorsement   An endorsement to an insurance policy of an insured party that names another individual or entity as an additional insured party. In real estate management, an endorsement to the building owner's insurance policy or policies that names the manager or managing agent as an additional insured party.

adjuster   In insurance, an individual employed by a property and/or casualty insurer to settle loss claims filed by insured parties on behalf of the insurance company; also called *insurance adjuster*. The adjuster investigates individual claims and makes recommendations to the insurance company regarding their settlement. See also *public adjuster*.

ad valorem tax.   A tax levied according to the value of the object taxed; a tax in proportion to the value. Most often refers to taxes levied by municipalities and counties against real property and personal property.

agent   A person authorized to transact some business or perform some act for another (the principal) within the limits of the authority bestowed by the latter. A *managing agent* is one who supervises the operation of a property on behalf of the owner in consideration of a management fee.

aggregate rent   The total or gross rent amount for the lease term.

agreed amount insurance   A policy under which a coinsurance clause is waived if the insured carries insurance in an agreed amount. The insurer then agrees to pay the face amount on the policy in the event of total loss of property covered or upon occurrence of a stated contingency.

all risk coverage   Insurance that covers losses caused by all perils except those specifically excluded in the policy contract; also called *special property coverage*.

amenities   Features that enhance and add to a property's desirability and perceived value. These might include: gated entry, clubhouse, pool, tennis court, relaxation garden.

Americans with Disabilities Act (ADA) of 1990   A federal law that prohibits discrimination in employment on the basis of disability and requires places of public accommodation and commercial facilities to be designed, constructed, and altered in compliance with specified accessibility standards. The accommodation portion of this law may apply to "common areas" of residential properties (e.g., rental offices).

ancillary income   See *unscheduled income.*

annual budget   A twelve-month estimate of income and expenses for a property. See also *operating budget.*

arbitration   The submitting of a matter in dispute to the judgment of one, two, or more disinterested persons called arbitrators, whose decision, called an award, is binding on the parties.

asset manager   One who is charged with supervising an owner's real estate assets at the investment level. In addition to real estate management responsibilities that include maximizing net operating income and property value, an asset manager may recommend or be responsible for or participate in property acquisition, development, and divestiture. An asset manager may have only superficial involvement with day-to-day operations at the site (e.g., supervision of personnel, property maintenance, tenant relations). Compare *property manager.*

assignment   The transfer of an interest in a bond, mortgage, lease, or other instrument, in writing.

assisted housing   Privately owned rental property that either receives government assistance in the form of mortgage insurance, a reduced mortgage interest rate, or tax incentives, or houses residents who receive some form of rental subsidy.

below market interest rate (BMIR)   A rate offered by a government agency (e.g., HUD) for mortgage insurance on certain types of housing.

betterment   Improvements upon real property other than mere repairs.

blanket policy   An insurance policy covering all of a specified quantity or class of property, or a variety of risks, or both.

budget   An itemized estimate of income and expenses over a specific time period for a particular property, project, or institution. See also *annual budget; operating budget.*

budget variance   The differences between projected and actual amounts of income and expenses. Higher income and lower expenditures than expected constitute favorable variances, while lower income and higher expenditures are reported as unfavorable variances. Usually a component of the monthly management report sent to ownership.

cannibalization   To strip equipment or housing units of parts for use in other equipment or units to help keep the latter in service.

capital expenditure   Spending on capital assets, such as major improvements, large equipment, additions to buildings, buildings themselves, and land.

capital improvement   A structural addition or betterment to real property other than a repair or replacement; also, the use of capital for a betterment that did not exist before.

capitalization rate   A rate of return used to estimate a property's value based on that property's net operating income (NOI). This rate is based on the rates of return prevalent in the marketplace for similar properties and intended to reflect the investment risk associated with a particular property. It is derived from market data on similar, recent, sales (NOI ÷ property value/sales price = capitalization rate) or from calculations based on expected returns to debt and equity. Also called *cap rate.*

cash accounting   The method of accounting that recognizes income and expenses when money is received or paid. Compare *accrual accounting.*

cash flow   The amount of cash available after all payments have been made for operating expenses and mortgage principal and interest.

cash-on-cash return   A measure of the productivity of an investor's initial investment that compares the yearly cash flow of a property with its initial investment base: cash flow ÷ initial investment base; sometimes also called *return on equity.* The result is given as a percentage.

certificate of occupancy   A document issued by an appropriate governmental agency certifying that the premises (new construction, rehabilitation, alterations) complies with local building codes and/or zoning ordinances. Some jurisdictions require a certificate of occupancy for apartments based on inspection of units between each tenancy.

Certified Apartment Manager (CAM)   A professional designation conferred by the National Apartment Association (NAA) on apartment managers who have demonstrated a level of experience and proficiency.

Certified Property Manager® (CPM®)   A professional designation conferred by the Institute of Real Estate Management on individuals who distinguish themselves in the areas of education, experience, and ethics in property management. See also *Accredited Residential Manager®.*

chart of accounts   A classification or arrangement of account items by type of income or expense (e.g., rent, advertising, insurance, maintenance), as well as assets and liabilities, accounts receivable, and accounts payable.

coinsurance   An insurance option under which the insured (e.g., the property owner) is obligated to maintain insurance coverage at a stipulated level (e.g., 80 percent of the property's value) in order to receive the full value up to the limits of the policy in case of a loss, in exchange for a lowered premium rate. (Coverage is based on actual cash value of the improvements, which reflects a deduction for depreciation.) Failure to maintain that level of insurance coverage will reduce the amount reimbursed (in proportion to the property value). In the event of a loss, the insured shares in losses in proportion to the amount that the insurance coverage was *less* than the required percentage. See also *actual cash value.*

collateral   Security given as a pledge for the fulfillment of an obligation.

collateral materials   As applied to advertising and promotion, includes printed items such as brochures, leaflets, floor plans, and posters as well as photographs, lapel pins, book matches, etc.

commingle   To mix or combine; combining the money of more than one person or entity into a common fund is *commingling* of funds. (A prohibited practice in real estate.)

common interest realty association (CIRA)   A term commonly used by accountants and real estate managers to describe real estate that is operated for the mutual benefit of the owners. Condominiums, cooperatives, townhouses, zero-lot-line homes, and manor homes are the more popular examples.

comparison grid   A form used to compare the features of a property with those of other properties in the same market that are similar in size and use. The form lists features and amenities of the properties in a column at the left and includes columns to identify the characteristics of the subject property and to evaluate those same characteristics in the comparable properties. The user usually also assigns a value to each item, an estimate of how much additional rent a tenant might willingly pay to have the feature. For rental apartments, a comparison grid should be completed for each different type and size of apartment. Usual practice is to identify at least three comparable properties. The form is often used in determining a market rent for the subject property and usually included as part of a management plan.

comparison grid analysis   A method of price analysis in which the features of a subject property are compared to similar features in three or more comparable properties in the same market. The price (or rent) for each comparable property helps to determine an appropriate price (or rent) for the subject. This method involves assigning values for different attributes such as square footage, amenities, parking, floor and window treatments, age, location, and view. In making a rent comparison for rental apartments, features are compared for a specific type or size of unit (e.g., one-bedroom apartments). The process should take market trends into consideration and is obviously subjective. Each comparable property is compared to the subject, feature by feature. When the feature being examined is superior in the comparable property, the comparable rent should be reduced by the amount that a particular feature is worth in the marketplace. When the feature being examined is superior in the subject property, the comparable rent should be appropriately increased. Rent for the subject property is determined by adding up the adjustments to the rent of each comparable and then either averaging the adjusted rents or using the final rent of the comparable that has had the fewest adjustments (because this comparable is most like the subject property).

condemnation   The taking of private property for public use; also, the official act to terminate the use of real property for nonconformance with governmental regulations or because of hazards to public health and safety.

condemnation clause   A provision in a lease stating the agreed rights, privileges, and limitations of the owner and tenant, respectively, in the event of the taking of the subject property for public use.

condominium   Outright or fee ownership of an individual unit within a multiple-unit structure along with a prorated share of the undivided ownership of the land and common areas.

condominium association   A private, usually not-for-profit corporation comprised of the unit owners of a condominium that is responsible for the operation of the condominium community. The operation of a condominium association is governed by legal documents known as the declaration, bylaws, and articles of incorporation.

Consumer Price Index (CPI)   A way of measuring consumer purchasing power by comparing the current costs of goods and services to those of a selected base period (currently 1982–1984). Sometimes used as a reference point for rent escalations as a measure of inflation. The CPI is published monthly by the U.S. Department of Labor, Bureau of Labor Statistics.

contract   An agreement entered into by two or more persons which creates an obligation to do (or not do) a particular thing. The document that serves as proof of such an obligation. The essentials of a contract are legally competent parties, the obligation created between them, consideration or compensation (e.g., a fee), and mutuality of agreement. Examples in real estate management include management agreements, leases, and maintenance service agreements related to building systems and equipment.

contract rent   The rent stipulated in an existing lease, which may differ from the economic or market rent. See also *market rent; street rent.*

conversion ratio   The number of prospect contacts in a defined period compared to the number of leases that result from those contacts. For example, if 20 prospects visit a property, resulting in 4 leases, the conversion ratio would be 5:1. This may also be expressed as a percentage: 1:5 = 20%.

cooperative   Ownership of a share or shares of stock in a corporation that holds the title to a multiple-unit residential structure; shareholders do not own their units outright but have the right to occupy them.

corporation   A legal entity that is chartered by a state and treated by courts as an individual entity with the ability to buy, sell, sue, and be sued separate and distinct from the persons who own its stock.

credit score   A numerical value that measures the relative degree of risk of a potential borrower. A credit score takes into account payment history, amounts owed, length of time credit has been established, acquisition of new credit, and types of credit established (credit cards, installment loans, mortgage, etc.).

curb appeal   General cleanliness, neatness, and attractiveness of a building as exemplified by the appearance of the exterior and grounds and the general level of housekeeping. The aesthetic image and appearance projected by a property; the first impression it creates.

death clause   A special clause in a lease that provides for termination of the lease before its expiration date in the event of the tenant's death.

debt service   Regular payments of the principal and interest on a loan.

deferred maintenance   Ordinary maintenance of a building that, because it has not been performed, negatively affects the use, occupancy, and value of the property. Also, an amount needed for repairs, restoration, or rehabilitation of an asset (e.g., real property) but not yet expended.

degree-day   A unit that represents one degree difference in the mean outdoor temperature for one day. Temperatures above 65° F represent *cooling degree-days;* those below 65° F represent *heating degree-days.*

demographics   The statistical analysis of populations, using information derived primarily from census records, including overall population size, density, and distribution, birth and death rates, and the impact of inmigration and outmigration. Also included are age, gender, nationality, religion, education, occupation, and income characteristics of people who live in a geographically defined area. Used to characterize discrete markets. Residential property owners and managers are also interested in such concurrent data as household size, numbers of children and their ages, and levels of homeownership because they relate to requirements for living space in the form of rental apartments.

Department of Housing and Urban Development (HUD)   See *U.S. Department of Housing and Urban Development.*

depreciation   Loss of value due to all causes, usually considered to include: (1) physical deterioration (ordinary wear and tear), (2) functional depreciation, and (3) economic obsolescence; see also *obsolescence.* The tax deduction that allows for exhaustion of property; also called *cost recovery.*

directors' and officers' liability insurance   Protection against financial loss arising out of alleged errors in judgment, breaches of duty, and wrongful acts of a board of directors and/or officers in carrying out their prescribed duties. A recommended coverage for condominium associations.

disability   With respect to a person, a physical or mental impairment that substantially limits one or more major life activities, a record of such an impairment, or being regarded as having such an impairment. Further defined as such a condition which is expected to be of long, continued, and indefinite duration.

discrimination   Unfair treatment or denial of normal services or privileges to a person or persons because of their skin color, race, national origin, or religion. Sex, disability, and familial status are also protected classes in regard to some types of discrimination. See also *Americans with Disabilities Act (ADA); fair housing laws.*

economic life   The number of years during which a building will continue to produce an acceptable yield.

economic vacancy   Commonly used in rental housing to mean all vacant units that are not producing income. In addition to physical vacancies, this includes units that are not available for lease (e.g., apartments used as models or offices, staff apartments, cannibalized units) as well as leased units that are not yet occupied and occupied units that are not producing rent (i.e., delinquencies); usually expressed as a percentage of the total number of units.

effective gross income   The total amount of income actually collected during a reporting period; the gross receipts of a property. Gross potential rental income *less* vacancy and collection losses *plus* miscellaneous or unscheduled income.

efficiency apartment   A small, bedroomless apartment usually with a less-than-standard-size kitchen. See also *studio apartment.*

efficiency factor   The percentage of gross building area that is actually rentable.

$$\frac{\text{Net Rentable Area}}{\text{Gross Building Area}} = \text{Efficiency Factor}$$

electronic funds transfer (EFT)   Movement of funds between banking institutions and between individual accounts via computer transfer of credits rather than using a check or other payment instrument. Direct deposit is commonly handled electronically. Individual consumers can also use computer software to "bank online," transferring money from their personal accounts to the accounts of various creditors (e.g., utility, credit card, and rent payments).

e-mail   Short for electronic mail. Communication via the Internet.

eminent domain   The right of a government or municipal quasi-public body to acquire private property for public use through a court action called condemnation in which the court determines that the use is a public use and determines the price or compensation to be paid to the owner.

employee handbook   A compilation of a company's employment policies and procedures. It is advisable to include a notice that such handbook does not constitute a set of promises or an employment contract. Depending on state law, it might include a statement that employment is at the will of the company, and that the company or the employee may terminate the employment at any time for any reason. To protect the employer's interests, the contents of such a handbook should be reviewed by an attorney.

employment practices liability   A form of liability insurance to protect against employee claims arising from sexual harassment, wrongful discharge, discrimination, and disability suits.

empty-nesters   Persons whose children have left home permanently.

endorsement   An attachment to an insurance policy that provides or excludes a specific coverage for a specific portion or element of a property; also called a *rider*.

Environmental Protection Agency (EPA)   An independent agency of the U.S. government established in 1970 to enforce laws that preserve and protect the environment.

Equal Employment Opportunity Commission (EEOC)   A U.S. governmental body that enforces Title VII of the Civil Rights Act of 1964, which prohibits discrimination in the workplace.

errors and omissions (E&O) insurance   Insurance to protect against liabilities resulting from honest mistakes and oversights (no protection is provided in cases of gross negligence).

escalator clause   A clause in a contract, lease, or mortgage providing for increases in wages, rent, or interest based on fluctuations in certain economic indexes, costs, or taxes. Also called *rent escalator clause*.

escrow   An agreement that something of value (money, security, a deed) should be held in trust by a third party until certain conditions are met. Upon fulfillment of the specified conditions, the money or other item(s) in escrow is conveyed to the respective parties.

eviction   A legal process to reclaim possession of real estate from a tenant who has not performed under the agreed-upon terms. Eviction is a complex undertaking. The tenant may be sent a *notice to vacate* or *notice to quit* (i.e., legal notice requiring a tenant to remove himself or herself and all removable possessions from the premises and to surrender the premises to the owner). Action to obtain possession or repossession of real property which had been transferred from one party to another under a contract is referred to as *forcible detainer*. Failure of a tenant to move out at the end of a tenancy or following lawful eviction is *unlawful detainer*.
    Constructive eviction is the inability of a tenant to obtain or maintain possession because of conditions of a property that make occupancy hazardous or make the premises unfit for its intended use; to apply in a landlord-tenant dispute, the tenant must vacate the premises prematurely because of the conditions. *Retaliatory eviction* is a requirement by the landlord that a tenant vacate leased premises in response to a complaint from the tenant concerning the condition of the building or other reasons; landlord-tenant laws in many states forbid such evictions.

eviction notice   A written notice to a tenant to cure a breach of the lease immediately or vacate the premises within a specified period. Also called *demand to pay or quit* or *demand for compliance or possession*.

exclusion   A provision in an insurance contract detailing perils that are not covered.

exculpate   To free from blame. Hold-harmless clauses are exculpatory.

Fair Credit Reporting Act (FCRA)   A federal law that gives people the right to see and correct their credit records at credit reporting bureaus. It also requires property managers to inform applicants if a credit bureau is contracted to investigate their credit and to identify the source of credit information that resulted in their being denied a lease.

Fair Debt Collection Practices Act (FDCPA) A federal law that created a series of guidelines for debt collectors to follow and was designed to prevent collection agencies from harassing debtors. The law was later expanded to include any organization that collects consumer debt (including property managers). The law is governed and regulated by the Federal Trade Commission (FTC).

fair housing laws Any law that prohibits discrimination against people seeking housing. There are federal, state, and local fair housing laws. Specifically, Title VIII of the Civil Rights Act of 1968 prohibits discrimination in the sale or rental of housing based on race, color, religion, national origin, or sex; the *Fair Housing Amendments Act* of 1988 further prohibits discrimination on the basis of familial status (children) or physical or mental disability.

Fair Labor Standards Act (FLSA) The federal law that establishes minimum wages per hour and maximum hours of work. It also provides that employees who work in excess of 40 hours per week are to be paid one and one-half times their regular hourly wage. This is frequently referred to as *Wage and Hour Law*.

familial status The presence in a household of children under age 18 living with parents or guardians, pregnant women, or people seeking custody of children under age 18.

family Most commonly used in referring to a group of persons consisting of parents (father and mother) and their children. A group of blood relatives (extended family). Compare *household*.

Federal Housing Administration (FHA) An agency—part of the U.S. Department of Housing and Urban Development (HUD)—that administers a variety of housing loan programs.

fidelity bond A casualty insurance guaranteeing one individual against financial loss that might result from dishonest acts of another specific individual.

fiduciary One charged with a relationship of trust and confidence, as between a principal and agent, trustee and beneficiary, or attorney and client.

financing The availability, amount, and terms under which money may be borrowed to assist in the purchase of real property and using the property itself as the security for such borrowing.

fixture An article of personal property attached permanently to a building or to land so that it becomes part of the real estate.

floor plan Drawings showing the floor layout of a building and including room sizes and their interrelationships. The arrangement of the rooms on a single floor of a building, or within a specific apartment, including walls, windows, and doors.

general partnership The business activity of two or more persons who agree to pool capital, talents, and other assets according to some agreed-to formula, and similarly to divide profits and losses, and to commit the partnership to certain obligations. General partners assume unlimited liability. Compare *limited partnership*.

gentrification Inmigration of middle and upper income people into a deteriorating or recently renewed area so they gradually displace lower income residents. A form of urban neighborhood renewal.

government-assisted housing   Residential rental property in which the lessor (landlord) receives part of the rent payment from a governmental body, either directly from the government on behalf of a resident or indirectly from a grant to a public housing authority, or from the residents in the form of a voucher. Compare *subsidized housing.*

graduated rent   Rent that has two or more levels in the same lease term.

gross building area   Area equal to length times width of the building(s) times the number of living floors, expressed in square feet.

gross potential rental income   The sum of the rental rates of all spaces available to be rented in a property, regardless of occupancy. The maximum amount of rent a property can produce. Also called *gross possible rental income.*

gross receipts   The total cash income from all sources during a specific period of time such as monthly or annually.

group relamping   Systematic replacement of all lamps in a building or lighting system after a specific period, based on when the lamps were installed and the rated life for the type of lamp, as opposed to replacing individual lamps as they burn out.

guarantor   One who agrees to assume responsibility for a financial obligation of another in the event the other person cannot perform (e.g., payment of rent under a lease).

guest   In apartments, a nonresident who stays in a resident's private dwelling (with that resident's consent) for one or more nights. See also *visitor.*

habitability   A state of being fit for occupancy (e.g., sanitary, safe, in compliance with applicable codes). Under landlord-tenant law, the landlord is bound by an implied warranty of habitability, by which he/she warrants the condition of the leased premises at the time the tenant takes possession and during the period of tenancy.

half-bath   A bathroom with a basin and toilet but no bathing facilities such as a tub or shower.

hazardous materials   Any of a variety of gaseous, liquid, or solid materials that can pose a potential hazard (e.g., flammability, combustibility, toxicity, corrosivity) to persons who are exposed to them or damage property in the event of a spill. Some types of materials have been declared as specific hazards by federal, state, or local laws.

head rent   Rent charged to a person or persons occupying the same premises independently of each other.

heating, ventilating, and air-conditioning (HVAC) system   The combination of equipment and ductwork for producing, regulating, and distributing heat, refrigeration, and fresh air throughout a building.

highest and best use   That use of real property which will produce the highest property value and develop a site to its fullest economic potential. The four criteria for highest and best use are: physical possibility, legal permissibility, financial feasibility, and maximum profitability.

high-rise apartment building   A multiple-unit dwelling that is ten or more stories in height.

hold harmless   A declaration that one is not liable for things beyond his/her control. A clause in contracts (e.g., management agreements) through which one party assumes liability inherent in a situation and thereby eliminates the liability of the other party. See also *indemnification*.

holdover tenancy   A situation in which a tenant retains possession of leased premises after the lease has expired, and the landlord, by continuing to accept rent from the tenant, thereby agrees to the tenant's continued occupancy as defined by state law.

host liquor liability insurance   Protection against loss arising out of the insured party's legal responsibility as a result of an accident attributed to the use of liquor dispensed (but not sold) on the premises at functions incidental to the insured party's business. Recommended coverage for properties where liquor may be served in the common areas of the premises. May be purchased to cover specific events.

household   All persons, related or not, who occupy a housing unit. Compare *family*.

housekeeping   The regular duties involved in keeping a property clean and in good order. Also used in referring to the level of care given to a leased space by the occupant.

Immigration Reform and Control Act (IRCA)   Federal law requiring employers to verify an employee's identity and eligibility to work in the United States at the time of employment. Employees must complete Immigration and Naturalization Service (INS) form I-9.

income capitalization approach   The process of estimating the value of an income-producing property by capitalization of the annual net income expected to be produced by the property during its remaining useful life. See also *capitalization rate*.

independent contractor   A person who contracts to do work for others by using his/her own methods and without being under the control of the other person(s) regarding how and when the work should be done. Unlike an employee, an independent contractor is responsible for paying all expenses including income and Social Security taxes, receives no employee benefits, and is not covered by workers' compensation.

inflation   An economic condition occurring when the money supply increases in relation to the amount of goods available, resulting in substantial and continuing increases in prices. Inflation is associated with increasing wages and costs and decreasing purchasing power.

inspection checklist   A printed form used when property managers or other staff members inspect a building and its leased spaces. Usually set up in a grid format with the items to be inspected being listed with space provided to note the condition of the item and identify repair work to be done. Some forms include columns that facilitate scheduling of the work and estimating repair costs.

Institute of Real Estate Management (IREM®)   A professional association of men and women who meet established standards of experience, education, and ethics with the objective of continually improving their respective managerial skills by mutual education and exchange of ideas and experiences. The Institute is affiliated with the National Association of REALTORS®.

insured   The person or other entity for whom insurance is provided. The person whose property, life, or physical well-being is covered by insurance.

interest   A share in the ownership of property; a payment for the use of money borrowed.

Internet   A worldwide open information network of computer links that allows users to access and search databases, advertise services, and deliver messages.

IRV formula   A basic equation in real estate that relates three variables—income, rate, value—to calculate a property's value. As a formula, its basic form is Income ÷ Rate = Value. The investor's equation—the income-to-value ratio—is the same terms, rearranged (income ÷ value = rate of return).

joint venture   An association of two or more persons or businesses to carry out a single business enterprise for profit, for which purpose they combine their assets and agree to share the risks. In real estate, a combination of owners and money partners may be involved in a joint venture.

landlord-tenant law   Laws enacted by various jurisdictions (at the state or local level) that regulate the relationship between landlord and tenant.

landscaping   The improvements made to and maintenance done on a specific parcel of land. Landscaping may involve contouring the land; planting grass, flowers, trees, and shrubs; and installing items to enhance the appearance or utility of the land (e.g., a fountain, a pathway). Regular upkeep (cutting grass, trimming hedges, weeding, picking up litter, etc.) is also considered landscaping.

late fee   A fee charged for late payment of rent.

late notice   Notification that payment of rent is past due. While sometimes handled informally, such notification may be provided for specifically in a lease. When that is the case, the usual requirement is that notice be presented in writing to a specified address and include a statement of what additional charges (i.e., late fee) apply if the delinquency is not cured immediately (or within a specified time period).

laws of supply and demand   In relation to pricing, when demand exceeds supply, prices rise. If supply exceeds demand, prices drop. Prices are stable when supply equals demand. In regard to rental real estate, when demand exceeds supply, absorption of space is favorable (vacancy decreases); when supply exceeds demand, absorption is unfavorable. Stabilization occurs when landlords are able to increase rents in parallel with inflation rates.

lease   A contract for the possession of a landowner's land or property for a stipulated period of time in return for the payment of rent or other consideration by the tenant; sometimes called an *occupancy agreement.*

lease extension agreement   A written and executed agreement extending the lease term beyond the expiration date and stating the rental amount for the new term.

lease renewal   The process of encouraging qualified residents to renew their leases.

leasing agent   The individual in a real estate brokerage firm (or management organization or development company) who is directly responsible for renting space in assigned properties. In some states, leasing agents must have a real estate license unless they are employed directly by the property owner. Residential leasing agents are often called *leasing consultants.*

legal description   The description of real property by metes and bounds, lot and block numbers of a recorded plat, or government survey, including any easement or reservation, used to locate and identify a particular parcel of land in legal instruments (e.g., leases, sale/purchase contracts).

liability insurance   Insurance protection against claims arising out of injury or death of people or physical or financial damage to other people's property that is a consequence of an incident occurring on or about an owner's property.

limited liability company (LLC)   Created by state statute, a business ownership form that functions like a corporation (its members are protected from liability) but for income tax purposes is classified as a partnership. Income and expenses flow through to the individual members. The arrangement offers considerable flexibility in its organization and structure.

limited partnership (LP)   A partnership arrangement in which the liability of certain partners is limited to the amount of their investment. Limited partnerships are managed and operated by one or more general partners whose liability is not limited; *limited partners* have no voice in management. Compare *general partnership*.

location   Commonly used in real estate to refer to the comparative advantages of one site over another in consideration of such factors as transportation, convenience, social benefits, specific use, and anticipated pattern of change.

low-income household   A household whose annual income is 80 percent or less of median income for the jurisdiction as defined by HUD and adjusted for household size by HUD.

low-rise apartment building   Multiple-unit residential dwelling of four or fewer stories.

majority   The age set by state law at which individuals have the legal right to manage their own affairs and are responsible for their own actions. The age of majority varies from state to state. See also *minor*.

management agreement   A contractual arrangement between the owner(s) of a property and the designated managing agent, describing the duties and establishing the authority of the agent and detailing the responsibilities, rights, and obligations of both agent and owner(s).

management company   A real estate organization that specializes in the professional management of real properties for others as a gainful occupation; a *management firm*.

management fee   The monetary consideration paid monthly or otherwise for the performance of management duties, usually defined in the management agreement as a percentage of the gross receipts (actual collections less security deposits) of the property and/or as a minimum monthly amount.

management plan   The fundamental document for the operation of a property that represents a statement of facts, objectives, and policies and details how the property is to be operated during the coming years. Such a plan usually includes the appropriate budgets.

marketing   In apartment leasing, methods used to attract new renters and to retain current residents.

market rent   Rent that a property is capable of yielding if leased under prevailing market conditions. Also, the amount that comparable space (i.e., an apartment unit of a particular type and size) would command in a competitive market.

mid-rise apartment building   A multiple-unit dwelling ranging from five to nine stories tall.

minor   One who has not reached the age set by state law to be legally recognized as an adult; therefore, one not legally responsible for contracting debts or signing contracts. See also *majority*.

miscellaneous income   See *unscheduled income*.

month-to-month tenancy   An agreement to rent or lease for consecutive and continuing monthly periods until terminated by proper prior notice by either the landlord or the tenant.

mortgage   A pledge of real property conveyed by a written instrument as security for the payment of a debt. Often used in referring to the loan itself, the debt instrument usually creates a *lien* against the property (i.e., the property becomes security for the debt owed) until the debt has been paid in full. The lender in a mortgage loan transaction is the *mortgagee;* the borrower is the *mortgagor.*

move-in checklist   An inspection checklist used to document the condition of an apartment at the time a new resident moves in. Usual practice is for a member of the management staff to conduct this inspection in the presence of the resident and for both management and resident to sign the completed form acknowledging its accuracy. This will be compared to a *move-out checklist* to determine if there has been any excessive damage (beyond normal wear and tear) that the resident is responsible for repairing.

move-out checklist   An inspection checklist used to document the condition of an apartment at the time a resident moves out. This is compared to a previously used *move-in checklist* to identify repairs to be made and responsibility for the cost of such repairs. Often combined with the former as a *move-in/move-out checklist* that facilitates comparison of the before and after condition. Here again, usual practice is to have the management person and the resident sign the completed form and acknowledge responsibility for repair costs to be deducted from the resident's security deposit.

named insured   The entity or entities specifically identified in an insurance contract as the insured parties. One of several parties provided coverage, which may include others in addition to the purchaser of the policy. Managing agents are automatically included as a named insured.

negligence   Failure to use the level of care a reasonable and prudent person would use under the same circumstances, characterized by inattention, inadvertence, and thoughtlessness that results in harm. Failure to exercise reasonable care which, though not accompanied by harmful intent, directly results in an injury to an innocent party or damage to property. A person (e.g., a property manager) or a business entity (e.g., a property management company) can be held liable for negligent acts.

neighborhood   An area within which there are common characteristics of population and land use. A district or locality, often defined by referring to its character or inhabitants. In real estate market analysis, a section of a larger region or market area, within which buildings generally compete with one another for residents. The area surrounding and adjacent to a property, especially as it is characterized by similarity of demographic, economic, and other parameters.

net operating income (NOI)   Total collections (gross receipts) *less* operating expenses; may be calculated on an annual or a monthly basis. More broadly, cash available after all operating expenses have been deducted from collected income and before debt service and capital expenses have been deducted.

nonsufficient funds (NSF)   Usually used as the acronym in referring to a check drawn on a bank account that does not contain enough cash to cover the draft; an NSF check. Also sometimes called *insufficient funds*.

nonyield space   Space that is essential to the operation of a building but does not produce direct revenue. See also *efficiency factor*.

obsolescence   Generally speaking, a loss of value brought about by a change in design, technology, taste, or demand. *Physical obsolescence* (deterioration) is a result of aging (wear and tear) or deferred maintenance. *Functional obsolescence* is a condition of a property related to its design or use. *Economic obsolescence* is an inability to generate enough income to offset operating expenses, usually due to conditions external to the property (changes in populations and/or land uses, legislation, etc.). Also used in referring to the process by which property loses its economic usefulness to the owner/taxpayer due to causes other than physical deterioration (e.g., technological advancements, changes in public taste); an element of depreciation.

occupancy agreement   See *lease*.

occupancy report   A statement of the number of occupied units in a building and, correspondingly, the number of non-revenue-producing units (usually generated every Monday and commonly referred to as the Monday Report). A usual component of the periodic management report to ownership.

Occupational Safety and Health Act (OSHA)   A law requiring employers to comply with job safety and health standards issued by the U.S. Department of Labor.

off-site management   Management of a property by persons not residing or keeping office hours at the subject property.

on-site manager   See *resident manager*.

operating budget   A listing of all anticipated income from and expenses of operating a property, usually projected on an annual basis. While funds for accumulation of reserves would be deducted from net operating income (NOI) in an operating budget, actual expenditures of such reserve funds would be anticipated in a capital budget.

operating expenses   In real estate, the expenditures for real estate taxes, salaries, insurance, maintenance, utilities, and similar items paid in connection with the operation of a rental property that are properly charged against income. More broadly, all expenditures made in connection with operating a property with the exception of debt service, capital reserves (and/or capital expenditures), and income taxes.

operating reserves   Funds set aside for the payment of a major expense.

operations manual   An authoritative collection of information that describes the organization and its goals, explains policies that guide its operations, outlines specific procedures for implementing those policies on a day-to-day basis, assigns responsibility for performing various functions, and contains the various documents (forms) for performing the work; also called *standard operating procedures manual*. In real estate management, an operations manual is usually developed to guide the management and business operations of a specific property.

option   The right to purchase or lease something at a future date for a specified price and terms; the right may or may not be exercised at the option holder's (optionee's) discretion. Options may be received or purchased. In a lease, the right to obtain a specific condition within a specified time (e.g., to renew at the same or a pre-agreed rate when the lease term expires; to cancel the lease under certain circumstances). Options are often incorporated in the lease as an addendum.

owner, landlord, and tenant (OLT) liability Insurance covering claims against a property owner, a landlord, or a tenant arising from personal injury to a person or persons in or about a subject property and including the improvements on the land and any other contiguous areas for which the insured is legally responsible, such as sidewalks. This coverage is generally included in "all risk" policies.

peaceful enjoyment A lease provision, often only implied, which grants the tenant the right of possession of the leased premises without illegal or unreasonable interference by the landlord or undue disturbance by others; also referred to as *quiet enjoyment.*

personal property Movable property belonging to an individual, family, or other entity that is not permanently affixed to real property, such as clothing, fixtures, and furnishings; distinguished from real property. In real estate, the furniture, blinds and drapes, office equipment, appliances, and other items that belong to the property owner apart from the land and the improvements to it. Also, the items owned outright by the tenant in leased premises.

pet agreement A lease addendum that authorizes a tenant to keep a specific pet on the premises as long as certain conditions are met. A pet agreement is actually a separate document that constitutes a license granted by the landlord to the tenant. As such, it can be revoked or canceled without affecting the lease itself.

physical vacancy The number of vacant units in a building or development that are available for rent, usually expressed numerically and/or as a percentage of the total number of units. See also *economic vacancy.*

principal In real estate, one who owns property. In real estate management, the property owner who contracts for the services of an agent. In finance, the amount of money that is borrowed in a loan as distinct from the interest on such loan; the original amount or remaining balance of a loan. Also, the original amount of capital invested. In law, the individual being represented in a business transaction by an agent authorized to do so.

professional liability insurance Insurance against a monetary loss caused by failure to meet a professional standard or resulting from negligent actions (e.g., malpractice). Policies that protect directors and officers of corporations are also available. See *directors' and officers' liability insurance.*

pro forma A projection of gross income, operating expenses, and net operating income of a property; a budget.

property management A professional activity in which someone other than the owner supervises the operation of a property according to the owner's objectives; also referred to as *real estate management.* The operation of income-producing real estate as a business, including leasing, rent collection, maintenance of the property, and general administration. Usually, this is performed by someone who acts as the owner's agent (i.e., a professional property manager).

property manager A knowledgeable professional who has the experience and skills to operate real estate and understands the fundamentals of business management. The person who supervises the day-to-day operation of a property, making sure it is properly leased, well maintained, competitive with other sites, and otherwise managed according to the owner's objectives. The chief operating officer or administrator of a particular property or group of properties.

protected class A group, usually a minority in the population, specifically protected against discrimination under the U.S. Civil Rights Act of 1964 and later amendments to that law. Protected classes include race, religion, color, national origin, and sex; in regard to housing, familial status and disability are also protected classes. Other protected classes may be created under state and local laws. See also *fair housing laws*. Color, race, national origin, sex, and disability are also protected classes in regard to employment; specific protections are delineated in the Civil Rights Acts of 1964/1968 and the Americans with Disabilities Act (ADA).

public adjuster The name commonly used to refer to the individual or company that represents the insured party in an insurance claim. See also *adjuster*.

Pullman kitchen A small non-walk-in kitchen, with appliances and equipment aligned in a row along a wall or in a small area. Named after the narrow kitchen areas on Pullman train cars.

purchase order (P.O.) Written authorization to an outside vendor to provide certain goods or services in a given amount, at a given price, to be delivered at a certain time and place. Purchase orders are usually preprinted, sequentially numbered forms with multiple copies to ensure that appropriate departments of the company have a record of all such transactions.

real estate Land; a portion of the earth's surface extending downward to the center of the earth and upward into space including all things permanently attached to the land by nature or by mankind; also, freehold estates in land.

real estate investment trust (REIT) An entity that sells shares of beneficial interest to investors and uses the funds to invest in real estate or mortgages. Real estate investment trusts must meet certain requirements such as a minimum number of investors and widely dispersed ownership. No corporate taxes need to be paid as long as a series of complex IRS qualifications are met. See also *shares of beneficial interest*.

recapture An income tax term describing money taken back or forfeited; a kind of tax penalty. For example, if a tax deduction was taken but does not meet all conditions, the deduction will be disallowed and the taxpayer will be required to pay tax on the income that had been offset by the deduction. This money is said to be recaptured by the taxing body.

recurring expenses Operating expenses that recur monthly or periodically, such as those for utilities, supplies, salaries, waste disposal services, insurance, and taxes.

recycling Minimizing the generation of waste by recovering usable materials that might otherwise be disposed. Also, the reprocessing of various materials (e.g., paper, glass, aluminum, and various types of plastic) into usable new products.

Registered in Apartment Management (RAM) A professional certification granted by the National Association of Home Builders (NAHB).

rentable area The combined rentable area of all dwelling units. The rentable area of a unit is calculated by multiplying length times width of the apartment, with no discounts for interior partitions, plumbing chases, and other small niches. Balconies, patios, and unheated porches are not included in these measurements. Sometimes called *net rentable area*.

rent control Laws that regulate rental rates, usually to limit the amount of rent increases and their frequency.

renters by choice   People who prefer to rent, either for flexibility, economic advantage, limited commitment, or freedom from home maintenance. Renters by choice include career professionals, senior citizens, and parents of grown children (empty-nesters).

renters by circumstance   Persons and households whose current situations require them to rent, at least on a temporary basis; also called *renters by necessity*. These are people who cannot afford to buy a home or are trying to save enough money for a downpayment, as well as students and people in changing circumstances.

renters' insurance   Insurance coverage for tenants' personal possessions, which are not covered by a landlord's insurance policies, including reimbursement of out-of-pocket costs if they cannot live in their rented unit.

rent loss   The deficiency increment resulting from vacancies, bad debts, etc., between total projected rental income (for a given period) and the actual rents collected or collectible.

rent roll   A list of each rental unit described by size and type and including the following information if the unit is rented: amount of monthly rent, tenant name, and lease expiration date; also called *rent schedule*. Rent received, date of receipt, period covered, and other related information for each individual tenant is recorded in a *rent ledger* or *tenant ledger*.

rent-up budget   Projection of income and expenses for a newly developed property; also called *lease-up budget*. Having such a separate budget allows the developer or property manager to account for the wide variances in income and expenses that occur before there is sufficient occupancy to stabilize its financial picture.

replacement cost   The estimated cost to replace or restore a building to its pre-existing condition and appearance (and in compliance with applicable current building codes); a common method of determining insurance coverage. In insurance, replacement cost coverage reimburses the total cost of rebuilding; no deductions are made for depreciation.

replacement cost coverage   Insurance to replace or restore a building or its contents to its pre-existing condition and appearance. Compare *actual cash value (ACV)*.

replacement reserves   Funds set aside for future repair and replacement of major building components (e.g., roof, HVAC system).

request for proposal (RFP)   Written specifications for services to be provided by a bidder, often including the scope of work and details of design and use and asking for specifics regarding materials, labor, pricing, delivery, and payment.

resident   One who lives (or resides) in a place. Referring to residential tenants as "residents" is preferred by many real estate professionals.

resident guidebook   Minimally, a compilation of house rules and other information apartment occupants need for ready reference; a *resident handbook*. Ideally, such a guidebook will inform residents of their basic rights and responsibilities, covering basic lease provisions as well as management's policies regarding use of supporting facilities (swimming pool, exercise room, laundry room), the keeping of pets, and requests for maintenance or other services.

Residential Lead-Based Paint Hazard Reduction Act   Federal law enacted in 1992 that requires all owners of residential properties built *before* 1978 to notify new renters and potential buyers about the presence of lead-based paint. New rules regarding particulars of disclosure came into effect in December 1996. Rental applicants and residents who renew leases must be given a government pamphlet on lead paint hazards, a disclosure form detailing lead paint hazards at the property, and any reports that describe lead paint hazards at the property.

resident manager An employee residing on site for the purpose of overseeing and administering the day-to-day building affairs in accordance with directions from the manager or owner; also called *on-site manager, site manager,* and *residential manager.*

resident organization See *tenant organization.*

resident profile A study and listing of the similar and dissimilar characteristics of the present occupants of a residential property; used in positioning the property in the market. May also be called *tenant profile.*

return on investment (ROI) The ratio of net operating income to the total investment amount, for a given time period, which provides a measure of the financial performance of the investment. A measure of profitability expressed as a percentage and calculated by comparing periodic income to the owner's equity in the property (income ÷ equity = % ROI). It can be calculated either before or after deduction of income tax. ROI measures overall effectiveness of management in generating profits from available assets; however, it does not consider the time value of money.

right of re-entry A common lease provision, subject to prevailing landlord-tenant laws, granting the right to inspect, maintain, update, and exhibit the unit for renting; sometimes called *right of access.*

risk management The process of controlling risks and managing losses. There are four methods of risk management: *Avoidance* is the act or practice of avoiding something or preventing its occurrence. *Control* involves actions or practices undertaken to reduce the frequency or severity of loss. *Retention* is acceptance of a certain amount of potential economic loss (rather than pay the cost of insurance premiums). *Transfer* involves shifting the burden of risk to a third party (i.e., an insurance provider who assumes the risk in return for payment of a premium).

seasonal rent Rent that is adjusted by season, often used in resort areas. *High season* is the busiest season at a resort area, when rental rates are highest; *low season* is an intermediate period (the months just before and after high season) that is differentiated from *off season* when demand is lowest.

security deposit A preset amount of money advanced by the tenant before occupancy and held by an owner or manager for a specific period to ensure the faithful performance of the lease terms by the tenant; also called *lease deposit.* (Local or state law may require the landlord to pay the tenant interest on the security deposit during the lease term and/or hold the money in an *escrow account.*) Part or all of the deposit may be retained to pay for rent owed, miscellaneous charges owed, unpaid utility bills, and damage to the leased space that exceeds normal wear and tear. Limitations on withholding may be imposed by local and state ordinances, which often also stipulate penalties for failing to return the security deposit in a timely manner.

self-service storage facilities A rental property comprising individual storage spaces with individual doors and locks, used for storage of personal property. Sometimes constructed as part of an apartment complex to provide supplementary storage that can be leased to residents or others for a fee.

service contract   An agreement to perform certain work, as to maintain specific operating systems (e.g., preventive maintenance of HVAC, elevators) or for general upkeep (e.g., janitorial or custodial maintenance), in exchange for specific compensation. Services may be contracted for a flat fee for a designated period or on a time and materials (T&M) basis (e.g., a rate per hour plus the cost of replacement parts).

service request   A form for documenting the specifics of a resident's request for maintenance work; sometimes combined with a work order form. A *work order* is a written form, letter, or other instrument for authorizing work to be performed. The completed form documents the nature of the work, where it was done, who performed it, and the materials used and time required to complete it.

shares of beneficial interest   Shares sold by real estate investment trusts (REITs), they are traded on the stock markets similar to corporate common stock. See also *real estate investment trust.*

shopper   A person who is commissioned to visit a property in the guise of a rental prospect and whose identity is unknown to the property staff. His or her assignment is to accurately report, in a written narrative, the rental experience (both positive and negative) for the purpose of improving future leasing presentations.

signature block   Usually the final section of a lease (or other contract) containing a statement that all parties have read and understand the lease (or contract), with space for signatures.

site manager   See *resident manager.*

site plan   A plan, prepared to scale, showing locations of buildings, roadways, parking areas, and other improvements.

special multi-peril (SMP) insurance policy   See *all risk coverage.*

specifications   A written description of equipment maintenance or other services that describes the scope of work, materials and methods to be employed, and other specifics used as a basis for estimating project or service costs. Also, a written description of construction work to be done that describes the kind and quality of materials to be used, the mode of construction (type and extent of work), and dimensions and other particulars that define the job as the basis for estimating costs.

spreadsheet   A table of numbers listed in columns and rows and related by formulas. Used in reference to computer software that creates such tables and automatically performs the calculations according to predetermined formulas.

street rent   The rental rate quoted to new prospects; also called *market rent.*

studio apartment   Commonly used term to describe an efficiency or bedroomless apartment. In certain areas, the term refers to a small apartment with two levels. See also *efficiency apartment.*

sublet   The leasing of part or all of the premises by a tenant to a third party for part or all of the tenant's remaining term.

subordination clause   A lease covenant in which the tenant agrees that the landlord may act on the tenant's behalf in certain legal matters, so long as it does not affect the tenant's right to possession.

subsidized housing   Usually privately owned rental property for which a portion of the return on the owner's investment may result from additional tax advantages granted for development, for leasing part of the property to residents who are eligible for housing subsidies, or for leasing to a local housing authority. The National

Housing Act, which has been amended substantially over time, includes provisions for subsidies to landlords via low mortgage rate loans and for payment of rent on behalf of qualified individuals. Compare *government-assisted housing.*

sundry income   See *unscheduled income.*

tenant   One who pays rent to occupy or gain possession of real estate. The estate or interest held is called a *tenancy.*

tenant organization   A group of tenants formed to use their collective powers against an owner to achieve certain goals such as improved conditions, expanded facilities, and lower rent.

tenant retention   A defined program that attempts to maintain harmony between tenants and management, often related to sound maintenance procedures; at a residential property, often called *resident retention.* In actual practice, a tenant retention program includes measurement of tenant satisfaction, often via written surveys, and efforts to encourage lease renewals by providing a superior product and better service.

term   A limited or defined period of time. The duration of a tenant's lease; the duration of a mortgage (e.g., a thirty-year term); the duration of a contract for services.

termination   The ending of a contract, usually when the conditions of the agreement have been carried out. Ending of an employee's employment; firing. Also used in referring to the process of voluntarily leaving a job.

term rent   A type of rent sometimes collected in resort areas for a specified term, usually the high season, and payable in full in advance. Also, the total amount of rent due over the period (term) of the lease.

townhouse   A one-, two-, or three-story dwelling with a separate outside entryway sharing common or partitioning walls with other similar dwellings.

traffic   The number of prospects seen by a leasing agent in reference to a particular property or rental space within a given time.

traffic report   A record of the number of prospects who visit or make inquiries at a property and the factors that attracted them to it, often used to measure the effectiveness of advertisements and other marketing vehicles.

turnover   The number of units vacated during a specific period of time, usually one year. Most *turnover rates* are expressed as the ratio between the number of move-outs (or the number of new tenancies) and the total number of units in a property.

umbrella liability insurance   Extra liability coverage that exceeds the limits of the primary liability policy.

U.S. Department of Housing and Urban Development (HUD)   A federal department created to supervise the Federal Housing Administration (FHA) and other government agencies charged with administering various housing programs.

unit mix   The combination of apartment types within a property. The number or percentage of the total of each unit size or type contained in a particular property.

unit size   A listing of the number of bedrooms and bathrooms an apartment contains; the square footage of an apartment.

unscheduled income   Income a property produces from sources other than rent, such as coin-operated laundry equipment, vending machines, late fees, etc.; also called *ancillary, miscellaneous,* or *sundry income.*

useful life   The period of time during which a building is expected to yield a competitive return. For purposes of cost recovery under U.S. tax code, useful life is based on property type (e.g., residential or commercial building) and does not necessarily coincide with the building's actual physical or economic life.

vacancy   An area in a building that is unoccupied and available for rent.

vacancy rate   The ratio of vacant space to total rentable area, expressed as a percentage. On a larger scale, the amount of vacant rental space available in the market expressed as a percentage of the total supply of rental space.

visitor   In apartments, a nonresident who spends time at the home of a resident (with that resident's consent) but does not stay overnight. Compare *guest*.

Wage and Hour Law   See *Fair Labor Standards Act.*

waiting list   A list of people who are interested in renting an apartment at a specific property.

walk-up   An apartment building of two or more floors in which the only access to the upper floors is by means of stairways.

warranty   A form of guarantee, usually in writing, given to a buyer by a seller stating that the goods (or services) purchased are free of defects and will perform as promised or the seller will repair any defect at no charge or replace the item or refund the purchase price. Warranties are usually effective from the date of purchase (or when a manufacturer receives a notice of purchase or other application for warranty from the buyer). Often they include specific limitations as to time (e.g., 90 days, 3 years, 10 years), depending on the item and its anticipated use life, and they usually exclude defects not caused by the manufacturer.

workers' compensation insurance   Insurance which, by law, must be carried by an employer to cover the expenses that arise from employee sicknesses and injuries that occur in the course of employment, usually including medical and disability benefits and lost wages.

working drawings   Final drawings (both architectural and mechanical) that contain the information needed to construct a building or a component of a building; sometimes also called *construction drawings*. See also *specifications.*

zero lot line housing   A type of residential development in which individual dwelling units are placed on separately defined lots, but the units are physically attached to one another or share a common wall.

zoning   A legal mechanism whereby local (municipal) governments regulate the use of privately owned real property to prevent conflicting land uses, promote orderly development, and regulate such conditions as noise, safety, and density. Zoning regulations are specified in *zoning ordinances.*

Index

A

Abandonment, 111–112, 351
Abatement, 125, 351
Absorption rate, 265, 279, 334, 351
Access control systems, 351
Accessibility, 203, 351
Accounting, 337–346
  accrual versus cash, 339
  bill payments, 339–342
  chart of accounts, 344
  income, types, 337–338
  owners' custodial account, 338
  purchase orders, 339
  security deposit funds, 338
  taxes and reporting forms, 342
ACCREDITED MANAGEMENT
  ORGANIZATION® (AMO®), 351–352
ACCREDITED RESIDENTIAL MANAGER®
  (ARM®), 352
Accrual accounting, 339, 352
Actual cash value, 305–306, 315, 352
Addendum, 352
Additional insured, insurance endorse-
  ment, 308, 352
Adequate-income group, 257–258, 281
Adjuster, 313–314, 352
Ad valorem tax, 348, 352

Advance payment, rent, 138
Advertising, 321
  budgeting, 321, 325, 329
  creating name recognition, 231
  marketing tool, 194
  size of ads, 220–221
Advertising media, 213–231
  airport displays, 229
  apartment guides, 223
  banners, 230
  benches, 230
  billboards, 228–229
  cable television, 225
  direct mail, 226–227
  event programs, 225–226
  handbills and flyers, 227–228
  human directionals, 230
  newsletters, 228
  newspapers, 213–223
  radio, 224–225
  television, 225
  transit, 230–231
  web site, 223–224
  Yellow Pages, 227
Age
  rental applicants, 91
  rental housing stock, 2, 228, 289

Agency relationship, 32
Agent, managing, 24, 33, 34–35, 102, 352
Aggregate rent, 103–104, 352
Agreed amount endorsement, 305, 352
Agreed value amount insurance, 305
Airport display advertising, 229
All risk insurance, 304, 305, 352
Alternate employer, 33, 311
Amenities, 193, 201, 207, 215–216, 220, 228, 236, 241, 286, 332, 334, 352
    recreational facilities, 71–72
    supporting, 72–75
Americans with Disabilities Act (ADA), 46, 352–353
Ample-income group, 258, 281
Ancillary income, 29–30, 319, 337. *See also* Unscheduled income
Annual budget, 320, 353
Annual cash return, 32
Answering service, 70
Apartment buildings
    efficiency factor, 6–7
    high-rise, 3, 360
    low-rise, 3, 363
    mid-rise, 3, 363
Apartment guides, advertising, 213, 223
Apartment locator services, 208–210, 214
Apartment management, business aspects, 1–7
Apartment manager. *See* Property manager
Apartments
    accessing, 170
    area, measuring, 5
    bruised, 275–276
    changes, updating, 301–302
    features, reason for renting, 183–184
    layout, 4–5, 262, 270, 290, 294, 297
    maintenance, 162–167
    numbering, 6
    room count, 4
    showing, 242–243
    size, 4–5, 259, 261, 269, 371
    type, 259, 261, 262, 269, 270, 271, 284, 321
    vacant, accessing, 78

Apartment-to-lobby intercommunication systems, 79
Appearance
    employee, 40
    office, 68
    property, 183
Application deposit, 95, 247–248
Application form, rental, 90–95
Application process, rental, 90–100
Appointment, leasing, 237, 248
Appreciation in value, ownership goal, 17
Arbitration, 129
Artwork, lobby, 158
Asphalt tile, 166
Asset manager, 26, 343, 353
Assignment, 112, 353
Assisted housing, 128, 353
Assistive animals, 87
Automated telephones, 69–70
Automobile insurance, resident qualification, 85

B
Backing up computer records, 350
Bank deposits, 59, 137
    receipts, 349–350
Bankruptcy, 113
Banners, advertising, 230
Base rent, 266, 273
Bathroom, 4
Below market interest rate (BMIR), 256, 353
Benches, advertising, 230
Benchmarks
    management progress, 335
    rental prospect, 239
    rent increases, 280–287
Best-of-type pricing, 262–265
    absorption rate and rent level, 265
    compared to pattern pricing, 265–269
    status and rent, 263–264
    views, 264–265
Betterment, 307, 353
Billboards, 228–229. *See also* Directional signs
    examples, 229

Bill payments, 339–342
   tips for handling, 340
Blanket policy, insurance, 307, 308, 353
Boats, parking for resident, 76
Boiler and machinery insurance, 306
Boilerplate language, lease, 110
Bond, fidelity, 310
Bonding, job applicants, 39
Bonuses, 50
   employee, 35, 46
   vendor-offered, 57
Boulders, use in landscaping, 153
Breaks, employee policy, 53
Breezeways, 158, 159, 160
Brochures, 194, 206–208, 224
   competing properties, 201
Bruised apartments, rent discount, 275–276
Budget analysis, 331–333
   cents/dollars per square foot, 332
   cost per apartment, 332–333
   cost per plumbing fixture, 333
   dollars per room, 332
   last year comparisons, 331
   percentage of income, 331–332
   slippage, 331
Budgeting, 317–330
   advertising, 321, 325, 329
   collection losses, 318, 319
   contingency, 322–323
   impact of property age, 330
   major expenditures, 321–322
   periodic income, 318–319
   property size considerations, 327–330
   seasonality considerations, 325–326
   types of budgets, 318–323
Budgets, 353
   analysis, 331–333
   annual, 320
   cash flow, 318, 320
   categories of line items, 324–325
   negative cash flow, 320
   net operating income (NOI), 318, 319
   preparing, 323–330
   quarterly, 320–321
   rent-up, 321
   why needed, 317–318

Budget variance, 323, 330–331, 353
   acceptable, 324
Building codes, 161, 293
Bulletin board, resident, 73
Burnout, employee, 43
Business cards, 194
Business centers, amenities, 300
Business plan, 333–335
Bus stop shelter advertising, 230

C
Cable television advertising, 225
Campers, parking for resident, 76
Canceled checks, 349–350
Cancellation, 35–36. *See also*
   Termination
Canine patrols, 79
Cannibalization, 179, 353
Canvassing, resident policy, 121
Capital expenditure, 321–322, 344, 353
Capital improvement, 353
Capitalization rate, 30–31, 353–354
Carbon monoxide (CO) detectors, 80, 170
Career professionals as renters, 11
Carpeting, 168
   apartments, 163, 165–166
   dyeing, 166
   indoor-outdoor, 160, 173
   stairs, 159–160
Cash accounting, 339, 354
Cash flow, 25, 28, 32, 318, 320, 354
Cash flow budget, 318, 320
Cashier's checks, rent payment, 137
Cash-on-cash return, 32, 254–255, 354
Cash on delivery (COD), 341
Cash payments, rent payment, 137
Casual Friday, 56
Celebrity appearances, traffic builder, 231
Cell phones, 176, 198, 222
Central air conditioning, maintenance, 176
Cents per square foot, budget analysis, 332
Certificate of insurance, 311, 312, 348
Certificate of occupancy, 347, 354
Certified Apartment Manager (CAM), 354

CERTIFIED PROPERTY MANAGER® (CPM®), 354
Charitable activities, traffic builder, 231–232
Chart of accounts, 344, 354
Checkbook eviction, 142
Checks
    canceled, 349–350
    cashier's, 137
    personal, 137–138
    post-dated, 138
    third-party, 138
City row house, 3
Classified ads, 215, 216
Climate, impact on operating efficiency, 7
Closing, leasing procedure, 247
Coinsurance, 306, 354
Collateral, loan, 304, 307, 354
Collateral materials, 321, 354
    leasing handout, 243
    marketing tool, 206–208
Collection losses, 28–29, 278, 318, 319
Collections, 30, 331, 337, 345
Command signs, 198
Commingling, funds, 338, 354
Commissions, 35, 46
    employee policy, 57–58
    leasing, 49
    salary versus, 48–49
Common interest realty association (CIRA), 23–24, 309, 354
Communications
    resident, policy, 114–116
    staff, 176
Community newspapers, 221
Compact disks (CDs), 337, 350
Comparison grid, 260, 354–355
Comparison grid analysis, 261–262, 355
Compensation
    employee policies, 47–49
    real estate management, 33, 35
    real estate managers, 26, 27
    salary versus commission, 48–49
Competing properties
    assessing, 189–191
    brochures, 201
    visiting, 190–191

Competition for prospects, identifying, 188
Competitive bids, 168
Complaints, resident, 123–124, 126, 127, 128, 145, 184
Computers, 336–337
    backing up records, 350
    compact disks (CDs), 337, 350
    digital video disks (DVDs), 337, 350
    equipment and programs, 336–337
    insurance coverage, 306
Concessionaire, 73, 74
Concessions, rent, 257, 265, 272–276
    factor in raising rents, 278
    free rent, 272, 279, 323
    history, 273
    leasing tool, 273
    personal accommodation in leasing, 274
    rent discounts, 275–276
Condemnation clause, 113, 355
Condominium association, 24, 128, 355
Condominiums, 23, 24, 136, 257, 293, 307, 355
Consistency, importance in marketing, 193
Construction drawings, 347
Consumer Price Index (CPI), 106, 281–282, 355
Contents insurance, 306
Contests
    timely rent payment incentive, 140
    traffic builder, 232
Contingency, budgeting consideration, 322–323
Contractors
    independent, 34
    meeting, 168
    restoration, 315
Contract rent, 28, 356
Contracts, 346, 347, 355–356. *See also* Maintenance contracts
    service, 177
Control categories, budget, 325
Controlling purchases, employee policies, 57
Control of investment, ownership goal, 17–18, 255

Conversion rate, 250
Conversion ratio, 252, 253, 329, 356
Convertible apartment, 4
Converting prospects to residents, 234–253
Cooling degree-days, 326, 327, 356
Cooperatives, 23, 356
Corporate ownership, 21–22
Corporate units, 86, 136
Corporation, 21–22, 356
Correspondence, records, 347–348
Corridors, maintenance, 158, 161
Cosigner, 102
Cost per apartment, budget analysis, 332–333
Cost per plumbing fixture, budget analysis, 333
Cost recovery, 322
Could-do improvements, 291–292
Coupons, rent, 274–275
Court settlement, rent payment, 141–142
Covered parking, 4
Cracks, sealing pavement, 155
Credit card, rent payment, 138
Credit check
   job applicants, 38
   property, by vendors, 341
   rental prospects, 95–96
Credit score, 96, 356
Crime insurance, 310
Criminal activity, 80, 126–127
Criminal background check, job applicants, 38–39
Curb appeal, 145, 152, 356
Custodial maintenance, 42–43
Customized classified ad, 215

D
Damage, resident policy, 125–126
Damage deductions, rent payment, 141
Damages
   awards, 308
   claims, 313
Daylight saving time, 156
Dead-bolt locks, 79
Death clause, 109, 356
Death of a relative, employee policy, 54
Debit card, use in laundry rooms, 73

Debt service, 25, 28, 31–32, 318, 320, 330, 344, 356
Deductibles, insurance, 306, 307, 309
Deferred maintenance, 178, 356
Deficiency discount, rent, 275
Degree days, 326, 356
   calculating, 327
Delinquencies
   factor in raising rents, 278–279
   gauging, 142–143
Demeanor, employee, 40
Demographics, 292, 356
Department of Housing and Urban Development (HUD). *See* U.S. Department of Housing and Urban Development
Depreciation, 315, 322, 356
Determining rent increases, 280–287
   amount of last increase, 282
   first increase, 280
   income group influence, 281–282
   typical rent versus street rent, 282–287
Difference in condition (DIC) endorsement, 307
Digital video disks (DVDs), 337, 350
Directional signs, 195, 228. *See also* Billboards
   examples, 196, 197
Directions to property, 237–238
Direct mail, 226–227
Directories, apartment building, 157–158
Directors and officers liability insurance, 309, 357
Direct payment, rent, 137
Disability, 87, 311, 357
Discounts
   apartment deficiency, 275
   bill payments, 341
   bruised apartments, 275–276
   deficiency, 275
   employee, 47–48
   rent payment, 140
Discrimination, 357
   employment, 37, 63, 309
   leasing, 83–84, 90, 91, 92–93, 98, 309

Disbursements, 343, 344, 345
Display ads, 215, 217
Display-classified ads, 215, 218
Divorced and divorcing, rental prospects, 13
Dollars per room, budget analysis, 332
Dollars per square foot, budget analysis, 332
Door-to-door sales, resident policy, 121
Downward rent adjustment, 271–272
Drafting, rent setting, 285–286
Dram shop insurance, 310
Draperies, 165
Dress code, 40
Drive-by traffic, 145, 213, 214, 222, 251
Drive pattern, finding prospects, 187–188
Driver's license, qualifying prospects, 92
Drug testing, job applicants, 39
Dryers, laundry, 73
Dumpsters, 157

E
Economic life, 357
Economic vacancy, 28–29, 277, 357
Education and tuition, employee policy, 55
Effective gross income, 28, 30, 318, 319, 357
Efficiency apartment, 4, 201, 357
Efficiency factor, 6, 357
    apartment buildings, 6–7
    impact of climate, 7
Electronic equipment, leasing policy, 89–90
Electronic funds transfer (EFT), 136, 137, 138, 357
Electronic locks, 78. *See also* Keycards
Elevator cabs, inspection, 158–159
Elevators, maintenance, 176
E-mail, 70, 71, 125, 128, 250, 357. *See also* Internet; Web site
    address, 194, 207
    resident policy, 115
Emergencies, 124–125
Emergency lighting packs, 80, 160
Emergency procedures, 316

Eminent domain, 113, 357
Employee benefits
    education and tuition, 55
    holidays, 53
    insurance, 55
    personal days, 54
    professional memberships, 55–56
    sick days, 54
    vacations, 53–54
Employee burnout, 61–62
Employee compensation, 47–49
    discounts, 47–48
    exchange for service, 44–45
    free rent, 47
    free utilities, 48
    incentives and bonuses, 50
    noncash benefits, 48
    salary, 48
    salary versus commission, 48–49, 239
Employee handbook, 41, 81, 357
Employee identification, policy regarding, 56
Employee licensing, 46–47
Employee manual. *See* Employee handbook
Employee notices, posting, 45
Employee policies, 41–59
    breaks, 53
    death of a relative, 54
    gifts, vendor, 57–58
    identification as staff, 56
    kickbacks, vendor, 57–58
    living on site versus off site, 43–44
    personal hygiene, 57
    pilfering and petty theft, 58–59
    purchase controls, 57
    radios, 56–57
    reporting to work, 53
    scheduling alternatives, 42–43
    socializing with residents, 45
    tools, 56
    uniforms, 56
    vendor commissions, 57–58
    weapons, 57
    work scheduling, 41–42
Employee records, 46, 349
Employee selection, 38–40

Employee termination, 62–63
Employee time records, 349
Employee turnover, 59–60
Employers, local, source for rental prospects, 187
Employment applicants, screening, 38–39
Employment contract, 32
Employment practices liability insurance, 309, 358
Employment record, rental applicants, 93
Empty-nesters as renters, 10
Endorsements, insurance policies, 305, 358
Entry restriction, 78–79
Entryways, 158
Environmental Protection Agency (EPA), 81, 173, 358
Equal Employment Opportunity Commission (EEOC), 37, 358
Equal Housing Opportunity (EHO), 223
Errors and omissions (E&O) insurance, 309, 358
Escalator clauses, lease, 106–107
Escrow, 127, 141, 338, 345, 358
Established properties, rent increases, 276–280
Evacuation drills, 316
Evacuation plans, 81
Event programs, advertising, 225–226
Eviction, 126, 140, 141–142, 242, 300, 329, 358
  checkbook, 142
Eviction notice, 141, 358
Exchange for service, employee policy, 44–45, 79
Exclusion, 305, 358
Exculpate, 358. *See also* Waivers
Excuses, late rent payment, 140–141
Executive property manager, 25–26, 39
Executive summary, management statement, 343
Exhaust fans, 161–162
Exhibits, rental information center, 200–201
Exits and exit signs, maintenance, 160–161

F
Facelift, building improvement, 297
Fair Credit Reporting Act (FCRA), 38, 96, 97, 358–359
Fair Debt Collection Practices Act (FDCPA), 138, 139, 359
Fair Housing Amendments Act, 12, 91, 359
Fair housing laws, 83–84, 87, 223, 309, 359
Fair Isaac Company (FICO) Credit Scoring System, 96
Fair Labor Standards Act (FLSA), 45, 50, 359. *See also* Wage and Hour Law
Familial status, 12, 91, 359
Families with children, 11–12
Family, 209, 359
Fans, maintenance, 169
Fast-track approval, prospects, 84–85
Federal Housing Administration (FHA), 98, 359
Federal Insurance Contributions Act (FICA), 342
Federal Unemployment Tax Act (FUTA), 342
Fidelity bond, 310, 359
Fiduciary, 33, 359
Filters, maintenance, 169–170
Financing, 359
  leverage, ownership goal, 18–19
Fine arts insurance coverage, 306
Fire and casualty insurance, 112
Fire doors, 80–81
Fire extinguishers, 80, 161
  recharging and maintenance, 177
Fire hoses, 161
Fire legal liability insurance, 310
First aid, 81
Fixture, 359
Flammable articles, leasing policy, 90
Flood insurance, 307
Floor coverings. *See also* Carpeting
  apartments, 165–167
  entryways, 159–160
Floor mats, 159
Floor plans, 208, 223, 224, 359

Flower beds, 148–149, 153, 154
Flyers, advertising, 227–228
Follow-up action, leasing, 250
Forced turnover, residents, 132
Foreign ownership of real estate, 24
Form 1099, 338, 342
Free rent, 272, 279, 323
  employee compensation, 47
Free utilities, employee compensation, 48
Frequency, advertising, 221–222
Full bath, 4
Furnished units, 85–86
Furnishings
  lobby, 158
  rental information center, 199

G
Garage, 4
  rental profit margin, 301
Garden apartment, 264
Gated setback entries, 301
Gatekeepers, 79
General partnership, 21, 359
Gentrification, 292, 359
Gifts, employee policy, 57–58
Giveaways, traffic builders, 231
Goal setting, leasing agents, 253
Government-assisted housing, 322, 338, 360
Graduated rent, 104, 284, 360
Graffiti, 159
Grand opening, 231
  ads, 217, 222, 224, 227
Graphics manual, 194, 195
Grass, landscaping, 152
Great room, 293, 294
Gross building area, 332, 360
Gross negligence, 309
Gross potential rental income, 28, 318, 319, 331, 332, 360
Gross receipts, 360
Ground fault interrupter (GFI), 80
Group relamping, 147, 360
Guarantor, 102, 360
Guest cards, 239, 243
Guests, 71, 72, 304, 360

H
Habitability, 110, 127, 360
Half-bath, 4, 360
Handbills, 157
  advertising, 227–228
Handicapped parking, 75
Hardwood flooring, 166–167
Hazardous materials, 90, 360
  examples, 81
  regulations, 82
Headlines, ads, 220
Head rent, 104–105, 360
Health and safety concerns, 80–82
Health insurance, employees, 55
Health Maintenance Organization (HMO), 55
Heat detectors, 160
Heating degree-days, 326, 327, 356
Heating, ventilating, and air-conditioning (HVAC) system, 360
Hedge on inflation, ownership goal, 19, 255
High ceilings, 206
Highest and best use, 334, 335, 360
High-rise apartment buildings, 3, 7, 360
Hiring property staff, 37–41
Hold-harmless provisions, 35, 360–361
Holdover tenancy, 108, 361
Holidays, employee policy, 53
Home purchase clause, lease, 108
Host liquor liability insurance, 310
Household, 189, 361
Housekeeping, 316, 361
  poor, 202, 209, 242
Housing directors, rental referrals, 211
Housing record, rental applicants, 93
Housing styles, changes, 293–294
Human directionals, advertising, 230

I
Identification signs, 196–198
  examples, 198
  permanent, 196–197
Illegal and immoral uses, resident policy, 126–127
Immigrants as renters, 12–13, 92–93

Immigration Reform and Control Act (IRCA), 361
Improvements
  apartment, related to rent increases, 287
  charging for apartment, 285
  insurance coverage, 307
Incentives
  direct mail advertising, 226
  employee compensation, 50
Incidents, reporting to insurer, 312–313
Income
  ancillary, 29–30, 319, 337
  gross potential rental, 28, 318, 319, 331, 332
  scheduled, 337–338
  security deposit funds, 337
  types, 337–338
  unscheduled, 28, 29–30, 323, 324, 337–338
Income capitalization approach, 30, 276, 361
Income groups, 13, 15, 255–258, 281
Income tax shelter, ownership goal, 19
Independent contractor, 34, 177, 311, 361
Indoor lighting, 160
Indoor-outdoor carpeting, 160, 173
Inflation, 19, 330, 361
Inflation guard provision, insurance, 306
Informational signs, 198–199
  examples, 200
Inspection checklist, maintenance, 175
Inspection report, move-in, 117
Institute of Real Estate Management (IREM®), 175, 361
Institutional owners, 22
Insurance, 303–316
  blanket policies, 307–308
  deductibles, 307
  endorsements, 305
  handling losses, 312–315
  liability, 308–310
  premiums, 309, 311
  property loss, 305–308
  risk management, 315–316

  settlements, 315
  snow-plowing contractor, 174
  volume purchases, 307–308
Insurance adjuster, 313–314, 315, 352
Insurance adjustment and restoration, 315
Insurance companies, real estate owners, 22
Insurance coverages
  all risk, 305
  boiler and machinery, 306
  computers and printers, 306
  contents, 306
  crime, 310
  directors and officers liability, 309
  employment practices liability, 309
  errors and omissions, 309
  fire legal liability, 310
  host liquor liability, 310
  improvements and betterments, 307
  long-term disability, 311
  natural disasters, 306–307
  non-owned and hired automobile, 309–310
  plate glass, 306
  rent loss, 307
  short-term disability, 311
  tenant discrimination liability, 309
  umbrella liability, 308–309
  workers' compensation, 311–312
Insurance policies, property records, 348
Insured, 314, 361
Interactive electronic messaging, 201
Intercoms, 157–158
Interest, 361
Interior designer, 203
Internal Revenue Service (IRS), 34, 47, 48, 322, 338, 339, 342
Internet, 78, 137, 213, 223, 337, 350, 362. *See also* Web site
Inventory
  apartment furnishings, 111, 125–126
  building equipment, 148, 149, 152
  parts and supplies, 178–180
  property, 334
  vacant apartments, 242

Investment control, ownership goal,
    17–18
Investment economics, real estate, 27–
    32
Invoices, property records, 349, 350
IRV formula, 31, 362
Issues report, 178, 343

J

Job applicants, screening, 38–39
Job descriptions, 32, 41, 46
Joint venture, 21, 362

K

Keycard, access control, 72, 73, 78
Keys and lockouts, resident policy,
    120
Keys and locks, property policy, 77–78
Keystone-entry sign, 196
Kickbacks, vendor, 57–58

L

Labor unions, 63–64
Landscape architect, 152
Landscaping, 152–154, 362
Landlord-tenant law, 127, 139, 362
Late fee, 140, 362
Late notice, 139, 362
Laundry room, 72–73
Lawn sprinklers, 154
Laws, rules, and regulations, 81–82
Laws of supply and demand, 257, 258,
    265, 281, 362
Lawsuits, liability, 308, 309, 310
Lead-based paint, 81, 368–369
Lease agreement, 101–113
    common clauses, 110–113
    special provisions, 108–110
    terms of occupancy, 102–108
Lease extension agreement, 129, 362
Lease extension rider, 108
Leasehold interest, 112
Lease provisions, 102–113
    abandonment, 111–112
    assignment, 112
    bankruptcy, 113
    condemnation, 113
    condition of premises, 110

death clause, 109
    eminent domain, 113
    fire and casualty, 112
    home purchase clause, 108
    identification of premises, 103
    limitations, 110
    option to renew, 109–110
    parties to the agreement, 102
    peaceful enjoyment, 110
    rent, 103–107
    repairs and breakdowns, 110
    repossession, 111
    right of re-entry, 111
    rules and regulations, 113
    signatures and delivery, 113
    subletting, 112
    subordination, 112
    term, 107–108
    transfer clause, 108
    use, 110
    waivers and exculpation, 112
Lease renewal, 107–108, 129–130, 265,
    274, 362
    option, 109–110
    rent increases, 283–284, 287
Leases, 101–102, 362
    property records, 346
Leasing agents, 42, 235, 362
    commission-only, 49
    conversion rate, 250
    evaluating performance, 251–253
    hiring, 40
    product knowledge, 240–241, 246
    property tour, 241–243
    role, seller or helper, 240
    salary versus commission, 239
    setting goals, 253
    suggesting competing properties,
        240, 245
    telephone inquiries, 236–239
    using guest cards, 243
    visiting competing properties, 241
Leasing office. *See* Rental information
    center
Leasing policies, 83–100
    lifestyle choices, 90
    pets, 86–89
    possessions, 89–90

rental application process, 90–100
resident selection, 83–90
Leasing presentation, 243–249. *See also*
   Tour
  closing, 247
  deposit application, 247–248
  evaluating, 248–249
  introductions, 244
  motivation to move, 245
  new appointment, 248
  prospect's rent budget, 244–245
  questions and objections, 246–247
  readiness to rent, 244
  surprise, 246
  urgency, 245–246
Legal description, 362
Legal expense, budgeting, 329
Lending institutions, real estate owners,
  22
Length of stay, residents, 130
Letters of agreement, 347
Levels of rehab. *See* Rehabilitation
Liability insurance, 308
Licensing, employee, 46–47
Lifestyle choices, 90
Lien, 339
Lift, asphalt paving, 155
Lightbulbs, 147, 156, 160, 161, 179
Lighting, 152
  emergency, 80, 160
  indoor, 160
  outdoor, 156
  parking lot, 148, 151, 152, 156
Lighting fixtures, resident policy, 119
Limited-edition units, 264
Limited-income group, 256–257, 258,
  281, 331
Limited liability company (LLC), 21, 363
Limited partnership, 21, 363
Lobbies, maintenance, 158
Local area trends, 333–334
Location, property, 2–3, 183, 363
Locator services, 210–211, 214
Lock boxes, rent payment, 136
Locking devices, 79
Lockouts, resident policy, 120
Locks and keys, 77–78
Long-term disability insurance, 311

Low-income group, 256, 258, 281
Low-income household, 13, 363
Low-rise apartment buildings, 3, 363

M
Ma and pa management, 27, 43
Mailboxes, resident, 157–158
Mailing lists, 226
Maintenance, 144–181
  deferred, 178
  equipment, 180
  equipment rooms, 167
  inspection, conducting, 152–162
  property, ongoing, 167–177
  programmed, 180–181
  specialized tools, 180
Maintenance contracts, 175–177
  air conditioning, 176
  elevators, 176
  painting, 170–172
  pest control, 173
  recharging fire extinguishers, 177
  satellite dishes and antennas, 177
  sewer rodding, 177
  snow plowing, 173–174, 177
  swimming pools, 177
  window washing, 177
Maintenance personnel
  finding qualified, 41
  outside, versus property staff, 175–
  177
Maintenance program, 167–177, 180–
  181
Maintenance room, 167, 171
Maintenance schedule, 149, 175
Maintenance service requests, 42–43,
  71
Major expenditure budget, 321–322,
  345
Majority, 91, 363
Major renewal, building rehab, 297
Management agreement, 27, 32–36,
  308, 363
  associated risks, 35
  cancellation, 35–36
  compensation, 35
  powers, 33–34
  termination, 35–36

Management company, 25–26, 27, 32, 65, 123, 338, 339, 343, 363
  liability, 308, 312, 314, 315
Management fee, 27, 330, 363
Management office, 67–71
  automated telephones, 69–70
  appearance, 68
  hours, 69
  locations, 67
  one versus two, 68
  web site, 70–71
Management plan, 16, 335, 363
Management statement, 343–346
Managers
  finding qualified applicants, 40–41
  obligations, 34–35
  types, 24–27
Managing agent, powers, 33–34
Market boundaries, 186–187
Market feedback, 209–210
Market identification, 185–192
Marketing, 363. *See also* Advertising; Marketing tools
Marketing campaign, preparing 182–212
Marketing map, 185–189
  creating, 185–186
  sample, 187
  using, 186–189
Marketing plan, 190
Marketing program, 251
Marketing tools, 192–208
  brochures and collateral material, 206–208
  directional signs, 195–196
  identification signs, 196–198
  informational signs, 198–199
  model apartments, 201–206
  property name, 193–194
  property theme, 192–194
  rental information center, 199–201
  signage, 194–199
  symbols, 193–194
  unified graphics system, 194
Market-ready condition, 163, 184, 205, 241
  checklist, 163–165
Market rent, 28, 363

Market softening, 141, 143. *See also* Soft markets
Master key, 77–78
Mechanical equipment, 149
Medicare, 46, 342
Memos to the file, 348
Mid-rise apartment buildings, 3, 7, 363
Mildew, 161, 169
  control, 172–173
Mini-master keys, 78
Minor, 91, 364
Miscellaneous income. *See* Unscheduled income
Miscellaneous receipts, 343, 344
Mission statement, 335
Model apartments, 201–206, 242
Mold, 172–173
  insurance exclusion, 305
Monday morning reports, 132, 365
Money orders, rent payment, 137
Monthly disbursements, 344
Month-to-month tenancy, 108, 364
Monument sign, 196
Morale, employee, 60–61
Mortgage, 318, 320, 321, 340, 364
Mortgage payments. *See* Debt service
Motorcycles, parking for resident, 76
Move-in, 116–118
  checklist, 117, 364
  early, 274
  resident policy, 116–118
Move-in condition, 184
Move-outs, 118, 119, 121, 328
  causes of resident, 145
  checklist, 364
  delayed, 117
  impact on bottom line, 257, 274, 278, 281–282, 283, 286, 287
  inspection, 121–122
  resident policy, 121
  security deposit return, 121–122
Multifamily housing business, 22
Multifamily rental housing stock, age, 288, 289
Must-do improvements, 290
Mutual agreement, lease cancellation, 109, 127

N

Named insured, 308, 310, 364
National Flood Insurance Program, 307
Natural disasters, insurance coverage,
    306–307
Natural turnover, residents, 132
Negligence, 364
    manager, 340
Neighborhood, 364
    analysis for management plan, 333–
    334
    reason for renting, 183
    turnarounds, 292
Nerve factor, setting rent, 259
Net operating income (NOI), 11, 24–25,
    28, 30–31, 86, 318, 322, 364
Net operating income (NOI) budget,
    318
    sample format, 319
Net worth, 308
New construction, factor in raising rent,
    279
Newsletters, 80, 228
Newspaper advertising, 213–223
Noisy equipment, leasing policy, 90
Noncash employee benefits, 48
Non-owned and hired auto insurance,
    309–310
Nonrecourse loans, 307
Nonyield space, 6–7, 332, 365
Notices, posting requirements, 45–46

O

Obsolescence, 288, 365
Occupancy agreement, 101. *See also*
    Lease agreement
Occupancy certificates, 347
Occupancy durations, improving resi-
    dent, 129–134
Occupancy report, 365
Occupational Safety and Health Act, 35,
    45, 46, 56, 365
Occupational Safety and Health Admin-
    istration (OSHA), 46, 81
Odor, 161–162
Office. *See* Management office
Off-season, 105, 129–130
Off-site management, 365

One-bedroom apartment, 4–5
One-person household, 12
One unit at a time property rehab, 296–
    297
On-site manager, 17, 43–44. *See also*
    Resident manager
    required by law, 44
Operating budget, 317, 321, 323, 365
Operating expenses, 31, 318, 319, 322,
    333, 365
Operating reserves, 365
Operations manual, 67, 365
Option, 100–101, 365–366
Optional coverage, insurance, 306
Outdoor lighting, 156
Overall upgrade, property rehab, 297
Overtime pay, 46, 49–53, 340
    exemptions, 51
    sample calculation, 52
Owner, landlord, and tenant (OLT)
    liability, 366
Owner's custodial account, 338
Ownership disadvantages, 19–20
Ownership forms, 20–24. *See also*
    Types of owners
    corporation, 21–22
    joint venture, 21
    limited liability company, 21
    partnerships, 20–21
    real estate investment trust (REIT),
    22–23
    sole owner, 20
Ownership goals, 15–19
    appreciation in value, 17
    control of investment, 17
    financing leverage, 18–19
    hedge on inflation, 19
    income tax shelter, 19
    periodic income, 16–17
    personal use, 18
    pride of ownership, 18
Owner's manuals, 346–347. *See also*
    Warranties

P

Pagers, 176
Painting, 170–172
Parking, 75–76

Parking lots. *See also* Paved areas
lighting, 156
maintenance, 149
security, 75
striping, 155
Partnerships, 20–21
Parts, repair, 179–180
Pattern pricing, 259
compared to best-of-type pricing,
265–269
Paved areas, 154–156
deferred maintenance, 178
Payment plan, rent, 141
Payroll, budgeting, 328–329
Peaceful enjoyment, 110, 366
Penalty charges, rent payments, 140
Percentage of income, budget analysis,
331–332
Perimeter plantings, 153
Periodic income, ownership goal, 16–
17
Periodic maintenance, 169–170
Permanent identification sign, 196
Personal checks, rent payment, 137–138
Personal days, employee policy, 54
Personal hygiene, employee policy, 57
Personal presentation evaluation, 249
Personal property, 366
taxes, 348, 349
Pest control, 173
Pet agreement, 89, 366
Pet policies
fair housing law, 87
number of pets, 88
owners' responsibilities, 88–89
refundable deposit, 88
size of pets, 88
types of pets, 88
Pets, 86–89, 223
assistive animals, 87
Petty cash, 341
Petty theft, 58–59. *See also* Pilferage;
Theft
Photo cells, lighting control, 156
Physical vacancy, 28–29, 277, 366
Pilferage, 179, 329. *See also* Theft
employee policy, 58–59
reducing, 180
Plans, property records, 347

Plants, lobby decor, 158
Plate glass insurance, 306
Playgrounds, maintenance, 154
Plumbing, 119, 169
Police involvement, property security,
80
Policies
employee, 41–59
leasing, 83–90
property, 65–82
rent collection, 138–143
rent payment, 135–138
resident, 114–134
Politics, resident policy, 120
Polygraph tests, job applicants, 39
Positioning, web site, 71
Possessions, leasing policy, 89–90
Postcards, promotional, 208
Post-dated checks, rent payment, 138
Preferred employer program, 211
Preleasing, 222
Premiums
insurance, 309, 311
traffic builders, 231
Presentation, leasing, 243–248
evaluation form, 249
personal evaluation, 248–249
Pricing by floor, 265–266
Pride of ownership, ownership goal, 18
Principal, 366
Printers, insurance for computer, 306
Private garages, amenity, 301
Problem-solving, 122–229
Professional associations, 191
memberships, employee policy, 55–
56
Professional liability insurance, 366
Pro formas, 258, 366
Programmed maintenance, 180–181
Promotional signs, 195. *See also* Bill-
boards
Proof of insurance, 85
Property
age, budget impact, 330
description, business plan compo-
nent, 334
directions to find, 237–238
location, 2–3
loss, insuring against, 305–308

maintenance, ongoing, 167–177
name, marketing tool, 193–194
protecting after loss, 314–315
reputation, 184
size, budget impact, 326–327
types of rental, 3–4
Property appearance, 183. *See also* Curb
  appeal
Property assets
  documenting, 147–152
  identifying, 146–147
Property management, 366
Property manager, 26–27, 366
Property patrols, 79
Property policies, 65–82
  automated telephones, 69–70
  laundry room, 72–73
  laws, rules, and regulations, 81–82
  office appearance, 68
  office hours, 69
  office location, 67
  one office versus two, 68
  parking, 75–76
  public telephone, 74
  recreational facilities, 71–72
  safety and health concerns, 80–82
  security, 76–80
  storage, 74–75
  supporting amenities, 72–75
  vending machines, 74
  web site, 70–71
Property staff
  employee policies, 41–59
  hiring, 37–41
  maintenance personnel, 175–177
  managing, 59–64
Property taxes. *See* Real estate taxes
Property value, impact of rent level,
  276
Prospects, rental
  arrival at the property, 243–251
  converting to residents, 234–253
  finding, 208–212
Prospect tracking software, 238
Prospect traffic, 251
Protected class, 367
Public adjuster, insurance, 313–314,
  367
Public relations, 232–233, 321

Public service activities, traffic builder,
  231–232
Public telephone, 74
Pullman kitchen, 4, 367
Purchase order (PO), 57, 180, 339, 367
Purchasing, 167–169

Q
Qualifications, job applicants, 37, 40–
  41
Qualifying rental prospects, 236, 244–
  245, 247
Quarterly budget, 320–321

R
Radio advertising, 224–225
Radios, employee policy, 56–57
Raising rent, 269–280. *See also* Rent;
  Setting rent
  apartment improvements, 285, 287
  benchmarks, rent-specific, 280–287
  drafting, 285–286
  established properties, 276–280
  graduated increases, 284
  market indicators, 277–280
  new properties, making adjustments,
    269–276
  odd dollar amounts, 283
  testing increases after rehab, 296
  testing increases on vacancies, 284–
    285
  timing increases, 282–283, 286–
    287
  typical rent versus street rent, 282–
    287
Rate of return, 16
Rating residents, 14–15
Real estate, 367
Real estate investment economics, 27–
  32, 254–255
Real estate investment trust (REIT), 22–
  23, 367
Real estate management, 1–7
  management agreement, 32–36
  types of managers, 24–27
Real estate ownership
  disadvantages, 19–20
  forms, 20–24
  goals, 15–19

Real estate taxes, 320, 321, 323, 324, 325, 326, 330, 331, 345, 347, 348–349
Reasons for renting, 182–185
  apartment condition, 183–184
  apartment features, 183–184
  apartment layout, 183–184
  property appearance, 183
  property location, 183
  property reputation, 184
  rent level, 184–185
Reassurance sign, 195
Recapture, 19, 367
Record keeping, employer requirements, 45–46, 349
Records, 346–350
  canceled checks, 349–350
  computer back-up, 350
  contracts, 347
  correspondence, 347–348
  deposit receipts, 349–350
  employee time records, 349
  insurance policies, 348
  leases, 346
  memos to the file, 347–348
  occupancy certificates, 347
  paid invoices, 349–350
  property plans, 347
  property taxes, 348–349
  warranties and owner's manuals, 346–347
Recreational facilities, 71–72
Recurring expenses, 321, 367
Recycling, 81, 156, 367
References, job applicants, 38
Referral rewards, 210–211, 275
Referrals, rental, 214
  competing properties, 240, 245
  housing directors, 211
  residents, 210–211
Refinancing, 289
Registered in Apartment Management (RAM), 367
Rehabilitation, property
  adding amenities, 300–302
  apartment changes, 301
  changes in housing styles, 293–294
  could-do improvements, 291–292
  examples, 298–299

  facelift, 297
  four levels, 296–300
  major renewal, 297
  must-do improvements, 290
  one unit at a time, 296–297
  overall upgrade, 297
  remodel or demolish, 293
  should-do improvements, 290–291
  variety and change, 294–296
Relaxation gardens, 259, 300
Relocation assistance, 209
Renewal, lease, 107–108
Renewal options, 109–110
Renewal rewards, 134, 274
  resident policy, 130–131
Rent, 103–107. *See also* Raising rent
  adjusting upward, 270
  aggregate, 103–104
  concessions, 272–276
  downward adjustment, 271–272
  graduated, 104, 284
  head, 104–105
  seasonal, 105
  setting and raising, 254–287
  street, 27, 28, 282
Rentable area, 6, 367
Rentable square feet, 5, 332
Rental agreement, 101
Rental application, 247
  form, contents, 90–95
Rental cycles, 7
Rental housing stock
  age, 288, 289
  condition, 2
Rental information center, 68, 195, 197, 210, 233, 243, 244, 253
  exhibits, 200–201
  furnishings, 199
  marketing tool, 199–201
Rental properties, types, 3–4
Rent bills, 136
Rent collection. *See* Fair Debt Collection Practices Act
Rent collection policies, 138–143
  checkbook eviction, 142
  contests, 140
  damage deductions, 141
  discounts, 140
  enforcement, 139

excuses, 140–141
gauging delinquencies, 142–143
payment plan, 141
penalty charges, 140
settle in court, 141–142
spotting trouble, 139–140
Rent control, 24, 277, 367
Rent discounts
apartment deficiency, 275
bruised apartments, 275–276
employee policy, 47–48
Renters by choice, 8–11, 368
Renters by circumstance, 8, 11–13,
368
Renters' insurance, 368
Rent holidays, concessions, 273
Rent increases, 129
achieving, 330
determining, 280–287
market indicators, 276–280
Rent level, impact on property value,
276
Rent loss, 368
insurance coverage, 307
Rent payment policies, 135–138
Rent payments, 135–143
forms of payment, 136–138
Rent reductions, 271–272
Rent revenue, budgeting, 329
Rent roll, 28, 272, 275, 337, 343, 344,
368
Rent schedule, 259, 261, 265, 269, 270,
271, 331
Rent-up budget, 321, 368
Rent-up specialists, 211–212
Repairs, budgeting, 329
Replacement cost, 368
Replacement cost coverage, 305, 306,
368
Replacement reserves, 322, 345, 368
Reporting to work, employee policy,
53
Repossession, lease clause, 111
Reputation, property, 184
Request for proposal (RFP), 168, 368
Reserve account, 345
Reserved parking, 75
Reserve fund, 289, 290
Resident communications, 114–116

Resident guidebook, 81, 115–116, 124,
368
Resident handbook. *See* Resident
guidebook
Residential Lead-Based Paint Hazard
Reduction Act, 368–369
Resident manager, 27, 369
Resident manual. *See* Resident
guidebook
Resident mix, shaping, 85–86
Resident organization. *See* Tenant
organization
Resident policies, 114–134
apartment improvements, 118–119
apartment transfers, 119–120
communications, 114–116
complaints, 123–124, 126
damage to units, 125–126
disregard for others, 126
door-to-door sales and canvassing,
121
emergencies, 124–125
illegal and immoral uses, 126
keys and lockouts, 120
move-in, 116–118
move-out, 121
move-out inspection, 121–122
politics and voting, 120
rent, 135–143
security deposit return, 121–122
Resident notices, posting, 45
Resident profile, 252, 287, 291, 292,
302, 369
choosing employees, 38–40
developing a business plan, 334
Resident referrals, 210–211
Resident retention. *See* Tenant retention
Resident rights, 127
Residents
prospective, 234–253
profile, factor in employee selection,
38–40
rating, 14–15
responsibility for own security, 80
socializing with employees, 45
types, 7–13, 15
Resident selection, 83–90
automobile insurance, 85
criteria, 284

Resident turnover, 106, 129, 132–133, 283
  costs, 131, 133, 134
Resilient flooring, 166, 168
Restoration contractor, 315
Return on investment (ROI), 16, 291, 300, 318, 369
Right of re-entry, landlord's, 111, 242, 369
Risk management, 315–316, 369
Roofing, 152
Room count, 4–5, 332
Rubbish, 156–157
Rules and regulations, lease clause, 113

S

Safety equipment, 81
Safety inspections, 81
Salary, employee policies, 48
  commission versus, 48–49
  wage adjustments, 49–50
Sales taxes on rents, 342, 349
Satellite dishes and antennas, maintenance, 177
Scheduled income, 337–338
Scheduled receipts, 28
Scheduling, employee policy, 41–43
Seal coating, paved areas, 155
Seasonality, factor in budgeting, 325–326
Seasonal rent, 105, 287, 369
Security, 76–80, 294, 301
  breach, 67, 79, 80
  entry restriction, 78–79
  laundry room, 73
  liability, 80
  locks and keys, 77–78
  management responsibility, 80
  officers, 77
  parking, 75
  police involvement, 80
  policies, 77
  property patrols, 77, 79
  resident responsibility, 80
  video surveillance, 79–80
Security deposit funds, accounting, 338
Security deposits, 86, 98–100, 121, 125–126, 127, 134, 211, 324, 338, 369
  acknowledgment in lease, 108

reduction, resident retention strategy, 134
Self-service storage facilities, 75, 369
Senior citizens as renters, 11
Service contracts, 177, 370
Service request, 117, 128, 370
Setting rent, first time, 258–269. *See also* Raising rent
  making adjustments, 269–276
Sewer lines, locating, 149
Sewer rodding, 177
Sexual harassment, 309
Shares of beneficial interest, 23, 370
Shock advertising, 222–223
Shoppers, 252–253, 370
Short-term disability insurance, 311
Should-do improvements, 290–291
Sick days, employee policy, 54
Signage, 194–199
Signature block, 113, 370
Sinking fund, 322
Site manager, 27. *See also* Resident manager
Site office, paying rent, 136
Site plan, 208, 370
Sliding glass doors, 79
Smoke alarms, 80
Smoke detectors, 170
Smoking policy, 68
Snow and ice control, 149, 173–174
Snow plowing, 177
Soap and detergent dispensers, 73
Socializing with residents, employee policy, 45
Social Security, 46, 342
Social Security number, job applicants, 92
Soft markets, 143, 212, 251
Sole owner, 20
Specifications, 168, 347, 370
Spray painting, 171
Spreadsheet, 370
Sprinklers, 81
Staff. *See also* Employee benefits; Employee compensation; Employee policies
  hiring, 37–41
  managing, 59–64
  scheduling, 41–42

Staff communications, 176
Staffing alternatives, 42–43
Stairs, carpeting, 159–160
Statement, management, 343–346
Stationery as marketing tool, 194
Status, factor in setting rent, 263–264
Stick-built buildings, 3
Storage, resident lockers, 74–75
Street rent, 27, 28, 282, 370
Student housing, 105–106
    furnished apartments, 86
    rent increases, 287
Students as renters, 13
Studio apartment, 4, 370. *See also*
    Efficiency apartment
Subletting, 112, 370
Subordination clause, 112, 370
Subsidized housing, 256, 281, 370–371
Sunday, staff scheduling, 41–42
Sundry income, 29–30, 318. *See also*
    Unscheduled income
Supplies and parts, 179–180
    budgeting, 329
Supporting amenities, 72–75
Swimming pools
    maintenance, 177
    opening and closing, 149
Symbols, marketing tools, 193–194

T
Targeted marketing
    direct mail advertising, 226–227
    human resources directors, 187
Telephone calls, tracking prospect, 238
Telephone inquiries, prospects, 236–239
Telephone number
    importance in advertising, 222
    inclusion on rental signs, 198
Telephones
    automated, 69–70
    public, 74
Television advertising, 225
Tenant, 102, 371. *See also* Resident
Tenant discrimination liability insurance, 309
Tenant organizations, 252, 371
    resident policy, 127–128
Tenant retention, 129–134, 371

Term, 107–108, 371
Termination, 371
    employees, 62–63
    lease, 109, 113, 126, 127
    management agreement, 33, 35–36
    wrongful, 63, 309
Term rent, 103, 371. *See also* Seasonal
    rent
Terrorism, coinsurance, 306
Testing, job applicants, 39
Thank you note, 250
Theft, 58–59, 137, 158, 161, 179, 180,
    338, 341. *See also* Pilferage
    insurance coverage, 305, 310
Theme, selection of marketing, 192–193
Third-party checks, rent payment, 138
Tickler files, 348, 349
Timers, lighting control, 156
Timing
    move-in, 84–85
    rent increases, 286–287
Tools, employee policy, 56
Tour, 241–243. *See also* Leasing
    presentation
Townhouses, 6–7, 23, 210, 257, 293,
    307, 371
Traffic, rental prospects, 213, 214, 371
Traffic builders, 231–232
Traffic report, 371
Transfer clause, lease, 108
Transit ads, 230–231
Trips, traffic builders, 232
Trust account, 338
Tub and shower caulking, 169
Turnover, 371
    costs of resident, 131, 133, 134
    employee, 59–60
    resident, 106, 129, 132–133, 283
Turnover rate, 130, 132, 181, 212, 332,
    371
Two-person households, 12
Two-story garden apartment, 4
Two-story unit, design, 3
Two-way radio, 176
Type size in ads, 221
Types of owners. *See also* Ownership
    forms
    common interest realty associations,
        23–24

Types of owners (*continued*)
  foreign investors, 22
  institutions, 22, 343
Typical rent, 282

U
Umbrella liability insurance, 308–309, 371
Underground utilities, 149
Unfurnished units, 85–86
Unified graphics system, 194, 208, 228
Uniforms, employee policy, 56
U.S. Department of Housing and Urban Development (HUD), 13, 84, 128, 137, 338, 371
Unit layout, 4–5, 262, 270, 290, 294, 297
Unit mix, 5–6, 371
Unit size, 4–5, 259, 261, 269, 371
Unit type, 259, 261, 262, 269, 270, 271, 284, 321
Unscheduled income, 28, 29–30, 323, 324, 337–338, 371
Upgrading and renovation, 288–302. *See also* Rehabilitation
  planning ahead, 289–296
Upward rent adjustments, 269–270
Useful life, 322, 334, 372
  equipment and fixtures, 147, 178
  model apartments, 205

V
Vacancies, 28–29, 30, 318, 372
  accessing, 78
  budgeting consideration, 327–328
  economic, 28–29
  factor in raising rents, 277–278
  physical, 28–29, 277
  testing rent increases, 284–285
Vacancy rate, 185, 372
Vacations, employee policy, 53–54
Value added, 205
Vandalism, 74, 76
  insurance coverage, 305
Variances, budget, 323, 324, 330–331
Vehicles as marketing tool, 194
Vending machines, 58, 59, 74
Ventilation, corridors, 162

Vertical blinds, 165
Video surveillance, 79–80
Views, factor in setting rent, 264–265
Vinyl tile, 166
Virtual tours, 201, 207, 209, 337
Visitors, 159, 285, 372
Volume ceilings, 293, 295, 301
Volume purchases, insurance, 307–308
Voting, resident policy, 120

W
Wage and Hour Law, 33, 35, 50–53, 349. *See also* Fair Labor Standards Act
  exemptions from overtime, 51
  overtime requirements, 49–50
Waiting list, leasing, 250–251, 372
Waivers, lease clause, 112
Walking paths, amenity, 153–154
Walk-in kitchen, 4
Walk-up apartments, 7, 372
Warranties, 148, 167, 330, 346–347, 372
Washer, laundry, 73
Waterbeds, leasing policy, 89
Water leaks, 169
Water supply, 149
Weak markets, 232, 278. *See also* Soft markets
Weapons, employee policy, 57
Web site, 70–71, 80, 194, 207, 213, 223–224. *See also* Internet
Wheel stops, 155
White space in ads, 221
Wide-angle viewer, 79
Window coverings, 165
Window washing, 177
Workers' compensation, 311–312
Working drawings, 347, 372
Wrongful discharge, 309

Y
Yard fixtures, insurance exclusion, 305
Yellow Pages advertising, 227
Yield, investment, 32

Z
Zero-lot-line housing, 23, 372
Zoning, 347, 372